Great Battles of World War Two

Battle of the Britain

Compiled by

Eldon Mcmillian

Scribbles

Year of Publication 2018

ISBN : 9789352979325

Book Published by

Scribbles

(An Imprint of Alpha Editions)

email - alphaedis@gmail.com

Produced by: PediaPress GmbH
Limburg an der Lahn
Germany
http://pediapress.com/

Contents

Introduction

Battle of Britain

Battle of Britain	
Part of the Second World War	

An Observer Corps spotter
scans the skies of London.

Date	10 July – 31 October 1940[1] German historians usually place the beginning of the battle in May 1940 and end it mid-August 1941, with the withdrawal of the bomber units in preparation for Operation *Barbarossa*, the campaign against the Soviet Union, which began on 22 June 1941.</ref> (3 months and 3 weeks)
Location	British airspace
Result	British victory[2] Other references that can be consulted include::Shulman 2004, p. 63.:Bungay 2000, p. 368.:Hough and Richards 2007, p. XV.:Overy 2001, p. 267.:Deighton 1980, p. 213.:Keegan 1997, p. 81.:Buell 2002, p. 83.:Terraine 1985, p. 181.</ref>

Belligerents	
United Kingdom Canada[3,4] Although under RAF operational control, RCAF pilots in the BoB were technically flying for the RCAF</ref>	Germany Italy

Commanders and leaders	
Hugh Dowding Keith Park T. Leigh-Mallory Quintin Brand Richard Saul L. Samuel Breadner Zdzisław Krasnodębski	Hermann Göring Albert Kesselring Hugo Sperrle Hans-Jürgen Stumpff R. C. Fougier

Units involved	
[icon] Royal Air Force [icon] Royal Canadian Air Force	✚ *Luftwaffe* ⊕ *Corpo Aereo Italiano*
Strength	
1,963 serviceable aircraft[5]	2,550 serviceable aircraft.[6]</-ref>[7]</ref>
Casualties and losses	
1,542 aircrew killed[8,9]</ref> 422 aircrew wounded[10] 1,744 aircraft destroyed[11] 376 bombers, 148 aircraft (RAF Coastal Command) </ref>	2,585 aircrew killed and missing, 925 captured, 735 wounded[12] 1,977 aircraft destroyed, 1,634 in combat and 343 non-combat[13]
41,480 civilians killed (including 16,775 women and 5,184 children) Total: 90,000 civilian casualties	
1,400,245 buildings destroyed or damaged (London)	

The **Battle of Britain** (German: *Luftschlacht um England*, literally "The Air Battle for England") was a military campaign of the Second World War, in which the Royal Air Force (RAF) defended the United Kingdom (UK) against large-scale attacks by Nazi Germany's air force, the Luftwaffe. It has been described as the first major military campaign fought entirely by air forces.[14] The British officially recognise the battle's duration as being from 10 July until 31 October 1940, which overlaps the period of large-scale night attacks known as the Blitz, that lasted from 7 September 1940 to 11 May 1941. German historians do not accept this subdivision and regard the battle as a single campaign lasting from July 1940 to June 1941, including the Blitz.[15]

The primary objective of the German forces was to compel Britain to agree to a negotiated peace settlement. In July 1940 the air and sea blockade began, with the Luftwaffe mainly targeting coastal-shipping convoys, ports and shipping centres, such as Portsmouth. On 1 August, the Luftwaffe was directed to achieve air superiority over the RAF with the aim of incapacitating RAF Fighter Command; 12 days later, it shifted the attacks to RAF airfields and infrastructure.[16] As the battle progressed, the Luftwaffe also targeted factories involved in aircraft production and strategic infrastructure. Eventually it employed terror bombing on areas of political significance and on civilians.[17]</ref>

The Germans had rapidly overwhelmed France and the Low Countries, leaving Britain to face the threat of invasion by sea. The German high command knew the difficulties of a seaborne attack and its impracticality while the Royal Navy controlled the English Channel and the North Sea.[18]Wikipedia:Citing sources On 16 July, Adolf Hitler ordered the preparation of Operation *Sea Lion* as a potential amphibious and airborne assault on Britain, to follow once the Luftwaffe had air superiority over the UK. In September, RAF Bomber Command night raids disrupted the German preparation of converted barges, and the Luftwaffe's failure to overwhelm the RAF forced Hitler to postpone and eventually cancel Operation *Sea Lion*. Germany proved unable to sustain daylight raids, but their continued night-bombing operations on Britain became known as the Blitz.

Historian Stephen Bungay cited Germany's failure to destroy Britain's air defences to force an armistice (or even outright surrender) as the first major German defeat in World War II and a crucial turning point in the conflict. The Battle of Britain takes its name from a speech by Winston Churchill to the House of Commons on 18 June: "What General Weygand has called The Battle of France is over. The Battle of Britain is about to begin."[19]

Background

Strategic bombing during World War I introduced air attacks intended to panic civilian targets and led in 1918 to the amalgamation of British army and navy air services into the Royal Air Force (RAF). Its first Chief of the Air Staff Hugh Trenchard was among the military strategists in the 1920s like Giulio Douhet who saw air warfare as a new way to overcome the stalemate of trench warfare. Interception was nearly impossible with fighter planes no faster than bombers. Their view (expressed vividly in 1932) was that the bomber will always get through, and the only defence was a deterrent bomber force capable of matching retaliation. Predictions were made that a bomber offensive would quickly cause thousands of deaths and civilian hysteria leading to capitulation, but widespread pacifism contributed to a reluctance to provide resources.[20]

Developing air strategies

Germany was forbidden to have a military air force by the 1919 Treaty of Versailles, but developed air crew training in civilian and sport flying. Following a 1923 memorandum, the Deutsche Luft Hansa airline developed designs for aircraft which could carry passengers and freight, and also be readily adapted into bombers, including the Junkers Ju 52. In 1926 the secret Lipetsk fighter-pilot school began operating.[21] Erhard Milch organised rapid expansion, and following the 1933 Nazi seizure of power his subordinate Robert Knauss formulated a deterrence theory incorporating Douhet's ideas and Tirpitz's "risk theory", which proposed a fleet of heavy bombers to deter a preventive attack by France and Poland before Germany could fully rearm.[22] A 1933–34 war game indicated a need for fighters and anti-aircraft protection as well as bombers. On 1 March 1935 the Luftwaffe was formally announced, with Walther Wever as Chief of Staff. The 1935 Luftwaffe doctrine for "Conduct of the Air War"

(*Die Luftkriegführung*) set air power within the overall military strategy, with critical tasks of attaining (local and temporary) air superiority and providing battlefield support for army and naval forces. Strategic bombing of industries and transport could be decisive longer term options, dependent on opportunity or preparations by the army and navy, to overcome a stalemate or used when only destruction of the enemy's economy would be conclusive.[23,24] The list excluded bombing civilians to destroy homes or undermine morale, as that was considered a waste of strategic effort, but the doctrine allowed revenge attacks if German civilians were bombed. A revised edition was issued in 1940, and the continuing central principle of Luftwaffe doctrine was that destruction of enemy armed forces was of primary importance.[25]

The RAF responded to Luftwaffe developments with its 1934 Expansion Plan A rearmament scheme, and in 1936 it was restructured into Bomber Command, Coastal Command, Training Command and Fighter Command. The latter was under Hugh Dowding, who opposed the doctrine that bombers were unstoppable: the invention of radar at that time could allow early detection, and prototype monoplane fighters were significantly faster. Priorities were disputed, but in December 1937 the Minister in charge of defence coordination Sir Thomas Inskip decided in Dowding's favour, that "The role of our air force is not an early knock-out blow" but rather was "to prevent the Germans from knocking us out" and fighter squadrons were just as necessary as bomber squadrons.[26,27]

In the Spanish Civil War, the Luftwaffe in the Condor Legion tried out air fighting tactics and their new aeroplanes. Wolfram von Richthofen became an exponent of air power providing ground support to other services.[28] The difficulty of accurately hitting targets prompted Ernst Udet to require that all new bombers had to be dive bombers, and led to the development of the Knickebein system for night time navigation. Priority was given to producing large numbers of smaller aeroplanes, and plans for a long range four engined strategic bomber were delayed.[29]

First stages of World War II

The early stages of World War II saw successful German invasions on the continent aided decisively by the air power of the Luftwaffe, which was able to establish tactical air superiority with great efficiency. The speed with which German forces defeated most of the defending armies in Norway in early 1940 created a significant political crisis in Britain. In early May 1940, the Norway Debate questioned the fitness for office of the British Prime Minister Neville Chamberlain. On 10 May, the same day Winston Churchill became British Prime Minister, the Germans initiated the Battle of France with an aggressive invasion of French territory. RAF Fighter Command was desperately short of

Figure 1: *Winston Churchill, British Prime Minister, in 1941*

trained pilots and aircraft, but despite the objections of its commander Hugh Dowding that the diversion of his forces would leave home defences under-strength, Churchill sent fighter squadrons, the Air Component of the British Expeditionary Force, to support operations in France, where the RAF suffered heavy losses.

After the evacuation of British and French soldiers from Dunkirk and the French surrender on 22 June 1940, Hitler mainly focused his energies on the possibility of invading the Soviet Union in the belief that the British, defeated on the continent and without European allies, would quickly come to terms. The Germans were so convinced of an imminent armistice that they began constructing street decorations for the homecoming parades of victorious troops. Although the British Foreign Secretary, Lord Halifax, and certain elements of the British public favoured a negotiated peace with an ascendant Germany, Churchill and a majority of his Cabinet refused to consider an armistice. Instead, Churchill used his skilful rhetoric to harden public opinion against capitulation and to prepare the British for a long war.

The Battle of Britain has the unusual distinction that it gained its name before being fought. The name is derived from the *This was their finest hour* speech delivered by Winston Churchill in the House of Commons on 18 June, more than three weeks prior to the generally accepted date for the start of the battle:

Figure 2: *Adolf Hitler, Chancellor of Germany, in 1933*

... What General Weygand has called The Battle of France is over. The battle of Britain is about to begin. Upon this battle depends the survival of Christian civilisation. Upon it depends our own British life and the long continuity of our institutions and our Empire. The whole fury and might of the enemy must very soon be turned on us. Hitler knows that he will have to break us in this island or lose the war. If we can stand up to him, all Europe may be free and the life of the world may move forward into broad, sunlit uplands. But if we fail, then the whole world, including the United States, including all that we have known and cared for, will sink into the abyss of a new Dark Age made more sinister, and perhaps more protracted, by the lights of a perverted science. Let us therefore brace ourselves to our duties, and so bear ourselves that, if the British Empire and its Commonwealth last for a thousand years, men will still say, 'This was their finest hour".[30,31]

— *Winston Churchill*

German aims and directives

From the outset of his rise to power, Hitler expressed admiration for Britain, and throughout the Battle period he sought neutrality or a peace treaty with Britain.[32] In a secret conference on 23 May 1939, Hitler set out his rather contradictory strategy that an attack on Poland was essential and "will only be successful if the Western Powers keep out of it. If this is impossible, then it will be better to attack in the West and to settle Poland at the same time" with a surprise attack. "If Holland and Belgium are successfully occupied and held, and if France is also defeated, the fundamental conditions for a successful war against England will have been secured. England can then be blockaded from Western France at close quarters by the Air Force, while the Navy with its submarines extend the range of the blockade."[33]

When war commenced, Hitler and the OKW (*Oberkommando der Wehrmacht* or "High Command of the Armed Forces") issued a series of Directives ordering planning and stating strategic objectives. "Directive No. 1 for the Conduct of the War" dated 31 August 1939 instructed the invasion of Poland on 1 September as planned. Potentially, Luftwaffe "operations against England" were to "dislocate English imports, the armaments industry, and the transport of troops to France. Any favourable opportunity of an effective attack on concentrated units of the English Navy, particularly on battleships or aircraft carriers, will be exploited. The decision regarding attacks on London is reserved to me. Attacks on the English homeland are to be prepared, bearing in mind that inconclusive results with insufficient forces are to be avoided in all circumstances."[34] Both France and the UK declared war on Germany; on 9 October Hitler's "Directive No. 6" planned the offensive to defeat these allies and "win as much territory as possible in the Netherlands, Belgium, and northern France to serve as a base for the successful prosecution of the air and sea war against England".[35] On 29 November OKW "Directive No. 9 – Instructions For Warfare Against The Economy Of The Enemy" stated that once this coastline had been secured, the Luftwaffe together with the Kriegsmarine (German Navy) was to blockade UK ports with sea mines, attack shipping and warships, and make air attacks on shore installations and industrial production. This directive remained in force in the first phase of the Battle of Britain.[36] It was reinforced on 24 May during the Battle of France by "Directive No. 13" which authorised the Luftwaffe "to attack the English homeland in the fullest manner, as soon as sufficient forces are available. This attack will be opened by an annihilating reprisal for English attacks on the Ruhr Basin."[37]

By the end of June 1940, Germany had defeated Britain's allies on the continent, and on 30 June the OKW Chief of Staff Alfred Jodl issued his review of options to increase pressure on Britain to agree to a negotiated peace. The first priority was to eliminate the RAF and gain air supremacy. Intensified air attacks against shipping and the economy could affect food supplies and civilian morale in the long term. Reprisal attacks of terror bombing had the potential to cause quicker capitulation, but the effect on morale was uncertain. Once the Luftwaffe had control of the air, and the UK economy had been weakened, an invasion would be a last resort or a final strike (*"Todesstoss"*) after Britain had already been conquered, but could have a quick result.Wikipedia:Please clarify On the same day, the Luftwaffe Commander-in-Chief Hermann Göring issued his operational directive; to destroy the RAF, thus protecting German industry, and also to block overseas supplies to Britain.[38] The German Supreme Command argued over the practicality of these options.

In "Directive No. 16 – On preparations for a landing operation against England" on 16 July, Hitler required readiness by mid-August for the possibility of an invasion he called Operation Sea Lion, unless the British agreed to negotiations. The Luftwaffe reported that it would be ready to launch its major attack early in August. The Kriegsmarine Commander-in-Chief, Grand Admiral Erich Raeder, continued to highlight the impracticality of these plans, and said sea invasion could not take place before early 1941. Hitler now argued that Britain was holding out in hope of assistance from Russia, and the Soviet Union was to be invaded by mid 1941.[39] Göring met his air fleet commanders, and on 24 July issued "Tasks and Goals" of firstly gaining air supremacy, secondly protecting invasion forces and attacking the Royal Navy's ships. Thirdly, they were to blockade imports, bombing harbours and stores of supplies.[40]

Hitler's "Directive No. 17 – For the conduct of air and sea warfare against England" issued on 1 August attempted to keep all the options open. The Luftwaffe's *Adlertag* campaign was to start around 5 August, subject to weather, with the aim of gaining air superiority over southern England as a necessary precondition of invasion, to give credibility to the threat and give Hitler the option of ordering the invasion. The intention was to incapacitate the RAF so much that the UK would feel open to air attack, and would begin peace negotiations. It was also to isolate the UK and damage war production, beginning an effective blockade.[41] Following severe Luftwaffe losses, Hitler agreed at a 14 September OKW conference that the air campaign was to intensify regardless of invasion plans. On 16 September, Göring gave the order for this change in strategy,[42] to the first independent strategic bombing campaign.[43]

Negotiated peace or neutrality

Adolf Hitler's *Mein Kampf* of 1923 mostly set out his hatreds: he only admired ordinary German World War I soldiers and Britain, which he saw as an ally against communism. In 1935 Hermann Göring welcomed news that Britain as a potential ally was rearming. In 1936 he promised assistance to defend the British Empire, asking only a free hand in Eastern Europe, and repeated this to Lord Halifax in 1937. That year, von Ribbentrop met Churchill with a similar proposal; when rebuffed, he told Churchill that interference with German domination would mean war. To Hitler's great annoyance, all his diplomacy failed to stop Britain from declaring war when he invaded Poland. During the fall of France, he repeatedly discussed peace efforts with his generals.[32]

When Churchill came to power, there was still wide support for Halifax, who as Foreign Secretary openly argued for peace negotiations in the tradition of British diplomacy, to secure British independence without war. On 20 May, Halifax secretly requested a Swedish businessman to make contact with Göring to open negotiations. Shortly afterwards, in the May 1940 War Cabinet Crisis, Halifax argued for negotiations involving the Italians, but this was rejected by Churchill with majority support. An approach made through the Swedish ambassador on 22 June was reported to Hitler, making peace negotiations seem feasible. Throughout July, as the battle started, the Germans made wider attempts to find a diplomatic solution.[44] On 2 July, the day the armed forces were asked to start preliminary planning for an invasion, Hitler got von Ribbentrop to draft a speech offering peace negotiations. On 19 July Hitler made this speech to the German Parliament in Berlin, appealing "to reason and common sense", and said he could "see no reason why this war should go on". His sombre conclusion was received in silence, but he did not suggest negotiations and this was effectively an ultimatum which was rejected by the British government.[45,46] Halifax kept trying to arrange peace until he was sent to Washington in December as ambassador,[47] and in January 1941 Hitler expressed continued interest in negotiating peace with Britain.[48]

Blockade and siege

A May 1939 planning exercise by Luftflotte 3 found that the Luftwaffe lacked the means to do much damage to Britain's war economy beyond laying naval mines.[49] The Head of Luftwaffe intelligence Joseph "Beppo" Schmid presented a report on 22 November 1939, stating that "Of all Germany's possible enemies, Britain is the most dangerous."[50] This "Proposal for the Conduct of Air Warfare" argued for a counter to the British blockade and said "Key is to paralyse the British trade". Instead of the Wehrmacht attacking the French, the Luftwaffe with naval assistance was to block imports to Britain and attack seaports. "Should the enemy resort to terror measures—for example, to attack our towns in western Germany" they could retaliate by bombing industrial centres and London. Parts of this appeared on 29 November in "Directive No. 9" as future actions once the coast had been conquered. On 24 May 1940 "Directive No. 13" authorised attacks on the blockade targets, as well as retaliation for RAF bombing of industrial targets in the Ruhr.

After the defeat of France the OKW felt they had won the war, and some more pressure would persuade Britain. On 30 June the OKW Chief of Staff Alfred Jodl issued his paper setting out options: the first was to increase attacks on shipping, economic targets and the RAF: air attacks and food shortages were expected to break morale and lead to capitulation. Destruction of the RAF was the first priority, and invasion would be a last resort. Göring's operational directive issued the same day ordered destruction of the RAF to clear the way for attacks cutting off seaborne supplies to Britain. It made no mention of invasion.[51]

Invasion plans

In November 1939, the OKW reviewed the potential for an air- and seaborne invasion of Britain: the Kriegsmarine (German Navy) was faced with the threat the Royal Navy's larger Home Fleet posed to a crossing of the English Channel, and together with the German Army viewed control of airspace as a necessary precondition. The German navy thought air superiority alone was insufficient; the German naval staff had already produced a study (in 1939) on the possibility of an invasion of Britain and concluded that it also required naval superiority.[52] The Luftwaffe said invasion could only be "the final act in an already victorious war."[53]

Hitler first discussed the idea of an invasion at a 21 May 1940 meeting with Grand Admiral Erich Raeder, who stressed the difficulties and his own preference for a blockade. OKW Chief of Staff Jodl's 30 June report described invasion as a last resort once the British economy had been damaged and the Luftwaffe had full air superiority. On 2 July, OKW requested preliminary plans.[16,46] In Britain, Churchill described "the great invasion scare" as "serving a very useful purpose" by "keeping every man and woman tuned to a high pitch of readiness".[54] On 10 July, he advised the War Cabinet that invasion could be ignored, as it "would be a most hazardous and suicidal operation".[55]

On 11 July, Hitler agreed with Raeder that invasion would be a last resort, and the Luftwaffe advised that gaining air superiority would take 14 to 28 days. Hitler met his army chiefs, von Brauchitsch and Halder, who presented detailed plans on the assumption that the navy would provide safe transport.[56] Hitler showed no interest in the details, but on 16 July he issued Directive No. 16 ordering preparations for Operation Sea Lion.[57]

The navy insisted on a narrow beachhead and an extended period for landing troops; the army rejected these plans: the Luftwaffe could begin an air attack in August. Hitler held a meeting of his army and navy chiefs on 31 July. The navy said 22 September was the earliest possible date, and proposed postponement until the following year, but Hitler preferred September. He then told von Brauchitsch and Halder that he would decide on the landing operation eight to fourteen days after the air attack began. On 1 August he issued Directive No. 17 for intensified air and sea warfare, to begin with Adlertag on or after 5 August subject to weather, keeping options open for negotiated peace or blockade and siege.[58]

Independent air attack

Under the continuing influence of the 1935 "Conduct of the Air War" doctrine, the main focus of the Luftwaffe command (including Göring) was in concentrating attacks to destroy enemy armed forces on the battlefield, and "blitzkrieg" close air support of the army succeeded brilliantly. They reserved strategic bombing for a stalemate situation or revenge attacks, but doubted if this could be decisive on its own and regarded bombing civilians to destroy homes or undermine morale as a waste of strategic effort.[59,60]

The defeat of France in June 1940 introduced the prospect for the first time of independent air action against Britain. A July *Fliegercorps I* paper asserted that Germany was by definition an air power: "Its chief weapon against England is the Air Force, then the Navy, followed by the landing forces and the Army." In 1940, the Luftwaffe would undertake a *"strategic offensive ... on its own and independent of the other services"*, according to an April 1944 German account of their military mission. Göring was convinced that strategic bombing could win objectives which were beyond the army and navy, and gain political advantages in the Third Reich for the Luftwaffe and himself.[61] He expected air warfare to decisively force Britain to negotiate, as all in the OKW hoped, and the Luftwaffe took little interest to planning to support an invasion.[62]

Opposing forces

The *Luftwaffe* faced a more capable opponent than any it had previously met: a sizeable, highly coordinated, well-supplied, modern air force.

Fighters

The *Luftwaffe*'s Messerschmitt Bf 109E and Bf 110C fought against the RAF's workhorse Hurricane Mk I and the less numerous Spitfire Mk I; Hurricanes outnumbered Spitfires in RAF Fighter Command by about 2:1 when war broke out. The Bf 109E had a better climb rate and was up to 40 mph faster in level flight than the Rotol (constant speed propeller) equipped Hurricane Mk I, depending on altitude.[63] The speed and climb disparity with the original non-Rotol Hurricane was even greater. By mid-1940, all RAF Spitfire and Hurricane fighter squadrons converted to 100 octane aviation fuel,[64] which allowed their Merlin engines to generate significantly more power and an approximately 30 mph increase in speed at low altitudes[65,66] through the use of an Emergency Boost Override. In September 1940, the more powerful Mk IIa series 1 Hurricanes started entering service in small numbers. This version was capable of a maximum speed of 342 mph (550 km/h), some 20 mph more than the original (non-Rotol) Mk I, though it was still 15 to 20 mph slower than a Bf 109 (depending on altitude).[67]

Figure 3: *Hawker Hurricane R4118 fought in the Battle of Britain. Here it arrives at the 2014 Royal International Air Tattoo, England.*

Figure 4: *X4382, a late production Spitfire Mk I of 602 Squadron flown by P/O Osgood Hanbury, Westhampnett, September 1940*

Figure 5: *Messerschmitt Bf 109E-3*

The performance of the Spitfire over Dunkirk came as a surprise to the *Jagdwaffe*, although the German pilots retained a strong belief that the 109 was the superior fighter. The British fighters were equipped with eight Browning .303 (7.7mm) machine guns, while most Bf 109Es had two 7.92mm machine guns supplemented by two 20mm cannons.[68] The latter was much more effective than the .303; during the Battle it was not unknown for damaged German bombers to limp home with up to two hundred .303 hits.[69] At some altitudes, the Bf 109 could outclimb the British fighter. It could also engage in vertical-plane negative-*g* manoeuvres without the engine cutting out because its DB 601 engine used fuel injection; this allowed the 109 to dive away from attackers more readily than the carburettor-equipped Merlin. On the other hand, the Bf 109E had a much larger turning circle than its two foes. In general, though, as Alfred Price noted in *The Spitfire Story*:

> ... *the differences between the Spitfire and the Me 109 in performance and handling were only marginal, and in a combat they were almost always surmounted by tactical considerations of which side had seen the other first, which had the advantage of sun, altitude, numbers, pilot ability, tactical situation, tactical co-ordination, amount of fuel remaining, etc.*

The Bf 109E was also used as a *Jabo* (*jagdbomber*, fighter-bomber)—the E-4/B and E-7 models could carry a 250 kg bomb underneath the fuselage, the later model arriving during the battle. The Bf 109, unlike the *Stuka*, could fight on equal terms with RAF fighters after releasing its ordnance.

Figure 6: *Four 264 Squadron Defiants (PS-V was
shot down on 28 August 1940 over Kent by Bf 109s.)*

At the start of the battle, the twin-engined Messerschmitt Bf 110C long range
Zerstörer ("Destroyer") was also expected to engage in air-to-air combat while
escorting the *Luftwaffe* bomber fleet. Although the 110 was faster than the
Hurricane and almost as fast as the Spitfire, its lack of manoeuvrability and
acceleration meant that it was a failure as a long-range escort fighter. On 13
and 15 August, thirteen and thirty aircraft were lost, the equivalent of an entire
Gruppe, and the type's worst losses during the campaign. This trend continued
with a further eight and fifteen lost on 16 and 17 August.

The most successful role of the Bf 110 during the battle was as a *Schnellbomber*
(fast bomber). The Bf 110 usually used a shallow dive to bomb the target and
escape at high speed. One unit, *Erprobungsgruppe 210* – initially formed as
the service test unit (*Erprobungskommando*) for the emerging successor to the
110, the Me 210 – proved that the Bf 110 could still be used to good effect in
attacking small or "pinpoint" targets.

The RAF's Boulton Paul Defiant had some initial success over Dunkirk because of its resemblance to the Hurricane; Luftwaffe fighters attacking from
the rear were surprised by its unusual gun turret. During the Battle of Britain,
it proved hopelessly outclassed. For various reasons, the Defiant lacked any
form of forward-firing armament, and the heavy turret and second crewman
meant it could not outrun or outmanoeuvre either the Bf 109 or Bf 110. By

Figure 7: *Heinkel He 111 bombers during the Battle of Britain*

the end of August, after disastrous losses, the aircraft was withdrawn from daylight service.

Bombers

The Luftwaffe's primary bombers were the Heinkel He 111, Dornier Do 17, and Junkers Ju 88 for level bombing at medium to high altitudes, and the Junkers Ju 87 *Stuka* for dive bombing tactics. The He 111 was used in greater numbers than the others during the conflict, and was better known, partly due to its distinctive wing shape. Each level bomber also had a few reconnaissance versions accompanying them that were used during the battle.

Although it had been successful in previous Luftwaffe engagements, the *Stuka* suffered heavy losses in the Battle of Britain, particularly on 18 August, due to its slow speed and vulnerability to fighter interception after dive bombing a target. As the losses went up along with their limited payload and range, *Stuka* units were largely removed from operations over England and diverted to concentrate on shipping instead until they were eventually re-deployed to the Eastern Front in 1941. For some raids, they were called back, such as on 13 September to attack Tangmere airfield.[70]

The remaining three bomber types differed in their capabilities; the Heinkel 111 was the slowest; the Ju 88 was the fastest once its mainly external bomb

Figure 8: *German propaganda photo purporting to show a Spitfire I flying very close to a Dornier 17Z*[71]

load was dropped; and the Do 17 had the smallest bomb load. All three bomber types suffered heavy losses from the home-based British fighters, but the Ju 88 disproportionately so. The German bombers required constant protection by the Luftwaffe's fighter force. German escorts were not sufficiently numerous. Bf 109Es were ordered to support more than 300–400 bombers on any given day. Later in the conflict, when night bombing became more frequent, all three were used. Due to its smaller bomb load, the lighter Do 17 was used less than the He 111 and Ju 88 for this purpose.

On the British side, three bomber types were mostly used on night operations against targets such as factories, invasion ports and railway centres; the Armstrong Whitworth Whitley, the Handley-Page Hampden and the Vickers Wellington were classified as heavy bombers by the RAF, although the Hampden was a medium bomber comparable to the He 111. The twin-engined Bristol Blenheim and the obsolescent single-engined Fairey Battle were both light bombers; the Blenheim was the most numerous of the aircraft equipping RAF Bomber Command and was used in attacks against shipping, ports, airfields and factories on the continent by day and by night. The Fairey Battle squadrons, which had suffered heavy losses in daylight attacks during the Battle of France, were brought up to strength with reserve aircraft and continued to operate at night in attacks against the invasion ports, until the Battle was withdrawn from UK front line service in October 1940.[72,73]</ref>

Figure 9: *A Spitfire pilot recounts how he shot
down a Messerschmitt, Biggin Hill, September 1940*

Pilots

Before the war, the RAF's processes for selecting potential candidates were
opened to men of all social classes through the creation in 1936 of the RAF
Volunteer Reserve, which "... was designed to appeal, to ... young men ...
without any class distinctions ..." The older squadrons of the Royal Auxiliary
Air Force did retain some of their upper-class exclusiveness, but their numbers
were soon swamped by the newcomers of the RAFVR; by 1 September 1939,
6,646 pilots had been trained through the RAFVR.

By mid-1940, there were about 9,000 pilots in the RAF to man about 5,000 aircraft, most of which were bombers.Wikipedia:Citation needed Fighter Command was never short of pilots, but the problem of finding sufficient numbers
of fully trained fighter pilots became acute by mid-August 1940. With aircraft
production running at 300 planes each week, only 200 pilots were trained in
the same period. In addition, more pilots were allocated to squadrons than
there were aircraft, as this allowed squadrons to maintain operational strength
despite casualties and still provide for pilot leave. Another factor was that only
about 30% of the 9,000 pilots were assigned to operational squadrons; 20% of
the pilots were involved in conducting pilot training, and a further 20% were
undergoing further instruction, like those offered in Canada and in Southern
Rhodesia to the Commonwealth trainees, although already qualified. The rest
were assigned to staff positions, since RAF policy dictated that only pilots

Figure 10: *South African Adolph "Sailor" Malan led No. 74 Squadron RAF and was, at the time, the RAF's leading ace, with 27 planes destroyed, 7 shared, 2 unconfirmed, 3 probables and 16 damaged.*

could make many staff and operational command decisions, even in engineering matters. At the height of fighting, and despite Churchill's insistence, only 30 pilots were released to the front line from administrative duties.[74]

For these reasons, and the permanent loss of 435 pilots during the Battle of France alone[75] along with many more wounded, and others lost in Norway, the RAF had fewer experienced pilots at the start of the initial defence of their home. It was the lack of trained pilots in the fighting squadrons, rather than the lack of aircraft, that became the greatest concern for Air Chief Marshal Hugh Dowding, Commander of Fighter Command. Drawing from regular RAF forces, the Auxiliary Air Force and the Volunteer Reserve, the British were able to muster some 1,103 fighter pilots on 1 July. Replacement pilots, with little flight training and often no gunnery training, suffered high casualty rates, thus exacerbating the problem.

The Luftwaffe, on the other hand, were able to muster a larger number (1,450) of more experienced fighter pilots. Drawing from a cadre of Spanish Civil War veterans, these pilots already had comprehensive courses in aerial gunnery and instructions in tactics suited for fighter-versus-fighter combat. Training manuals discouraged heroism, stressing the importance of attacking only when the

Figure 11: *126 German aircraft or "Adolfs" were claimed
by Polish pilots of 303 Squadron during the Battle of Britain*

odds were in the pilot's favour. Despite the high levels of experience, German fighter formations did not provide a sufficient reserve of pilots to allow for losses and leave, and the Luftwaffe was unable to produce enough pilots to prevent a decline in operational strength as the battle progressed.

International participation

76

Allies

About 20% of pilots who took part in the battle were from non British countries. The Royal Air Force roll of honour for the Battle of Britain recognises 595 non-British pilots (out of 2,936) as flying at least one authorised operational sortie with an eligible unit of the RAF or Fleet Air Arm between 10 July and 31 October 1940. These included 145 Poles, 127 New Zealanders, 112 Canadians, 88 Czechoslovaks, 10 Irish, 32 Australians, 28 Belgians, 25 South Africans, 13 French, 9 Americans, 3 Southern Rhodesians and one each from Jamaica and Mandatory Palestine.[77] "Altogether in the fighter battles, the bombing raids, and the various patrols flown between 10 July and 31 October 1940 by the Royal Air Force, 1495 aircrew were killed, of whom 449 were fighter pilots, 718 aircrew from Bomber Command, and 280 from Coastal

Command. Among those killed were 47 airmen from Canada, 24 from Australia, 17 from South Africa, 35 from Poland, 20 from Czechoslovakia and six from Belgium. Forty-seven New Zealanders lost their lives, including 15 fighter pilots, 24 bomber and eight coastal aircrew. The names of these Allied and Commonwealth airmen are inscribed in a memorial book which rests in the Battle of Britain Chapel in Westminster Abbey. In the chapel is a stained glass window which contains the badges of the fighter squadrons which operated during the battle and the flags of the nations to which the pilots and aircrew belonged."[78]

These pilots, some of whom had to flee their home countries because of the Nazi war-machine, fought with great distinction. The No. 303 Polish Fighter Squadron for example was not just the highest scoring of the Hurricane squadrons during the Battle of Britain, but also had the highest ratio of enemy aircraft destroyed to their own losses.[79,80,81]

Axis

An element of the Italian Royal Air Force (*Regia Aeronautica*) called the Italian Air Corps (*Corpo Aereo Italiano* or CAI) first saw action in late October 1940. It took part in the latter stages of the battle, but achieved limited success. The unit was redeployed in early 1941.

Luftwaffe strategy

The high command's indecision over which aim to pursue was reflected in shifts in Luftwaffe strategy. Their Air War doctrine of concentrated close air support of the army at the battlefront succeeded in the *blitzkrieg* offensives against Poland, Denmark and Norway, the Low Countries and France, but incurred significant losses. The Luftwaffe now had to establish or restore bases in the conquered territories, and rebuild their strength. In June 1940 they began regular armed reconnaissance flights and sporadic *Störangriffe*, nuisance raids of one or a few bombers, both day and night. These gave crews practice in navigation and avoiding air defences, and set off air raid alarms which disturbed civilian morale. Similar nuisance raids continued throughout the battle, into late 1940. Scattered naval mine–laying sorties began at the outset, and increased gradually over the battle period.[82,83]

Göring's operational directive of 30 June ordered destruction of the RAF as a whole, including the aircraft industry, with the aims of ending RAF bombing raids on Germany and facilitating attacks on ports and storage in the Luftwaffe blockade of Britain. Attacks on Channel shipping in the *Kanalkampf* began on 4 July, and were formalised on 11 July in an order by Hans Jeschonnek which added the arms industry as a target.[84,85]

Figure 12: *Hermann Göring, the commander of the Luftwaffe*

Figure 13: *Hugo Sperrle, the commander of Luftflotte 3*

On 16 July Directive No. 16 ordered preparations for Operation Sea Lion, and on the next day the luftwaffe was ordered to stand by in full readiness. Göring met his air fleet commanders, and on 24 July issued "Tasks and Goals" of gaining air supremacy, protecting the army and navy if invasion went ahead, and attacking the Royal Navy's ships as well as continuing the blockade. Once the RAF had been defeated, Luftwaffe bombers were to move forward beyond London without the need for fighter escort, destroying military and economic targets.[40]

At a meeting on 1 August the command reviewed plans produced by each *Fliegerkorps* with differing proposals for targets including whether to bomb airfields, but failed to focus priorities. Intelligence reports gave Göring the impression that the RAF was almost defeated: the intent was that raids would attract British fighters for the Luftwaffe to shoot down.[86] On 6 August he finalised plans for this "Operation Eagle Attack" with Kesselring, Sperle and Stumpff: destruction of RAF Fighter Command across the south of England was to take four days, with lightly escorted small bomber raids leaving the main fighter force free to attack RAF fighters. Bombing of military and economic targets was then to systematically extend up to the Midlands until daylight attacks could proceed unhindered over the whole of Britain.[87,88]

Bombing of London was to be held back while these night time "destroyer" attacks proceeded over other urban areas, then in culmination of the campaign a major attack on the capital was intended to cause a crisis when refugees fled London just as the Operation Sea Lion invasion was to begin.[89] With hopes fading for the possibility of invasion, on 4 September Hitler authorised a main focus on day and night attacks on tactical targets with London as the main target, in what the British called the Blitz. With increasing difficulty in defending bombers in day raids, the Luftwaffe shifted to a strategic bombing campaign of night raids aiming to overcome British resistance by damaging infrastructure and food stocks, though intentional terror bombing of civilians was not sanctioned.[90]

Regrouping of Luftwaffe in Luftflotten

The Luftwaffe was forced to regroup after the Battle of France into three *Luftflotten* (Air Fleets) on Britain's southern and northern flanks. *Luftflotte 2*, commanded by *Generalfeldmarschall* Albert Kesselring, was responsible for the bombing of southeast England and the London area. *Luftflotte 3*, under *Generalfeldmarschall* Hugo Sperrle, targeted the West Country, Wales, the Midlands, and northwest England. *Luftflotte 5*, led by *Generaloberst* Hans-Jürgen Stumpff from his headquarters in Norway, targeted the north of England and

Scotland. As the battle progressed, command responsibility shifted, with *Luft-flotte* 3 taking more responsibility for the night-time *Blitz* attacks while the main daylight operations fell upon *Luftflotte* 2's shoulders.

Initial Luftwaffe estimates were that it would take four days to defeat the RAF Fighter Command in southern England. This would be followed by a four-week offensive during which the bombers and long-range fighters would destroy all military installations throughout the country and wreck the British aircraft industry. The campaign was planned to begin with attacks on airfields near the coast, gradually moving inland to attack the ring of sector airfields defending London. Later reassessments gave the Luftwaffe five weeks, from 8 August to 15 September, to establish temporary air superiority over England. To achieve this goal, Fighter Command had to be destroyed, either on the ground or in the air, yet the Luftwaffe had to be able to preserve its own strength to be able to support the invasion; this meant that the Luftwaffe had to maintain a high "kill ratio" over the RAF fighters. The only alternative to the goal of air superiority was a terror bombing campaign aimed at the civilian population, but this was considered a last resort and it was (at this stage of the battle) expressly forbidden by Hitler.

The Luftwaffe kept broadly to this scheme, but its commanders had differences of opinion on strategy. Sperrle wanted to eradicate the air defence infrastructure by bombing it. His counterpart, Kesselring, championed attacking London directly— either to bombard the British government into submission, or to draw RAF fighters into a decisive battle. Göring did nothing to resolve this disagreement between his commanders, and only vague directives were set down during the initial stages of the battle, with Göring seemingly unable to decide upon which strategy to pursue. He seemed at times obsessed with maintaining his own power base in the Luftwaffe and indulging his outdated beliefs on air fighting, which would later lead to tactical and strategic errors.Wikipedia:Citation needed

Tactics

Fighter formations

Luftwaffe formations employed a loose section of two (nicknamed the *Rotte* (pack)), based on a leader (*Rottenführer*) followed at a distance of about 200 metres[91] by his wingman (nicknamed the *Rottenhund* (pack dog) or *Katschmarek*), who also flew slightly higher and was trained always to stay with his leader. With more room between them, both pilots could spend less time maintaining formation and more time looking around and covering each other's blind spots. Attacking aircraft could be sandwiched between the two 109s.[92] for similar reasons, though Luftwaffe' pilots during the Spanish Civil

War (led by Günther Lützow and Werner Mölders, among others) are generally given credit.</ref> The *Rotte* allowed the *Rottenführer* to concentrate on getting kills, but few wingmen had the chance, leading to some resentment in the lower ranks where it was felt that the high scores came at their expense. Two sections were usually teamed up into a *Schwarm*, where all the pilots could watch what was happening around them. Each *Schwarm* in a *Staffel* flew at staggered heights and with about 200 metres of room between them, making the formation difficult to spot at longer ranges and allowing for a great deal of flexibility. By using a tight "cross-over" turn, a *Schwarm* could quickly change direction.

The Bf 110s adopted the same *Schwarm* formation as the 109s, but were seldom able to use this to the same advantage. The Bf 110's most successful method of attack was the "bounce" from above. When attacked, *Zerstör-ergruppen* increasingly resorted to forming large "defensive circles", where each Bf 110 guarded the tail of the aircraft ahead of it. Göring ordered that they be renamed "offensive circles" in a vain bid to improve rapidly declining morale. These conspicuous formations were often successful in attracting RAF fighters that were sometimes "bounced" by high-flying Bf 109s. This led to the often repeated misconception that the Bf 110s were escorted by Bf 109s.

Higher-level dispositions

Luftwaffe tactics were influenced by their fighters. The Bf 110 proved too vulnerable to the nimble single-engined RAF fighters. This meant the bulk of fighter escort duties fell on the Bf 109. Fighter tactics were then complicated by bomber crews who demanded closer protection. After the hard-fought battles of 15 and 18 August, Göring met with his unit leaders. During this conference, the need for the fighters to meet up on time with the bombers was stressed. It was also decided that one bomber *Gruppe* could only be properly protected by several *Gruppen* of 109s. In addition, Göring stipulated that as many fighters as possible were to be left free for *Freie Jagd* ("Free Hunts": a free-roving fighter sweep preceded a raid to try to sweep defenders out of the raid's path). The Ju 87 units, which had suffered heavy casualties, were only to be used under favourable circumstances. In early September, due to increasing complaints from the bomber crews about RAF fighters seemingly able to get through the escort screen, Göring ordered an increase in close escort duties. This decision shackled many of the Bf 109s to the bombers and, although they were more successful at protecting the bomber forces, casualties amongst the fighters mounted primarily because they were forced to fly and manoeuvre at reduced speeds.

The Luftwaffe consistently varied its tactics in its attempts to break through the RAF defences. It launched many *Freie Jagd* to draw up RAF fighters.

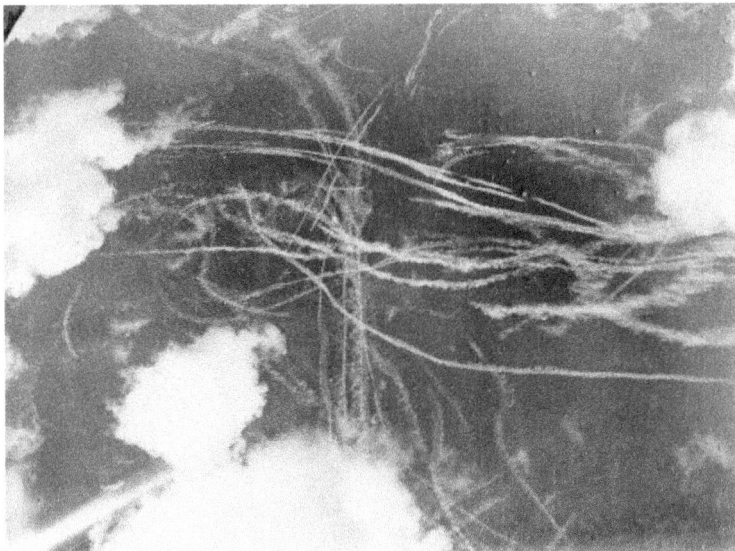

Figure 14: *Pattern of condensation trails left
by British and German aircraft after a dogfight.*

RAF fighter controllers were often able to detect these and position squadrons to avoid them, keeping to Dowding's plan to preserve fighter strength for the bomber formations. The Luftwaffe also tried using small formations of bombers as bait, covering them with large numbers of escorts. This was more successful, but escort duty tied the fighters to the bombers' slow speed and made them more vulnerable.

By September, standard tactics for raids had become an amalgam of techniques. A *Freie Jagd* would precede the main attack formations. The bombers would fly in at altitudes between 16,000 feet (4,900 m) and 20,000 feet (6,100 m), closely escorted by fighters. Escorts were divided into two parts (usually *Gruppen*), some operating in close contact with the bombers, and others a few hundred yards away and a little above. If the formation was attacked from the starboard, the starboard section engaged the attackers, the top section moving to starboard and the port section to the top position. If the attack came from the port side the system was reversed. British fighters coming from the rear were engaged by the rear section and the two outside sections similarly moving to the rear. If the threat came from above, the top section went into action while the side sections gained height to be able to follow RAF fighters down as they broke away. If attacked, all sections flew in defensive

Figure 15: *Adolf Galland, the successful leader of III./JG 26, became Geschwaderkommodore of JG 26 on 22 August*

circles. These tactics were skilfully evolved and carried out, and were difficult to counter.[93]

Adolf Galland noted:

> *We had the impression that, whatever we did, we were bound to be wrong. Fighter protection for bombers created many problems which had to be solved in action. Bomber pilots preferred close screening in which their formation was surrounded by pairs of fighters pursuing a zigzag course. Obviously, the visible presence of the protective fighters gave the bomber pilots a greater sense of security. However, this was a faulty conclusion, because a fighter can only carry out this purely defensive task by taking the initiative in the offensive. He must never wait until attacked because he then loses the chance of acting.*

> *We fighter pilots certainly preferred the free chase during the approach and over the target area. This gives the greatest relief and the best protection for the bomber force.*

The biggest disadvantage faced by Bf 109 pilots was that without the benefit of long-range drop tanks (which were introduced in limited numbers in the late stages of the battle), usually of 300 litres (66 imp gal; 79 US gal) capacity, the 109s had an endurance of just over an hour and, for the 109E, a 600 km (370 mi) range. Once over Britain, a 109 pilot had to keep an eye on a red "low fuel" light on the instrument panel: once this was illuminated, he was forced to turn back and head for France. With the prospect of two long flights over water, and knowing their range was substantially reduced when escorting bombers or during combat, the *Jagdflieger* coined the term *Kanalkrankheit* or "Channel sickness".

Intelligence

The Luftwaffe was ill-served by its lack of military intelligence about the British defences. The German intelligence services were fractured and plagued by rivalries; their performance was "amateurish". By 1940, there were few German agents operating in Great Britain and a handful of bungled attempts to insert spies into the country were foiled.

As a result of intercepted radio transmissions, the Germans began to realise that the RAF fighters were being controlled from ground facilities; in July and August 1939, for example, the airship *Graf Zeppelin*, which was packed with equipment for listening in on RAF radio and RDF transmissions, flew around the coasts of Britain. Although the Luftwaffe correctly interpreted these new ground control procedures, they were incorrectly assessed as being rigid and ineffectual. A British radar system was well known to the Luftwaffe from intelligence gathered before the war, but the highly developed "Dowding system" linked with fighter control had been a well-kept secret.[94] Even when good information existed, such as a November 1939 *Abwehr* assessment of Fighter Command strengths and capabilities by *Abteilung V*, it was ignored if it did not match conventional preconceptions.

On 16 July 1940, *Abteilung V*, commanded by *Oberstleutnant* "Beppo" Schmid, produced a report on the RAF and on Britain's defensive capabilities which was adopted by the frontline commanders as a basis for their operational plans. One of the most conspicuous failures of the report was the lack of information on the RAF's RDF network and control systems capabilities; it was assumed that the system was rigid and inflexible, with the RAF fighters being "tied" to their home bases.[95] An optimistic and, as it turned out, erroneous conclusion reached was:

> **D. Supply Situation**... *At present the British aircraft industry produces about 180 to 300 first line fighters and 140 first line bombers a month. In view of the present conditions relating to production (the appearance of raw material difficulties, the disruption or breakdown of production at factories owing to air attacks, the increased vulnerability to air attack owing to the fundamental reorganisation of the aircraft industry now in*

progress), it is believed that for the time being output will decrease rather than increase.

In the event of an intensification of air warfare it is expected that the present strength of the RAF will fall, and this decline will be aggravated by the continued decrease in production.

Because of this statement, reinforced by another more detailed report, issued on 10 August, there was a mindset in the ranks of the Luftwaffe that the RAF would run out of frontline fighters. The Luftwaffe believed it was weakening Fighter Command at three times the actual attrition rate. Many times, the leadership believed Fighter Command's strength had collapsed, only to discover that the RAF were able to send up defensive formations at will.

Throughout the battle, the Luftwaffe had to use numerous reconnaissance sorties to make up for the poor intelligence. Reconnaissance aircraft (initially mostly Dornier Do 17s, but increasingly Bf 110s) proved easy prey for British fighters, as it was seldom possible for them to be escorted by Bf 109s. Thus, the Luftwaffe operated "blind" for much of the battle, unsure of its enemy's true strengths, capabilities, and deployments. Many of the Fighter Command airfields were never attacked, while raids against supposed fighter airfields fell instead on bomber or coastal defence stations. The results of bombing and air fighting were consistently exaggerated, due to inaccurate claims, over-enthusiastic reports and the difficulty of confirmation over enemy territory. In the euphoric atmosphere of perceived victory, the Luftwaffe leadership became increasingly disconnected from reality. This lack of leadership and solid intelligence meant the Germans did not adopt consistent strategy, even when the RAF had its back to the wall. Moreover, there was never a systematic focus on one type of target (such as airbases, radar stations, or aircraft factories); consequently, the already haphazard effort was further diluted.[96]

Navigational aids

While the British were using radar for air defence more effectively than the Germans realised, the Luftwaffe attempted to press its own offensive with advanced radio navigation systems of which the British were initially not aware. One of these was *Knickebein* ("bent leg"); this system was used at night and for raids where precision was required. It was rarely used during the Battle of Britain.

Air-sea rescue

The Luftwaffe was much better prepared for the task of air-sea rescue than the RAF, specifically tasking the *Seenotdienst* unit, equipped with about 30 Heinkel He 59 floatplanes, with picking up downed aircrew from the North Sea, English Channel and the Dover Straits. In addition, Luftwaffe aircraft were equipped with life rafts and the aircrew were provided with sachets of a chemical called fluorescein which, on reacting with water, created a large, easy-to-see, bright green patch. In accordance with the Geneva Convention, the He 59s were unarmed and painted white with civilian registration markings and red crosses. Nevertheless, RAF aircraft attacked these aircraft, as some were escorted by Bf 109s.

After single He 59s were forced to land on the sea by RAF fighters, on 1 and 9 July respectively, a controversial order was issued to the RAF on 13 July; this stated that from 20 July, *Seenotdienst* aircraft were to be shot down. One of the reasons given by Churchill was:

> We did not recognise this means of rescuing enemy pilots so they could come and bomb our civil population again ... all German air ambulances were forced down or shot down by our fighters on definite orders approved by the War Cabinet.

The British also believed that their crews would report on convoys, the Air Ministry issuing a communiqué to the German government on 14 July that Britain was

> unable, however, to grant immunity to such aircraft flying over areas in which operations are in progress on land or at sea, or approaching British or Allied territory, or territory in British occupation, or British or Allied ships. Ambulance aircraft which do not comply with the above will do so at their own risk and peril

The white He 59s were soon repainted in camouflage colours and armed with defensive machine guns. Although another four He 59s were shot down by RAF aircraft, the *Seenotdienst* continued to pick up downed Luftwaffe and Allied aircrew throughout the battle, earning praise from Adolf Galland for their bravery.

RAF strategy

Figure 16: *Commander-in-Chief, Air Chief Marshal Sir Hugh Dowding*

Figure 17: *10 Group Commander, Sir Quintin Brand*

Figure 18: *11 Group Commander, Keith Park*

Figure 19: *12 Group Commander, Trafford Leigh-Mallory*

Figure 20: *13 Group Commander, Richard Saul*

Figure 21: *Chain Home radar cover*

The Dowding system

During early tests of the Chain Home system, the slow flow of information from the CH radars and observers to the aircraft often caused them to miss their "bandits". The solution, today known as the "Dowding system", was to create a set of reporting chains to move information from the various observation points to the pilots in their fighters. It was named after its chief architect, "Stuffy" Dowding.

Reports from CH radars and the Observer Corps were sent directly to Fighter Command Headquarters (FCHQ) at Bentley Priory where they were "filtered" to combine multiple reports of the same formations into single tracks. Telephone operators would then forward only the information of interest to the Group headquarters, where the map would be re-created. This process was repeated to produce another version of the map at the Sector level, covering a much smaller area. Looking over their maps, Group level commanders could select squadrons to attack particular targets. From that point the Sector operators would give commands to the fighters to arrange an interception, as well as return them to base. Sector stations also controlled the anti-aircraft batteries in their area; an army officer sat beside each fighter controller and directed the gun crews when to open and cease fire.

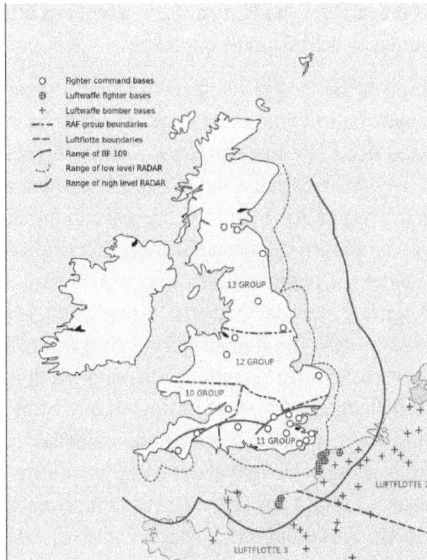

Figure 22: *RAF and Luftwaffe bases, group and Luftflotte boundaries, and range of Luftwaffe Bf 109 fighters. Southern part of British radar coverage: radar in North of Scotland not shown.*

The Dowding system dramatically improved the speed and accuracy of the information that flowed to the pilots. During the early war period it was expected that an average interception mission might have a 30% chance of ever seeing their target. During the battle, the Dowding system maintained an average rate over 75%, with several examples of 100% rates – every fighter dispatched found and intercepted its target.Wikipedia:Citation needed In contrast, Luftwaffe fighters attempting to intercept raids had to randomly seek their targets and often returned home having never seen enemy aircraft. The result is what is now known as an example of "force multiplication"; RAF fighters were as effective as two or more Luftwaffe fighters, greatly offsetting, or overturning, the disparity in actual numbers.

Intelligence

While Luftwaffe intelligence reports underestimated British fighter forces and aircraft production, the British intelligence estimates went the other way: they overestimated German aircraft production, numbers and range of aircraft available, and numbers of Luftwaffe pilots. In action, the Luftwaffe believed from their pilot claims and the impression given by aerial reconnaissance that the

RAF was close to defeat, and the British made strenuous efforts to overcome the perceived advantages held by their opponents.[97]

It is unclear how much the British intercepts of the Enigma cipher, used for high-security German radio communications, affected the battle. Ultra, the information obtained from Enigma intercepts, gave the highest echelons of the British command a view of German intentions. According to F. W. Winterbotham, who was the senior Air Staff representative in the Secret Intelligence Service, Ultra helped establish the strength and composition of the Luftwaffe's formations, the aims of the commanders and provided early warning of some raids. In early August it was decided that a small unit would be set up at FCHQ, which would process the flow of information from Bletchley and provide Dowding only with the most essential Ultra material; thus the Air Ministry did not have to send a continual flow of information to FCHQ, preserving secrecy, and Dowding was not inundated with non-essential information. Keith Park and his controllers were also told about Ultra. In a further attempt to camouflage the existence of Ultra, Dowding created a unit named No. 421 (Reconnaissance) Flight RAF. This unit (which later became No. 91 Squadron RAF), was equipped with Hurricanes and Spitfires and sent out aircraft to search for and report Luftwaffe formations approaching England. In addition the radio listening service (known as Y Service), monitoring the patterns of Luftwaffe radio traffic contributed considerably to the early warning of raids.

Air-sea rescue

One of the biggest oversights of the entire system was the lack of adequate air-sea rescue organisation. The RAF had started organising a system in 1940 with High Speed Launches (HSLs) based on flying boat bases and at some overseas locations, but it was still believed that the amount of cross-Channel traffic meant that there was no need for a rescue service to cover these areas. Downed pilots and aircrew, it was hoped, would be picked up by any boats or ships which happened to be passing by. Otherwise the local life boat would be alerted, assuming someone had seen the pilot going into the water.[98]

RAF aircrew were issued with a life jacket, nicknamed the "Mae West," but in 1940 it still required manual inflation, which was almost impossible for someone who was injured or in shock. The waters of the English Channel and Dover Straits are cold, even in the middle of summer, and clothing issued to RAF aircrew did little to insulate them against these freezing conditions. The RAF also imitated the German practice of issuing fluorescein. A conference in 1939 had placed air-sea rescue under Coastal Command. Because pilots had been lost at sea during the "Channel Battle", on 22 August, control of RAF rescue launches was passed to the local naval authorities and 12 Lysanders were given to Fighter Command to help look for pilots at sea. In all some 200

Figure 23: *X4474, a late production Mk I Spitfire of 19 Squadron, September 1940. During the battle 19 Squadron was part of the Duxford Wing*

pilots and aircrew were lost at sea during the battle. No proper air-sea rescue service was formed until 1941.

Tactics

Fighter formations

In the late 1930s, Fighter Command expected to face only bombers over Britain, not single-engined fighters. A series of "Fighting Area Tactics" were formulated and rigidly adhered to, involving a series of manoeuvres designed to concentrate a squadron's firepower to bring down bombers. RAF fighters flew in tight, v-shaped sections ("vics") of three aircraft, with four such "sections" in tight formation. Only the squadron leader at the front was free to watch for the enemy; the other pilots had to concentrate on keeping station. Training also emphasised by-the-book attacks by sections breaking away in sequence. Fighter Command recognised the weaknesses of this structure early in the battle, but it was felt too risky to change tactics during the battle, because replacement pilots—often with only minimal flying time—could not be readily retrained, and inexperienced pilots needed firm leadership in the air only rigid formations could provide. German pilots dubbed the RAF formations *Idiotenreihen* ("rows of idiots") because they left squadrons vulnerable to attack.

Front line RAF pilots were acutely aware of the inherent deficiencies of their own tactics. A compromise was adopted whereby squadron formations used much looser formations with one or two "weavers" flying independently above and behind to provide increased observation and rear protection; these tended to be the least experienced men and were often the first to be shot down without the other pilots even noticing that they were under attack. During the battle,

74 Squadron under Squadron Leader Adolph "Sailor" Malan adopted a vari-
ation of the German formation called the "fours in line astern", which was a
vast improvement on the old three aircraft "vic". Malan's formation was later
generally used by Fighter Command.

Squadron- and higher-level deployment

The weight of the battle fell upon 11 Group. Keith Park's tactics were to
dispatch individual squadrons to intercept raids. The intention was to subject incoming bombers to continual attacks by relatively small numbers of
fighters and try to break up the tight German formations. Once formations
had fallen apart, stragglers could be picked off one by one. Where multiple squadrons reached a raid the procedure was for the slower Hurricanes to
tackle the bombers while the more agile Spitfires held up the fighter escort.
This ideal was not always achieved, resulting in occasions when Spitfires and
Hurricanes reversed roles. Park also issued instructions to his units to engage
in frontal attacks against the bombers, which were more vulnerable to such attacks. Again, in the environment of fast moving, three-dimensional air battles,
few RAF fighter units were able to attack the bombers from head-on.

During the battle, some commanders, notably Leigh-Mallory, proposed
squadrons be formed into "Big Wings," consisting of at least three squadrons,
to attack the enemy *en masse*, a method pioneered by Douglas Bader.

Proponents of this tactic claimed interceptions in large numbers caused greater
enemy losses while reducing their own casualties. Opponents pointed out the
big wings would take too long to form up, and the strategy ran a greater risk of
fighters being caught on the ground refuelling. The big wing idea also caused
pilots to overclaim their kills, due to the confusion of a more intense battle
zone. This led to the belief big wings were far more effective than they actually
were.

The issue caused intense friction between Park and Leigh-Mallory, as 12
Group was tasked with protecting 11 Group's airfields whilst Park's squadrons
intercepted incoming raids. The delay in forming up Big Wings meant the
formations often did not arrive at all or until after German bombers had hit
11 Group's airfields. Dowding, to highlight the problem of the Big Wing's
performance, submitted a report compiled by Park to the Air Ministry on 15
November. In the report, he highlighted that during the period of 11 September – 31 October, the extensive use of the Big Wing had resulted in just 10
interceptions and one German aircraft destroyed, but his report was ignored.
Post-war analysis agrees Dowding and Park's approach was best for 11 Group.

Dowding's removal from his post in November 1940 has been blamed on this
struggle between Park and Leigh-Mallory's daylight strategy. The intensive

Figure 24: *Douglas Bader commanded 242 Squadron during the battle. He also led the Duxford Wing.*

raids and destruction wrought during the Blitz damaged both Dowding and Park in particular, for the failure to produce an effective night-fighter defence system, something for which the influential Leigh-Mallory had long criticised them.

Bomber and Coastal Command contributions

Bomber Command and Coastal Command aircraft flew offensive sorties against targets in Germany and France during the battle.

An hour after the declaration of war, Bomber Command launched raids on warships and naval ports by day, and in night raids dropped leaflets as it was considered illegal to bomb targets which could affect civilians. After the initial disasters of the war, with Vickers Wellington bombers shot down in large numbers attacking Wilhelmshaven and the slaughter of the Fairey Battle squadrons sent to France, it became clear that they would have to operate mainly at night to avoid incurring very high losses. Churchill came to power on 10 May 1940, and night raids on German towns began with the bombing of Mönchen-Gladbach on the night of 11 May. The War Cabinet on 12 May agreed that German actions justified "unrestricted warfare", and on 14 May they authorised an attack on the night of 14/15 May against oil and rail targets in Germany. At the urging of Clement Attlee, the Cabinet on 15 May authorised a

Figure 25: *A Bristol Blenheim Mk IV of 21 Squadron*

full bombing strategy against "suitable military objectives", even where there could be civilian casualties. That evening, a night time bomber campaign began against the German oil industry, communications, and forests/crops, mainly in the Ruhr area. The RAF lacked accurate night navigation, and carried small bomb loads.[99] As the threat mounted, Bomber Command changed targeting priority on 3 June 1940 to attack the German aircraft industry. On 4 July, the Air Ministry gave Bomber Command orders to attack ports and shipping. By September, the build-up of invasion barges in the Channel ports had become a top priority target.

On 7 September, the government issued a warning that the invasion could be expected within the next few days and, that night, Bomber Command attacked the Channel ports and supply dumps. On 13 September, they carried out another large raid on the Channel ports, sinking 80 large barges in the port of Ostend. 84 barges were sunk in Dunkirk after another raid on 17 September and by 19 September, almost 200 barges had been sunk. The loss of these barges may have contributed to Hitler's decision to postpone Operation *Sea Lion* indefinitely. The success of these raids was in part because the Germans had few Freya radar stations set up in France, so that air defences of the French harbours were not nearly as good as the air defences over Germany; Bomber Command had directed some 60% of its strength against the Channel ports.

The Bristol Blenheim units also raided German-occupied airfields throughout July to December 1940, both during daylight hours and at night. Although

Figure 26: *Wellington crews studying maps at a brief-
ing with the station commander, September 1940*

most of these raids were unproductive, there were some successes; on 1 August, five out of twelve Blenheims sent to attack Haamstede and Evere (Brussels) were able to destroy or heavily damage three Bf 109s of II./JG 27 and apparently kill a *Staffelkapitän* identified as a *Hauptmann* Albrecht von Ankum-
Frank. Two other 109s were claimed by Blenheim gunners.[100] Another successful raid on Haamstede was made by a single Blenheim on 7 August which
destroyed one 109 of 4./JG 54, heavily damaged another and caused lighter
damage to four more.

There were some missions which produced an almost 100% casualty rate
amongst the Blenheims; one such operation was mounted on 13 August 1940
against a Luftwaffe airfield near Aalborg in north-eastern Denmark by 12 aircraft of 82 Squadron. One Blenheim returned early (the pilot was later charged
and due to appear before a court martial, but was killed on another operation);
the other eleven, which reached Denmark, were shot down, five by flak and six
by Bf 109s. Of the 33 crewmen who took part in the attack, 20 were killed
and 13 captured.

As well as the bombing operations, Blenheim-equipped units had been formed
to carry out long-range strategic reconnaissance missions over Germany and
German-occupied territories. In this role, the Blenheims again proved to be
too slow and vulnerable against Luftwaffe fighters, and they took constant ca-
sualties.Wikipedia:Citing sources

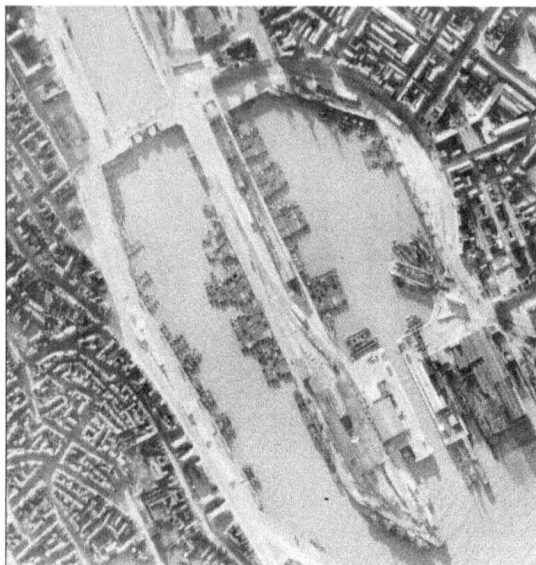

Figure 27: *German invasion barges waiting at Boulogne Harbour, France during the Battle of Britain*

Coastal Command directed its attention towards the protection of British shipping, and the destruction of enemy shipping. As invasion became more likely, it participated in the strikes on French harbours and airfields, laying mines, and mounting numerous reconnaissance missions over the enemy-held coast. In all, some 9,180 sorties were flown by bombers from July to October 1940. Although this was much less than the 80,000 sorties flown by fighters, bomber crews suffered about half the total casualties borne by their fighter colleagues. The bomber contribution was, therefore, much more dangerous on a loss-per-sortie comparison.

Bomber, reconnaissance, and antisubmarine patrol operations continued throughout these months with little respite and none of the publicity accorded to Fighter Command. In his famous 20 August speech about "The Few", praising Fighter Command, Churchill also made a point of mentioning Bomber Command's contribution, adding that bombers were even then striking back at Germany; this part of the speech is often overlooked, even today.[101] The Battle of Britain Chapel in Westminster Abbey lists in a roll of honour, 718 Bomber Command crew members, and 280 from Coastal Command who were killed between 10 July and 31 October.

Bomber and Coastal Command attacks against invasion barge concentrations in Channel ports were widely reported by the British media during Septem-

Figure 28: *German Heinkel He 111 bombers over the English Channel 1940*

ber and October 1940. In what became known as 'the Battle of the Barges' RAF attacks were claimed in British propaganda to have sunk large numbers of barges, and to have created widespread chaos and disruption to German invasion preparations. Given the volume of British propaganda interest in these bomber attacks during September and earlier October, it is striking how quickly this was overlooked once the Battle of Britain had been concluded. Even by mid-war the bomber pilots' efforts had been largely eclipsed by a continuing focus on the Few, this a result of the Air Ministry's continuing valorisation of the "fighter boys", beginning with the March 1941 Battle of Britain propaganda pamphlet.

Phases of the battle

The battle covered a shifting geographical area, and there have been differing opinions on significant dates: when the Air Ministry proposed 8 August as the start, Dowding responded that operations "merged into one another almost insensibly", and proposed 10 July as the onset of increased attacks.[102] With the caution that phases drifted into each other and dates are not firm, the Royal Air Force Museum states that five main phases can be identified:

- 26 June – 16 July: *Störangriffe* ("nuisance raids"), scattered small scale probing attacks both day and night, armed reconnaissance and mine-laying sorties. From 4 July, daylight *Kanalkampf* ("the Channel battles") against shipping.
- 17 July – 12 August: daylight *Kanalkampf* attacks on shipping intensify through this period, increased attacks on ports and coastal airfields, night raids on RAF and aircraft manufacturing.
- 13 August – 6 September: *Adlerangriff* ("Eagle Attack"), the main assault; attempt to destroy the RAF in southern England, including massive daylight attacks on RAF airfields, followed from 19 August by heavy night bombing of ports and industrial cities, including suburbs of London.
- 7 September – 2 October: the Blitz commences, main focus day and night attacks on London.
- 3–31 October: large scale night bombing raids, mostly on London; day-light attacks now confined to small scale fighter-bomber *Störangriffe* raids luring RAF fighters into dogfights.

Small scale raids

The RAF night bombing campaign against military objectives in German towns began on 11 May. The small forces available were given ambitious objectives, but lacked night navigation capability and their isolated inaccurate attacks were thought by the Germans to be intended to terrorise civilians. From 4 July the RAF achieved some successes with raids on Channel ports, anticipating the build up for an invasion.[99,103]

Following Germany's rapid territorial gains in the Battle of France, the Luftwaffe had to reorganise its forces, set up bases along the coast, and rebuild after heavy losses. It began small scale bombing raids on Britain on the night of 5/6 June, and continued sporadic attacks throughout June and July.[104] The first large-scale attack was at night, on 18/19 June, when small raids scattered between Yorkshire and Kent involved in total 100 bombers.[105] These *Störangriffe* ("nuisance raids") which involved only a few aeroplanes, sometimes just one, were used to train bomber crews in both day and night attacks, to test defences and try out methods, with most flights at night. They found that, rather than carrying small numbers of large high explosive bombs, it was more effective to use more small bombs, similarly incendiaries had to cover a large area to set effective fires. These training flights continued through August and into the first week of September.[106] Against this, the raids also gave the British time to assess the German tactics, and invaluable time for the RAF fighters and anti-aircraft defences to prepare and gain practice.[107]

Figure 29: *Interior of RAF Fighter Command's Sector 'G' Operations Room at Duxford, 1940*

The attacks were widespread: over the night of 30 June alarms were set off in 20 counties by just 20 bombers, then next day the first daylight raids occurred during 1 July, on both Hull in Yorkshire and Wick, Caithness. On 3 July most flights were reconnaissance sorties, but 15 civilians were killed when bombs hit Guildford in Surrey.[108] Numerous small *Störangriffe* raids, both day and night, were made daily through August, September and into the winter, with aims including bringing RAF fighters up to battle, destruction of specific military and economic targets, and setting off air-raid warnings to affect civilian morale: four major air-raids in August involved hundreds of bombers, in the same month 1,062 small raids were made, spread across the whole of Britain.[109]

Channel battles

The *Kanalkampf* comprised a series of running fights over convoys in the English Channel. It was launched partly because Kesselring and Sperrle were not sure about what else to do, and partly because it gave German aircrews some training and a chance to probe the British defences. Dowding could provide only minimal shipping protection, and these battles off the coast tended to favour the Germans, whose bomber escorts had the advantage of altitude and outnumbered the RAF fighters. From 9 July reconnaissance probing by

Dornier Do 17 bombers put a severe strain on RAF pilots and machines, with high RAF losses to Bf 109s. When nine 141 Squadron Defiants went into action on 19 July six were lost to Bf 109s before a squadron of Hurricanes intervened. On 25 July a coal convoy and escorting destroyers suffered such heavy losses to attacks by Stuka dive bombers that the Admiralty decided convoys should travel at night: the RAF shot down 16 raiders but lost 7 aircraft. By 8 August 18 coal ships and 4 destroyers had been sunk, but the Navy was determined to send a convoy of 20 ships through rather than move the coal by railway. After repeated Stuka attacks that day, six ships were badly damaged, four were sunk and only four reached their destination. The RAF lost 19 fighters and shot down 31 German aircraft. The Navy now cancelled all further convoys through the Channel and sent the cargo by rail. Even so, these early combat encounters provided both sides with experience.

Main assault

The main attack upon the RAF's defences was code-named *Adlerangriff* ("Eagle Attack"). Intelligence reports gave Göring the impression that the RAF was almost defeated, and raids would attract British fighters for the Luftwaffe to shoot down.[86] The strategy agreed on 6 August was to destroy RAF Fighter Command across the south of England in four days, then bombing of military and economic targets was to systematically extend up to the Midlands until daylight attacks could proceed unhindered over the whole of Britain, culminating in a major bombing attack on London.[87,110]

Assault on RAF: radar and airfields

Poor weather delayed *Adlertag* ("Eagle Day") until 13 August 1940. On 12 August, the first attempt was made to blind the Dowding system, when aircraft from the specialist fighter-bomber unit *Erprobungsgruppe* 210 attacked four radar stations. Three were briefly taken off the air but were back working within six hours. The raids appeared to show that British radars were difficult to knock out. The failure to mount follow-up attacks allowed the RAF to get the stations back on the air, and the Luftwaffe neglected strikes on the supporting infrastructure, such as phone lines and power stations, which could have rendered the radars useless, even if the towers themselves (which were very difficult to destroy) remained intact.

Adlertag opened with a series of attacks, led again by *Erpro* 210, on coastal airfields used as forward landing grounds for the RAF fighters, as well as 'satellite airfields'[111] (including Manston and Hawkinge). As the week drew on, the airfield attacks moved further inland, and repeated raids were made on the radar chain. 15 August was "The Greatest Day" when the Luftwaffe mounted the largest number of sorties of the campaign. *Luftflotte* 5 attacked the north

Figure 30: *East Coast Chain Home radar station*

of England. Believing Fighter Command strength to be concentrated in the south, raiding forces from Denmark and Norway ran into unexpectedly strong resistance. Inadequately escorted by Bf 110s, bombers were shot down in large numbers. North East England was attacked by 65 Heinkel 111s escorted by 34 Messerschmitt 110s, and RAF Great Driffield was attacked by 50 unescorted Junkers 88s. Out of 115 bombers and 35 fighters sent, 75 planes were destroyed and many others damaged beyond repair. Furthermore, due to early engagement by RAF fighters many of the bombers dropped their payloads ineffectively early.[112] As a result of these casualties, *Luftflotte* 5 did not appear in strength again in the campaign.

18 August, which had the greatest number of casualties to both sides, has been dubbed "The Hardest Day". Following this grinding battle, exhaustion and the weather reduced operations for most of a week, allowing the Luftwaffe to review their performance. "The Hardest Day" had sounded the end for the Ju 87 in the campaign. This veteran of *Blitzkrieg* was too vulnerable to fighters to operate over Britain. So as to preserve the *Stuka* force, Göring withdrew them from the fighting. This removed the main Luftwaffe precision-bombing weapon and shifted the burden of pinpoint attacks on the already-stretched *Erpro* 210. The Bf 110 proved too clumsy for dogfighting with single-engined fighters, and its participation was scaled back. It would be used only when

Figure 31: *Czechoslovak fighter pilots of No.
310 Squadron RAF at RAF Duxford in 1940*

range required it or when sufficient single-engined escort could not be provided
for the bombers.

Göring made yet another important decision: to order more bomber escorts
at the expense of free-hunting sweeps. To achieve this, the weight of the attack now fell on *Luftflotte* 2, and the bulk of the Bf 109s in *Luftflotte 3* were
transferred to Kesselring's command, reinforcing the fighter bases in the Pas-
de-Calais. Stripped of its fighters, *Luftflotte 3* would concentrate on the night
bombing campaign. Göring, expressing disappointment with the fighter performance thus far in the campaign, also made sweeping changes in the command structure of the fighter units, replacing many *Geschwaderkommodore*
with younger, more aggressive pilots like Adolf Galland and Werner Mölders.

Finally, Göring stopped the attacks on the radar chain. These were seen as
unsuccessful, and neither the *Reichsmarschall* nor his subordinates realised
how vital the Chain Home stations were to the defence systems. It was known
that radar provided some early warning of raids, but the belief among German
fighter pilots was that anything bringing up the "Tommies" to fight was to be
encouraged. Wikipedia:Citation needed

Figure 32: *Pilots of No. 19 Squadron RAF relax in the crew room at RAF Fowlmere, 1940*

Raids on British cities

On the afternoon of 15 August, *Hauptmann* Walter Rubensdörffer leading *Erprobungsgruppe* 210 mistakenly bombed Croydon airfield (on the outskirts of London) instead of the intended target, RAF Kenley.

German intelligence reports made the Luftwaffe optimistic that the RAF, thought to be dependent on local air control, was struggling with supply problems and pilot losses. After a major raid attacking Biggin Hill on 18 August, Luftwaffe aircrew said they had been unopposed, the airfield was "completely destroyed", and asked "Is England already finished?" In accordance with the strategy agreed on 6 August, defeat of the RAF was to be followed by bombing military and economic targets, systematically extending up to the Midlands.[113]

Göring ordered attacks on aircraft factories on 19 August 1940.[114] Sixty raids on the night of 19/20 August targeted the aircraft industry and harbours, and bombs fell on suburban areas around London: Croydon, Wimbledon and the Maldens.[115] Night raids were made on 21/22 August on Aberdeen, Bristol and South Wales. That morning, bombs were dropped on Harrow and Wealdstone, on the outskirts of London. Overnight on 22/23 August, the output of an aircraft factory at Filton near Bristol was drastically affected by a raid in which Ju88 bombers released over 16 tons of high explosive bombs. On

Figure 33: *Polish 303 squadron pilots, 1940. Left to right: P/O Ferić, Flt Lt Kent, F/O Grzeszczak, P/O Radomski, P/O Zumbach, P/O Łokuciewski, F/O Henneberg, Sgt. Rogowski, Sgt. Szaposznikow.*

the night of 23/24 August over 200 bombers attacked the Fort Dunlop tyre factory in Birmingham, with a significant effect on production. A sustained bombing campaign began on 24 August with the largest raid so far, killing 100 in Portsmouth, and that night, several areas of London were bombed; the East End was set ablaze and bombs landed on central London. Some historians believe that these bombs were dropped accidentally by a group of Heinkel He 111s which had failed to find their target; this account has been contested.[116]

More night raids were made around London on 24/25 August, when bombs fell on Croydon, Banstead, Lewisham, Uxbridge, Harrow and Hayes. London was on red alert over the night of 28/29 August, with bombs reported in Finchley, St Pancras, Wembley, Wood Green, Southgate, Old Kent Road, Mill Hill, Ilford, Chigwell and Hendon.[88]

Attacks on airfields from 24 August

Göring's directive issued on 23 August 1940 ordered ceaseless attacks on the aircraft industry and on RAF ground organisation to force the RAF to use its fighters, continuing the tactic of luring them up to be destroyed, and added that focussed attacks were to be made on RAF airfields.

From 24 August onwards, the battle was a fight between Kesselring's *Luft-flotte* 2 and Park's 11 Group. The Luftwaffe concentrated all their strength on knocking out Fighter Command and made repeated attacks on the airfields. Of the 33 heavy attacks in the following two weeks, 24 were against airfields. The key sector stations were hit repeatedly: Biggin Hill and Hornchurch four times each; Debden and North Weald twice each. Croydon, Gravesend, Rochford, Hawkinge and Manston were also attacked in strength. Coastal Command's Eastchurch was bombed at least seven times because it was believed to be a Fighter Command aerodrome. At times these raids caused some damage to the sector stations, threatening the integrity of the Dowding system.

To offset some losses, some 58 Fleet Air Arm fighter pilot volunteers were seconded to RAF squadrons, and a similar number of former Fairey Battle pilots were used. Most replacements from Operational Training Units (OTUs) had as little as nine hours flying time and no gunnery or air-to-air combat training. At this point, the multinational nature of Fighter Command came to the fore. Many squadrons and personnel from the air forces of the Dominions were already attached to the RAF, including top level commanders – Australians, Canadians, New Zealanders, Rhodesians and South Africans. In addition, there were other nationalities represented, including Free French, Belgian and a Jewish pilot from the British mandate of Palestine.

They were bolstered by the arrival of fresh Czechoslovak and Polish squadrons. These had been held back by Dowding, who mistakenly thought non-English speaking aircrew would have trouble working within his control system: Polish and Czech fliers proved to be especially effective. The pre-war Polish Air Force had lengthy and extensive training, and high standards; with Poland conquered and under brutal German occupation, the pilots of No. 303 (Polish) Squadron, the highest-scoring Allied unit,[117] were strongly motivated. Josef František, a Czech regular airman who had flown from the occupation of his own country to join the Polish and then French air forces before arriving in Britain, flew as a guest of 303 Squadron and was ultimately credited with the highest "RAF score" in the Battle of Britain.

The RAF had the advantage of fighting over home territory. Pilots who bailed out of their downed aircraft could be back at their airfields within hours, while if low on fuel and/or ammunition they could be immediately rearmed.[118] One RAF pilot interviewed in late 1940 had been shot down five times during the Battle of Britain, but was able to crash land in Britain or bail out each time. For Luftwaffe aircrews, a bailout over England meant capture – in the critical August period, almost exactly as many Luftwaffe pilots were taken prisoner as were killed – while parachuting into the English Channel often meant drowning or death from exposure. Morale began to suffer, and [*Kanalkrankheit*] ("Channel sickness") – a form of combat fatigue – began to appear among the German pilots. Their replacement problem became even worse than the British.

Assessment of attempt to destroy the RAF

The effect of the German attacks on airfields is unclear. According to Stephen Bungay, Dowding, in a letter to Hugh Trenchard[119] accompanying Park's report on the period 8 August – 10 September 1940, states that the Luftwaffe "achieved very little" in the last week of August and the first week of September. The only Sector Station to be shut down operationally was Biggin Hill, and it was non-operational for just two hours. Dowding admitted 11 Group's efficiency was impaired but, despite serious damage to some airfields, only two out of 13 heavily attacked airfields were down for more than a few hours. The German refocus on London was not critical.

Retired air marshal Peter Dye, head of the RAF Museum, discussed the logistics of the battle in 2000 and 2010,[120] dealing specifically with the single-seat fighters. Dye contends that not only was British aircraft production replacing aircraft, but replacement pilots were keeping pace with losses. The number of pilots in RAF Fighter Command increased during July, August and September. The figures indicate the number of pilots available never decreased: from July, 1,200 were available, and from 1 August, 1,400 were available. Just over that number were in the field by September. In October the figure was nearly 1,600. By 1 November 1,800 were available. Throughout the battle, the RAF had more fighter pilots available than the Luftwaffe. Although the RAF's reserves of single seat fighters fell during July, the wastage was made up for by an efficient Civilian Repair Organisation (CRO), which by December had repaired and put back into service some 4,955 aircraft, and by aircraft held at Air Servicing Unit (ASU) airfields.

Richard Overy agrees with Dye and Bungay. Overy asserts only one airfield was temporarily put out of action and "only" 103 pilots were lost. British fighter production produced 496 new aircraft in July and 467 in August, and another 467 in September (not counting repaired aircraft), covering the losses of August and September. Overy indicates the number of serviceable and total strength returns reveal an *increase* in fighters from 3 August to 7 September, 1,061 on strength and 708 serviceable to 1,161 on strength and 746 serviceable. Moreover, Overy points out that the number of RAF fighter pilots grew by one-third between June and August 1940. Personnel records show a constant supply of around 1,400 pilots in the crucial weeks of the battle. In the second half of September it reached 1,500. The shortfall of pilots was never above 10%. The Germans never had more than between 1,100 and 1,200 pilots, a deficiency of up to one-third. "If Fighter Command were 'the few', the German fighter pilots were fewer".

Figure 34: *Pilots of No. 66 Squadron at Gravesend, September 1940*

Other scholars assert that this period was the most dangerous of all. In *The Narrow Margin*, published in 1961, historians Derek Wood and Derek Dempster believed that the two weeks from 24 August to 6 September represented a real danger. According to them, from 24 August to 6 September 295 fighters had been totally destroyed and 171 badly damaged, against a total output of 269 new and repaired Spitfires and Hurricanes. They assert that 103 pilots were killed or missing and 128 were wounded, which represented a total wastage of 120 pilots per week out of a fighting strength of just fewer than 1,000. They conclude that during August no more than 260 fighter pilots were turned out by OTUs and casualties in the same month were just over 300. A full squadron establishment was 26 pilots whereas the average in August was 16. In their assessment, the RAF was losing the battle.[121] Denis Richards, in his 1953 contribution to the official British account *History of the Second World War*, agreed that lack of pilots, especially experienced ones, was the RAF's greatest problem. He states that between 8 and 18 August 154 RAF pilots were killed, severely wounded, or missing, while only 63 new pilots were trained. Availability of aircraft was also a serious issue. While its reserves during the Battle of Britain never declined to a half dozen planes as some later claimed, Richards describes 24 August to 6 September as the critical period because during these two weeks Germany destroyed far more aircraft through its attacks on 11 Group's southeast bases than Britain was producing. Three more weeks of such a pace would indeed have exhausted aircraft reserves. Germany had seen heavy losses of pilots and aircraft as well, thus its shift to night-time attacks in September. On 7 September RAF aircraft losses fell below British production and remained so until the end of the war.

Day and night attacks on London: start of the Blitz

Hitler's "Directive No. 17 – For the conduct of air and sea warfare against England" issued on 1 August 1940, reserved to himself the right to decide on terror attacks as measures of reprisal. Hitler issued a directive that London was not to be bombed save on his sole instruction. In preparation, detailed target plans under the code name Operation *Loge* for raids on communications, power stations, armaments works and docks in the Port of London were distributed to the *Fliegerkorps* in July. The port areas were crowded next to residential housing and civilian casualties would be expected, but this would combine military and economic targets with indirect effects on morale. The strategy agreed on 6 August was for raids on military and economic targets in towns and cities to culminate in a major attack on London.[122] In mid August raids were made on targets on the outskirts of London.

Luftwaffe doctrine included the possibility of retaliatory attacks on cities, and since 11 May small scale night raids by RAF Bomber Command had frequently bombed residential areas. The Germans assumed this was deliberate, and as the raids increased in frequency and scale the population grew impatient for measures of revenge.[122] On 25 August 1940, 81 bombers of Bomber Command were sent out to raid industrial and commercial targets in Berlin. Clouds prevented accurate identification and the bombs fell across the city, causing some casualties among the civilian population as well as damage to residential areas.[123] Continuing RAF raids on Berlin led to Hitler withdrawing his directive on 30 August, and giving the go-ahead to the planned bombing offensive.[122] On 3 September Göring planned to bomb London daily, with General Albert Kesselring's enthusiastic support, having received reports the average strength of RAF squadrons was down to five or seven fighters out of twelve and their airfields in the area were out of action. Hitler issued a directive on 5 September to attack cities including London.[124,125] In his widely publicised speech delivered on 4 September 1940, Hitler condemned the bombing of Berlin and presented the planned attacks on London as reprisals. The first daylight raid was titled *Vergeltungsangriff* (revenge attack).[126]

On 7 September, a massive series of raids involving nearly four hundred bombers and more than six hundred fighters targeted docks in the East End of London, day and night. The RAF anticipated attacks on airfields and 11 Group rose to meet them, in greater numbers than the Luftwaffe expected. The first official deployment of 12 Group's Leigh-Mallory's Big Wing took twenty

Figure 35: *Smoke rising from fires in the London docks, following bombing on 7 September*

Figure 36: *Heinkel He 111 bomber over the Surrey Commercial Docks in South London and Wapping and the Isle of Dogs in the East End of London on 7 September 1940*

Figure 37: *Air-raid shelter in London, 1940*

minutes to form up, missing its intended target, but encountering another formation of bombers while still climbing. They returned, apologetic about their limited success, and blamed the delay on being scrambled too late.[127,128]

The German press jubilantly announced that "one great cloud of smoke stretches tonight from the middle of London to the mouth of the Thames." Reports reflected the briefings given to crews before the raids – "Everyone knew about the last cowardly attacks on German cities, and thought about wives, mothers and children. And then came that word 'Vengeance!'" Pilots reported seeing ruined airfields as they flew towards London, appearances which gave intelligence reports the impression of devastated defences. Göring maintained that the RAF was close to defeat, making invasion feasible.[129]

Fighter Command had been at its lowest ebb, short of men and machines, and the break from airfield attacks allowed them to recover. 11 Group had considerable success in breaking up daytime raids. 12 Group repeatedly disobeyed orders and failed to meet requests to protect 11 Group airfields, but their experiments with increasingly large Big Wings had some success. The Luftwaffe began to abandon their morning raids, with attacks on London starting late in the afternoon for fifty-seven consecutive nights.[130]

The most damaging aspect to the Luftwaffe of targeting London was the increase in range. The Bf 109E escorts had a limited fuel capacity resulting in only a 660 km (410 mile) maximum range solely on internal fuel,[131] and when they arrived had only 10 minutes of flying time before turning for home,

Figure 38: *Members of the London Auxiliary Firefighting Service*

leaving the bombers undefended by fighter escorts. Its eventual stablemate, the Focke-Wulf Fw 190A, was flying only in prototype form in mid-1940; the first 28 Fw 190s were not delivered until November 1940. The Fw 190A-1 had a maximum range of 940 km (584 miles) on internal fuel, 40% greater than the Bf 109E.[132] The Messerschmitt Bf 109E-7 corrected this deficiency by adding a ventral centre-line ordnance rack to take either an SC 250 bomb or a standard 300 litre Luftwaffe drop tank to double the range to 1,325 km (820 mi). The ordnance rack was not retrofitted to earlier Bf 109Es until October 1940.

On 14 September, Hitler chaired a meeting with the OKW staff. Göring was in France directing the decisive battle, so Erhard Milch deputised for him. Hitler asked "Should we call it off altogether?" General Hans Jeschonnek, Luftwaffe Chief of Staff, begged for a last chance to defeat the RAF and for permission to launch attacks on civilian residential areas to cause mass panic. Hitler refused the latter, perhaps unaware of how much damage had already been done to civilian targets. He reserved for himself the power to unleash the terror weapon. Instead political will was to be broken by destroying the material infrastructure, the weapons industry, and stocks of fuel and food.

On 15 September, two massive waves of German attacks were decisively repulsed by the RAF by deploying every aircraft in 11 Group. Sixty German and twenty-six RAF aircraft were shot down. The action was the climax of the Battle of Britain.[133]

Figure 39: *Zehbe's Dornier falling on Victoria Station after being rammed by Ray Holmes, 15 September 1940*

Two days after the German defeat Hitler postponed preparations for the invasion of Britain. Henceforth, in the face of mounting losses in men, aircraft
and the lack of adequate replacements, the Luftwaffe completed their gradual
shift from daylight bomber raids and continued with nighttime bombing. 15
September is commemorated as Battle of Britain Day.

Night time Blitz, fighter-bomber day raids

At the 14 September OKW conference, Hitler acknowledged that the Luftwaffe had still not gained the air superiority needed for the Operation Sealion
invasion. In agreement with Raeder's written recommendation, Hitler said the
campaign was to intensify regardless of invasion plans: "The decisive thing is
the ceaseless continuation of air attacks." Jeschonnek proposed attacking residential areas to cause "mass panic", but Hitler turned this down: he reserved
to himself the option of terror bombing. British morale was to be broken by
destroying infrastructure, armaments manufacturing, fuel and food stocks. On
16 September, Göring gave the order for this change in strategy.[42] This new
phase was to be the first independent strategic bombing campaign, in hopes of
a political success forcing the British to give up.[43] Hitler hoped it might result
in "eight million going mad" (referring to the population of London in 1940),
which would "cause a catastrophe" for the British. In those circumstances,
Hitler said, "even a small invasion might go a long way". Hitler was against
cancelling the invasion as "the cancellation would reach the ears of the enemy
and strengthen his resolve".[134,135]</ref> On 19 September, Hitler ordered a re-
duction in work on Sealion.[136] He doubted if strategic bombing could achieve
its aims, but ending the air war would be an open admission of defeat. He had
to maintain the appearance of concentration on defeating Britain, to conceal
from Joseph Stalin his covert aim to invade the Soviet Union.[137]

Throughout the battle, most Luftwaffe bombing raids had been at night.[138]
They increasingly suffered unsustainable losses in daylight raids, and the last

Figure 40: *Gun camera film shows tracer ammunition from a Supermarine Spitfire Mark I of 609 Squadron, flown by Flight Lieutenant J H G McArthur, hitting a Heinkel He 111 on its starboard quarter. These aircraft were part of a large formation from KG 53 and 55 which attacked the Bristol Aeroplane Company's works at Filton, Bristol, just before midday on 25 September 1940.*

massive daytime attacks were on 15 September. A raid of 70 bombers on 18 September also suffered badly, and day raids were gradually phased out leaving the main attacks at night. Fighter command still lacked any successful way of intercepting night-time raiders, the night fighter force was mostly Blenheims and Beaufighters, and lacked airborne radar so had no way of finding the bombers. Anti-aircraft guns were diverted to London's defences, but had a much reduced success rate against night attacks.[139]

From mid September, Luftwaffe daylight bombing was gradually taken over by a Bf 109 fighters, adapted to take one 250 kg bomb. Small groups of fighter-bombers would carry out *Störangriffe* raids escorted by large escort formations of about 200 to 300 combat fighters. They flew at altitudes over 20,000 feet (6,100 m) where the Bf109 had an advantage over RAF fighters, except the Spitfire.[140]</ref>[141]</ref>[142] The raids disturbed civilians, and continued the war of attrition against Fighter Command. The raids were intended to carry out precision bombing on military or economic targets, but it was hard to achieve sufficient accuracy with the single bomb. Sometimes, when attacked, the fighter-bombers had to jettison the bomb to function as fighters. The RAF was at a disadvantage, and changed defensive tactics by introducing standing patrols of Spitfires at high altitude to monitor incoming raids. On a sighting, other patrols at lower altitude would fly up to join the battle.[143,137]

A Junkers Ju 88 returning from a raid on London was shot down in Kent on 27 September resulting in the Battle of Graveney Marsh, the last action between British and foreign military forces on British mainland soil.[144]

German bombing of Britain reached its peak in October and November 1940. In post war interrogation, Wilhelm Keitel described the aims as economic blockade, in conjunction with submarine warfare, and attrition of Britain's military and economic resources. The Luftwaffe wanted to achieve victory on its own, and was reluctant to cooperate with the navy. Their strategy for blockade was to destroy ports and storage facilities in towns and cities. Priorities were based on the pattern of trade and distribution, so for these months London was the main target. In November their attention turned to other ports and industrial targets around Britain.[145]

Hitler postponed the Sealion invasion on 13 October "until the spring of 1941". It was not until Hitler's Directive 21 was issued, on 18 December 1940, that the threat to Britain of invasion finally ended.

Royal family

During the battle, and for the rest of the war, an important factor in keeping public morale high was the continued presence in London of King George VI and his wife Queen Elizabeth. When war broke out in 1939, the King and Queen decided to stay in London and not flee to Canada, as had been suggested.[146] George VI and Elizabeth officially stayed in Buckingham Palace throughout the war, although they often spent weekends at Windsor Castle to visit their daughters, Elizabeth (the future queen) and Margaret.[147] Buckingham Palace was damaged by bombs which landed in the grounds on 10 September and, on 13 September, more serious damage was caused by two bombs which destroyed the Royal Chapel. The royal couple were in a small sitting room about 80 yards from where the bombs exploded. On 24 September, in recognition of the bravery of civilians, King George VI inaugurated the award of the George Cross.

Attrition statistics

Overall, by 2 November, the RAF fielded 1,796 pilots, an increase of over 40% from July 1940's count of 1,259 pilots. Based on German sources (from a Luftwaffe intelligence officer Otto Bechtle attached to KG 2 in February 1944) translated by the Air Historical Branch, Stephen Bungay asserts German fighter and bomber "strength" declined without recovery, and that from

August–December 1940, the German fighter and bomber strength declined by 30 and 25 percent. In contrast, Williamson Murray, argues (using translations by the Air Historical Branch) that 1,380 German bombers were on strength on 29 June 1940, 1,420 bombers on 28 September, 1,423 level bombers on 2 November and 1,393 bombers on 30 November 1940. In July–September the number of Luftwaffe pilots available fell by 136, but the number of operational pilots had shrunk by 171 by September. The training organisation of the Luftwaffe was failing to replace losses. German fighter pilots, in contrast to popular perception, were not afforded training or rest rotations unlike their British counterparts. The first week of September accounted for 25% of Fighter Command's and 24% of the *Luftwaffe's* overall losses. Between the dates 26 August – 6 September, on only one day (1 September) did the Germans destroy more aircraft than they lost. Losses were 325 German and 248 British.[148]

Luftwaffe losses for August numbered 774 aircraft to all causes, representing 18.5% of all combat aircraft at the beginning of the month. Fighter Command's losses in August were 426 fighters destroyed,[149] amounting to 40 per cent of 1,061 fighters available on 3 August.[150] In addition, 99 German bombers and 27 other types were destroyed between 1 and 29 August.[151]

From July to September, the Luftwaffe's loss records indicate the loss of 1,636 aircraft, 1,184 to enemy action. This represented 47% of the initial strength of single-engined fighters, 66% of twin-engined fighters, and 45% of bombers. This indicates the Germans were running out of aircrew as well as aircraft.

Throughout the battle, the Germans greatly underestimated the size of the RAF and the scale of British aircraft production. Across the Channel, the Air Intelligence division of the Air Ministry consistently overestimated the size of the German air enemy and the productive capacity of the German aviation industry. As the battle was fought, both sides exaggerated the losses inflicted on the other by an equally large margin. The intelligence picture formed before the battle encouraged the Luftwaffe to believe that such losses pushed Fighter Command to the very edge of defeat, while the exaggerated picture of German air strength persuaded the RAF that the threat it faced was larger and more dangerous than was the case. This led the British to the conclusion that another fortnight of attacks on airfields might force Fighter Command to withdraw their squadrons from the south of England. The German misconception, on the other hand, encouraged first complacency, then strategic misjudgement. The shift of targets from air bases to industry and communications was taken because it was assumed that Fighter Command was virtually eliminated.

Between 24 August and 4 September, German serviceability rates, which were acceptable at *Stuka* units, were running at 75% with Bf 109s, 70% with bombers and 65% with Bf 110s, indicating a shortage of spare parts. All units were well below established strength. The attrition was beginning to affect the fighters in particular." By 14 September, the Luftwaffe's Bf 109 *Geschwader* possessed only 67% of their operational crews against authorised aircraft. For Bf 110 units it was 46 per cent; and for bombers it was 59 per cent. A week later the figures had dropped to 64 per cent, 52% and 52 per cent. Serviceability rates in Fighter Command's fighter squadrons, between 24 August and 7 September, were listed as: 64.8% on 24 August; 64.7% on 31 August and 64.25% on 7 September 1940.

Due to the failure of the Luftwaffe to establish air supremacy, a conference assembled on 14 September at Hitler's headquarters. Hitler concluded that air superiority had not yet been established and "promised to review the situation on 17 September for possible landings on 27 September or 8 October. Three days later, when the evidence was clear that the German Air Force had greatly exaggerated the extent of their successes against the RAF, Hitler postponed *Sea Lion* indefinitely."

Propaganda

Propaganda was an important element of the air war which began to develop over Britain from 18 June 1940 onwards, when the *Luftwaffe* began small, probing daylight raids to test RAF defences. One of many examples of these small-scale raids was the destruction of a school at Polruan in Cornwall, by a single raider. Into early July, the British media's focus on the air battles increased steadily, the press, magazines, BBC radio and newsreels daily conveying the contents of Air Ministry communiques. The German OKW communiques matched Britain's efforts in claiming for the upper hand.

Central to the propaganda war on both sides of the Channel were aircraft claims, this discussed under 'Attrition statistics'. These daily claims were important both for sustaining British home front morale and persuading America to support Britain, and were produced by the Air Ministry's Air Intelligence branch. Under pressure from American journalists and broadcasters to prove that the RAF's claims were genuine, RAF intelligence compared pilots' claims with actual aircraft wrecks and those seen to crash into the sea. It was soon realised that there was a discrepancy between the two, but the Air Ministry decided not to reveal this. In fact, it was not until May 1947 that the actual figures were released to the public, by which time it was of far less importance. Many though refused to believe the revised figures, including Douglas Bader.

The place of the Battle of Britain in British popular memory is due in no small part to the successful propaganda campaign waged by the Air Ministry, between July–October 1940, but also in valorising the Few from March 1941 onwards. The publication of the immensely successful 3d pamphlet, *The Battle of Britain*, saw huge international sales, leading even Goebbels to admire its propaganda value. Focusing only upon the Few, with no mention of RAF bomber attacks against invasion barges, the Battle of Britain was soon established as a major victory for Fighter Command. This in turn inspired a wide range of feature films, books, magazines, works of art, poetry, radio plays and MOI short films.

It is notable that this most impressive of British victories had, in essence, been proclaimed within only five months of the cessation of large-scale daylight air battles, and without reference to Hitler and the OKW's reasoning for not proceeding with Operation *Sea Lion*. The continuing post-war popularity of the Battle of Britain is in fact directly attributable to the Air Ministry's latter-1940 air communiques, the media in turn broadcasting or publishing RAF aircraft claims. Noted above, this in turn led to the March 1941 pamphlet, which inspired a wide range of cultural responses to the Few, and the Battle of Britain. The Air Ministry built upon this with the development of the Battle of Britain Sunday commemoration, also supported the Battle of Britain clasp for issue to the Few in 1945, and from 1945 Battle of Britain Week. The Battle of Britain window in Westminster Abbey was also encouraged by the Air Ministry, Lords Trenchard and Dowding on its committee. By July 1947 when the window was unveiled, the Battle of Britain had already attained central prominence as Fighter Command's most notable victory, the Few alone credited with preventing invasion in 1940. Although given widespread media coverage in September and October 1940, RAF Bomber and Coastal Command raids against invasion barge concentrations had already been forgotten by war's end.

Aftermath

The Battle of Britain marked the first major defeat of Germany's military forces, with air superiority seen as the key to victory. Pre-war theories had led to exaggerated fears of strategic bombing, and UK public opinion was buoyed by coming through the ordeal. For the RAF, Fighter Command had achieved a great victory in successfully carrying out Sir Thomas Inskip's 1937 air policy of preventing the Germans from knocking Britain out of the war.

The battle also significantly shifted American opinion. During the battle, many Americans accepted the view promoted by Joseph Kennedy, the American ambassador in London, who believed that the United Kingdom could not survive. Roosevelt wanted a second opinion, and sent "Wild Bill" Donovan on a brief visit to the UK; he became convinced the UK would survive and should be supported in every possible way.[152] Before the end of the year American journalist Ralph Ingersoll, after returning from Britain, published a book concluding that "Adolf Hitler met his first defeat in eight years" in what might "go down in history as a battle as important as Waterloo or Gettysburg". The turning point was when the Germans reduced the intensity of the Blitz after 15 September. According to Ingersoll, "[a] majority of responsible British officers who fought through this battle believe that if Hitler and Göring had had the courage and the resources to lose 200 planes a day for the next five days, nothing could have saved London"; instead, "[the Luftwaffe's] morale in combat is definitely broken, and the RAF has been gaining in strength each week."

Both sides in the battle made exaggerated claims of numbers of enemy aircraft shot down. In general, claims were two to three times the actual numbers, because of the confusion of fighting in dynamic three-dimensional air battles. Postwar analysis of records has shown that between July and September, the RAF claimed 2,698 kills, while the Luftwaffe fighters claimed 3,198 RAF aircraft downed.Wikipedia:Citation needed Total losses, and start and end dates for recorded losses, vary for both sides. Luftwaffe losses from 10 July to 30 October 1940 total 1,977 aircraft, including 243 twin- and 569 single-engined fighters, 822 bombers and 343 non combat types. In the same period, RAF Fighter Command aircraft losses number 1,087, including 53 twin-engined fighters.Wikipedia:Citation needed To the RAF figure should be added 376 Bomber Command and 148 Coastal Command aircraft lost conducting bombing, mining, and reconnaissance operations in defence of the country.

There is a consensus among historians that the Luftwaffe were unable to crush the RAF. Stephen Bungay described Dowding and Park's strategy of choosing when to engage the enemy whilst maintaining a coherent force as vindicated; their leadership, and the subsequent debates about strategy and tactics, had created enmity among RAF senior commanders and both were sacked from their posts in the immediate aftermath of the battle. All things considered, the RAF proved to be a robust and capable organisation which was to use all the modern resources available to it to the maximum advantage. Richard Evans wrote:

> *Irrespective of whether Hitler was really set on this course, he simply lacked the resources to establish the air superiority that was the sine qua non-of a successful crossing of the English Channel. A third of the initial strength of the German air force, the Luftwaffe, had been lost in the western campaign in the spring. The Germans lacked the trained pilots, the effective fighter aircraft, and the heavy bombers that would have been needed.*[153,154] *</ref>*

The Germans launched some spectacular attacks against important British industries, but they could not destroy the British industrial potential, and made little systematic effort to do so. Hindsight does not disguise the fact the threat to Fighter Command was very real, and for the participants it seemed as if there was a narrow margin between victory and defeat. Nevertheless, even if the German attacks on the 11 Group airfields which guarded southeast England and the approaches to London had continued, the RAF could have withdrawn to the Midlands out of German fighter range and continued the battle from there.[155] The victory was as much psychological as physical. Writes Alfred Price:

> *The truth of the matter, borne out by the events of 18 August is more pro-*
> *saic: neither by attacking the airfields, nor by attacking London, was the*
> *Luftwaffe likely to destroy Fighter Command. Given the size of the British*
> *fighter force and the general high quality of its equipment, training and*
> *morale, the Luftwaffe could have achieved no more than a Pyrrhic vic-*
> *tory. During the action on 18 August it had cost the Luftwaffe five trained*
> *aircrew killed, wounded or taken prisoner, for each British fighter pilot*
> *killed or wounded; the ratio was similar on other days in the battle. And*
> *this ratio of 5:1 was very close to that between the number of German air-*
> *crew involved in the battle and those in Fighter Command. In other words*
> *the two sides were suffering almost the same losses in trained aircrew, in*
> *proportion to their overall strengths. In the Battle of Britain, for the first*
> *time during the Second World War, the German war machine had set it-*
> *self a major task which it patently failed to achieve, and so demonstrated*
> *that it was not invincible. In stiffening the resolve of those determined to*
> *resist Hitler the battle was an important turning point in the conflict.*

The British victory in the Battle of Britain was achieved at a heavy cost. Total British civilian losses from July to December 1940 were 23,002 dead and 32,138 wounded, with one of the largest single raids on 19 December 1940, in which almost 3,000 civilians died. With the culmination of the concentrated daylight raids, Britain was able to rebuild its military forces and establish itself as an Allied stronghold, later serving as a base from which the Liberation of Western Europe was launched.

Battle of Britain Day

Winston Churchill summed up the effect of the battle and the contribution of RAF Fighter Command, RAF Bomber Command, RAF Coastal Command and the Fleet Air Arm with the words, "Never in the field of human conflict was so much owed by so many to so few".[156] Pilots who fought in the battle have been known as *The Few* ever since; at times being specially commemorated on 15 September, "Battle of Britain Day". On this day in 1940, the Luftwaffe embarked on their largest bombing attack yet, forcing the engagement of the

Figure 41: *World War II poster containing the famous lines by Winston Churchill*

Figure 42: *The Battle of Britain anniversary parade at Buckingham Palace in 1943.*

entirety of the RAF in defence of London and the South East, which resulted in a decisive British victory that proved to mark a turning point in Britain's favour.[157,158]

Within the Commonwealth, Battle of Britain Day has been observed more usually on the third Sunday in September, and even on the 2nd Thursday in September in some areas in the British Channel Islands.

The day has been observed by many artists over the years, often with works that show the battle itself. Many mixed media artists have also created pieces in honour of the Battle of Britain.

Memorials and museums

Plans for the Battle of Britain window in Westminster Abbey were begun during wartime, the committee chaired by Lords Trenchard and Dowding. Public donations paid for the window itself, this officially opened by King George VI on 10 July 1947. Although not actually an 'official' memorial to the Battle of Britain in the sense that government paid for it, the window and chapel have since been viewed as such. During the late 1950s and 1960, various proposals were advanced for a national monument to the Battle of Britain, this also the focus of several letters in The Times. In 1960 the Conservative government decided against a further monument, taking the view that the credit should be shared more broadly than Fighter Command alone, and there was little public appetite for one. All subsequent memorials are the result of private subscription and initiative, as discussed below.

There are numerous memorials to the battle. The most important ones are the Battle of Britain Monument in London and the Battle of Britain Memorial at Capel le Ferne in Kent. Westminster Abbey and St James's Church, Paddington both have memorial windows to the battle, replacing windows that were destroyed during the campaign. There is also a memorial at the former Croydon Airport, one of the RAF bases during the battle, and a memorial to the pilots at Armadale Castle on the Isle of Skye in Scotland, which is topped by a raven sculpture.

There are also two museums to the battle: one at Hawkinge in Kent and one at Stanmore in London, at the former RAF Bentley Priory.

In 2015 the RAF created an online 'Battle of Britain 75th Anniversary Commemorative Mosaic' composed of pictures of "the few" – the pilots and aircrew who fought in the battle – and "the many" – 'the often unsung others whose contribution during the Battle of Britain was also vital to the RAF's victory in the skies above Britain', submitted by participants and their families.

Figure 43: *Monument of Polish Pilots, Northolt*

In popular culture

Media adaptations

The battle was the subject of the 1969 film *Battle of Britain*. The cast included Laurence Olivier as Hugh Dowding and Trevor Howard as Keith Park.[159] It also starred Michael Caine, Christopher Plummer and Robert Shaw as Squadron Leaders. Former participants of the battle served as technical advisors including Douglas Bader, Adolf Galland and Hugh Dowding. An Italian film around the same time entitled *Eagles Over London* (1969) also featured the Battle of Britain. The 1988 ITV mini-series *Piece of Cake*, an aerial drama about a fictional Second World War RAF fighter squadron in 1940, features the battle. The Czech film *Dark Blue World* (2001) also featured the battle, focusing on the Czech pilots who fought in the battle. A fictional version of the battle is shown in the 2001 movie, *Pearl Harbor*, in which the battle is depicted as still going on into 1941.Wikipedia:Citation needed

It has also been the subject of many documentaries, including the 1941 Allied propaganda film *Churchill's Island*, winner of the first Academy Award for Documentary Short Subject.[160] There was also the 1943 *The Battle of Britain* in Frank Capra's *Why We Fight* series. It was included in an episode of 2004 BBC television documentary series *Battlefield Britain*. In 2010, actor Julian Glover played a 101-year-old Polish veteran RAF pilot in the short film *Battle for Britain*.[161]

In books

The Few, a novel by Alex Kershaw, tells the stories of the men who flew in the Battle of Britain. As of 2003[162], a Hollywood film similarly named *The Few* was in preparation for release in 2008, based on the story of real-life US pilot Billy Fiske, who ignored his country's neutrality rules and volunteered for the RAF. A *Variety* magazine outline of the film's historical content was said in *The Independent* to have been described by Bill Bond, who conceived the Battle of Britain Monument in London, as "Totally wrong. The whole bloody lot."[163] The project was later cancelled.

Miscellaneous

* *Battle of Britain (video game)*, a 1987 video game
* *Their Finest Hour: The Battle of Britain*, a 1989 video game
* *Microsoft Combat Flight Simulator*, a 1998 combat flight simulator
* *Rowan's Battle of Britain*, a 2000 video game
* *Battle of Britain II: Wings of Victory*, a 2005 video game
* *Blazing Angels: Squadrons of WWII*, a 2006 video game
* *IL-2 Sturmovik: Cliffs of Dover*, a 2011 combat flight simulator
* The song *Aces in Exile* from Sabaton's album Coat of Arms is about foreign pilots who fought in the Battle of Britain.

Bibliography

General

<templatestyles src="Template:Refbegin/styles.css" />

* Allen, Hubert Raymond "Dizzy", Wing Commander, RAF. *Who Won the Battle of Britain?* London: Arthur Barker, 1974. ISBN 0-213-16489-2.
* Bishop, Edward. *Their Finest Hour: The Battle of Britain 1940*. London: Ballantine Books, 1968.
* Bishop, Patrick (2010). *Battle of Britain : a day-by-day chronicle, 10 July 1940 to 31 October 1940*. London: Quercus. ISBN 978-1-84916-224-1.
* Buckley, John. *Air Power in the Age of Total War*. London: UCL Press, 1999. ISBN 1-85728-589-1.
* Buell, Thomas. *The Second World War: Europe and the Mediterranean*. New York: Square One Publishers, 2002. ISBN 978-0-7570-0160-4.
* Bungay, Stephen (2000). *The Most Dangerous Enemy : A History of the Battle of Britain*. London: Aurum Press. ISBN 1-85410-721-6. (hardcover), 2002, ISBN 1-85410-801-8 (paperback).
* Collier, Basil. *The Defence of the United Kingdom* (1962, Official history)

- Collier, Basil. *The Battle of Britain* (1962, Batsford's British Battles series)
- Collier, Richard. *Eagle Day: The Battle of Britain, 6 August – 15 September 1940*. London: Pan Books, 1968.
- Churchill, Winston S (1949), *The Second World War – Their Finest Hour (Volume 2)*, London: Cassell
- Churchill, Winston S. *The Second World War – The Grand Alliance (Volume 3)*. Bantam Books, 1962.
- Corum, James. *The Luftwaffe: Creating the Operational Air War, 1918–1940*. Lawrence, Kansas: Kansas University Press, 1997. ISBN 0-7006-0836-2.
- Crosby, Francis. *A Handbook of Fighter Aircraft*. London: Hermes House, 2002. ISBN 978-1-8430-9444-9.
- Deighton, Len (1996). *Fighter: The True Story of the Battle of Britain*. London: Pimlico. ISBN 0-7126-7423-3. (Originally published: London: Jonathan Cape, 1977.) ISBN 0-7126-7423-3.
- Deighton, Len. *Battle of Britain*. London: Cape, 1980. ISBN 0-224-01826-4.
- de Zeng, Henry L., Doug G. Stankey and Eddie J. Creek. *Bomber Units of the Luftwaffe 1933–1945: A Reference Source, Volume 1*. Hersham, Surrey, UK: Ian Allen Publishing, 2007. ISBN 978-1-85780-279-5.
- Dönitz, Karl. *Ten years and Twenty Days*. New York: Da Capo Press, First Edition, 1997. ISBN 0-306-80764-5.
- Dye, Air Commodore Peter J. (Winter 2000), "Logistics and the Battle of Britain"[164], *Air Force Journal of Logistics*, Vol 4 (No. 24), archived from the original[165] on 26 September 2010
- Ellis, John. *Brute Force: Allied Strategy and Tactics in the Second World War*. London: Andre Deutsch, 1990. ISBN 0-8264-8031-4.
- Evans, Michael. "Never in the field of human conflict was so much owed by so many to ... the Navy."[166] *The Times*, 24 August 2006. Retrieved: 3 March 2007.
- Goodenough, Simon. *War Maps: World War II, From September 1939 to August 1945, Air, Sea, and Land, Battle by Battle*. New York: St. Martin's Press, 1982, ISBN 978-0-3128-5584-0.
- Halpenny, Bruce Barrymore. *Action Station 4: Military Airfields of Yorkshire*. Cambridge, UK: Patrick Stevens, 1984. ISBN 0-85059-532-0.
- Harding, Thomas. "Battle of Britain was won at sea."[167] *The Telegraph*, 25 August 2006. Retrieved: 25 August 2006.
- Holland, James. *The Battle of Britain*. London: Bantam, 2011. ISBN 978-0-593-05913-5.
- Hooton, E.R. *Luftwaffe at War: Blitzkrieg in the West, Vol. 2*. London: Chevron/Ian Allen, 2007. ISBN 978-1-85780-272-6.

- Hough, Richard and Denis Richards. *The Battle of Britain: The Greatest Air Battle of World War II*. New York: W.W. Norton & Co Inc, 2007. ISBN 978-0-393-02766-2.
- Ingersoll, Ralph (1940), *Report on England, November 1940*[168], New York: Simon & Schuster
- Irving, David (1974), *The Rise and Fall of the Luftwaffe: The Life of Field Marshal Erhard Milch*, Dorney, Windsor, UK: Focal Point Publications, ISBN 978-0-297-76532-5
- Keegan, John. *The Second World War* London: Pimlico, 1997. ISBN 978-0-7126-7348-8.
- Kieser, Egbert. *Operation Sea Lion; The German Plan to Invade Britain 1940*. London: Cassel Military Paperbacks, 1999. ISBN 0-304-35208-X.
- Kieser, Egbert. *Unternehmen Seelöwe: Die geplante Invasion in England 1940* (in German). Berlin: Becthle, 2000. ISBN 3-7628-0457-5.
- Korda, Michael (2010), *With Wings Like Eagles: The Untold Story of the Battle of Britain*, New York: Harper Perennial, ISBN 978-0-06-112536-2
- Macksey, Kenneth. *Invasion: The German Invasion of England, July 1940*. London: Greenhill Books, 1990. ISBN 0-85368-324-7.
- Magenheimer, Heinz (10 September 2015). *Hitler's War: Germany's Key Strategic Decisions 1940–45*. Orion. ISBN 978-1-4746-0275-4.
- Manchester, William and Reid, Paul (2012) *Defender of the Realm* New York: Little, Brown & Company, ISBN 978-0-316-54770-3.
- Mason, Francis K.*Battle Over Britain: A History of the German Air Assaults on Great Britain, 1917–18 and July–December 1940, and the Development of Air Defences Between the World Wars*. New York: Doubleday, 1969. ISBN 978-0-901928-00-9.
- Murray, Williamson (2002). *Strategy for defeat : the Luftwaffe, 1933–1945*[169]. Honolulu, Hawaii: University Press of the Pacific. ISBN 0-89875-797-5.
- Overy, Richard J. (2001). *The Battle of Britain: The Myth and the Reality*. New York: W.W. Norton. ISBN 0-393-02008-8. (hardcover, ISBN 0-393-32297-1 paperback, 2002)
- Overy, Richard J. (2013). *The Bombing War : Europe 1939–1945*. London & New York: Allen Lane. ISBN 978-0-7139-9561-9.
- Owen, R.E, New Zealanders with the Royal Air Force[170] Government Printer, Wellington, New Zealand 1953.
- Peszke, Michael Alfred (October 1980), "A Synopsis of Polish-Allied Military Agreements During World War Two"[171], *The Journal of Military History*, Volume 44 (No. 3): 128–134
- Ponting, Clive. *1940: Myth and Reality*. Chicago: Ivan R. Dee, 1991. ISBN 978-1-56663-036-8.

- Pope, Stephan. "Across the Ether: Part One". *Aeroplane*, Vol. 23, No. 5, Issue No. 265, May 1995.
- Price, Alfred (1980), *The Hardest Day: 18 August 1940*, New York: Charles Scribner's Sons, ISBN 0-684-16503-1
- Raeder, Erich. *Erich Rader, Grand Admiral*. New York: Da Capo Press; United States Naval Institute, 2001. ISBN 0-306-80962-1.
- Ramsay, Winston, ed. (1987), *The Blitz Then and Now: Volume 1*, London: Battle of Britain Prints International, ISBN 0-900913-45-2
- Ramsay, Winston, ed. (1988), *The Blitz Then and Now: Volume 2*, London: Battle of Britain Prints International, ISBN 0-900913-54-1
- Ramsay, Winston, ed. (1989), *The Battle of Britain Then and Now Mk V*, London: Battle of Britain Prints International, ISBN 0-900913-46-0
- Richards, Denis. *Royal Air Force 1939–1945, Vol. I: The Fight at Odds*. London: His Majesty's Stationery Office, 1953.
- Robinson, Derek, *Invasion, 1940: Did the Battle of Britain Alone Stop Hitler?* New York: Carroll & Graf, 2005. ISBN 0-7867-1618-5.
- Shulman, Milton. *Defeat in the West*. London: Cassell, 2004 (First edition 1947). ISBN 0-304-36603-X.
- Shirer, William (1964), *The Rise and Fall of the Third Reich: A History of Nazi Germany*, London: Ballantine, ISBN 978-0-449-21977-5
- Smith, Howard K. *Last Train from Berlin*. New York: Knopf, 1942.
- Stacey, C P. (1955) The Canadian Army 1939–1945 An Official Historical Summary[172] Queen's Printer, Ottawa
- Stacey, C P. (1970) Arms, Men and Governments: The War Policies of Canada, 1939–1945[173] Queen's Printer, Ottawa (Downloadable PDF)
- Taylor, A. J. P. and S. L. Mayer, eds. *A History of World War Two*. London: Octopus Books, 1974. ISBN 0-7064-0399-1.
- Terraine, John, *The Right of the Line: The Royal Air Force in the European War, 1939–1945*. New York: Sceptre, 1985. ISBN 0-340-41919-9.
- Terraine, John, *A Time for Courage: The Royal Air Force in the European War, 1939–1945*. London: Macmillan, 1985. ISBN 978-0-02-616970-7.
- Wagner, Ray and Heinz Nowarra. *German Combat Planes: A Comprehensive Survey and History of the Development of German Military Aircraft from 1914 to 1945*. New York: Doubleday & Company, 1971.
- Winterbotham, F. W. (1975), *The Ultra Secret*, London: Futura Publications, ISBN 0-86007-268-1
- Wood, Derek, and Derek Dempster, *The Narrow Margin: The Battle of Britain and the Rise of Air Power, 1930–1949*. London: Pen & Sword, 2003, First edition 1961. ISBN 978-0-85052-915-9.
- Wright, Gordon, *The Ordeal of Total War: 1939–1945*. New York: Harper & Row, 1968.

Autobiographies and biographies

<templatestyles src="Template:Refbegin/styles.css" />

- Collier, Basil. *Leader of the Few: the Authorised Biography of Air Chief Marshal Lord Dowding of Bentley Priory*. London: Jarrolds, 1957.
- Deere, Alan Christopher (1974), *Nine Lives*, London: Hodder Paperbacks Ltd for Coronet Books, ISBN 0-340-01441-5
- Duncan Smith, Group Captain W.G.G., *Spitfire into Battle*. London: John Murray, 2002. ISBN 0-7195-5484-5.
- Franks, Norman, *Wings of Freedom: Twelve Battle of Britain Pilots*. London: William Kimber, 1980. ISBN 0-7183-0197-8.
- Galland, Adolf *The First and the Last: Germany's Fighter Force in WWII* (Fortunes of War) South Miami, Florida: Cerberus Press, 2005. ISBN 1-84145-020-0.
- Halpenny, Bruce, *Fight for the Sky: Stories of Wartime Fighter Pilots*. Cambridge, UK: Patrick Stephens, 1986. ISBN 0-85059-749-8.
- Halpenny, Bruce, *Fighter Pilots in World War II: True Stories of Front-line Air Combat (paperback)*. Barnsley, UK: Pen and Sword Books Ltd, 2004. ISBN 1-84415-065-8.
- Orange, Vincent, *Park: The Biography of Air Chief Marshal Sir Keith Park*. London: Grub Street, 2001. ISBN 1-902304-61-6.

Aircraft

<templatestyles src="Template:Refbegin/styles.css" />

- Ansell, Mark, *Boulton Paul Defiant: Technical Details and History of the Famous British Night Fighter*. Redbourn, Herts, UK: Mushroom Model Publications, 2005. pp. 712–714. ISBN 83-89450-19-4.
- de Zeng, Henry L., Doug G. Stankey and Eddie J. Creek, *Bomber Units of the Luftwaffe 1933–1945: A Reference Source, Volume 2*. Hersham, Surrey, UK: Ian Allen Publishing, 2007. ISBN 978-1-903223-87-1.
- Feist, Uwe, *The Fighting Me 109*. London: Arms and Armour Press, 1993. ISBN 1-85409-209-X.
- Goss, Chris, *Dornier 17: In Focus*. Surrey, UK: Red Kite Books, 2005. ISBN 0-9546201-4-3.
- Green, William, *Famous Fighters of the Second World War*. London: Macdonald, 1962.
- Harvey-Bailey, Alec. *Merlin in Perspective: The Combat Years* Derby, UK: Rolls-Royce Heritage Trust, 1995. ISBN 978-1-8729-2206-5.
- Holmes, Tony, *Hurricane Aces 1939–1940* (Aircraft of the Aces). Botley, Oxford, UK: Osprey Publishing, 1998. ISBN 1-85532-597-7.

- Holmes, Tony (2007), *Spitfire vs Bf 109: Battle of Britain*, Oxford: Osprey, ISBN 978-1-84603-190-8
- Huntley, Ian D., *Fairey Battle, Aviation Guide 1*. Bedford, UK: SAM Publications, 2004. ISBN 0-9533465-9-5.
- Jones, Robert C., *Camouflage and Markings Number 8: Boulton Paul Defiant, RAF Northern Europe 1936–45*. London: Ducimus Book Limited, 1970.
- Lloyd, Sir Ian and Pugh, Peter., *Hives and the Merlin*. Cambridge : Icon Books, 2004. ISBN 1840466448.
- Mason, Francis K., *Hawker Aircraft since 1920*. London: Putnam, 1991. ISBN 0-85177-839-9.
- McKinstry, Leo, *Hurricane: Victor of the Battle of Britain*. London: John Murray Publishers, 2010. ISBN 1-84854-339-5
- Molson, Kenneth M. *et al.*, *Canada's National Aviation Museum: Its History and Collections*. Ottawa: National Aviation Museum, 1988. ISBN 978-0-660-12001-0.
- Moyes, Philip, J. R., "The Fairey Battle." *Aircraft in Profile, Volume 2 (nos. 25–48)*. Windsor, Berkshire, UK: Profile Publications, 1971. ISBN 0-85383-011-8
- Parry, Simon W., *Intruders over Britain: The Story of the Luftwaffe's Night Intruder Force, the Fernnachtjager*. Washington, DC: Smithsonian Books, 1989. ISBN 0-904811-07-7.
- Price, Alfred (1996), *Spitfire Mark I/II Aces 1939–41 (Aircraft of the Aces 12)*, London: Osprey Books, ISBN 1-85532-627-2
- Price, Alfred (2002), *The Spitfire Story: Revised second edition*, Enderby, Leicester, UK: Silverdale Books, ISBN 1-85605-702-X
- Sarkar, Dilip, *How the Spitfire Won the Battle of Britain*. London: Amberly, 2011. ISBN 1-84868-868-7.
- Scutts, Jerry, *Messerschmitt Bf 109: The Operational Record*. Sarasota, Florida: Crestline Publishers, 1996. ISBN 978-0-7603-0262-0.
- Ward, John, *Hitler's Stuka Squadrons*. London: Brown Reference, 2004. ISBN 0-7603-1991-X.
- Warner, G (2005), *The Bristol Blenheim: A Complete History* (2nd ed.), London: Crécy Publishing, ISBN 0-85979-101-7
- Weal, John (1999), *Messerschmitt Bf 110 'Zerstörer' Aces of World War 2*, Botley, Oxford, UK: Osprey Publishing, ISBN 1-85532-753-8

Additional references

<templatestyles src="Template:Refbegin/styles.css" />

Books

- Addison, Paul and Jeremy Crang. *The Burning Blue: A New History of the Battle of Britain.* London: Pimlico, 2000. ISBN 0-7126-6475-0.
- Bergström, Christer. *Barbarossa – The Air Battle: July–December 1941.* London: Chervron/Ian Allen, 2007. ISBN 978-1-85780-270-2.
- Bishop, Patrick. *Fighter Boys: The Battle of Britain, 1940.* New York: Viking, 2003 (hardcover, ISBN 0-670-03230-1); Penguin Books, 2004. ISBN 0-14-200466-9. As *Fighter Boys: Saving Britain 1940.* London: Harper Perennial, 2004. ISBN 0-00-653204-7.
- Brittain, Vera. *England's Hour.* London: Continuum International Publishing Group, 2005 (paperback, ISBN 0-8264-8031-4); Obscure Press (paperback, ISBN 1-84664-834-3).
- Campion, Garry. *The Good Fight: Battle of Britain Wartime Propaganda and The Few.* Basingstoke, Hampshire, UK: Palgrave Macmillan, 2010, First edition 2008. ISBN 978-0-230-27996-4.
- Campion, Garry. *The Battle of Britain, 1945–1965: The Air Ministry and the Few:* Palgrave Macmillan, 2015. ISBN 978-0230284548
- Cooper, Matthew. *The German Air Force 1933–1945: An Anatomy of Failure.* New York: Jane's Publishing Incorporated, 1981. ISBN 0-531-03733-9.
- Craig, Phil and Tim Clayton. *Finest Hour: The Battle of Britain.* New York: Simon & Schuster, 2000. ISBN 0-684-86930-6 (hardcover); 2006, ISBN 0-684-86931-4 (paperback).
- Cumming, Anthony J. *The Royal Navy and The Battle of Britain.* Annapolis, Maryland: Naval Institute Press, 2010. ISBN 978-1-59114-160-0.
- Fiedler, Arkady. *303 Squadron: The Legendary Battle of Britain Fighter Squadron.* Los Angeles: Aquila Polonica, 2010. ISBN 978-1-60772-004-1.
- Fisher, David E. *A Summer Bright and Terrible: Winston Churchill, Lord Dowding, Radar and the Impossible Triumph of the Battle of Britain.* Emeryville, CA: Shoemaker & Hoard, 2005. (hardcover, ISBN 1-59376-047-7); 2006, ISBN 1-59376-116-3 (paperback).
- Foreman, John (1989), *Battle of Britain: The Forgotten Months, November And December 1940,* Wythenshawe, Lancashire, UK: Crécy, ISBN 1-871187-02-8
- Gaskin, Margaret. *Blitz: The Story of 29 December 1940.* New York: Harcourt, 2006. ISBN 0-15-101404-3.
- Haining, Peter. *The Chianti Raiders: The Extraordinary Story of the Italian Air Force in the Battle of Britain.* London: Robson Books, 2005. ISBN 1-86105-829-2.
- Haining, Peter. *Where the Eagle Landed: The Mystery of the German Invasion of Britain, 1940.* London: Robson Books, 2004. ISBN 1-86105-

750-4.

- Halpenny, Bruce Barrymore. *Action Stations: Military Airfields of Greater London v. 8*. Cambridge, UK: Patrick Stephens, 1984. ISBN 0-85039-885-1.
- Harding, Thomas. "It's baloney, say RAF aces". *The Telegraph*, 24 August 2006. Retrieved: 3 March 2007.
- Hough, Richard. *The Battle of Britain: The Greatest Air Battle of World War II*. New York: W.W. Norton, 1989. ISBN 0-393-02766-X (hardcover); 2005, ISBN 0-393-30734-4(paperback).
- James, T.C.G. *The Battle of Britain (Air Defence of Great Britain; vol. 2)*. London/New York: Frank Cass Publishers, 2000. ISBN 0-7146-5123-0(hardcover); ISBN 0-7146-8149-0 (paperback,).
- James, T.C.G. *Growth of Fighter Command, 1936–1940 (Air Defence of Great Britain; vol. 1)*. London; New York: Frank Cass Publishers, 2000. ISBN 0-7146-5118-4.
- James, T.C.G. *Night Air Defence During the Blitz*. London/New York: Frank Cass Publishers, 2003. ISBN 0-7146-5166-4.
- McGlashan, Kenneth B. with Owen P. Zupp. *Down to Earth: A Fighter Pilot Recounts His Experiences of Dunkirk, the Battle of Britain, Dieppe, D-Day and Beyond*. London: Grub Street Publishing, 2007. ISBN 1-904943-84-5.
- March, Edgar J. *British Destroyers; a History of Development 1892–1953*. London: Seely Service & Co. Limited, 1966.
- Olson, Lynne and Stanley Cloud. *A Question of Honor: The Kościuszko Squadron: Forgotten Heroes of World War II*. New York: Knopf, 2003. ISBN 0-375-41197-6. NB: This book is also published under the following title:
  - *For Your Freedom and Ours: The Kościuszko Squadron – Forgotten Heroes of World War II*.
- Prien, Jochen and Peter Rodeike.*Messerschmitt Bf 109 F, G, and K: An Illustrated Study*. Atglen, Pennsylvania: Schiffer Publishing, 1995. ISBN 0-88740-424-3.
- Ray, John. *Battle of Britain*. London: The Orion Publishing Co., 2003. ISBN 1-85409-345-2.
- Ray, John Philip. *The Battle of Britain: Dowding and the First Victory 1940*. London: Cassel & Co., 2001. ISBN 0-304-35677-8.
- Ray, John Philip. *The Battle of Britain: New Perspectives: Behind the Scenes of the Great Air War*. London: Arms & Armour Press, 1994 (hardcover, ISBN 1-85409-229-4); London: Orion Publishing, 1996 (paperback, ISBN 1-85409-345-2).
- Rongers, Eppo H. *De oorlog in mei '40*, Utrecht/Antwerpen: Uitgeverij Het Spectrum N.V., 1969, No ISBN

- Townsend, Peter. *Duel of Eagles (new edition)*. London: Phoenix, 2000. ISBN 1-84212-211-8.
- Wellum, Geoffrey. *First Light: The Story of the Boy Who Became a Man in the War-Torn Skies Above Britain*. New York: Viking Books, 2002. ISBN 0-670-91248-4 (hardcover); Hoboken, NJ: Wiley & Sons, 2003. ISBN 0-471-42627-X (hardcover); London: Penguin Books, 2003. ISBN 0-14-100814-8 (paperback).
- Zaloga, Steven J. and Richard Hook. *The Polish Army 1939–45*. London: Osprey, 1982. ISBN 0-85045-417-4.

General

- The Battle of Britain Historical Timeline[174]
- Day by Day blog charting the progress of the Battle by ex RAF veteran[175]
- Battle Of Britain Historical Society[176]
- video: *Battle of Britain*[177] on YouTube, (52 min.) complete film documentary by Frank Capra made for U.S. Army
- The Battle of Britain "In Photos"[178]
- Royal Air Force history[179]
- Battle of Britain Memorial[180]
- BBC History Overview of Battle[181]
- Historical recording BBC: Churchill's "This Was Their Finest Hour" speech[182]
- Radio New Zealand 'Sounds Historical' ANZAC Day, 25 April 2008: Historical recording of Sir Keith Park describing the Battle of Britain. (Scroll down to 10:50 am).[183]
- Air Chief Marshal Hugh Dowding on the Battle of Britain (despatch to the Secretary of State, August 1941)[184]
- Royal Engineers Museum: Royal Engineers during the Second World War (airfield repair)[185]
- Shoreham Aircraft Museum[186]
- Tangmere Military Aviation Museum[187]
- Kent Battle of Britain Museum[188]
- ADLG Visits RAF Uxbridge Battle of Britain Operations Room[189]
- British Invasion Defences[190]
- The Falco and Regia Aeronautica in the Battle of Britain[191]
- History of North Weald Airfield[192]
- The Royal Mint Memorial website[193]
- New Zealanders in the Battle of Britain (NZHistory.net.nz)[194]
- New Zealanders in the Battle of Britain (official history)[195]
- Battle for Britain, short film starring Julian Glover[196]
- Interactive map showing Battle of Britain airfields and squadrons by date[197]
- http://garry-campion.com/

Operation Sea Lion

Operation Sea Lion

Operation Sea Lion	
Part of the Western Front of the Second World War	
Operational scope	Normandy, the Belgian coast line, the English Channel and the English coast line from Kent to Dorset, Isle of Wight and parts of Devon, but principally in Sussex and Kent
Planned	September 1940
Planned by	OKW
Objective	Elimination of the United Kingdom as a base of military operations against the Axis powers[198]
Outcome	Eventual cancellation and diversion of German, Italian, and other Axis forces for Operation Barbarossa

Operation Sea Lion, also written as **Operation Sealion** (German: *Unternehmen Seelöwe*), was Nazi Germany's code name for the plan for an invasion of the United Kingdom during the Battle of Britain in the Second World War. Following the Fall of France, Adolf Hitler, the German Führer and Supreme Commander of the Armed Forces, hoped the British government would seek a peace agreement and he reluctantly considered invasion only as a last resort if all other options failed. As a precondition, he specified the achievement of both air and naval superiority over the English Channel and the proposed landing sites, but the German forces did not achieve either at any point during the war, and both the German High Command and Hitler himself had serious doubts about the prospects for success. A large number of barges were gathered together on the Channel coast, but, with air losses increasing, Hitler postponed Sea Lion indefinitely on 17 September 1940 and it was never put into action.

Background

Adolf Hitler hoped for a negotiated peace with the UK and made no preparations for amphibious assault on Britain until the Fall of France. At the time, the only forces with experience of or modern equipment for such landings were the Japanese, at the Battle of Wuhan in 1938.[199]

Outbreak of war and fall of Poland

In September 1939, the German invasion of Poland was a success, but this infringed on both a French and a British alliance with Poland and both countries declared war on Germany. On 9 October, Hitler's "Directive No. 6 for the Conduct of the War" planned an offensive to defeat these allies and "win as much territory as possible in Holland, Belgium, and northern France to serve as a base for the successful prosecution of the air and sea war against England".[200]

With the prospect of the Channel ports falling under *Kriegsmarine* (German Navy) control, Grand Admiral (*Großadmiral*) Erich Raeder (head of the *Kriegsmarine*) attempted to anticipate the obvious next step that might entail and instructed his operations officer, *Kapitän* Hansjürgen Reinicke, to draw up a document examining "the possibility of troop landings in England should the future progress of the war make the problem arise". Reinicke spent five days on this study and set forth the following prerequisites:

- Eliminating or sealing off Royal Navy forces from the landing and approach areas.
- Eliminating the Royal Air Force.
- Destroying all Royal Navy units in the coastal zone.
- Preventing British submarine action against the landing fleet.[201]

On 22 November 1939, the Head of *Luftwaffe* (German Air Force) intelligence Joseph "Beppo" Schmid presented his "Proposal for the Conduct of Air Warfare", which argued for a counter to the British blockade and said "Key is to paralyse the British trade" by blocking imports to Britain and attacking seaports. The OKW (*Oberkommando der Wehrmacht* or "High Command of the Armed Forces") considered the options and Hitler's 29 November "Directive No. 9 – Instructions For Warfare Against The Economy Of The Enemy" stated that once the coast had been secured, the *Luftwaffe* and *Kriegsmarine* were to blockade UK ports with sea mines, attack shipping and warships, and make air attacks on shore installations and industrial production. This directive remained in force in the first phase of the Battle of Britain.[202]

In December 1939, the German Army issued its own study paper (designated *Nordwest*) and solicited opinions and input from both *Kriegsmarine* and *Luftwaffe*. The paper outlined an assault on England's eastern coast between The Wash and the River Thames by troops crossing the North Sea from ports in the Low Countries. It suggested airborne troops as well as seaborne landings of 100,000 infantry in East Anglia, transported by the *Kriegsmarine*, which was also to prevent Royal Navy ships from getting through the Channel, while the *Luftwaffe* had to control airspace over the landings. The *Kriegsmarine* response was focused on pointing out the many difficulties to be surmounted if invading England was to be a viable option. It could not envisage taking on the Royal Navy Home Fleet and said it would take a year to organise shipping for the troops. *Reichsmarschall* Hermann Göring, head of the *Luftwaffe*, responded with a single-page letter in which he stated, "[A] combined operation having the objective of landing in England must be rejected. It could only be the final act of an already victorious war against Britain as otherwise the preconditions for success of a combined operation would not be met".[203,204]

The fall of France

Germany's swift and successful occupation of France and the Low Countries gained control of the Channel coast, facing what Schmid's 1939 report called their "most dangerous enemy". Raeder met Hitler on 21 May 1940 and raised the topic of invasion, but warned of the risks and expressed a preference for blockade by air, submarines and raiders.[205,206]

By the end of May, the *Kriegsmarine* had become even more opposed to invading Britain following its Pyrrhic victory in Norway: after Operation *Weserübung*, the *Kriegsmarine* had only one heavy cruiser, two light cruisers, and four destroyers available for operations.[207] Raeder was strongly opposed to Sea Lion, for almost the entire *Kriegsmarine* surface fleet had been either sunk or badly damaged in *Weserübung*, and his service was hopelessly outnumbered by the ships of the Royal Navy.[208] British parliamentarians still arguing for peace negotiations were defeated in the May 1940 War Cabinet Crisis, but throughout July the Germans continued with attempts to find a diplomatic solution.[209]

Invasion planning

In a report presented on 30 June, OKW Chief of Staff Alfred Jodl reviewed
options to increase pressure on Britain to agree to a negotiated peace. The first
priority was to eliminate the Royal Air Force and gain air supremacy. Intensified air attacks against shipping and the economy could affect food supplies
and civilian morale in the long term. Reprisal attacks of terror bombing had the
potential to cause quicker capitulation but the effect on morale was uncertain.
Once the Luftwaffe had control of the air and the British economy had been
weakened, an invasion would be a last resort or a final strike (*"Todesstoss"*)
after England had already been practically defeated, but could have a quick
result.[205,210] At a meeting that day, OKW Chief of General Staff Franz Halder
heard from Secretary of State Ernst von Weizsäcker that Hitler had turned
his attention to Russia. Halder met Admiral Otto Schniewind on 1 July, and
they shared views without understanding each other's position. Both thought
that air superiority was needed first, and could make the invasion unnecessary. They agreed that minefields and U-boats could limit the threat posed by
the Royal Navy; Schniewind emphasised the significance of weather conditions.[211]

On 2 July, the OKW asked the services to start preliminary planning for an
invasion, as Hitler had concluded that invasion would be achievable in certain
conditions, the first of which was command of the air, and specifically asked
the *Luftwaffe* when this would be achieved. On 4 July, after asking General
Erich Marcks to begin planning an attack on Russia, Halder heard from the
Luftwaffe that they planned to eliminate the RAF, destroying its aircraft manufacturing and supply systems, with damage to naval forces as a secondary
aim. A *Luftwaffe* report presented to the OKW at a meeting on 11 July said
that it would take 14 to 28 days to achieve air superiority. The meeting also
heard that England was discussing an agreement with Russia. On the same
day, Grand Admiral Raeder visited Hitler at the Berghof to persuade him that
the best way to pressure the British into a peace agreement would be a siege
combining air and submarine attacks. Hitler agreed with him that invasion
would be a last resort.[212]

Jodl set out the OKW proposals for the proposed invasion in a memorandum
issued on 12 July, which described operation *Löwe* (Lion) as "a river crossing
on a broad front", irritating the *Kriegsmarine*. On 13 July, Hitler met Field
Marshal von Brauchitsch and Halder, who presented detailed plans prepared
by the army on the assumption that the navy would provide safe transport.[213]
Against his previous practice, Hitler showed no interest in the details, but said
preparations were to begin.[214]

Directive No. 16: Operation Sea Lion

On 16 July 1940 Hitler issued Führer Directive No. 16, setting in motion preparations for a landing in Britain. He prefaced the order by stating: "As England, in spite of her hopeless military situation, still shows no signs of willingness to come to terms, I have decided to prepare, and if necessary to carry out, a landing operation against her. The aim of this operation is to eliminate the English Motherland as a base from which the war against Germany can be continued, and, if necessary, to occupy the country completely." The code name for the invasion was *Seelöwe*, "Sea Lion".[215]

Hitler's directive set four conditions for the invasion to occur:[216]

- The RAF was to be "beaten down in its morale and in fact, that it can no longer display any appreciable aggressive force in opposition to the German crossing".
- The English Channel was to be swept of British mines at the crossing points, and the Strait of Dover must be blocked at both ends by German mines.
- The coastal zone between occupied France and England must be dominated by heavy artillery.
- The Royal Navy must be sufficiently engaged in the North Sea and the Mediterranean so that it could not intervene in the crossing. British home squadrons must be damaged or destroyed by air and torpedo attacks.

This ultimately placed responsibility for Sea Lion's success squarely on the shoulders of Raeder and Göring, neither of whom had the slightest enthusiasm for the venture and, in fact, did little to hide their opposition to it.[217] Nor did Directive 16 provide for a combined operational headquarters, similar to the Allies' creation of the Supreme Headquarters Allied Expeditionary Force (SHAEF) for the later Normandy landings, under which all three service branches (Army, Navy, and Air Force) could work together to plan, coordinate, and execute such a complex undertaking.[218]

The invasion was to be on a broad front, from around Ramsgate to beyond the Isle of Wight. Preparations, including overcoming the RAF, were to be in place by mid August.[212]

Discussion

Grand Admiral Raeder sent a memorandum to OKW on 19 July, complaining about the onus placed on the navy in relation to the army and air force, and stating that the navy would be unable to achieve its objectives.[213]

The first joint services conference on the proposed invasion was held by Hitler in Berlin on 21 July, with Raeder, Field Marshal von Brauchitsch, and *Luftwaffe* Chief of Staff Hans Jeschonnek. Hitler told them that the British had no hope of survival, and ought to negotiate, but were hoping to get Russia to intervene and halt German oil supplies. Invasion was very risky, and he asked them if direct attacks by air and submarine could take effect by mid September. Jeschonnek proposed large bombing attacks so that responding RAF fighters could be shot down. The idea that invasion could be a surprise "river crossing" was dismissed by Raeder, and the navy could not complete its preparations by mid August. Hitler wanted the air attack to commence early in August and, if it succeeded, the invasion was to start around 25 August before weather deteriorated. Hitler's main interest was the question of countering potential Russian intervention. Halder outlined his first thoughts on defeating Russian forces. Detailed plans were to be made to attack the Soviet Union.[219]

Raeder met Hitler on 25 July to report on navy progress: they were not sure if preparations could be completed during August: he was to present plans at a conference on 31 July. On 28 July he told OKW that ten days would be needed to get the first wave of troops across the Channel, even on a much narrower front. Planning was to resume. In his diary, Halder noted that if what Raeder had said was true, "all previous statements by the navy were so much rubbish and we can throw away the whole plan of invasion". On the next day, Halder dismissed the navy's claims and required a new plan.[220,221]

The *Luftwaffe* announced on 29 July that they could begin a major air attack at the start of August, and their intelligence reports gave them confidence of a decisive result. Half of their bombers were to be kept in reserve to support the invasion. At a meeting with the army, the navy proposed delay until May 1941, when the new battleships *Bismarck* and *Tirpitz* would be ready. A navy memorandum issued on 30 July said invasion would be vulnerable to the Royal Navy, and autumn weather could prevent necessary maintenance of supplies. The OKW assessed alternatives, including attacking the British in the Mediterranean, and favoured extended operations against England while remaining on good terms with Russia.[220]

At the Berghof conference on 31 July, the *Luftwaffe* were not represented. Raeder said barge conversions would take until 15 September, leaving the only possible 1940 invasion dates as 22-26 September, when weather was likely to be unsuitable. Landings would have to be on a narrow front, and would be better in spring 1941. Hitler wanted the invasion in September as the British army was increasing in strength. After Raeder left, Hitler told von Brauchitsch and Halder that the air attack was to start around 5 August; eight to fourteen days after that, he would decide on the landing operation. London was showing new-found optimism, and he attributed this to their hopes of intervention by Russia, which Germany was to attack in the spring of 1941.[222]

Directive No. 17: air and sea warfare against England

On 1 August 1940, Hitler instructed intensified air and sea warfare to "establish the necessary conditions for the final conquest of England". From 5 August, subject to weather delays, the *Luftwaffe* was "to overpower the English Air Force with all the forces at its command, in the shortest possible time." Attacks were then to be made on ports and food stocks, while leaving alone ports to be used in the invasion, and "air attacks on enemy warships and merchant ships may be reduced except where some particularly favourable target happens to present itself." The *Luftwaffe* was to keep sufficient forces in reserve for the proposed invasion, and was not to target civilians without a direct order from Hitler in response to RAF terror bombing. No decision had been reached on the choice between immediate decisive action and a siege. The Germans hoped the air action would force the British to negotiate, and make invasion unnecessary.[223]

Land forces

In the plan finalised in August 1940, the invasion force was organised into two army groups drawn from the 6th Army, the 9th Army and the 16th Army. The first wave of the landing would have consisted of eleven infantry and mountain divisions, the second wave of eight panzer and motorised infantry divisions and finally, the third wave was formed of six further infantry divisions. The initial assault would have also included two airborne divisions and the special forces of the Brandenburg Regiment.

The landings would have been initially opposed by XII Corps of Eastern Command with three infantry divisions and two independent brigades and V Corps of Southern Command with three infantry divisions. In reserve were two more Corps under GHQ Home Forces; located south of London was the VII Corps with the 1st Canadian Infantry Division, an armoured division and an independent armoured brigade, while north of London was IV Corps with an armoured division, infantry division and independent infantry brigade.[224]

Air power

Battle of Britain

The Battle of Britain began in early July 1940, with attacks on shipping and ports in the *Kanalkampf* which forced RAF Fighter Command into defensive action. In addition, wider raids gave aircrew experience of day and night navigation, and tested the defences.Wikipedia:Citation needed On 13 August, the German *Luftwaffe* began a series of concentrated aerial attacks (designated *Unternehmen Adlerangriff* or Operation Eagle Attack) on targets throughout the United Kingdom in an attempt to destroy the RAF and establish air superiority over Great Britain. The change in emphasis of the bombing from RAF bases to bombing London, however, turned *Adlerangriff* into a short-range strategic bombing operation.

The effect of the switch in strategy is disputed. Some historians argue the change in strategy lost the Luftwaffe the opportunity of winning the air battle, or air superiority.[225] Others argue the *Luftwaffe* achieved little in the air battle and the RAF was not on the verge of collapse, as often claimed.[226] Another perspective has also been put forward, which suggests the Germans could not have gained air superiority before the weather window closed.[227] Others have said that it was unlikely the *Luftwaffe* would ever be able to destroy RAF Fighter Command. If British losses became severe, the RAF could simply have withdrawn northward and regrouped. It could then deploy when, or if, the Germans launched an invasion. Most historians agree Sea Lion would have failed regardless, because of the weaknesses of German sea power compared to the Royal Navy.[228]

Limitations of the *Luftwaffe*

The track record of the *Luftwaffe* against naval combat vessels up to that point in the war was poor. In the Norwegian Campaign, despite eight weeks of continuous air supremacy, the *Luftwaffe* sank only two British warships. The German aircrews were not trained or equipped to attack fast-moving naval targets, particularly agile naval destroyers or Motor Torpedo Boats (MTB). The Luftwaffe also lacked armour-piercing bombs and had almost no aerial torpedo capability, essential for defeating larger warships. The *Luftwaffe* made 21 deliberate attacks on small torpedo boats during the Battle of Britain, sinking none. The British had between 700 and 800 small coastal craft (MTBs, Motor Gun Boats and smaller vessels), making them a critical threat if the *Luftwaffe* could not deal with the force. Only nine MTBs were lost to air attack out of 115 sunk by various means throughout the Second World War. Only nine destroyers were sunk by air attack in 1940, out of a force of over 100 operating in

British waters at the time. Only five were sunk while evacuating Dunkirk, despite large periods of German air superiority, thousands of sorties flown, and hundreds of tons of bombs dropped. The *Luftwaffe*'s record against merchant shipping was also not impressive: It sank only one in every 100 British vessels passing through British waters in 1940, and most of this total was achieved using mines.[229]

Luftwaffe Special Equipment

Had an invasion taken place, the Bf 110 equipped *Erprobungsgruppe 210* would have dropped *Seilbomben* just prior to the landings. This was a secret weapon which would have been used to blackout the electricity network in south-east England. The equipment for dropping the wires was fitted to the Bf 110 aeroplanes and tested. It involved dropping wires across high voltage wires, and was probably as dangerous to the aircraft crews as to the British.[230]

Italian air force

Upon hearing of Hitler's intentions, Italian dictator Benito Mussolini, through his Foreign Minister Count Galeazzo Ciano, quickly offered up to ten divisions and thirty squadrons of Italian aircraft for the proposed invasion.[231] Hitler initially declined any such aid but eventually allowed a small contingent of Italian fighters and bombers, the Italian Air Corps (*Corpo Aereo Italiano* or CAI), to assist in the *Luftwaffe*'s aerial campaign over Britain in October and November 1940.[232]

Navy

The most daunting problem for Germany in protecting an invasion fleet was the small size of its navy. The *Kriegsmarine*, already numerically far inferior to Britain's Royal Navy, had lost a sizeable portion of its large modern surface units in April 1940 during the Norwegian Campaign, either as complete losses or due to battle damage. In particular, the loss of two light cruisers and ten destroyers was crippling, as these were the very warships most suited to operating in the Channel narrows where the invasion would likely take place.[233] Most U-boats, the most powerful arm of the *Kriegsmarine*, were meant for destroying ships, not supporting an invasion.

Although the Royal Navy could not bring the whole of its naval superiority to bear—as most of the fleet was engaged in the Atlantic and Mediterranean—the British Home Fleet still had a very large advantage in numbers. It was debatable whether British ships were as vulnerable to enemy air attack as the Germans hoped. During the Dunkirk evacuation, few warships were actually sunk, despite being stationary targets. The overall disparity between the

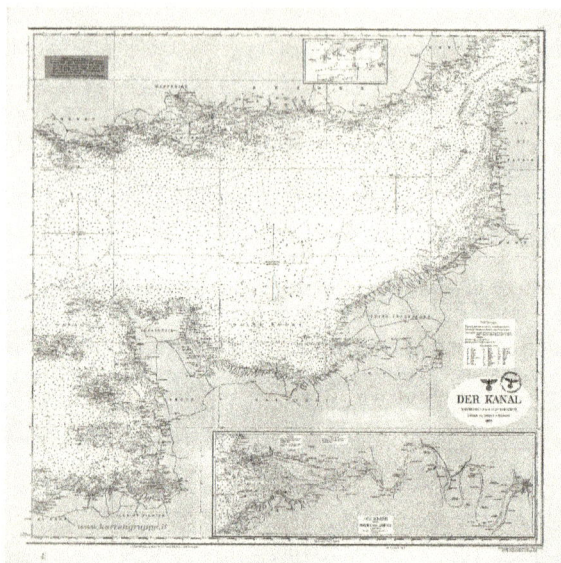

Figure 44: *The Channel (Der Kanal), D.66 Kriegsmarine nautical chart, 1943*

opposing naval forces made the amphibious invasion plan extremely risky, regardless of the outcome in the air. In addition, the *Kriegsmarine* had allocated
its few remaining larger and more modern ships to diversionary operations in
the North Sea.

The fleet of defeated France, one of the most powerful and modern in the
world, might have tipped the balance against Britain if it had been captured
by the Germans. However, the pre-emptive destruction of a large part of the
French fleet by the British at Mers-el-Kébir, and the scuttling of the remainder
by the French themselves at Toulon two years later, ensured that this could not
happen.

Even if the Royal Navy had been neutralised, the chances of a successful amphibious invasion across the Channel were remote. The Germans had no specialised landing craft, and would have had to rely primarily on river barges to
lift troops and supplies for the landing. This would have limited the quantity of
artillery and tanks that could be transported and restricted operations to times
of good weather. The barges were not designed for use in open sea and, even in
almost perfect conditions, they would have been slow and vulnerable to attack.
There were also not enough barges to transport the first invasion wave nor the
following waves with their equipment. The Germans would have needed to immediately capture a port in full working order, a highly unlikely circumstance

considering the strength of the British coastal defences around the southeastern harbors at that time and the likelihood the British would have demolished the docks in any port from which they had to withdraw. The British also had several contingency plans, including the use of poison gas.

The view of those who believed, regardless of a potential German victory in the air battle, that Sea Lion was still not going to succeed included a number of German General Staff members. After the war, Admiral Karl Dönitz said he believed air superiority was "not enough". Dönitz stated, "[W]e possessed neither control of the air or the sea; nor were we in any position to gain it".[234] In his memoirs, Erich Raeder, commander-in-chief of the *Kriegsmarine* in 1940, argued:

> .....the emphatic reminder that up until now the British had never thrown the full power of their fleet into action. However, a German invasion of England would be a matter of life and death for the British, and they would unhesitatingly commit their naval forces, to the last ship and the last man, into an all-out fight for survival. Our Air Force could not be counted on to guard our transports from the British Fleets, because their operations would depend on the weather, if for no other reason. It could not be expected that even for a brief period our Air Force could make up for our lack of naval supremacy.[235]

On 13 August 1940, Alfred Jodl, Chief of Operations in the OKW (*Oberkommando der Wehrmacht*) wrote his "Assessment of the situation arising from the views of the Army and Navy on a landing in England." His first point was that "The landing operation must under no circumstances fail. A failure could leave political consequences, which would go far beyond the military ones." He believed that the *Luftwaffe* could meet its essential objectives, but if the *Kriegsmarine* could not meet the operational requirements of the Army for an attack on a broad front with two divisions landed within four days, followed promptly by three further divisions irrespective of weather, "then I consider the landing to be an act of desperation, which would have to be risked in a desperate situation, but which we have no reason whatsoever to undertake at this moment."[236]

Landing craft

In 1940 the German Navy was ill-prepared for mounting an amphibious assault the size of Operation Sea Lion. Lacking purpose-built landing craft and both doctrinal and practical experience with amphibious warfare, the *Kriegsmarine* was largely starting from scratch. Some efforts had been made during the interwar years to investigate landing military forces by sea, but inadequate funding severely limited any useful progress.[237]

Figure 45: *Invasion barges assembled at the German port of Wilhelmshaven.*

Figure 46: *A Pionierlandungsboot.*

The *Kriegsmarine* had taken some small steps in remedying the landing craft situation with construction of the *Pionierlandungsboot 39* (Engineer Landing Boat 39), a self-propelled shallow-draft vessel which could carry 45 infantry-men, two light vehicles or 20 tons of cargo and land on an open beach, unloading via a pair of clamshell doors at the bow. But by late September 1940 only two prototypes had been delivered.[238]

Recognising the need for an even larger craft capable of landing both tanks and infantry onto a hostile shore, the *Kriegsmarine* began development of the 220-ton *Marinefährprahm* (MFP) but these too were unavailable in time for a landing on British soil in 1940, the first of them not being commissioned until April 1941.

Given barely two months to assemble a large seagoing invasion fleet, the *Kriegsmarine* opted to convert inland river barges into makeshift landing craft. Approximately 2,400 barges were collected from throughout Europe (860 from Germany, 1,200 from the Netherlands and Belgium and 350 from France). Of these, only about 800 were powered (some insufficiently); the rest had to be towed by tugs.[239]

Barge types

Two types of inland river barge were generally available in Europe for use in Sea Lion: the *peniche*, which was 38.5 meters long and carried 360 tons of cargo, and the *Kampine*, which was 50 meters long and carried 620 tons of cargo. Of the barges collected for the invasion, 1,336 were classified as *peniches* and 982 as *Kampinen*. For simplicity's sake, the Germans designated any barge up to the size of a standard *peniche* as Type A1 and anything larger as Type A2.[240]

Type A

Converting the assembled barges into landing craft involved cutting an opening in the bow for off-loading troops and vehicles, welding longitudinal I-beams and transverse braces to the hull to improve seaworthiness, adding a wooden internal ramp and pouring a concrete floor in the hold to allow for tank transport. As modified, the Type A1 barge could accommodate three medium tanks while the Type A2 could carry four.[241]

Type B

This barge was a Type A altered to carry and rapidly off-load the submersible tanks (*Tauchpanzer*) developed for use in Sea Lion. They had the advantage of being able to unload their tanks directly into water up to 15 metres (49 ft) in depth, several hundred yards from shore, whereas the unmodified Type A had to be firmly grounded on the beach, making it more vulnerable to enemy fire. The Type B required a longer external ramp (11 meters) with a float attached to the front of it. Once the barge anchored, the crew would extend the internally stowed ramp using block and tackle sets until it was resting on the water's surface. As the first tank rolled forward onto the ramp, its weight would tilt the forward end of the ramp into the water and push it down onto the seabed. Once the tank rolled off, the ramp would bob back up to a horizontal position, ready for the next one to exit. The Navy High Command increased its initial order for 60 of these vessels to 70 in order to compensate for expected losses. A further five were ordered on 30 September as a reserve.[241]

Type C

The Type C barge was specifically converted to carry the Panzer II amphibious tank (*Schwimmpanzer*). Because of the extra width of the floats attached to this tank, cutting a broad exit ramp into the bow of the barge was not considered advisable as it would have compromised the vessel's seaworthiness to an unacceptable degree. Instead, a large hatch was cut into the stern, thereby allowing the tanks to drive directly into deep water before turning under their own motive power and heading towards shore. The Type C barge could accommodate up to four *Schwimmpanzern* in its hold. Approximately 14 of these craft were available by the end of September.[242]

Type AS

During the planning stages of Sea Lion, it was deemed desirable to provide the advanced infantry detachments (making the initial landings) with greater protection from small-arms and light artillery fire by lining the sides of a Type A barge with concrete. Wooden slides were also installed along the barge's hull to accommodate ten assault boats (*Sturmboote*), each capable of carrying six infantrymen and powered by a 30 hp outboard motor. The extra weight of this additional armour and equipment reduced the barge's load capacity to 40 tons. By mid-August, 18 of these craft, designated Type AS, had been converted, and another five were ordered on 30 September.

Type AF

The *Luftwaffe* had formed its own special command (*Sonderkommando*) under Major Fritz Siebel to investigate the production of landing craft for Sea Lion. Major Siebel proposed giving the unpowered Type A barges their own motive power by installing a pair of surplus 600 hp (610 PS; 450 kW) BMW aircraft engines, driving propellers. The *Kriegsmarine* was highly sceptical of this venture, but the *Heer* (Army) high command enthusiastically embraced the concept and Siebel proceeded with the conversions.[243]

The aircraft engines were mounted on a platform supported by iron scaffolding at the aft end of the vessel. Cooling water was stored in tanks mounted above-deck. As completed, the Type AF had a speed of six knots, and a range of 60 nautical miles unless auxiliary fuel tanks were fitted. Disadvantages of this set-up included an inability to back the vessel astern, limited maneuverability and the deafening noise of the engines which would have made voice commands problematic.

By 1 October, 128 Type A barges had been converted to airscrew propulsion and, by the end of the month, this figure had risen to over 200.[244]

The *Kriegsmarine* later used some of the motorized Sea Lion barges for landings on the Russian-held Baltic islands in 1941 and, though most of them were eventually returned to the inland rivers they originally plied, a reserve was kept for military transport duties and for filling out amphibious flotillas.[243]

Army

Panzers ashore

Providing armour support for the initial wave of assault troops was a critical concern for Sea Lion planners and much effort was devoted to finding practical ways of rapidly getting tanks onto the invasion beaches. Though the Type A barges could disembark several medium tanks onto an open beach, this could be accomplished only at low tide when the barges were firmly grounded. The time needed for assembling the external ramps also meant that both the tanks and the ramp assembly crews would be exposed to close-quarter enemy fire for a considerable time. A safer and faster method was needed and the Germans eventually settled on providing some tanks with floats and making others fully submersible.

Figure 47: *A Panzer III Tauchpanzer under test (1940)*

Schwimmpanzer

The *Schwimmpanzer* II was a modified version of the Panzer II which, at 8.9 tons, was light enough to float with the attachment of long rectangular buoyancy boxes on each side of the tank's hull. The boxes were machined from aluminium stock and filled with Kapok sacks for added buoyancy. Motive power came from the tank's own tracks which were connected by rods to a propeller shaft running through each float. The *Schwimmpanzer* II could make 5.7 km/h in the water. An inflatable rubber hose around the turret ring created a waterproof seal between the hull and turret. The tank's 2 cm gun and coaxial machinegun were kept operational and could be fired while the tank was still making its way ashore. Because of the great width of the pontoons, *Schwimmpanzer* IIs were to be deployed from specially-modified Type C landing barges, from which they could be launched directly into open water from a large hatch cut into the stern. The Germans converted 52 of these tanks to amphibious use prior to Sea Lion's cancellation.[245]

Tauchpanzer

The *Tauchpanzer* or deep-wading tank (also referred to as the *U-Panzer* or *Unterwasser Panzer*) was a standard Panzer III or Panzer IV medium tank with its hull made completely waterproof by sealing all sighting ports, hatches and air intakes with tape or caulk. The gap between the turret and hull was sealed with an inflatable hose while the main gun mantlet, commander's cupola and radio operator's machine gun were given special rubber coverings. Once the tank reached the shore, all covers and seals could be blown off via explosive cables, enabling normal combat operation.[246]

Fresh air for both the crew and engine was drawn into the tank via an 18m long rubber hose to which a float was attached to keep one end above the water's surface. A radio antenna was also attached to the float to provide communication between the tank crew and the transport barge. The tank's engine was converted to be cooled with seawater, and the exhaust pipes were fitted with overpressure valves. Any water seeping into the tank's hull could be expelled by an internal bilge pump. Navigation underwater was accomplished using a directional gyrocompass or by following instructions radioed from the transport barge.

Experiments conducted at the end of June and early July at Schilling, near Wilhelmshaven, showed that the submersible tanks functioned best when they were kept moving along the seabed as, if halted for any reason, they tended to sink into the sand. Obstacles such as underwater trenches or large rocks tended to stop the tanks in their tracks, and it was decided for this reason that they should be landed at high tide so that any mired tanks could be retrieved at low tide. Submersible tanks could operate in water up to a depth of 15 metres (49 ft).[247]

The *Kriegsmarine* initially expected to use 50 specially-converted motor coasters to transport the submersible tanks, but testing with the coaster *Germania* showed this to be impractical. This was due to the ballast needed to offset the weight of the tanks, and the requirement that the coasters be grounded to prevent them from capsizing as the tanks were transferred by crane onto the vessel's wooden side ramps. These difficulties led to development of the Type B barge.

By the end of August the Germans had converted 160 Panzer IIIs, 42 Panzer IVs, and 52 Panzer IIs to amphibious use. This gave them a paper strength of 254 machines, about the equivalent of an armoured division. The tanks were divided into four battalions or detachments labeled *Panzer-Abteilung* A, B, C and D. They were to carry sufficient fuel and ammunition for a combat radius of 200 km.[248]

Specialised landing equipment

As part of a *Kriegsmarine* competition, prototypes for a prefabricated "heavy landing bridge" or jetty (similar in function to later Allied Mulberry Harbours) were designed and built by Krupp Stahlbau and Dortmunder Union and successfully overwintered in the North Sea in 1941–42.[249] Krupp's design won out, as it only required one day to install, as opposed to twenty-eight days for the Dortmunder Union bridge. The Krupp bridge consisted of a series of 32m-long connecting platforms, each supported on the seabed by four steel columns. The platforms could be raised or lowered by heavy-duty winches in order to accommodate the tide. The German Navy initially ordered eight complete Krupp units composed of six platforms each. This was reduced to six units by the autumn of 1941, and eventually cancelled altogether when it became apparent that Sea Lion would never take place.[250]

In mid-1942, both the Krupp and Dortmunder prototypes were shipped to the Channel Islands and installed together off Alderney, where they were used for unloading materials needed to fortify the island. Referred to as the "German jetty" by local inhabitants, they remained standing for the next thirty-six years until demolition crews finally removed them in 1978–79, a testament to their durability.

The German Army developed a portable landing bridge of its own nicknamed *Seeschlange* (Sea Snake). This "floating roadway" was formed from a series of joined modules that could be towed into place to act as a temporary jetty. Moored ships could then either unload their cargo directly onto the roadbed or lower it down onto waiting vehicles via their heavy-duty booms. The *Seeschlange* was successfully tested by the Army Training Unit at Le Havre in France in the autumn of 1941 and later chosen for use in *Operation Herkules*, the proposed Italo-German invasion of Malta. It was easily transportable by rail.

A specialised vehicle intended for Sea Lion was the *Landwasserschlepper* (LWS), an amphibious tractor under development since 1935. It was originally intended for use by Army engineers to assist with river crossings. Three of them were assigned to Tank Detachment 100 as part of the invasion; it was intended to use them for pulling ashore unpowered assault barges and towing vehicles across the beaches. They would also have been used to carry supplies directly ashore during the six hours of falling tide when the barges were grounded. This involved towing a *Kässbohrer* amphibious trailer capable of transporting 10–20 tons of freight behind the LWS.[251] The LWS was demonstrated to General Halder on 2 August 1940 by the Reinhardt Trials Staff on the island of Sylt and, though he was critical of its high silhouette on land, he recognised the overall usefulness of the design. It was proposed to build enough tractors that one or two could be assigned to each invasion barge, but the late date and difficulties in mass-producing the vehicle prevented this.

Other equipment to be used for the first time

Operation Sea Lion would have been the first ever amphibious invasion by a mechanized army, and the largest amphibious invasion since Gallipoli. The Germans had to invent and improvise a lot of equipment. They also proposed to use some new weapons and use upgrades of their existing equipment for the first time. These included:

1. New antitank guns and ammunition. The standard German antitank gun, the 37 mm Pak 36, was capable of penetrating the armour of all 1940 British tanks except the Matilda and Valentine. Armour-piercing ballistic capped (tungsten-cored) ammunition (Pzgr. 40) for 37 mm Pak 36 had become available in time for the invasion.Wikipedia:Citation neededWikipedia:No original researchWikipedia:Identifying reliable sources The 37 mm Pzgr.40 would still have had trouble penetrating the Matilda II's armour so the first echelon units replaced theirs with French or Czechoslovak 47mm guns (which weren't much better).[252] The Pak 36 began to be replaced by the 50 mm Pak 38 in mid-1940. The Pak 38, which could penetrate a Matilda's armour, would probably have seen action first with Sea Lion as it would have been issued initially to the *Waffen-SS* and the *Heer*'s elite units, and all those units were in the Sea Lion force. These included the *SS Leibstandarte Adolf Hitler* regiment, the *Großdeutschland* regiment, 2 mountain, 2 *Jäger*, 2 *Fallschirmjäger*, 4 panzer, and 2 motorised divisions. In addition, the 7th Infantry division was considered one of the best in the *Heer*, and the 35th almost as good.Wikipedia:VerifiabilityWikipedia:No original research

2. Captured French armoured tractors.[253] The use of these tractors by the first wave units was intended to reduce their dependence upon horses and probably would have reduced the problems of getting supplies off the beaches. In addition to their proposed use on the beaches, the Germans later used them as tractors for antitank guns and munitions carriers, as self-propelled guns, and as armoured personnel carriers. There were two main types. The Renault UE Chenillette (German name: *Infanterie Schlepper UE 630 (f)*) was a light tracked armoured carrier and prime mover produced by France between 1932 and 1940. Five to six thousand were built, and about 3,000 were captured and overhauled by the Germans.[254] They had a storage compartment that could carry 350 kg, pull a trailer weighing 775 kg for a total of about 1000 kg, and could climb a 50% slope. The armour was 5–9 mm, enough to stop shell fragments and bullets. There was also the Lorraine 37L, which was larger, of which 360 fell into German hands. In that vehicle a load of 810 kilograms could be carried, plus a 690 kg trailer pulled for a total of 1.5 tonnes. The use of such captured equipment meant that the first wave divisions were largely

motorised,[255] with the first wave using 9.3% (4,200) of the 45,000 horses normally required.[256]

3. 48× Stug III Ausf B Assault Guns- 7.5 cm StuK 37 L/24, 50mm armour and improved suspension. Some were to be landed with the first wave.[257]

4. Panzer III F/G upgraded with more armour on the mantlet and progressively from 3.7 cm KwK 36 L/46.5 to 5 cm KwK 38 L/42.Wikipedia:Citation needed

5. 72 *Nebelwerfer*, to be landed with the second and third waves.[258]

6. 36× *Flammpanzer II* flamethrower tanks, 20 to land with the first wave.

7. 4 or more 75 mm *Leichtgeschütz* 40 recoilless guns, for use by paratroopers. The LG 40 could be split into four parts with each part being dropped on a single parachute.[259]

Broad versus narrow front

The German Army High Command (*Oberkommando des Heeres, OKH*) originally planned an invasion on a vast scale by landing over forty divisions from Dorset to Kent. This was far in excess of what the *Kriegsmarine* could supply, and final plans were more modest, calling for nine divisions to make an amphibious assault on Sussex and Kent with around 67,000 men in the first echelon and an airborne division to support them.[260] The chosen invasion sites ran from Rottingdean in the west to Hythe in the east.

The *Kriegsmarine* wanted a front as short as possible, as it regarded this as more defensible. Admiral Raeder wanted a front stretching from Dover to Eastbourne and stressed that shipping between Cherbourg/Le Havre and Dorset would be exposed to attacks from the Royal Navy based in Portsmouth and Plymouth. General Halder rejected this: "From the army's point of view I regard it as complete suicide, I might just as well put the troops that have landed straight through the sausage machine".[261]

One complication was the tidal flow in the English Channel, where high water moves from west to east, with high water at Lyme Regis occurring around six hours before it reaches Dover. If all the landings were to be made at high water across a broad front, they would have to be made at different times along different parts of the coast, with the landings in Dover being made six hours after any landings in Dorset and thus losing the element of surprise. If the landings were to be made at the same time, methods would have to be devised to disembark men, vehicles and supplies at all states of the tide. That was another reason to favour landing craft.

The battle plan called for German forces to be launched from Cherbourg to Lyme Regis, Le Havre to Ventnor and Brighton, Boulogne to Eastbourne, Calais to Folkestone, and Dunkirk and Ostend to Ramsgate. *Fallschirmjäger*

Figure 48: *The huge 21 cm K12 railway gun was only suitable for bombarding targets on land.*

(paratroopers) would land near Brighton and Dover. Once the coast was secured, they would push north and take Gloucester and encircle London.[262] There is reason to believe that the Germans would not attempt to assault the city but besiege and bombard it.[263] German forces would secure England up to the 52nd parallel (approximately as far north as Northampton), anticipating that the rest of the United Kingdom would then surrender.

German coastal guns

With Germany's occupation of the Pas-de-Calais region in Northern France, the possibility of closing the Strait of Dover to Royal Navy warships and merchant convoys by the use of land-based heavy artillery became readily apparent, both to the German High Command and to Hitler. Even the *Kriegsmarine*'s Naval Operations Office deemed this a plausible and desirable goal, especially given the relatively short distance, 34 km (21 mi), between the French and English coasts. Orders were therefore issued to assemble and begin emplacing every Army and Navy heavy artillery piece available along the French coast, primarily at Pas-de-Calais. This work was assigned to the *Organisation Todt* and commenced on 22 July 1940.[264]

By early August, four 28 cm (11 in) traversing turrets were fully operational as were all of the Army's railway guns. Seven of these weapons, six 28 cm K5 pieces and a single 21 cm (8.3 in) K12 gun with a range of 115 km (71 mi), could only be used against land targets. The remainder, thirteen 28 cm and five 24 cm (9.4 in) pieces, plus additional motorised batteries comprising twelve 24 cm guns and ten 21 cm weapons, could be fired at shipping but were of limited effectiveness due to their slow traverse speed, long loading time and ammunition types.[265]

Better suited for use against naval targets were the four heavy naval batteries installed by mid-September: *Friedrich August* with three 30.5 cm (12.0 in) barrels; *Prinz Heinrich* with two 28 cm guns; *Oldenburg* with two 24 cm weapons and, largest of all, *Siegfried* (later renamed *Batterie Todt*) with a pair of 38 cm (15 in) guns. Fire control for these weapons was provided by both spotter aircraft and by DeTeGerät radar sets installed at Blanc Nez and Cap d'Alprech. These units were capable of detecting targets out to a range of 40 km (25 mi), including small British patrol craft inshore of the English coast. Two additional radar sites were added by mid-September: a DeTeGerät at Cap de la Hague and a FernDeTeGerät long-range radar at Cap d'Antifer near Le Havre.[265]

To strengthen German control of the Channel narrows, the Army planned to quickly establish mobile artillery batteries along the English shoreline once a beachhead had been firmly established. Towards that end, 16th Army's *Artillerie Kommand 106* was slated to land with the second wave to provide fire protection for the transport fleet as early as possible. This unit consisted of twenty-four 15 cm (5.9 in) and seventy-two 10 cm (3.9 in) guns. About one third of them were to be deployed on English soil by the end of Sea Lion's first week.[266]

The presence of these batteries was expected to greatly reduce the threat posed by British destroyers and smaller craft along the eastern approaches as the guns would be sited to cover the main transport routes from Dover to Calais and Hastings to Boulogne. They could not entirely protect the western approaches, but a large area of those invasion zones would still be within effective range.

The British military was well aware of the dangers posed by German artillery dominating the Dover Strait and on 4 September 1940 the Chief of Naval Staff issued a memo stating that if the Germans "...could get possession of the Dover defile and capture its gun defences from us, then, holding these points on both sides of the Straits, they would be in a position largely to deny those waters to our naval forces". Should the Dover defile be lost, he concluded, the Royal Navy could do little to interrupt the flow of German supplies and reinforcements across the Channel, at least by day, and he further warned that "...there might really be a chance that they (the Germans) might be able to bring a serious weight of attack to bear on this country". The very next day the Chiefs of Staff, after discussing the importance of the defile, decided to reinforce the Dover coast with more ground troops.[267]

The guns started to fire in the second week of August 1940 and were not silenced until 1944, when the batteries were overrun by Allied ground forces. They caused 3,059 alerts, 216 civilian deaths, and damage to 10,056 premises in the Dover area. However, despite firing on frequent slow moving coastal convoys, often in broad daylight, for almost the whole of that period (there was an interlude in 1943), there is no record of any vessel being hit by them, although one seaman was killed and others were injured by shell splinters from near misses.[268] Whatever the perceived risk, this lack of ability to hit any moving ship does not support the contention that the German coastal batteries would have been a serious threat to fast destroyers or smaller warships.[269]

Indefinite postponement

During the summer of 1940, both the British public and the Americans believed that a German invasion was imminent, and they studied the forthcoming high tides of 5–9 August, 2–7 September, 1–6 October, and 30 October-4 November as likely dates. The British prepared extensive defences, and, in Churchill's view, "the great invasion scare" was "serving a most useful purpose" by "keeping every man and woman tuned to a high pitch of readiness".[270,271] He did not think the threat credible. On 10 July, he advised the War Cabinet that the possibility of invasion could be ignored, as it "would be a most hazardous and suicidal operation". That summer, Britain exported tanks to the campaign in Egypt.[272]

The Germans were confident enough to film a simulation of the intended invasion in advance. A crew turned up at the Belgian port of Antwerp in early September 1940 and, for two days, they filmed tanks and troops landing from barges on a nearby beach under simulated fire. It was explained that, as the invasion would happen at night, Hitler wanted the German people to see all the details.[273]

In early August, the German command had agreed that the invasion should begin on 15 September, but the Navy's revisions to its schedule set the date back to 20 September. At a conference on 14 September, Hitler praised the various preparations, but told his service chiefs that, as air superiority had still not been achieved, he would review whether to proceed with the invasion. At this conference, he gave the Luftwaffe the opportunity to act independently of the other services, with intensified continuous air attacks to overcome British resistance; on 16 September, Göring issued orders for this new phase of the air attack.[274] On 17 September 1940, Hitler held a meeting with *Reichsmarschall* Hermann Göring and *Generalfeldmarschall* Gerd von Rundstedt during which he became convinced the operation was not viable. Control of the skies was still lacking, and coordination among three branches of the armed forces was out of the question. Later that day, Hitler ordered the postponement of the operation. He ordered the dispersal of the invasion fleet in order to avert further damage by British air and naval attacks.

The postponement coincided with rumours that there had been an attempt to land on British shores on or about 7 September, which had been repulsed with large German casualties. The story was later expanded to include false reports that the British had set the sea on fire using flaming oil. Both versions were widely reported in the American press and in William L. Shirer's *Berlin Diary*, but both were officially denied by Britain and Germany. Author James Hayward has suggested that the whispering campaign around the "failed invasion" was a successful example of British black propaganda to bolster morale at home and in occupied Europe, and convince America that Britain was not a lost cause.[275]

On 12 October 1940, Hitler issued a directive releasing forces for other fronts. The appearance of preparations for Sea Lion was to be continued to keep political pressure on Britain, and a fresh directive would be issued if it was decided that invasion was to be reconsidered in the Spring of 1941.[276,277]

While the bombing of Britain intensified during the Blitz, Hitler issued his Directive No. 21 on 18 December 1940 instructing the Wehrmacht to be ready for a quick attack to commence his long planned invasion of the Soviet Union.[278] *Seelöwe* lapsed, never to be resumed.[279]

Chances of success

Reichsmarschall Hermann Göring, Commander-in-Chief of the *Luftwaffe*, believed the invasion could not succeed and doubted whether the German air force would be able to win control of the skies; nevertheless he hoped that an early victory in the Battle of Britain would force the UK government to negotiate, without any need for an invasion.[280] Adolf Galland, commander of *Luftwaffe* fighters at the time, claimed invasion plans were not serious and that there was a palpable sense of relief in the *Wehrmacht* when it was finally called off.[281] *Generalfeldmarschall* Gerd von Rundstedt also took this view and thought that Hitler never seriously intended to invade Britain, he was convinced that the whole thing was a bluff to put pressure on the British government to come to terms following the Fall of France.[282] He observed that Napoleon had failed to invade and the difficulties that confounded him did not appear to have been solved by the Sea Lion planners. In fact, in November 1939, the German naval staff produced a study on the possibility of an invasion of Britain and concluded that it required two preconditions, air and naval superiority, neither of which Germany ever had.[283] Grand Admiral Karl Dönitz believed air superiority was not enough and admitted, "We possessed neither control of the air or the sea; nor were we in any position to gain it."[284] Grand Admiral Erich Raeder thought it would be impossible for Germany to attempt an invasion until the spring of 1941;[285] he instead called for Malta and the Suez Canal to be overrun so German forces could link up with Japanese forces in the Indian Ocean to bring about the collapse of the British Empire in the Far East, and prevent the Americans from being able to use British bases if the United States entered the war.[286]

As early as 14 August 1940, Hitler had told his generals that he would not attempt to invade Britain if the task seemed too dangerous, before adding that there were other ways of defeating the UK than invading.

In *Memoirs of WWII*, Churchill stated, "Had the Germans possessed in 1940 well trained [and equipped] amphibious forces their task would still have been a forlorn hope in the face of our sea and air power. In fact they had neither the tools or the training".[287] He added, "There were indeed some who on purely technical grounds, and for the sake of the effect the total defeat of his expedition would have on the general war, were quite content to see him try."[288]

Although Operation Sea Lion was never attempted, there has been much speculation about its hypothetical outcome. The great majority of military historians, including Peter Fleming, Derek Robinson and Stephen Bungay, have expressed the opinion that it had little chance of success and would have most likely resulted in a disaster for the Germans. Len Deighton and some other writers have called the German amphibious plans a "Dunkirk in reverse".[289] Robinson argues the massive superiority of the Royal Navy over the *Kriegsmarine* would have made Sea Lion a disaster. Dr Andrew Gordon, in an article for the *Royal United Services Institute Journal*[290] agrees with this and is clear in his conclusion the German Navy was never in a position to mount Sealion, regardless of any realistic outcome of the Battle of Britain. In his fictional alternate history *Invasion: the German invasion of England, July 1940*, Kenneth Macksey proposes that the Germans might have succeeded if they had swiftly and decisively begun preparations even before the Dunkirk evacuations, and the Royal Navy for some reason had held back from large-scale intervention,[291] though in practice the Germans were unprepared for such a speedy commencement of their assault.[292]

Logistics

Four years later, the Allied D-Day landings showed just how much materiel had to be landed continuously to maintain an amphibious invasion. The problem for the Germans was worse, as the German Army was mostly horse-drawn. One of its prime headaches would have been transporting thousands of horses across the Channel. British intelligence calculated that the first wave of 11 divisions (including the airborne divisions) would require a daily average of 3,300 tons of supplies.[293] In fact, in Russia in 1941, when engaged in heavy fighting (at the end of a very long supply line), a single German infantry division required up to 1,100 tons of supplies a day, though a more usual figure would be 212-425 tons per day.[294] The smaller figure is more likely due to the very short distances the supplies would have to travel. Rations for two weeks were to be provided to the German troops of the first wave because the armies had been instructed to live off the land as far as possible in order to minimise supply across the Channel during the initial phase of the battle.[295] British intelligence further calculated that Folkestone, the largest harbour falling within the planned German landing zones, could handle 150 tons per day in the first week of the invasion (assuming all dockside equipment was successfully demolished and regular RAF bombing raids reduced capacity by 50%). Within seven days, maximum capacity was expected to rise to 600 tons per day, once German shore parties had made repairs to the quays and cleared the harbour of any blockships and other obstacles. This meant that, at best, the nine German infantry and two airborne divisions landed initially would receive less than 20% of the 3,300 tons of supplies they required each day through a port, and would have to rely heavily on whatever could be brought in directly over the beaches or air-dropped.[296]

The capture of Dover and its harbour facilities was expected to add another 800 tons per day, raising to 40% the amount of supplies brought in through ports. However, this rested on the rather unrealistic assumption of little or no interference from the Royal Navy and RAF with the German supply convoys which would have been made up of underpowered (or unpowered, i.e. towed) inland waterways vessels as they shuttled slowly between the Continent to the invasion beaches and any captured harbours.

Weather

From 19 to 26 September 1940, sea and wind conditions on and over the Channel where the invasion was to take place were good overall, and a crossing, even using converted river barges, was feasible provided the sea state remained at less than 4, which for the most part it did. Winds for the remainder of the month were rated as "moderate" and would not have prevented the German invasion fleet from successfully depositing the first wave troops ashore during the ten days needed to accomplish this.[297] From the night of 27 September, strong northerly winds prevailed, making passage more hazardous, but calm conditions returned on 11–12 October and again on 16–20 October. After that, light easterly winds prevailed which would have assisted any invasion craft travelling from the Continent towards the invasion beaches. But by the end of October, according to British Air Ministry records, very strong south-west winds (force 8) would have prohibited any non-seagoing craft from risking a Channel crossing.[298]

German intelligence

At least 20 spies were sent to England by boat or parachute to gather information on the British coastal defences under the codename "Operation Lena"; many of the agents spoke limited English. All agents were quickly captured and many were convinced to defect by MI5's Double-Cross System, providing disinformation to their German superiors. It has been suggested that the "amateurish" espionage efforts were a result of deliberate sabotage by the head of the army intelligence bureau in Hamburg, Herbert Wichmann, in an effort to prevent a disastrous and costly amphibious invasion; Wichmann was critical of the Nazi regime and had close ties to Wilhelm Canaris, the former head of the *Abwehr* who was later executed by the Nazis for treason.

While some errors might not have caused problems, others, such as the inclusion of bridges that no longer existed[299] and misunderstanding the usefulness of minor British roads, would have been detrimental to German operations, and would have added to the confusion caused by the layout of Britain's cities (with their maze of narrow roads and alleys)Wikipedia:Please clarify and the removal of road signs.[300]

Post-war wargaming of the plan

In the 1974 wargame conducted at Royal Military Academy Sandhurst, which assumed the *Luftwaffe* had not yet won air supremacy and continued to divert much of their efforts into bombing London,Wikipedia:Citation needed the Germans were able to establish a beachhead in south-east England. However, the German ground forces were delayed at the "Stop Lines" (such as the GHQ Line), a layered series of defensive positions that had been built, each a combination of Home Guard troops and physical barriers. At the same time, the regular troops of the British Army were forming up. After only a few days, the Royal Navy was able to reach the Channel from Scapa Flow, cutting off supplies and blocking further reinforcement. Isolated and facing regular troops with armour and artillery, the invasion force was forced to surrender.[301]

Planned occupation of Britain

Administration

According to the most detailed plans created for the planned post-invasion administration, Great Britain and Ireland were to be divided into six military-economic commands, with headquarters in London, Birmingham, Newcastle, Liverpool, Glasgow and Dublin.[302]   Hitler decreed that Blenheim Palace, the ancestral home of Winston Churchill, was to serve as the overall headquarters of the German occupation military government.[303] A certain sourceWikipedia:Manual of Style/Words to watch#Unsupported attributions indicated that the Germans only intended to occupy Southern England, and that draft documents existed on the regulation of the passage of British civilians back and forth between the occupied and unoccupied territories. Some Nazi planners envisaged the institution of a nationalities policy in Western Europe to secure German hegemony there, which entailed the granting of independence to various regions. This involved detaching Scotland from the United Kingdom, the creation of a United Ireland, and an autonomous status for Western England.[304]

The OKW, RSHA, (the *Reichssicherheitshauptamt*) and Foreign Ministry compiled lists of those they thought could be trusted to form a new government along the lines of that in occupied Norway. The list was headed by Oswald Mosley. The RSHA also felt that Harold Nicolson might prove useful in this role.[305] OKW also expected to face armed civilian resistance.

After the war rumours also emerged about the selection of two candidates for the "viceregal" office of *Reichskommissar für Großbritannien* ("Imperial Commissioner for Great Britain"), which in other occupied territories (such as Norway and the Netherlands) actually entailed the granting of near-dictatorial powers to its officeholders (Josef Terboven and Arthur Seyss-Inquart, respectively).[306] The first of these was Joachim von Ribbentrop, the German Foreign Minister and previously an ambassador to Great Britain, the second was Ernst Wilhelm Bohle, an undersecretary in the Foreign Office and the Gauleiter of the NSDAP/AO. However, no establishment by this name was ever approved by either Hitler or the *Reich* government during the Second World War, and was also denied by Bohle when he was interrogated by the victorious Allies (von Ribbentrop not having been questioned on the matter). After the Second Armistice at Compiègne with France, when he expected an imminent British capitulation, Hitler did however assure Bohle that he would be the next German ambassador to the Court of St. James's "if the British behave[d] sensibly".

Figure 49: *Dr. Franz Alfred Six at Nuremberg (1948)*

British monarchy

A Channel 5 documentary broadcast on 16 July 2009 repeated the claim that the Germans intended to restore Edward VIII to the throne in the event of a German occupation. Many senior German officials believed the Duke of Windsor to be highly sympathetic to the Nazi government, a feeling that was reinforced by his and Wallis Simpson's 1937 visit to Germany. However, despite German approaches, "The Duke never wavered in his loyalty to Great Britain during the war", according to a statement by the British Foreign Office.[307]

Death squads

Had Operation Sea Lion succeeded, *Einsatzgruppen* ("task forces" which operated as death squads) under Dr Franz Six were to follow the invasion force to establish the New Order. Six's headquarters were to be in London, with regional task forces in Birmingham, Liverpool, Manchester and Edinburgh. They were provided with a list (known as the Black Book) of 2,820 people to be arrested immediately. The *Einsatzgruppen* were also tasked with liquidating Britain's Jewish population, who numbered over 300,000.[308]

Artworks and newspapers

Six had also been entrusted with the task of securing "aero-technological re-search result and important equipment" as well as "Germanic works of art". There is also a suggestion that he toyed with the idea of moving Nelson's Column to Berlin.[309]

The RSHA planned to take over the Ministry of Information, to close the major news agencies and to take control of all of the newspapers. Anti-German newspapers were to be closed down.[310]

It appears, based on the German police plans, that the occupation was to be only temporary, as detailed provisions for the post-occupation period are mentioned.[311]

Deportation

According to captured German documents, the commander-in-chief of the German Army, Walther von Brauchitsch, directed that "The able-bodied male population between the ages of 17 and 45 will, unless the local situation calls for an exceptional ruling, be interned and dispatched to the Continent". This represented about 25% of male citizens. The UK was then to be plundered for anything of financial, military, industrial or cultural value,[312] and the remaining population terrorised. Civilian hostages would be taken, and the death penalty immediately imposed for even the most trivial acts of resistance.[313]

The deported male population would have most likely been used as industrial slave labour in areas of the *Reich* such as the factories and mines of the Ruhr and Upper Silesia. Although they might have been treated less brutally than slaves from the East (whom the Nazis regarded as sub-humans, fit only to be worked to death), living and working conditions would still have been severe.[314]

In late February 1943, Otto Bräutigam of the Reich Ministry for the Occupied Eastern Territories claimed he had the opportunity to read a personal report by General Eduard Wagner about a discussion with Heinrich Himmler, in which Himmler had expressed the intention for special forces of the SS to kill about 80% of the populations of France and England after the German victory.[315] In an unrelated event, Hitler had on one occasion called the English lower classes "racially inferior".[316]

In fiction

There is a large corpus of works set in an alternate history where the Nazi invasion of Britain is attempted or successfully carried out.

References

Notes

Bibliography

- Ansel, Walter (1960). *Hitler Confronts England*. Duke University Press.
- Bungay, Stephen (2000). *The Most Dangerous Enemy : A History of the Battle of Britain*. London: Aurum Press. ISBN 1-85410-721-6. (hardcover), 2002, ISBN 1-85410-801-8 (paperback).
- Burdick, Charles, Jacobsen, Hans-Adolf. (1988). *The Halder War Diary 1939–1942*. Novato Press, California. ISBN 1-85367-022-7
- Collier, Basil. *The Defence of the United Kingdom* (1962, Official history)
- Corum, James. *The Luftwaffe: Creating the Operational Air War, 1918–1940*. Kansas University Press. 1997. ISBN 978-0-7006-0836-2
- Cox, Richard (1977). *Operation Sea Lion*. Presidio Press. ISBN 0-89141-015-5
- Deighton, Len (1996). *Fighter: The True Story of the Battle of Britain*. London: Pimlico. ISBN 0-7126-7423-3. (Originally published: London: Jonathan Cape, 1977.) ISBN 0-7126-7423-3.
- Dönitz, Karl. *Ten years and Twenty Days*. New York: Da Capo Press, First Da Capo Edition, 1997. ISBN 0-306-80764-5.
- Evans, Martin Marix (2004). *Invasion! Operation Sealion 1940*. Pearson Education. ISBN 0-582-77294-X
- Evans, Martin Marix; Mcgeoch, Angus (10 July 2014). *Invasion!: Operation Sea Lion, 1940*[317]. Taylor & Francis. ISBN 978-1-317-86827-9.
- Fleming, Peter (1957). *Operation Sea Lion*. Simon & Schuster. ISBN 0-330-24211-3
- Greiner, H. 'Operation Seelowe and Intensified Air Warfare Against England up to the 30 October 1940', in Detweiler, D. *World War II German Military Studies*, Volume 7 of 24 (New York, 1979)
- Haining, Peter (2004). *Where the Eagle Landed: The Mystery of the German Invasion of Britain, 1940*. Robson. ISBN 1-86105-750-4
- Hewitt, Geoff (2008). *Hitler's Armada: The Royal Navy and the Defence of Great Britain, April - October 1940*. Pen & Sword Maritime. ISBN 978-1844157853
- Hewitt, Nick (2008). *Coastal Convoys 1939-1945: The Indestructible Highway*. Pen & Sword Maritime. ISBN 978-1-84415-861-4

* Hooton, E.R.. Hooton, E.R. *The Luftwaffe: A Study in Air Power,
  1933–1945*. Classic Publications, London. 2010. ISBN 978-1-906537-
  18-0
* Kieser, Egbert (1987). *Cassell Military Classics: Operation Sea Lion:
  The German Plan To Invade Britain, 1940*. Sterling. ISBN 0-304-35208-
  X.
* Kugler, Randolf (1989). *Das Landungswesen in Deutschland seit 1900*.
  Buchzentrum, Empfingen. ISBN 978-3-86755-000-0
* Larew, Karl. *The Royal Navy in the Battle of Britain*. The Historian 54:2
  (1992: Winter), pp. 243–254
* Macksey, Kenneth (1980). *Invasion: The German Invasion of England,
  July 1940*. MacMillan Publishing Co. ISBN 0-02-578030-1
* Overy, Richard (2010). *The Battle of Britain : Myth and Reality*. Lon-
  don: Penguin. ISBN 978-1-84614-356-4.
* Overy, Richard J. (2013). *The Bombing War : Europe 1939-1945*.
  London & New York: Allen Lane. ISBN 978-0-7139-9561-9.
* Parkinson, Roger (1977). *Summer, 1940: The Battle of Britain*. David
  McKay Co. ISBN 0-679-50756-6
* Raeder, Erich. *Erich Rader, Grand Admiral*: The Personal Memoir of
  the Commander in Chief of the German Navy From 1935 Until His Final
  Break With Hitler in 1943. *New York: Da Capo Press. United States
  Naval Institute, 2001. ISBN 0-306-80962-1.*
* Schenk, Peter (1990). *Invasion of England 1940: The Planning of Oper-
  ation Sealion*. Conway Maritime Press. ISBN 0-85177-548-9.
* Shirer, William L. (1960). *The Rise and Fall of the Third Reich*. Simon
  and Schuster, New York,.
* Taylor, Telford (1967). *The Breaking Wave: The Second World War in
  the Summer of 1940*. Simon and Schuster.
* Von der Porten, Edward P. (1976). *Pictorial History of the German Navy
  in World War II*. Thomas Y. Crowell Co.

External links

Wikimedia Commons has media related to *Operation Seelöwe*.

* British Invasion Defences[318]
* Why Sealion is not an option for Hitler to win the war[319] at the Wayback
  Machine (archived May 4, 2007) (essay)
* Second Why Operation Sealion Wouldn't Work[320] at the Wayback Ma-
  chine (archived April 16, 2008) (essay)

- *Sealion*: an orthodox view (includes quotes from participants)[321]
- Sea Lion vs. Overlord[322] (comparison)
- Operation Sealion[323]
- Operation Sealion[324] (*The German Threat to Britain in World War Two* by Dan Cruickshank, BBC)
- Kriegsmarine nautical charts, private collection[325] (Italy)
- Operation Sealion (argues that it was just a bluff) - BBC Timewatch 1998[326] on YouTube
- It's Startling How Close the Nazis Came to Invading Britain[327]
- Film made by a German engineer of various Sealion invasion craft[328]

Opposing forces

RAF Fighter Command Order of Battle 1940

This article lists the RAF Fighter Command order of battle at 15 September 1940, during the Battle of Britain.

Fighter Command

RAF Fighter Command Headquarters was located at RAF Bentley Priory, near Stanmore in North London. The commanding officer was Air Chief Marshal Hugh C.T. Dowding.

Fighter Groups

Group	Headquarters	Command-ing Officer	Area of Operations
9 Group	RAF Barton Hall, Preston, Lancashire	Not yet appointed	Not yet defined
10 Group	RAF Box,[329] Box, Wiltshire	Air Vice-Marshal Sir C J Quintin Brand	South West England and South Wales
11 Group	RAF Uxbridge,[330] Hillingdon, Middlesex	Keith Park	South East England and London
12 Group	RAF Watnall,[331] Notting-hamshire	Trafford Leigh-Mallory	East Anglia, the Midlands, Mid Wales and North Wales
13 Group	RAF Newcastle,[332] Kenton Bar, Newcastle upon Tyne	Richard Saul	North of England and Scotland
14 Group	Drumossie Hotel, Inverness	Malcolm Henderson	Scotland

Sector Stations and Satellite Aerodromes

Sector Stations had Sector Control Rooms as well as the usual features of RAF aerodromes; they were able to control RAF fighter formations during the battle. Sector stations were also able to disperse squadrons to satellite aerodromes, most of which were fully equipped.[333],[334]

Sector	Group	Sector Station	Radio call sign	Satellite Airfield or airfields
A	11	Tangmere	SHORTJACK	Westhampnett
B	11	Kenley	TOPHAT	Croydon
C	11	Biggin Hill	SAPPER	West Malling, Gravesend[335]
D	11	Hornchurch	LUMBA	Gravesend, Rochford, Manston, Hawkinge
E	11	North Weald	COWSLIP	Stapleford Tawney, Martlesham Heath
F	11	Debden	GARTER	Martlesham Heath[336]
G	12	Duxford		Fowlmere
K	12	Wittering		Coltishall
L	12	Digby		Ternhill
M	12	Kirton-in-Lindsey		
N	12	Church Fenton		Leconfield
O	13	Usworth		Catterick
P	13	Acklington		
Q	13	Turnhouse		Drem, Grangemouth
R	13	Dyce		Grangemouth
S	13	Wick		Grimsetter, Sumburgh
W	10	Filton		Boscombe Down, Colerne, Pembrey
Y	10	Middle Wallop	STARLIGHT	Boscombe Down, Warmwell, Exeter, some control over RNAS Roborough, St. Eval
Z	11	Northolt		Hendon

Stations and squadrons

337

Sector Station	Squadron	Aircraft Type	Squadron Code	Radio call sign	Aerodrome Assigned to	Commanding Officer
10 Group						
RAF Middle Wallop	No. 238 Sqn	Hawker Hurricane	VK		RAF Middle Wallop	Sqn Ldr Harold Arthur Fenton
RAF Middle Wallop	No. 609 Sqn	Supermarine Spitfire	PR	SORBO	RAF Warmwell	Sqn Ldr Horace Stanley Darley
RAF Middle Wallop	No. 604 (Night Fighter) Sqn	Bristol Blenheim & Bristol Beaufighter	NG		RAF Middle Wallop	Sqn Ldr Michael Frederick Anderson
RAF Middle Wallop	No. 23 Sqn (part)	Bristol Blenheim	YP		RAF Middle Wallop	Sqn Ldr George Francis Wheaton Heycock
RAF Middle Wallop	No. 152 Sqn	Supermarine Spitfire	UM	MAIDA	RAF Warmwell	Sqn Ldr Peter K Devitt
RAF Middle Wallop	No. 56 Sqn	Hawker Hurricane	US	BAFFIN	RAF Boscombe Down	Sqn Ldr Herbert Moreton Pinfold
RAF Filton	No. 79 Sqn	Hawker Hurricane	NV	PANSY	RAF Pembrey	Sqn Ldr J Hervey Heyworth
RAF Filton	No. 87 Sqn	Hawker Hurricane	LK	SUNCUP	RAF Exeter, RAF Bibury	Flt Lt R S Mills
RAF Filton	No. 601 Sqn	Hawker Hurricane	UF	WEAPON	RAF Filton	Flt Lt Sir Archibald Philip Hope (Acting CO)
RAF Filton	No. 234 Sqn	Supermarine Spitfire	AZ	CRESSY	RAF St Eval	Sqn Ldr Minden Vaughan Blake
RAF Filton	No. 236 (Coastal Command) Sqn	Bristol Blenheim	FA		RAF St Eval	Sqn Ldr G W Montagu
RAF Filton	No. 247 Sqn	Gloster Gladiator	HP		RNAS Roborough	Flight Lieutenant Hugh Addison Chater
11 Group						

RAF Biggin Hill	No. 72 Sqn	Super-marine Spitfire	RN	TENNIS	RAF Biggin Hill	Sqn Ldr A R Collins
RAF Biggin Hill	No. 92 Sqn	Super-marine Spitfire	QJ	GANNIC	RAF Biggin Hill	Sqn Ldr P J Sanders
RAF Biggin Hill	No. 141 Sqn (half)	Boulton Paul Defi-ant	TW		RAF Biggin Hill	Sqn Ldr W A Richardson
RAF Biggin Hill	No. 66 Sqn	Super-marine Spitfire	LZ	FIBUS	RAF Gravesend	Sqn Ldr Rupert Leigh
RAF North Weald	No. 249 Sqn	Hawker Hurricane	GN	GANER	RAF Middle Wallop	Sqn Ldr John Grandy
RAF North Weald	No. 23 Sqn (part)	Bristol Blenheim	YP		RAF North Weald	Sqn Ldr George Fran-cis Wheaton Heycock
RAF North Weald	No. 46 Sqn	Hawker Hurricane	PO	ANGEL	RAF Staple-ford	Sqn Ldr J R MacLachlan
RAF Ken-ley	No. 253 Sqn	Hawker Hurricane	SW		RAF Kenley	Sqn Ldr E R Bitmead
RAF Ken-ley	No. 501 Sqn	Hawker Hurricane	SD	VICEROY	RAF Kenley	Sqn Ldr Harry A V Hogan
RAF Ken-ley	No. 605 Sqn	Hawker Hurricane	UP	TURKEY	RAF Croy-don	Sqn Ldr Walter A Churchill
RAF Hornchurch	No. 603 Sqn	Super-marine Spitfire	XT	VIKEN	RAF Hornchurch	Sqn Ldr George Lovell Den-holm
RAF Hornchurch	No. 600 (Night Fighter) Sqn	Bristol Blenheim & Bristol Beaufighter	BQ		RAF Hornchurch	Sqn Ldr H L Maxwell
RAF Hornchurch	No. 41 Sqn	Super-marine Spitfire	EB	MITOR	RAF Hornchurch	Sqn Ldr Donald O. Finlay
RAF Hornchurch	No. 222 Sqn	Super-marine Spitfire	ZD	KOTEL	RAF Hornchurch	Sqn Ldr John H Hill
RAF Tang-mere	No. 213 Sqn	Hawker Hurricane	AK	BEARSKIN	RAF Tang-mere	Flt Lt D S Wilson-Macdonald
RAF Tang-mere	No. 607 Sqn	Hawker Hurricane	AF		RAF Tang-mere	Sqn Ldr James A Vick

RAF Tangmere	No. 602 Sqn	Supermarine Spitfire	LO	VILLA	RAF Westhampnett	Sqn Ldr A V R "Sandy" Johnstone DFC
RAF Tangmere	No. 23 Sqn (part)	Bristol Blenheim & Bristol Beaufighter	YP		RAF Ford	Sqn Ldr George Francis Wheaton Heycock
RAF Debden	No. 17 Sqn	Hawker Hurricane	YB	EDEY	RAF Debden	Sqn Ldr A G Miller
RAF Debden	No. 73 Sqn	Hawker Hurricane	TP		RAF Debden	Sqn Ldr Mike L Beytagh
RAF Debden	No. 257 Sqn	Hawker Hurricane	DT	ALERT	RAF Martlesham Heath	Sqn Ldr Robert Stanford Tuck DFC
RAF Debden	No. 25 Sqn (part)	Bristol Blenheim	ZK		RAF Martlesham Heath	Sqn Ldr Wilfred William Loxton
RAF Northolt	No. 1 Sqn RCAF	Hawker Hurricane	YO	CARIBOU	RAF Northolt	Sqn Ldr Ernest A McNab
RAF Northolt	No. 229 Sqn	Hawker Hurricane	RE	KETA	RAF Northolt	Sqn Ldr Harry J Maguire
RAF Northolt	No. 303 (Polish) Sqn	Hawker Hurricane	RF	APANY	RAF Northolt	Sqn Ldr Ronald Kellett DSO DFC
RAF Northolt	No. 264 Sqn (part)	Boulton Paul Defiant	PS		RAF Northolt	Sqn Ldr George Desmond Garvin
RAF Northolt	No. 504 Sqn	Hawker Hurricane	TM		RAF Hendon	Sqn Ldr John Sample
12 Group						
RAF Duxford	No. 242 Sqn	Hawker Hurricane	LE	LORAG	RAF Duxford	Sqn Ldr Douglas Bader
RAF Duxford	No. 302 (Polish) Sqn	Hawker Hurricane	WX	CALEB	RAF Duxford	Sqn Ldr W A Jack Satchell / Sqn Ldr M V M Mumler
RAF Duxford	No. 310 (Czech) Sqn	Hawker Hurricane,	NN	CALLA	RAF Duxford	Flt Lt G Douglas M Blackwood / Sqn Ldr A Sasha Hess

RAF Dux-ford	No. 19 Sqn	Super-marine Spitfire	QV	LUTON	RAF Fowlmere	Sqn Ldr Brian John Edward Lane DFC
RAF Coltishall	No. 74 Sqn	Super-marine Spitfire	ZP	DYSOE	RAF Witter-ing	Sqn Ldr Adolph G "Sailor" Malan
RAF Kirton-in-Lindsey	No. 616 Sqn	Super-marine Spitfire	QJ[338]	RADPOE	RAF Kirton-in-Lindsey	Flt Lt H F "Billy" Burton
RAF Kirton-in-Lindsey	No. 264 Sqn (part)	Boulton Paul Defi-ant	PS		RAF Kirton-in-Lindsey	Sqn Ldr George Desmond Garvin
RAF Digby	No. 151 Sqn	Hawker Hurricane	DZ		RAF Digby	
RAF Digby	No. 611 Sqn	Super-marine Spitfire	FY	CHARLIE	RAF Digby	Sqn Ldr Jim E McComb
RAF Digby	No. 29 (Night Fighter) Sqn	Bristol Blenheim & Bristol Beaufighter	RO		RAF Digby	Sqn Ldr Stan C Widdows
RAF Wit-tering	No. 1 Sqn	Hawker Hurricane	JX		RAF Witter-ing	Sqn Ldr David A Pemberton DFC
RAF Wit-tering	No. 266 Sqn	Super-marine Spitfire	UO		RAF Witter-ing	Flt Lt Patrick Geraint Jameson DFC
RAF Church Fenton	No. 85 Sqn	Hawker Hurricane	VY	HYDRO	RAF Church Fenton	Sqn Ldr Peter Wooldridge Townsend DFC
RAF Church Fenton	No. 306 (Polish) Sqn (part)	Hawker Hurricane	UZ		RAF Church Fenton	Sqn Ldr D R Scott
RAF Church Fenton	No. 64 Sqn	Super-marine Spitfire	SH	FREEMA	RAF Lecon-field / RAF Ringway	Sqn Ldr Don McDonell
13 Group						
RAF Us-worth	No. 54 Sqn	Super-marine Spitfire	KL	RABBIT	RAF Catter-ick	Flt Lt F P R Dunworth
RAF Us-worth	No. 219 (Night Fighter) Sqn (part)	Bristol Blenheim & Bristol Beaufighter	FK		RAF Catter-ick	Sqn Ldr J H Little

RAF Us-worth	No. 43 Sqn	Hawker Hurricane	FT		RAF Us-worth	Sqn Ldr Tom F Dalton Morgan DFC
RAF Ack-lington	No. 32 Sqn	Hawker Hurricane	GZ	JACKO	RAF Ack-lington	Flt Lt Mike N Crossley
RAF Ack-lington	No. 219 (Night Fighter) Sqn (part)	Bristol Blenheim	FK		RAF Ack-lington	Sqn Ldr J H Little
RAF Turn-house	No. 3 Sqn	Hawker Hurricane	QO		RAF Turn-house	Sqn Ldr S F Gooden
RAF Turn-house	No. 65 Sqn	Super-marine Spitfire	YT		RAF Turn-house,	Sqn Ldr A L Holland
RAF Turn-house	No. 141 Sqn	Boulton Paul Defi-ant	TW		RAF Turn-house	Sqn Ldr W A Richardson
RAF Turn-house	No. 111 Sqn	Hawker Hurricane	JU	WAGON	RAF Drem	Sqn Ldr John M Thompson DFC
RAF Turn-house	No. 263 Sqn	Hawker Hurri-cane & Westland Whirlwind	HE		RAF Drem	Fg Off T P Pugh
RAF Dyce	No. 145 Sqn	Hawker Hurricane	SO	PATIN	RAF Robor-ough	Sqn Ldr John R A Peel
RAF Wick	No. 232 Sqn	Hawker Hurricane	EF		RAF Robor-ough	Fg Off M M Stephens DFC & Bar
RAF Alder-grove	No. 245 Sqn	Hawker Hurricane	DX		RAF Robor-ough	Sqn Ldr E W Whitley DFC
RAF Biggin Hill	No.610 Sqn	Super marine Spitfire	DW		RAF Biggin Hill	Sqn ldr J Ellis DFC & Bar

References

Bibliography

- Ramsay, Winston (editor). *The Battle of Britain Then and Now Mk V*. London: Battle of Britain Prints International Ltd, 1989. ISBN 0-900913-46-0

External links

- BattleofBritain.com[339] - Retrieved: 4 August 2007.

Luftwaffe Order of Battle August 1940

For its Battle of Britain campaign against Great Britain during World War II, the German Luftwaffe had the following Order of Battle in the West. *Luftflotte 2* was responsible for the bombing of southeast England and the London area and based in the Pas-de-Calais area in France. *Luftflotte 3* targeted the West Country, Midlands, and northwest England, from bases a bit further north in France. *Luftflotte 5* targeted the north of England and Scotland, from bases in Norway. *Luftflotte 1* and *Luftflotte 4* were based in Germany, but most of their bomber formations had been reassigned to the three *Luftflotten* engaged in the Battle of Britain. Some fighters were retained to provide air cover over Germany, however.[340]

Luftflotte 2

Headquarters in Brussels, Belgium, commanded by Generalfeldmarschall Albert Kesselring, OOB from 13 August 1940.

Wettererkundungstaffel 26 (Weather reconnaissance unit under direct control of *Luftflotte 2*)	Brussels–Grimbergen	Independent Staffel	Dornier Do 17, Heinkel He 111, Messerschmitt Bf 110	Brussels-Grimbergen	Regierungsrat Krug

Parent unit	Geschwader Base	Unit (Gruppe/-Staffel)	Aircraft Type	Unit Airfield	Commanding Officer
I. Fliegerkorps (Generaloberst Ulrich Grauert), Beauvais					
Kampfgeschwader 1 (Major General Karl Angerstein)[341]					
	Rosières-en-Santerre	I. Gruppe	Heinkel He 111	Montdidier	Major Ludwig Maier
		II. Gruppe	Heinkel He 111	Montdidier	Obstlt. Benno Kosch

		III. Gruppe	Heinkel He 111	Rosières-en-Santerre	Major Hans Steinwig/ Major Willibald Fanelsa
Kampfgeschwader 76 (Oberst Stefan Fröhlich)					
	Cormeilles-en-Vexin	Stab. Gruppe	Dornier Do 17	Cormeilles-en-Vexin	Oberstleutnant Fröhlich
	Cormeilles-en-Vexin	I. Gruppe	Dornier Do 17	Beauvais	Hauptmann Alois Lindmayr
		II. Gruppe	Junkers Ju 88	Creil	Major Friedrich Möericke
		III. Gruppe	Dornier Do 17	Cormeilles-en-Vexin	Major Franz Von Benda
Aufklärungsgruppe 122 (Long-range reconnaissance)					
		5. Staffel	Junkers Ju 88, Heinkel He 111, Dornier Do 17P	Haute-Fontaine	Hauptmann Bohm
II. Fliegerkorps (General der Flieger Bruno Lörzer), Ghent.					
Kampfgeschwader 2 (Major-General Johannes Fink)					
	Arras	I. Gruppe	Dornier Do 17	Épinoy	Major Martin Gutzmann (POW 26 August), not replaced until 4 September.[342]
		II. Gruppe	Dornier Do 17	Arras	Major Paul Weitkus
		III. Gruppe	Dornier Do 17	Cambrai	Major Adolph Fuchs
Kampfgeschwader 3 (Oberstleutnant von Chamier-Glisczinski)					
	Le Culot	I. Gruppe	Dornier Do 17	Le Culot	Oblt. Gabelmann
		II. Gruppe	Dornier Do 17	Antwerp/-Deurne	Hptm. Pilger

		III. Gruppe	Dornier Do 17	Sint-Truiden	Hptm. Rathmann
Kampfgeschwader 53 (Oberstleutnant Stahl)					
	Lille-Nord	I. Gruppe	Heinkel He 111	Lille-Nord	Major Kauffmann
		II. Gruppe	Heinkel He 111	Lille-Nord	Major Winkler
		III. Gruppe	Heinkel He 111	Lille-Nord	Major Edler von Braun
Sturzkampfgeschwader 1 (Hauptmann Keil)					
	Pas-de-Calais	II. Gruppe	Junkers Ju 87	Pas de Calais	Hptm. A. Keil
		IV. Gruppe	Junkers Ju 87	Tramecourt	Hptm. Von Brauchitsch
Erprobungsgruppe 210 (Hauptmann Rubensdörffer)					
	Calais-Marck	1. Staffel	Messerschmitt Bf 110	Calais-Marck	Oblt. M. Lutz
		2. Staffel	Messerschmitt Bf 110	Calais-Marck	Oblt. W-R. Rössinger
		3. Staffel	Messerschmitt Bf 109	Calais-Marck	Oblt. O. Hintze
Lehrgeschwader 2					
	1–4 August: Unknown	I. (Jagd) Gruppe	Messerschmitt Bf109	Leeuwarden (to 4 August)/- Calais	Hptm Hanns Trübenbach (to 18 August), Hptm Bernhard Mieklke (21–30 August, KIA)
		II.(Schlacht) Gruppe	Messerschmitt Bf109	Most of the unit was based at Böblingen, elements moved to Calais on 13 August	Hptm Otto Weiß
		7(F). Gruppe	Messerschmitt Bf110	Ghent/- Brussels	Probably Hptm Hans Schäfer

		9.(H). Gruppe (Pz)	Messerschmitt Bf 110/ Henschel Hs 126	Unknown location in Belgium	Probably an Oblt Wöbbeking
IX. Fliegerkorps (Generalmajor Joachim Coeler), Soesterberg.					
Kampfgeschwader 4 (Oberstleutnant Hans-Joachim Rath)					
	Soesterberg	I. Gruppe	Heinkel He 111	Soesterberg	Hptm. Nikolaus-Wolfgang Meissner
		II. Gruppe	Heinkel He 111	Eindhoven	Major Dr. Gottlieb Wolf
		III. Gruppe	Junkers Ju 88	Amsterdam/-Schiphol	Hptm. Erich Bloedorn
Kampfgruppe 100 (Pathfinder bombers)		Autonomous Gruppe	Heinkel He 111	Vannes	Hauptmann Aschenbrenner
Küstengruppe 126 (Minelaying)	Various	Autonomous Gruppe	Heinkel He 111		
Aufklärungsgruppe 122		3. Staffel	Junkers Ju 88, Heinkel He 100	Eindhoven	Oberstleutnant Koehler
Jagdfliegerführer 2 (Generalmajor Theodor "Theo" Osterkamp), Wissant					
Jagdgeschwader 3 (Oberstleutnant Viek)					
	Samer	I. Gruppe	Messerschmitt Bf 109	Colombert	Hptm. Hans von Hahn
		II. Gruppe	Messerschmitt Bf 109	Samer	Hptm. Erich von Selle
		III. Gruppe	Messerschmitt Bf 109	Desvres	Hptm. W. Kienitz
Jagdgeschwader 26 (Major Handrick)					
	Audembert	I. Gruppe	Messerschmitt Bf 109	Audenbert	Hptm. K. Fischer

		II. Gruppe	Messer-schmitt Bf 109	Marquise	Hptm. K. Ebbighausen
		III. Gruppe	Messer-schmitt Bf 109	Caffiers	Major Adolf Galland
Jagdgeschwader 51 (Major Werner Mölders)					
	Wissant	I. Gruppe	Messer-schmitt Bf 109	Wissant	Hptm. Brustellin
		II. Gruppe	Messer-schmitt Bf 109	Wissant	Hptm. G. Matthes
		III. Gruppe	Messer-schmitt Bf 109	St.Omer	Major Hannes Trautloft
Jagdgeschwader 52 (Major von Bernegg)					
	Coquelles	I. Gruppe	Messer-schmitt Bf 109	Coquelles	Hptm. S. von Eschwege
		II. Gruppe	Messer-schmitt Bf 109	Peuplingne	Hptm. Von Kornatzki
Jagdgeschwader 54 (Major Mettig)					
	Campagne	I. Gruppe	Messer-schmitt Bf 109	Guînes	Hptm. Hu-bertus von Bonin
		II. Gruppe	Messer-schmitt Bf 109	Hermal-inghen	Hptm. Win-terer
		III. Gruppe	Messer-schmitt Bf 109	Guînes	Hptm. Ultsch
Lehrgeschwader 2					
	Calais-Marck	I. Gruppe	Messer-schmitt Bf 109	Calais-Marck	Major Hans Trubenbach
Zerstörergeschwader 26 (Oberstleutnant Joachim-Friedrich Huth)					
	Lille	Stab-schwarme	Messer-schmitt Bf 110	Lille	Oberstleut-nant Huth

	Lille	I. Gruppe	Messer-schmitt Bf 110	Yvrench	Hptm. Wilhelm Makrocki
		II. Gruppe	Messer-schmitt Bf 110	Crécy	Hptm. Ralph von Rettberg
		III. Gruppe	Messer-schmitt Bf 110	Barley	Hptm. Johann Schalk
Zerstörergeschwader 76 (Major Walter Grabmann)					
	Laval	Stab-schwarme	Messer-schmitt Bf 110	Laval	Major Grab-mann
	Laval	II. Gruppe	Messer-schmitt Bf 110	Abbeville	Maj Erich Groth
	Laval	III. Gruppe	Messer-schmitt Bf 110	Laval	Hptm. Friedrich-Karl Dickoré

Luftflotte 3

Headquarters in Paris, France, under Generalfeldmarschall Hugo Sperrle. OOB from 13 August 1940.

Wettererkundungstaffel 51 (Weather reconnaissance unit under direct control of *Luftflotte 3*)	Ver-sailles–Buc	Inde-pendent Staffel	Dornier Do 17, Heinkel He 111,	Versailles-Buc	Regierungsrat Dr. Felber

Parent unit	Gesh-wader Base	Unit (Gruppe/-Staffel)	Aircraft Type	Unit Airfield	Commanding Officer
IV. Fliegerkorps (Generalleutnant Kurt Pflugbeil), Dinard					
Lehrgeschwader 1 (Ober-stleutnant Alfred Bülow-ius)					
	Or-léans/-Bricy	I. Gruppe	Junkers Ju 88	Orléans/-Bricy	Hptm. W. Kern
		II. Gruppe	Junkers Ju 88	Orléans/-Bricy	Major Debratz

		III. Gruppe	Junkers Ju 88	Châteaudun	Major Dr. Ing. Ernst Bormann
Kampfgeschwader 27 (Oberst Gerhard Conrad)					
	Tours	I. Gruppe	Heinkel He 111	Tours	Major Gerhard Ulbricht
		II. Gruppe	Heinkel He 111	Dinard	Major Friedrich-Karl Schlichting
		III. Gruppe	Heinkel He 111	Rennes	Major Manfred *Freiherr* von Sternberg
Kampfgeschwader 40 (Long range reconnaissance) Oberst Ernst-August Roth (as of 1 August)					
		Stab-schwarme	Junkers Ju 88	Brest-Guipavas	Oberst Ernst-August Roth
		I. Gruppe	Focke Wulf Fw 200	Brest-Guipavas	Hptm Edmund Daser
Sturzkampfgeschwader 3 (Oberst Angerstein)					
		Stab-schwarme	Junkers Ju 87 and Dornier Do 17	Caen	
Kampfgruppe 806 (Maritime bombers) (Oberst)					
			Junkers Ju 88	Nantes	Hptm. W. Siegel
Aufklärungsgruppe 31 (Long-range reconnaissance)		3. Staffel	Dornier Do 17, Junkers Ju 88, Messer-schmitt Bf 110	Rennes	Hauptmann Sieckemus
Aufklärungsgruppe 121 (Long-range reconnaissance)		3. Staffel	Junkers Ju 88,	North-West France	Hauptmann Kerber
V. Fliegerkorps (General der Flieger Robert Ritter von Greim) Villacoublay					
Kampfgeschwader 51 (Major Schulz-Heyn)					
	Orly	I Gruppe	Junkers Ju 88	Melun	Major Schulz-Hein
		II Gruppe	Junkers Ju 88	Orly	Major Winkler

		III Gruppe	Junkers Ju 88	Étampes	Major W. Marienfeld
Kampfgeschwader 54 (Oberstleutnant Otto Höhne)					
	Évreux	I Gruppe	Junkers Ju 88	Évreux	Hptm. Jobst-Heinrich von Heydebrock
		II Gruppe	Junkers Ju 88	St. Andre-de-L'Eure	Major Kurt Leonhardy (MIA 11 August). Replaced by Hptm Karl-Bernhard Schlaeger (acting). Replaced by Htpm Hans Widmann.[343]
Kampfgeschwader 55 (Oberstleutnant Alois Stoeckl - KIA 14 August). Replaced by Obstlt Hans Korte 15 August[344]					
	Villa-coublay	I Gruppe	Heinkel He 111	Dreux	Major Joachim Roeber
		II Gruppe	Heinkel He 111	Chartres	Major Friedrich Kless
		III Gruppe	Heinkel He 111	Villacou-blay	Hptm Hans Schlemell
Aufklärungsgruppe 14 (Long-range reconnaissance)		4. Staffel	Dornier Do 17, Messerschmitt Bf 110	Cherbourg	Hauptmann von Dewitz
Aufklärungsgruppe 121 (Long-range reconnaissance)		4. Staffel	Dornier Do 17, Junkers Ju 88	Villacou-blay	Hauptmann Kerber (?)
VIII. Fliegerkorps (General der Flieger Wolfram Freiherr von Richthofen, Deauville					
Sturzkampfgeschwader 1 (Major Hagen)					
	Angers	I Gruppe	Junkers Ju 87	Angers	Major P. Hozzel
		II Gruppe	Junkers Ju 87	Angers	Hptm. H. Mahlke
Sturzkampfgeschwader 2 (Major Oskar Dinort)					
	Saint-Malo	I Gruppe	Junkers Ju 87	St. Malo	Hptm. H. Hitschold

		II Gruppe	Junkers Ju 87	Lannion	Major W. Enneccerus
Sturzkampfgeschwader 77 (Major Graf von Schönborn)					
	Caen	I Gruppe	Junkers Ju 87	Caen	Hptm. von D. zu Lichtenfels
		II Gruppe	Junkers Ju 87	Caen	Hptm. W. Plewig
		III Gruppe	Junkers Ju 87	Caen	Major H. Bode
Lehrgeschwader 1 (Oberstleutnant Bülowius)					
	Caen	V. Gruppe	Messerschmitt Bf 110	Caen	Hptm. Horst Liensberger
Aufklärungsgruppe 11 (Long-range reconnaissance)		2. Staffel	Dornier Do 17, Messerschmitt Bf 110	Bernay	
Aufklärungsgruppe 123 (Long-range reconnaissance)		2. Staffel	Dornier Do 17, Junkers Ju 88	Paris	
Jagdfliegerführer 3 (Oberst Werner Junck), Deauville					
Jagdgeschwader 2 (Major von Bülow)					
	Évreux,	Stabschwarme	Messerschmitt Bf 109	Beaumont-le-Roger	Major von Bülow
	Évreux	I. Gruppe	Messerschmitt Bf 109	Beaumont-le-Roger	Major H. Strumpell
		II. Gruppe	Messerschmitt Bf 109	Beaumont-le-Roger	Major Wolfgang Schellmann
		III. Gruppe	Messerschmitt Bf 109	Le Havre	Major Dr. Erich Mix
Jagdgeschwader 27 (Oberstleutnant Max Ibel)					
	Cherbourg-West	Stabschwarme	Messerschmitt Bf 109	Cherbourg-West	Oberstleutnant Max Ibel
	Cherbourg-West	I. Gruppe	Messerschmitt Bf 109	Plumetot	Hptm. Eduard Neumann

		II. Gruppe	Messer-schmitt Bf 109	Crépon	Hptm. Lippert
		III. Gruppe	Messer-schmitt Bf 109	Carquebut	Hptm. J. Schlichting
Jagdgeschwader 53 (Major Hans-Jürgen von Cramon-Taubadel)					
	Cher-bourg	Stab-schwarme	Messer-schmitt Bf 109	Cherbourg	Major von Cramon-Taubadel
	Cher-bourg	I. Gruppe	Messer-schmitt Bf 109	Rennes	Hptm. Blu-mensaat
		II. Gruppe	Messer-schmitt Bf 109	Dinan	Major Günther Freiherr von Maltzahn
		III. Gruppe	Messer-schmitt Bf 109	Sempy & Brest	Hptm. Harro Harder (Hptm. Wolf-Dietrich Wilcke from 13 August)
Zerstörergeschwader 2 (Oberstleutnant Friedrich Vollbracht)[345]					
	Toussus-le-Noble	Stab-schwarme	Messer-schmitt Bf 110	Toussus-le-Noble	Oberstleutnant Vollbracht
	Toussus-le-Noble	I. Gruppe	Messer-schmitt Bf 110	Amiens	Hptm. Hein-lein
		II. Gruppe	Messer-schmitt Bf 110	Guyancourt	Major Carl

Luftflotte 5

Headquarters in Stavanger, Norway, led by Generaloberst Hans-Jürgen Stumpff. OOB from 13 August 1940.

Parent unit	Geshwader Base	Unit (Gruppe/-Staffel)	Aircraft Type	Unit Airfield	Commanding Officer
X. Fliegerkorps (Generalleutnant Hans Geisler) Stavanger					
Wettererkundungskette X. Fl.Korps (Weather reconnaissance)	Unit under direct control of *X. Fliegerkorps*		Heinkel He 111	Stavanger	Regierungsrat Dr. Müller
Kampfgeschwader 26 (Oberstleutnant Karl *Frieherr* von Wechmar)					
	Stavanger	Stabschwarme	Heinkel He 111	Stavanger	Oberstleutnant Fuchs
		I. Gruppe	Heinkel He 111	Stavanger	Major Hermann Busch
		III. Gruppe	Heinkel He 111	Stavanger	Major Waldemar Lerche
Kampfgeschwader 30 (Oberstleutnant Walter Loebel, to 16 August. Replaced by Oberst Herbert Rieckhoff on 17 August.[346])					
	Aalborg	Stabschwarme	Junkers Ju 88	Aalborg	Oberstleutnant Loebel/Oberst Rieckhoff
		I. Gruppe	Junkers Ju 88	Aalborg	Major Fritz Doensch
		II. Gruppe	Junkers Ju 88	Aalborg	Hptm. Karl-Joachim von Symonski
		III. Gruppe	Junkers Ju 88	Aalborg-West	Hptm. Gerhard Kollewe
Zerstörergeschwader 76[347] (Major Walter Grabmann)					
	Stavanger	I. Gruppe	Messerschmitt Bf 110	Stavanger	Hptm. W. Restemeyer[348]
Jagdgeschwader 77 (Hauptmann Hentschel)					
	Stavanger	II. Gruppe	Messerschmitt Bf 109	Stavanger/-Trondheim	Hptm. Hentschel
Kustenfliegergruppe 506 (Major Eisenbach)					

	Stavanger	1. Staffel	Heinkel He 115	Stavanger	-
		2. Staffel	Heinkel He 115	Trondheim, Tromsø	
		3. Staffel	Heinkel He 115	List	-
Aufklärungsgruppe 22 (Long-range reconnaissance) (Oberstleutnant Thomas)		2. Staffel	Dornier Do 17,	Stavanger	
		3. Staffel	Dornier Do 17,	Stavanger	
Aufklärungsgruppe 120 (Long-range reconnaissance)		1. Staffel	Heinkel He 111, Junkers Ju 88	Stavanger	Major Schub
Aufklärungsgruppe 121 (Long-range reconnaissance)		1. Staffel	Heinkel He 111, Junkers Ju 88	Stavanger	Hauptmann Klinkicht
Aufklärungsgruppe Ob.d.L (Long-range reconnaissance)		1. Staffel	Dornier Do 215, Heinkel He 111, Messerschmitt Bf 110	Stavanger	
Seenotdienst (Air-sea rescue unit)			Heinkel He 59	Sola, Bergen, Trondheim	

Oberbefehlshaber der Luftwaffe

Headquarters in Berlin, Germany, led by Reichsmarschall Hermann Göring. OOB from 13 August 1940.

Parent unit	Gesh- wader Base	Unit (Gruppe/- Staffel)	Aircraft Type	Unit Airfield	Com- mand- ing Officer
Aufklärungsgruppe Ob.d.L (Ober- stleutnant Theodor Rowehl) Berlin					

	Various	1. Staffel	Blohm & Voss BV 142, Dornier Do 215, Dornier Do 217, Heinkel He 111, Junkers Ju 86P, Junkers Ju 88, Messerschmitt Bf 110	Autonomous, no fixed location	
		2. Staffel	Dornier Do 215, Heinkel He 111	Autonomous, no fixed location	
Wettererkundungskette Ob.d.L (Weather reconnaissance) Berlin					
	Oldenburg	1. Staffel	Dornier Do 17, Heinkel He 111	Oldenburg	
		2. Staffel	Heinkel He 111	Brest	
Seefliegerverbände (Maritime Patrol) (Generalmajor Ritter) Berlin					
Küstenfliegergruppe 406 (Major Stockmann)					
	Hörnum	3. Staffel	Dornier Do 18	Hörnum	
		2./106	Dornier Do 18	Rantum	
		2./906	Dornier Do 18	Hörnum	
Küstenfliegergruppe 706 (Major Lessing)					
	Stavanger	1./406	Dornier Do 18	Stavanger	
		2./406	Dornier Do 18	Stavanger	
Küstenfliegergruppe 606 (Major Hahn)					
	Brest	1. Staffel	Dornier Do 17	Brest	
		2. Staffel	Dornier Do 17	Brest	
		3. Staffel	Dornier Do 17	Brest	
Küstenfliegergruppe 106 (Major Hahn)					
	Norderney	1. Staffel	Heinkel He 115	Nordeney	

References

Bibliography

- Balke, Ulf. *Der Luftkrieg in Europa - Die Operativen Einsätze des Kampfgeschwaders 2 im Zweiten Weltkrieg*. Germany: Bernard and Graefe, 1989. ISBN 3-7637-5882-8
- Bungay, Stephen. *The Most Dangerous Enemy: A History of the Battle of Britain*. London: Aurum Press 2000. ISBN 1-85410-721-6(hardcover), ISBN 1-85410-801-8(paperback 2002).
- de Zeng, H.L; Stanket, D.G; Creek, E.J. *Bomber Units of the Luftwaffe 1933-1945; A Reference Source, Volume 1*. Ian Allan Publishing, 2007. ISBN 978-1-85780-279-5
- de Zeng, H.L; Stanket, D.G; Creek, E.J. *Bomber Units of the Luftwaffe 1933-1945; A Reference Source, Volume 2*. Ian Allan Publishing, 2007. ISBN 978-1-903223-87-1

External links

- BattleofBritain.com[349] - retrieved on 20 March 2007.

List of Battle of Britain squadrons

This is a list of the officially accredited Battle of Britain units with their aircraft types, code letters, call signs and casualties.

On 9 November 1960, the Air Ministry published Air Ministry Order N850 which officially defined the qualifications for aircrew to be classified as having participated in the Battle of Britain. The AMO also defined the squadrons that were deemed to have fought in the battle under the control of RAF Fighter Command between 0001 hours on 10 July and 2359 hours on 31 October 1940; the official beginning and end of the battle.

A total of 71 squadrons and other units from Fighter Command, Coastal Command and the Fleet Air Arm are listed.[350]

Figure 50: *A Royal Air Force Supermarine Spitfire trails smoke after attacking a German Heinkel He 111 bomber during the Battle of Britain.*

Accredited squadrons

Squadron	Squadron Code	Radio call sign	Aircraft Type	Number of Casualties
No. 1 (Cawnpore) Squadron RAF	JX	ACORN	Hurricane	7
No. 3 Squadron RAF	QO		Hurricane	1
No. 17 Squadron RAF	YB	EDEY	Hurricane	5
No. 19 Squadron RAF	QV	LUTON	Spitfire	6
No. 23 Squadron RAF	YP	LUTON	Blenheim	8
No. 25 Squadron RAF	ZK	LUTON	Blenheim, Beaufighter	5
No. 29 Squadron RAF	RO		Blenheim	8
No. 32 Squadron RAF	GZ	JACKO	Hurricane	2
No. 41 Squadron RAF	EB	MITOR	Spitfire	11[351]
No. 43 (China-British) Squadron RAF	FT		Hurricane	14
No. 46 (Uganda) Squadron RAF	PO	ANGEL	Hurricane	14
No. 54 Squadron RAF	KL	RABBIT	Spitfire	6

No. 56 (Punjab) Squadron RAF	US	BAFFIN	Hurricane	8
No. 64 Squadron RAF	SH	FREEMA	Spitfire	7
No. 65 (East India) Squadron RAF	YT		Spitfire	8
No. 66 Squadron RAF	LZ	FIBIUS	Spitfire	8
No. 72 (Basutoland) Squadron RAF	RN	TENNIS	Spitfire	9
No. 73 Squadron RAF	TP		Hurricane	4
No. 74 Squadron RAF	ZP	DYSOE	Spitfire	12
No. 79 (Madras Presidency) Squadron RAF	NV	PANSY	Hurricane	4
No. 85 Squadron RAF	VY	HYDRO	Hurricane	7
No. 87 (United Provinces) Squadron RAF	LK	SUNCUP	Hurricane	7
No. 92 (East India) Squadron RAF	QJ	GANNIC	Spitfire	14
No. 111 Squadron RAF	JU	WAGON	Hurricane	11
No. 141 Squadron RAF	TW		Boulton Paul Defiant	10
No. 145 Squadron RAF	SO	PATIN	Hurricane	13
No. 151 Squadron RAF	DZ		Hurricane	11
No. 152 (Hyderabad) Squadron RAF	UM	MAIDA	Spitfire	14
No. 213 (Ceylon) Squadron RAF	AK	BEARSKIN	Hurricane	15
No. 219 (Mysore) Squadron RAF	FK		Blenheim, Beaufightcr	6
No. 222 (Natal) Squadron RAF	ZD	KOTEL	Spitfire	9
No. 229 Squadron RAF	RE	KETA	Hurricane	5
No. 232 Squadron RAF	EF		Hurricane	–
No. 234 (Madras Presidency) Squadron RAF	AZ	CRESSY	Spitfire	5
No. 238 Squadron RAF	VK		Hurricane	17
No. 242 (Canadian) Squadron RAF	LE	LORAG	Hurricane	5
No. 245 (Northern Rhodesia) Squadron RAF	DX		Hurricane	2
No. 247 (China – British) Squadron RAF	HP		Gloster Gladiator	–

No. 249 (Gold Coast) Squadron RAF	GN	GANER	Hurricane	8
No. 253 (Hyderabad) Squadron RAF	SW	VICEROY	Hurricane	11
No. 257 (Burma) Squadron RAF	DT	ALERT	Hurricane	11
No. 263 (Fellowship of the Bellows) Squadron RAF	HE		Hurricane, Westland Whirlwind	1
No. 264 (Madras Presidency) Squadron RAF	PS		Boulton Paul Defiant	18
No. 266 (Rhodesia) Squadron RAF	UO		Spitfire	7
No. 421 Flight RAF	L-Z		Hurricane, Spitfire	1
No. 422 Flight RAF	–		Hurricane	–
Fighter Interception Unit	–		Hurricane, Blenheim, Beaufighter	–
Auxiliary Squadrons				
No. 501 (County of Gloucester) Squadron AuxAF	SD	MANDREL	Hurricane	19
No. 504 (City of Nottingham) Squadron AuxAF	TM		Hurricane	6
No. 600 (City of London) Squadron AuxAF	BQ		Blenheim, Beaufighter	9
No. 601 (County of London) Squadron AuxAF	UF	WEAPON	Hurricane, Spitfire	14
No. 602 (City of Glasgow) Squadron AuxAF	LO	VILLA	Spitfire	5
No. 603 (City of Edinburgh) Squadron AuxAF	XT	VIKEN	Spitfire	13
No. 604 (County of Middlesex) Squadron AuxAF	NG	TALLYHO	Blenheim, Beaufighter	3
No. 605 (County of Warwick) Squadron AuxAF	UP	TURKEY	Hurricane	8
No. 607 (County of Durham) Squadron AuxAF	AF		Hurricane	9
No. 609 (West Riding) Squadron AuxAF	PR	SORBO	Spitfire	7
No. 610 (County of Chester) Squadron AuxAF	DW	DOGROSE	Spitfire	11

No. 611 (West Lancashire) Squadron AuxAF	FY	CHARLIE	Spitfire	2
No. 615 (County of Surrey) Squadron AuxAF	KW	PANTA	Hurricane	6
No. 616 (South Yorkshire) Squadron AuxAF	QJ[352]	RADPOE	Spitfire	6
Commonwealth and Allied squadrons				
No. 1 Squadron RCAF (Canadian)	YO	CARIBOU	Hurricane	3
302 (City of Poznan) Squadron (Polish)[353]	WX	CALEB	Hurricane	6
303 (Warsaw – Kosciuszko) Squadron (Polish)[354]	RF	APANY	Hurricane	7
No. 310 (Czechoslovak) Squadron (Czech)	NN	CALLA	Hurricane	4
No. 312 (Czechoslovak) Squadron (Czech)	DU	SILVO	Hurricane	1
Coastal Command Squadrons				
No. 235 Squadron RAF	QY		Blenheim	9
No. 236 Squadron RAF	FA		Blenheim	10
No. 248 Squadron RAF	WR		Blenheim	16
Fleet Air Arm (FAA) Squadrons				
No. 804 Squadron FAA	5-		Gloster Sea Gladiator/Grumman Martlet	–
No. 808 Squadron FAA	5-		Fairey Fulmar[355]	–

References

Notes

Bibliography

- Ramsay, Winston (editor). *The Battle of Britain Then and Now Mk V*. London: Battle of Britain Prints International Ltd, 1989. ISBN 0-900913-46-0

External links

- BattleofBritain.com[356] – Retrieved: 4 August 2007.
- Battle of Britain at RAF website[357]

International participation

Non-British personnel in the RAF during the Battle of Britain

Nation	Number
Poland	141 or 145
New Zealand	127 or 135
Canada	112
Czechoslovakia	84 or 88
Belgium	28 or 30
Australia	26 or 32
South Africa	22 or 25
France	13 or 14
Ireland	10
United States	9 or 11
Southern Rhodesia	3 or 4
Jamaica	1
Barbados	1
Newfoundland	1
Northern Rhodesia	1

The Royal Air Force (RAF) and Fleet Air Arm (FAA) had included personnel from outside the United Kingdom from before the beginning of the Second World War and many served in the Battle of Britain in 1940. Many were volunteers from the British Empire[358] and refugees and exiles from German-occupied Europe.

The RAF Roll of Honour recognises 574 pilots, from countries other than the United Kingdom, as flying at least one authorized, operational sortie with an eligible unit during the period between 10 July to 31 October 1940, alongside 2,353 British pilots. The numbers differ slightly from the participants whose names are engraved on the Battle of Britain Monument in London, unveiled on 18 September 2005.

All pilots, regardless of nationality, who flew with British units during the Battle are known collectively, after a phrase coined by Winston Churchill, as "The Few".

Background

Prior to the outbreak of war, in view of the worsening European situation, the RAF had embarked on a series of expansion plans. These included Short-Service Commissions for pilots from the air forces of other British Commonwealth countries, namely Australia, Canada, New Zealand, South Africa and Southern Rhodesia.

The governments of Australia, Canada, New Zealand and the UK, under an agreement signed in December 1939, created the British Commonwealth Air Training Plan (BCATP), also known as the Empire Air Training Scheme. The plan had three main effects: first, joint military aircrew training facilities were set up in each member country, as well as Southern Rhodesia; second, these air forces also formed a common pool of aircrew and ground staff, who were posted to units according to operational needs and regardless of nationality and; third, under Article XV of the agreement, the Royal Australian Air Force (RAAF), Royal Canadian Air Force (RCAF) and Royal New Zealand Air Force (RNZAF) formed squadrons for service under RAF operational control. These so-called "Article XV squadrons" were given numbers in the 400-series, to avoid confusion with RAF units. Other squadrons from Dominion air forces served under RAF control during the Battle and other units, composed mostly of RAAF, RCAF and RNZAF personnel were formed within the RAF itself. Most of these squadrons and personnel were still in training and/or were not involved in fighter operations during the Battle of Britain, although No. 1 Squadron RCAF took part in operations from August 1940.

Contribution by country

Australia

When the war began, about 450 Australian pilots were serving in the RAF.[359]

Australia was among the first countries to declare war on Germany and the Royal Australian Air Force (RAAF; previously the Australian Flying Corps) was among the world's oldest air forces, having served during the First World War, in the Middle East and Europe. Under the Empire Air Training Scheme (EATS), a total of 37,000 aircrew were trained in Australia during 1939–45.

However, the flow of RAAF personnel to the European theatre was slowed by three factors: first, establishment of the massively expanded training process meant that first aircrews trained by the RAAF during the war did not graduate until November 1940; second, RAAF doctrine emphasised the army co-operation and maritime patrol roles; third, the Australian authorities placed great emphasis on a provision of EATS, that Dominion personnel should serve with units from their own air forces, wherever possible.Wikipedia:Citation needed RAAF Article XV fighter squadrons were not operational in Europe until mid-1941.[360]

Nevertheless, more than 30 Australians served in RAF Fighter Command during the Battle.[361] The highest scoring Australian ace of the Battle was Flight Lieutenant Pat Hughes, of No. 234 Squadron RAF, who claimed 14 kills before his death in September 1940.

No. 10 Squadron RAAF, a flying boat squadron was also based in Britain at the time, as part of Coastal Command.[362]

Barbados

At the start of the war, the small Caribbean island of Barbados was a British crown colony. Aubrey "Sinbad" de Lisle Inniss (1916-2003) was the sole Barbadian to serve as a pilot during the Battle of Britain. Inniss was born in Barbados to a British family and joined the RAF in 1939. During the Battle, he flew a Bristol Blenheim IF night fighter with No. 236 Squadron RAF and was responsible for shooting down a Heinkel He 111 in September 1940. Inniss, who became an ace during his subsequent war service, survived the conflict and retired from the RAF in 1957. The RAF Monument lists Inniss as Bajan, while the RAF Roll of Honour lists him as British.

Figure 51: *Belgian pilots of No. 609 Squadron RAF*

Belgium

At the time Belgium was invaded in May 1940, it had only a small airforce known as the *Aéronautique militaire* (AéMI). Although it played little role during the campaign in Belgium, a number of Belgian pilots succeeded in reaching Britain in the aftermath of the surrender. A significant number of Belgians were also undergoing flight training in France and, despite the reluctance of the Belgian government in Bordeaux, 124 reached Britain by August 1940 but few were able to participate in the Battle of Britain.[363]

As of December 2014, the RAF officially recognizes 30 Belgians as having participated in the Battle of Britain (of whom 18 did not survive the war) although the Battle of Britain monument (constructed in 2005) includes 28. At the time of the battle, Belgian pilots were mixed into British units and did not have their own squadrons. By the summer of 1940, Belgians made up around half of No. 609 Squadron RAF, a unit flying Spitfire fighters.[364,363] Nos. 235 and 236 Squadrons of RAF Coastal Command also had disproportionate numbers of Belgian pilots at 8 and 6 respectively. Altogether, Belgium provided the largest contingent of pilots during the Battle of Britain that were not from Eastern Europe or the Commonwealth.

During the course of the battle, Belgian pilots were responsible for shooting down 21 German aircraft.[363]   Between seven and 10 Belgians were

Figure 52: *Canadian pilots from No. 1*
Squadron RCAF, photographed in October 1940

killed.[364,363] In 1942, two all-Belgian squadrons were formed and, in total, 1,200 Belgians had served in the RAF during the course of the war.[363]

Canada

Many Canadians served in the fighter squadrons which repulsed the *Luftwaffe* in the summer of 1940. In fact, although the RAF only recognises 83 Canadian pilots as flying on fighter operations during the Battle of Britain, the RCAF claims the actual figure was over 100, and that of those 23 who died and 30 more were killed later in the war.[365,366] Much of this confusion can be attributed to the fact that apart from RCAF members flying in RCAF units, there were those RCAF members who were in RAF units as well as Canadians who were members of the RAF, not the RCAF. Another 200 Canadian pilots fought with RAF Bomber Command and RAF Coastal Command during the period and approx 2,000 Canadians served as ground crew.

Of these, 26 were in No. 1 Squadron RCAF, flying Hurricanes. The squadron arrived in Britain soon after Dunkirk with 27 officers and 314 ground staff. This squadron would later be re-numbered as No. 401 "City of Westmount" Squadron RCAF, in line with Article XV of the British Commonwealth Air

Training Plan (see above). It was the only fighter unit from the Commonwealth air forces to see combat in the Battle of Britain.

No. 1 Squadron made an inauspicious start to its service with Fighter Command, when on 24 August 1940 two of its Hurricanes mistook a flight of Bristol Blenheims for Junkers Ju 88s, shooting one down with the loss of its crew; an example of what is now known as friendly fire. No. 1 became the first RCAF unit to engage enemy aircraft in battle when it met a formation of German bombers over southern England on 26 August 1940, claiming three kills and four damaged, with the loss of one pilot and one aircraft. By mid-October the squadron had claimed 31 enemy aircraft destroyed and 43 probables or damaged for the loss of 16 aircraft and three pilots.

Other Canadians were spread across RAF squadrons, and on the second day of the Battle, 11 July, Canada suffered its first fighter casualty. In a *Luftwaffe* attack on the Royal Navy Dockyard naval base at Portland Harbour, Plt Offr D. A. Hewitt of Saint John, New Brunswick, flying a Hurricane with No. 501 Squadron RAF, attacked a Dornier Do-17 bomber and was hit himself. His aircraft plunged into the sea. Another Canadian pilot, Richard Howley, died eight days later.

The dispersed Canadian airmen included one who flew with No. 303 (Polish) Squadron. A total of 12 Canadian pilots in the Royal Air Force including Willie McKnight flew with No. 242 Squadron RAF at various times through the Battle. On 30 August, under the command of Squadron Leader Douglas Bader, nine 242 Squadron aircraft met 100 enemy aircraft over Essex. Attacking from above, the squadron claimed 12 victories for no loss.

Canadians also shared in repulsing the *Luftwaffe*'s last major daylight attack. On 27 September, 303 Squadron and 1 Squadron RCAF, attacked the first wave of enemy bombers. Seven aircraft were claimed destroyed, one probably destroyed and seven were damaged.

The top Canadian scorer during the Battle was Flt Lt H. C. Upton of No. 43 Squadron RAF, who claimed 10.25 aircraft shot down.

Czechoslovakia

Many of the Czechoslovak pilots had fled to France after Hitler's occupation of their country in March 1939 and had fought in the short *Armée de L'Air*[367] in the Battle of France, gaining important combat experience. The rapid fall of France caused Czechoslovak soldiers and airmen to leave for Britain, where they established their own squadrons.[368] Nearly 90 Czechoslovak pilots would fly in the Battle of Britain, with No. 310 and No. 312 (Czechoslovak)

Figure 53: *Pilots of No. 312 (Czechoslovak) Squadron RAF*

Squadrons, RAF, formed in the summer 1940 and operational during the battle.[369] Some Czechs also served in other Fighter Command squadrons. Both Czechoslovak squadrons were equipped with Hurricanes.

Czechoslovak fighters earned a reputation for aggressive aerial combat and for skills and bravery.[370] Together with Czechoslovak pilots serving in other RAF units, a total of 84 - 86 Czechs and 2 Slovaks - served, claiming almost 60 air kills. Nine pilots were killed. The top Czechoslovak ace was Sgt. Josef František, flying with No. 303 (Polish) Squadron, who claimed 17 confirmed kills, making him the highest scoring non-British pilot in the Battle of Britain.

France

French volunteers and Free French forces served in 245 and 615 Squadron. 13 are recognised in the Battle of Britain Roll of Honour.[371] In addition a French squadron, No. 346 Squadron RAF, was based at Elvington.[372]

Ireland

The Republic of Ireland (officially Called Ireland from 1937) seceded from the British rule in 1922 after a two-year war of independence. Relations between the two countries were still strained in 1940. Although technically a British dominion, Ireland remained neutral for the duration of the Second World War.

Figure 54: *Brendan "Paddy" Finucane, an Irish ace who is believed to have shot down four aircraft during the Battle of Britain and as many as 32 by his death in 1942*

Many individual Irish citizens did enlist in the British military, however, and ten pilots from the country fought in the RAF during the Battle of Britain. One of them, Brendan "Paddy" Finucane,[373] became an ace who would claim a total of 32 enemy aircraft before he was killed in 1942. The eldest of five children, Finucane grew up in County Dublin, where his father had taken part in the Easter Rising of 1916. He and his family moved to England in 1936, and he enlisted in the Royal Air Force aged 17. Finucane became operational in July 1940 and downed his first Bf 109 on 12 August, claiming a second the following day. During a 51-day period in 1941, Finucane claimed 16 Messerschmitt Bf 109 fighters shot down, while he was flying with an Australian squadron. Finucane became the youngest Wing Commander in the RAF, a rank he received at 21. He was shot down on 15 July 1942.[374,375]

Jamaica

In 1940, the island of Jamaica was crown colony under British rule. The sole Jamaican recognized as a participant in the Battle of Britain was Herbert Capstick, a Pilot Officer of British origin, who had been born in Jamaica in 1920. Capstick served in No. 236 Squadron RAF of Coastal Command. The Squadron was equipped with Bristol Blenheims and participated in antisubmarine operations in the English Channel. He survived the war and returned to live in Jamaica.[376]

Figure 55: *New Zealander Keith Park*

Newfoundland

Newfoundland was a separate dominion within the British Empire at the time of the Battle of Britain.[377] Pilot Officer R. A. Howley is recognized as the sole Newfoundlander to serve in the RAF during the period by the Battle of Britain monument. Howley served in No. 141 Squadron RAF, flying Boulton Paul Defiant turret fighters. He was shot down over Dover on 19 July 1940 and posted missing in action.[378]

New Zealand

The Royal New Zealand Air Force (RNZAF) was set up as a separate service in 1937, but numbered less than 1,200 personnel by September 1939. The Empire Air Training Scheme (as the BCATP was known in New Zealand and Australia), had resulted in about 100 RNZAF pilots being sent to Europe by the time the Battle started. Unlike the other Dominions, New Zealand did not insist on its aircrews serving with RNZAF squadrons, thereby speeding up the rate at which they entered service. An annual rate of 1,500 fully trained pilots was reached by January 1941.

The most prominent New Zealander in the Battle was Air Vice Marshal Keith Park, a high scoring air ace in the First World War and a member of the RAF since its creation. He was Commander of No. 11 Group RAF, which was tasked with the defence of London and south-east England.[379,380]

> *If any one man won the Battle of Britain, he did. I do not believe it is realised how much that one man, with his leadership, his calm judgment and his skill, did to save, not only this country, but the world.*
>
> —*Lord Tedder, Chief of the Royal Air Force, February 1947 about Keith Park.*

The RAF recognises 135 Fighter Command aircrew from New Zealand as having served in the Battle. Several New Zealanders became high scorers, including Plt Offr Colin Gray (No. 54 Squadron RAF) with 14 claims, Fg Offr Brian Carbury (No. 603 Squadron RAF) 14 claims and Plt Offr Alan "Al" Deere (54 Squadron), 12 claims. Carbury shot down the first German aircraft over British territory since 1918 and was also one of two aces in a day in the Battle.[381,382]

Northern Rhodesia

In 1940, Northern Rhodesia (today Zambia) was a British protectorate in Southern Africa. One Northern Rhodesian, of British origin, is recognised as a participant in the Battle of Britain. Pilot Officer John Ellacombe was born in Livingstone in 1920 and was educated in South Africa. He joined the RAF in 1939 and served in No. 151 Squadron during the Battle of Britain, flying Hurricanes. During the Battle, Ellacombe shot down several German bomber aircraft and was himself shot down on two occasions. He enjoyed a successful career in the RAF after 1940, retiring as an Air Commodore in 1973. He died in 2014.

Poland

Following the German invasion of Poland, many Polish pilots escaped and made their way to France and Britain. During the German invasion of France in May 1940, of the 1,600 Polish pilots available to the *Armée de l'Air* it is estimated that only about 150 took an active part in combat. This was mostly due to the fact that the French By June 1940, the Poles had over 85,000 men in France, including pilots and ground troops. Many of these personnel escaped to the UK around the time of the fall of France. By mid-1940 some 35,000 Polish airmen, soldiers and sailors had made their way to Britain, making up the largest foreign military force in the country after the French, as well as making it the largest Polish army ever formed abroad; of these some 8,500 were airmen.[383] Many were members of the Polish Air Force which had fought the *Luftwaffe*. However, the Air Ministry and the RAF underestimated their

Figure 56: *303 squadron pilots. L-R: Fg Offr Ferić, Flt Lt Kent, Fg Offr Grzeszczak, Plt Offr Radomski, Plt Offr Zumbach, Plt Offr Łokuciewski, Fg Offr Henneberg, Sgt Rogowski, Sgt Szaposznikow (in 1940)*

potential value in fighting against the *Luftwaffe*, as they felt that the Polish defeat on home soil was due to incompetence and lack of training. Most of the Poles were posted either to RAF bomber squadrons or the RAF Volunteer Reserve.[384]

Aside from being viewed as incompetent and unskilled in light of the fall of Poland, another one of the biggest barriers the Poles had to face was that of language. The fact that the majority of the Poles could not speak English made them unreliable in battle in the eyes of British commanders. One of the commanders stated that he would not have "people crashing around the sky until they understand what they're told to do." The Poles had to go through English language training before the majority of them could see action.

On 11 June 1940, the Polish Government in Exile signed an agreement with the British Government to form a Polish Air Force in the UK. Finally, in July 1940 the RAF announced that it would form two Polish fighter squadrons: 302 "Poznański" Squadron and 303 "Kościuszko" Squadron were composed of Polish pilots and ground crews, although their flight commanders and commanding officers were British.[385]

The two fighter squadrons went into action in August, with 89 Polish pilots. Another 50 Poles took part in the Battle, in RAF squadrons.

Polish pilots were among the most experienced in the Battle; most had hundreds of hours of pre-war flying experience and had fought in the 1939 Defensive War and/or the Battle of France. The Polish pilots had been well trained in formation flying and had learned from combat experience to fire from close range. By comparison, one Polish pilot referred to the close formation flying and set-piece attacks practiced in the RAF as "simply suicidal".[386]

The 147 Polish pilots claimed 201 aircraft shot down. 303 Squadron claimed the highest number of kills (126) of all Allied squadrons engaged in the Battle of Britain.[387] Witold Urbanowicz of 303 Squadron was the top Polish scorer with 15 claims. Sgt Tony Głowacki was one of two Allied pilots in the Battle to shoot down five German aircraft in one day, on 24 August (the other being New Zealander Brian Carbury). One Polish veteran, Stanislaw Skalski, became the top-scoring Polish fighter ace of the Second World War. With their combat experience, Polish pilots would have known that the quickest and most efficient way to destroy an enemy aircraft was to fire from close range, which often surprised their British counterparts. For instance:

> "After firing a brief opening burst at 150 to 200 yards, just to get on the enemy's nerves, the Poles would close almost to point-blank range. That was where they did their real work. "When they go tearing into enemy bombers and fighters they get so close you would think they were going to collide," observed Athol Forbes.[388]

In all, 30 Polish airmen were killed during the Battle. One of them died at the hands of an angry crowd in east London. He had baled out of his fighter and landed, injured in Wapping. His incoherent rambling was mistaken for German and he was set-upon by the people who had gathered round him. They were incensed by recent Nazi raids on civilian targets, but he was a member of the RAF.[389] Wikipedia:Accuracy dispute#Disputed statement

The close range tactics used by the Poles led to suggestions of recklessness, but there is little evidence for this view. For example, the death rate in 303 Squadron was lower than the average rate for other RAF squadrons, despite the squadron having been the highest-scoring Allied squadron during the Battle.[390]

The Polish War Memorial on the outskirts of RAF Northolt was dedicated in 1948 as a commemoration of the Polish contribution to Allied arms.

South Africa

One of the RAF's leading aces, and one of the highest scoring pilots during the Battle of Britain was Adolph "Sailor" Malan DFC, an RAF pilot since 1936, who led No. 74 Squadron RAF at the height of the Battle of Britain. Under his leadership No. 74 became one of the RAF's best units. Malan claimed his first two victories over Dunkirk on 21 May 1940, and had claimed five more

Figure 57: *Air Vice Marshal Quintin Brand, a South African and Commander in the Battle of Britain*

by the time the Battle started in earnest. Between 19 July and 22 October he shot down six German aircraft. His "Ten Rules for Air Fighting" were printed and pinned up in crew rooms all over Fighter Command. He was part of a group of about 25 pilots from South Africa that took part in the Battle, eight or nine of whom (depending on sources) died during the Battle.

Other notable pilots included P/O Albert "Zulu" Lewis, who opened his account over France in May with No. 85 Squadron, shooting down three Messerschmitt Bf 109s in one action. With No. 85 in August, and then in September with No. 249 Squadron under Squadron Leader (later Air Chief Marshal) Sir John Grandy, at North Weald. Lewis flew three, four and five times a day and 15 September 1940 got a He 111, and shared in the probable destruction of another. On 18 September he got his 12th confirmed enemy aircraft. By 27 September, flying GN-R, Lewis had 18 victories.[391] He was shot down and badly burned on 28 September. Lewis missed the rest of the Battle and his recovery to flying fitness took over three months. Basil Gerald "Stapme" Stapleton, with several probables to his credit, survived a crash on 7 September, trying to stop bombers getting through to London. Both men would later command RAF squadrons.

The most senior officer of South African origin during the Battle was Air Vice-Marshal Sir Christopher J. Quintin-Brand KBE, DSO, MC, DFC, Air Officer Commanding No. 10 Group RAF covering the South-West; a long service RAF officer, he had joined the RFC in 1916.

Figure 58: *Pilot Officer Billy Fiske - the first American pilot to be killed in World War II*

Southern Rhodesia

Southern Rhodesia (today Zimbabwe) was a British self-governing colony in Southern Africa at the time of the Battle of Britain. Three pilots born in Southern Rhodesia took part in the Battle of Britain: Squadron Leader Caesar Hull, Pilot Officer John Chomley, and Flight Lieutenant John Holderness.[392,393] Of these, Hull and Chomley lost their lives. Hull, the highest-scoring RAF ace of the Norwegian Campaign earlier in the year, was killed in a dogfight over south London on 7 September 1940, a week after taking command of No. 43 Squadron RAF.[394] Chomley went missing in action over the Channel on 12 August 1940 and was never found.[395]

United States

The RAF recognises seven aircrew personnel who were from the United States of America as having taken part in the Battle of Britain. American citizens were prohibited from serving under the various US Neutrality Acts; if an American citizen had defied strict neutrality laws, there was a risk of losing their citizenship and imprisonment. It is believed that another four Americans misled the British authorities about their origins, claiming to be Canadian or other nationalities.

(Acting) Plt Offr W. M. L. "Billy" Fiske was probably the most famous American pilot in the Battle of Britain, although he pretended to be a Canadian at the time. Fiske saw service with No. 601 (County of London) Squadron and claimed one (unconfirmed) kill. He crashed on 16 August 1940 and died the following day.[396]

Pilots

According to Kenneth G Wynn's *Men of the Battle of Britain* published in 1999, and the list currently held by the Royal Air Force, 11 American pilots qualified for the 1939-1945 Star with Battle of Britain clasp:

- De Peyster Brown – No. 401 Squadron RCAF
- Carl Raymond Davis – No. 601 Squadron (born in South Africa to American parents. Took British citizenship in 1932)**
- Arthur Gerald Donahue – No. 64 Squadron**
- William Meade Lindsley Fiske – No. 601 Squadron
- John Kenneth Haviland – No. 151 Squadron
- Vernon Charles Keough – No. 609 Squadron**
- Phillip Howard Leckrone – No. 616 Squadron**
- Andrew Mamedoff – No. 609 Squadron**
- Otto John Peterson – No. 401 Squadron RCAF
- Eugene Quimby Tobin – No. 609 Squadron**
- Alexander Roman Zatonski – No. 79 Squadron**

(** denotes pilot killed in action (KIA))

Wynn's list omits Whitney Straight, who although in Britain and a member of No. 601 Squadron, may have not flown an operational flight during the required dates (for the Battle of Britain clasp) due to recovering from injuries sustained in the Battle of Norway in 1940.

In popular culture

At the end of the 1969 film the *Battle of Britain* a list is shown containing the nationality of pilots that flew for the RAF. It incorrectly includes within this list a single person from Israel. This relates to George Goodman who was born in Haifa in 1920 and which was at the time British military-administered Palestine. Goodman was a British citizen and Israel did not become an independent country until November 1947. In some lists he is even recorded as Palestinian - also incorrectly.

During campaigning for the 2009 elections for the European Parliament, the far-right British National Party (BNP) used an image of a Spitfire, with the caption "Battle for Britain", in publicity to attempt to win support for the party's anti-immigration stance. The picture chosen, however, depicted a Spitfire flown by a Polish pilot from No. 303 (Polish) Squadron and the party was mocked in the British media as "absurd".

References

Bibliography

<templatestyles src="Template:Refbegin/styles.css" />

- Veranneman, Jean-Michel (2014). *Belgium in the Second World War.* Barnsley: Pen and Sword. ISBN 978-1-78337-607-0.
- Coulthard-Clark, Chris. *The Encyclopedia of Australia's Battles.* Sydney: Allen & Unwin, 2001. ISBN 1-86508-634-7.
- Eather, Steve (1995). *Flying Squadrons of the Australian Defence Force.* Weston Creek, Australian Capital Territory: Aerospace Publications. ISBN 1-875671-15-3.
- Fiedler, Arkady. *303 Squadron: The Legendary Battle of Britain Fighter Squadron.* Los Angeles: Aquila Polonica, 2010. ISBN 978-1-60772-004-1.
- Olson, Lynne; Cloud, Stanley (2003). *For Your Freedom and Ours: The Kościuszko Squadron: Forgotten Heroes of World War II.* London: Heinemann. ISBN 0-434-00868-0.
- Orange, Vincent. *Park: The Biography of Air Chief Marshal Sir Keith Park.* London: Grub Street, 2001. ISBN 1-902304-61-6.
- Polak, Thomas with Jiri Radlich and Pavel Vancata. *No. 310 (Czechoslovak) Squadron 1940-1945; Hurricane, Spitfire.* Boé Cedex, France: Graphic Sud, 2006. ISBN 2-9526381-1-X.
- Salt, Beryl (2001). *A Pride of Eagles: The Definitive History of the Rhodesian Air Force, 1920–1980.* Weltevredenpark, South Africa: Covos Day Books. ISBN 978-0-620-23759-8.
- Saunders, Andy (2003). *No 43 'Fighting Cocks' Squadron.* Aviation Elite Units. **9** (First ed.). Oxford: Osprey Publishing. ISBN 978-1-84176-439-9.
- Shores, Christopher and Clive Williams. *Aces High.* London: Grub Street, 1994. ISBN 1-898697-00-0.
- Wood, Derek; Dempster, Derek (1967). *The Narrow Margin: the Battle of Britain and the Rise of Air Power, 1930–1940.* London: Arrow Books. OCLC 459294[397].
- De Vos, Luc (2001). "The Reconstruction of Belgian Military Forces in Britain, 1940-1945". In Conway, Martin; Gotovitch, José. *Europe in Exile: European Exile Communities in Britain, 1940-1945.* New York: Berghahn. ISBN 1-57181-759-X.

Further reading

<templatestyles src="Template:Refbegin/styles.css" />

- Alexander, Kristen (2014). *Australia's Few and the Battle of Britain.* Sydney: University of New South Wales Press.

External links

- Battle of Britain Memorial, London website[398] - participants
- Northern Irish pilots in Battle of Britain[399]
- Irish pilots from the Republic of Ireland who fought in the Battle of Britain[400]

Corpo Aereo Italiano

The *Corpo Aereo Italiano* (literally, "Italian Air Corps"), or **CAI**, was an expeditionary force from the Italian *Regia Aeronautica* ("Royal Air Force") that participated in the Battle of Britain and the Blitz during the final months of 1940 during World War II. The CAI supported the German Air Force (*Luftwaffe*) and flew against the British Royal Air Force (RAF). The CAI achieved limited success during its brief existence, but it was generally hampered by the inadequacy of its equipment.

Formation

Italian dictator Benito Mussolini insisted on providing an element of the Italian Royal Air Force (*Regia Aeronautica*) to assist his German ally during the Battle of Britain.

On 10 September 1940, the CAI was formed, under the formal aegis of the *1a Squadra Aerea* di Milano ("First 'Milan' Air Command"). Generale di Squadra Aerea Rino Corso-Fougier was appointed Air Officer Commanding.

Figure 59: *An Italian Fiat CR.42 deployed in Belgium, 1940*

Aircraft

- Fiat CR.42 of 18° *Gruppo*, 56° *Stormo*. The Italian CR.42 was a manoeuvrable and fast biplane fighter. Despite its good manoeuvrability and speed (440+ km/h) it was technically outclassed by the faster and better armed Hurricanes and Spitfires of the British Royal Air Force.
- Fiat G.50 of 20° *Gruppo*, 56° *Stormo*. The Italian G.50 monoplane fighter was restricted by its range of 400 miles (640 km), which was roughly the same as that of Bf 109E models used by the *Luftwaffe*, and the lack of a radio unit in most participating aircraft.
- Fiat BR.20 bombers of 13° and 43° *Stormo*. The Italian BR.20 was a twin-engined bomber capable of carrying 1,600 kg (3,530 lb) of bombs.

Supporting aircraft included five CANT Z.1007 used for reconnaissance and Caproni Ca.133 transport planes.

On 25 September, the bombers arrived at their airfield in Melsbroek, Belgium after an eventful journey in which several planes force landed or even crashed due to malfunctions and poor weather. The fighter element arrived later at Ursel, Belgium.

Figure 60: *Fiat BR.20M MM.22267 of 242ª squadriglia on the airfield. This particular plane was shot down on 11 November 1940.*

Operations

On the night of 24 October 1940, the CAI conducted its first raid, when 18 BR.20s took off to attack Harwich and Felixstowe. Not all aircraft found their targets and three were lost in accidents.

The next major operation of the CAI was on 29 October. This date is regarded by some historians as the last day of the Battle of Britain. In response to a raid on several northern Italian cities, fifteen BR.20s with a strong fighter escort bombed Ramsgate by day. The Italian bombers were sighted crossing Kent at a relatively low level. The bombers flew in formation, wingtip to wingtip. The open-cockpit, fixed-undercarriage fighter escorts accompanied them in a similar immaculate order. The Italian aircraft were painted pale green and bright blue. This was camouflage more suitable for a more exotic climate than that found in Britain in late October.[401] Five Italian aircraft suffered damage due to anti-aircraft guns. At least one of the bombers was seen at 16:40 hours in Deal, Kent that afternoon, some 14 miles from Ramsgate and dropped three high-explosive bombs, one just outside the Officers' Mess at the Royal Marines Depot, killing Second Lieutenant Nelson, four Marines, and one private from the King's Shropshire Light Infantry. All but one were buried together in the Hamilton Road Cemetery, Deal.

The next few days saw several small raids.

On 11 November 1940, the day before the battle fleet of the *Regia Marina* (the Italian navy) was attacked at Taranto by the Royal Navy's aircraft and as a result lost half of its capital ships, the CAI saw its first major combat against the RAF. Ten bombers were escorted by forty-two CR.42s, G.50s, and some German Messerschmitt Bf 109s assigned to them. The G.50 mission was aborted due to bad weather that caused too much fuel consumption and the Fiat had to go, leaving only the CR.42 as escort. However, Hurricanes from several units, belonging to 257, 46, and 42[402] Squadrons intercepted the aircraft and destroyed three bombers and two fighters, while another was lost to mechanical fault or navigation herror, the pilot (Salvatori) was captured. In addition, four bombers eventually force landed, two fighters were destroyed on landing, and another eight fighters landed with damage, with over 20 aviators missing, dead or wounded. British had two fighters slightly damaged. One of the Fiats (MM.5701) was repaired by the British and subsequently evaluated by Eric Brown; this is one of the best conserved CR.42s, and it is owned by a UK museum (Hendon).

Fighter to fighter combat was no more successful for the CAI. On 23 November, the Italian biplanes were "bounced" by Spitfire Mk.IIs and two were shot down by Archibald Winskill with several others damaged, in return for one Spitfire damaged.

Further bombing raids were carried out by the CAI, mainly on the Ipswich and Harwich areas.

By the end of December, shortly before its redeployment, the CAI had flown 97 bomber sorties, for the loss of three aircraft. The Italian planes had dropped 44.87 tonnes of bombs in 77 night sorties, most of them over Harwich.[403]

Redeployment

Near the beginning of January 1941, all of the bombers and biplanes were redeployed. This left the CAI with only the Fiat G.50s, which remained until mid-April 1941, when they too were redeployed.

Impact

The first operation by the CAI was on 28 October. As late as 4 November, a *Time* magazine article only indicated that there was a possibility that an Italian air force unit might be sent to participate in the Battle of Britain.[404]

Figure 61: *A Falco biplane fighter after crash-landing near Lowestoft, Suffolk on 11 November 1940. The pilot successfully evaded three British Hurricanes, but was forced down by a propeller malfunction .*

Biplane versus monoplane

Although the main fighter used by the *Corpo Aereo Italiano* was a biplane, which, in purely technical terms, would be outclassed by more modern monoplanes, this was not the case all the time. On 11 and 23 November 1940, CR.42s flew two raids against Great Britain as part of the *Corpo Aereo Italiano*. Although the German *Luftwaffe* aircraft had difficulty flying in formation with the slower biplanes, the *Falcos*, though slower, and with an open cockpit, no radio, and armed with only two machine guns (a 12.7 mm/.5 in and a 7.7 mm/.303 in Breda-SAFAT), could easily out-turn Hurricanes and Spitfires, making them difficult to hit. "The CR 42 turned to fight using all the aeroplane's manoeuvrability. The pilot could get on my tail in a single turn, so tightly was he able to pull round."[405] As the RAF intelligence report stated, the *Falcos* were hard targets. "As I fired he half rolled very tightly and I was completely unable to hold him, so rapid were his manoeuvres. I attacked two or three more and fired short bursts, in each case the enemy aircraft half-rolled very tightly and easily and completely out-turned me. In two cases as they came out of their rolls, they were able to turn in almost on my tail and opened fire on me."[406]

Against British monoplanes, the CR.42s were not always outclassed. "I engaged one of the British fighters from a range of between 40 to 50 metres (130–165 ft). Then I saw a Spitfire, which was chasing another CR.42, and I got in a shot at a range of 150 metres (500 ft). I realised that in a manoeuvered flight, the CR.42 could win or survive against Hurricanes and Spitfires, though we had to be careful of a sweep from behind. In my opinion, the English .303 bullet was not very effective. Italian aircraft received many hits which did no material damage and one pilot even found that his parachute pack had stopped a bullet."[407]

Footnotes

Bibliography

- Gunston, Bill (2001), *The Illustrated Directory of Fighting Aircraft of World War II*, Salamander, ISBN 1-84065-092-3
- Haining, Peter *The Chianti Raiders The Extraordinary Story of the Italian Air Force in the Battle of Britain* London Robson 2005 ISBN 1-86105-829-2
- Hough, Richard, and Richards, Denis, *The Battle of Britain*, W.W. Norton Company, New York and London, 1989, ISBN 0-393-02766-X
- Mondey, David (1984), *The Concise Guide to Axis Aircraft of World War II*, Chancellor Press, ISBN 1-85152-966-7
- Ramsey, Winston C. (1988). *The Blitz*. Battle of Britain Prints International Limited. ISBN 0900913541.
- Townshend Bickers, Richard (1990, *The Battle of Britain*, Salamander, ISBN 0-86101-477-4

External links

- The Falco and Regia Aeronautica in the Battle of Britain[408]
- Time Magazine: Daily Damage[409]

The Dowding system

Dowding system

The **Dowding system**[410]</ref> was the world's first wide-area ground-controlled interception network, controlling the airspace across the United Kingdom from northern Scotland to the southern coast of England. It used a widespread dedicated land-line telephone network to rapidly collect information from Chain Home (CH) radar stations and the Royal Observer Corps (ROC) in order to build a single image of the entire UK airspace and then direct defensive interceptor aircraft and anti-aircraft artillery against enemy targets. The system was built by the Royal Air Force just before the start of World War II, and proved decisive in the Battle of Britain.

The Dowding system was developed after tests demonstrated problems relaying information to the fighters before it was out of date. Air Chief Marshal Hugh Dowding, commander of RAF Fighter Command, solved the problem through the use of hierarchical reporting chains. Information was sent to Fighter Command Headquarters (FCHQ) central *filter room* at Bentley Priory and used to prepare a map of the battle. Details of the map were then relayed to the Group and Sector headquarters, where operators re-created the map at a scale covering their area of operations. Looking at the maps, commanders could make decisions on how to employ their forces quickly and without clutter. Instructions were relayed to the pilots only from the squadron's sector control rooms, normally co-located at the fighters' operating bases.

The Dowding system is considered key to the success of the RAF against the German air force (*Luftwaffe*) during the Battle of Britain. The combination of early detection and rapid dissemination of that information acted as a force multiplier, allowing the fighter force to be used at extremely high rates of effectiveness. In the pre-war period, interception rates of 30% to 50% were considered excellent; that meant that over half the sorties sent out would return without having encountered the enemy. During the Battle, average rates

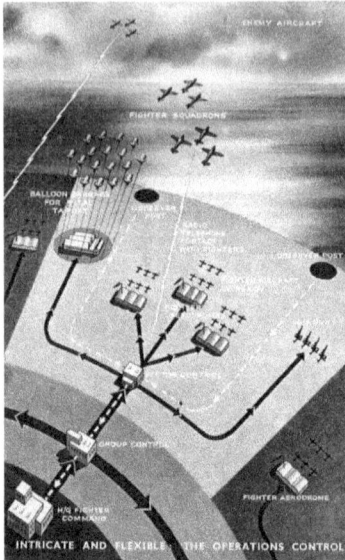

Figure 62: *This illustration shows the Dowding reporting chain for a
highlighted Sector. ROC reports flow back through the Sector controls
to FCHQ; it does not show the radars, which were still officially secret
when this was published. Information then flows back from FCHQ to
Group, between groups, and down to Sectors, and then to the defences.*

were around 90%, and several raids were met with 100% success rates.[411]
Lacking their own direction system, Luftwaffe fighters had little information
on the location of their RAF counterparts, and often returned to base having
never seen them. When they did, the RAF fighters were almost always in an
advantageous position.

Although many histories of the Battle of Britain comment on the role of radar,
it was in conjunction with the Dowding system that radar was truly effective.
This was not lost on Winston Churchill, who noted that:

*All the ascendancy of the Hurricanes and Spitfires would have been fruit-
less but for this system which had been devised and built before the war.
It had been shaped and refined in constant action, and all was now fused
together into a most elaborate instrument of war, the like of which existed
nowhere in the world.*

Development

Previous systems

To counter air raids on London during World War I, E. B. Ashmore constructed a system known as the London Air Defence Area (LADA).[412] Ashmore put defensive weapons into three rings around the city, searchlights and anti-aircraft artillery in the outer ring, fighter aircraft in the middle ring, and the innermost ring in the city contained more anti-aircraft guns.[413] Ashmore set up a large plotting table at Horse Guards in London. Information from spotters was relayed to this central room where wooden blocks were placed on a large map to indicate the location of aircraft and other information. Observers around the map could relay this information to one of 25 regional control rooms, who re-created the portions of the map relevant to them and passed the information to the various weapons in their region.[413]

After the war, LADA was run by a War Office department known as Air Defence of Great Britain (ADGB). ADGB was responsible for the defence of the entire British Isles during the 1920s and 30s. LADA became the Metropolitan Area, and ADGB expanded on Ashmore's system to deal with longer ranged and faster moving aircraft. Coloured markers matched coloured areas on a sector clock marking off five-minute intervals. As plots were called in, the plotters used markers with the colour pointed to by the clock, which produced multi-coloured paths of markers on the table making easily followed *tracks*; the freshness of the information could be determined the colour of the latest marker. An identical system was later set up in The Midlands.

The system lacked early detection, which was deemed essential as the performance of aircraft improved.[414] Experiments with acoustic mirrors and similar devices were carried out but these always proved unsatisfactory, with detection ranges often as low as 5 miles (8.0 km) even in good conditions. Lacking an alternative, in December 1934, the Air Ministry (AM) made plans to deploy sound detection devices around London as part of the Thames Estuary plan.[414]

RDF

A month after the Thames Estuary plan was approved, the Tizard Committee was formed to consider newspaper reports of Nikola Tesla's claims of a radio powered death ray. The committee consulted well-known radio expert Robert Watt for a judgement on the report.[415] Watt asked his assistant, Arnold Wilkins, to carry out the necessary calculations. Wilkins quickly concluded that it was impossible; the amount of radio energy needed would be well beyond the state of the art of existing electronics. When Watt asked about alternatives, Wilkins recalled a General Post Office (GPO) report on aircraft

Figure 63: *Chain Home coverage 1939–1940 extended over the entire British Channel area and some of France.*

causing fading in radio reception, and suggested that this effect might be used to detect aircraft at long range. The two wrote a joint memo on the concept and returned it to the Tizard Committee in time for their first formal meeting in late January 1935.[416]

The committee seized upon the concept as a potential solution to the problem of bomber detection and the fear that the bomber will always get through. A second memo with more detailed calculations arrived in February and was shown to the Air Member for Supply and Research, Hugh Dowding. He was impressed with the concept, but wanted a practical demonstration. This was carried out on 26 February 1935, now known as the Daventry Experiment, which clearly indicated the presence of a nearby aircraft. Dowding immediately released funding for development. By the summer of 1935 the system, code-named "RDF", was able to detect bomber-sized targets at ranges of 60 miles (97 km). Plans were made to build a chain of RDF stations at about 25 miles (40 km) intervals along the English coast in a system called Chain Home (CH).[417]

On 27 July, Henry Tizard suggested running a series of experiments of fighter interception, based on an estimated fifteen-minute warning time that RDF would provide. A seven-month-long series of tests began in the summer of

Figure 64: *Dowding's support for radar was matched by his understanding that radar alone was not a panacea.*

1936 at Biggin Hill, under the direction of Wing Commander Eustace Grenfell aided by a navigation expert, Squadron Leader Robert Linton Ragg.[417] Gloster Gauntlet fighters intercepted virtual aircraft, civilian airliners and then Bristol Blenheim light bombers.[418]

The first interceptions were calculated using trigonometry and mechanical calculators but eventually Grenfell had enough of the "confounded machines" and directed a perfect interception by eye.[419,420] Tizard introduced the *equal angles* method of rapidly estimating an interception point, by imagining the fighters and bombers at the opposite corners on the base of an isosceles triangle. The bombers were flying at a particular angle to the base and the controller sent the fighters along the opposite angle, to converge with the target at the apex of the triangle. With this *Tizzy Angle*, interception rates shot up and by the end of 1936 they were consistently above 90 percent when the altitude was known and did not change. If the bombers changed their altitude, or the fighters arrived below them, manoeuvring for the attack reduced the success rate to about 60 percent.[421,422]

Teething trouble

ADGB was disbanded in 1936, its duties were handed to the Air Ministry, and divided into Fighter Command and Bomber Command. Dowding was promoted to Air Officer Commanding-in-Chief of Fighter Command on its creation on 6 July 1936.[418]

The first operational CH station was set up at the radar researchers' new laboratory at Bawdsey Manor. In spite of rapid progress, RDF still had teething problems. On one occasion, Dowding was watching the displays of the test system for a sign of the attackers, when he heard them fly overhead.[423] These problems were remedied over the next year and in April 1937, tests using the prototype CH radar at Bawdsey demonstrated great promise, allowing the controllers to measure the altitude of the aircraft to within 2,000 feet (610 m)[421]

To increase warning time, the CH systems were built close to the shore facing out to sea, placing them as close to the enemy as possible. This meant they provided no information for friendly fighters on the way to the attack, or of enemy aircraft once they crossed the coast. For these areas, Dowding planned to rely on the existing Observer Corps (OC) system that Fighter Command inherited from ADGB.[424] Using different equipment, the reports from CH and the OC were sometimes contradictory, and the volume of information supplied by the national network was overwhelming.[425] An added problem was the lack of identification of the aircraft; CH could not discriminate between friendly and hostile aircraft at that time,[426] and the OC could not discriminate between friendly and enemy fighters when they were flying at high altitude.

To address the problem of identification, Dowding pressed for a supply of high-frequency direction finding (huff-duff) sets, which could locate the fighters using their existing radio sets. This led to the introduction of the "pip-squeak" system that was widely available from early 1940, along with the first identification friend or foe (IFF) transponders which were available in some quantity by October 1940. This solved the identification problem, but meant that there were now three sources of information, RDF, OC and huff-duff, none of which had a complete picture of the airspace.[421]

Building the system

Dowding recognised that the main problem was not technical but too many sources of information, none of them with complete coverage and none able quickly to report useful information to the fighters. Dowding, Tizard and a mathematician Patrick Blackett, another founding member of the committee, began to evolving a new system from that inherited from ADGB.[427]

To handle the mass of data and the potential for overlap, Dowding instituted a policy of sending all location reports from the radars to a new fighter direction centre at Fighter Command headquarters. This mimicked the system the OC had already set up for co-ordinating the reports from many individual spotters into a map covering a larger area. The new system did the same at a far larger scale, all of the UK. Telephone operators in contact with the CH and OC centers relayed reports to workers around the map, who used these reports to place small coloured markers on the map. The markers formed lines which, as they elongated, indicated the location and direction of the targets. Each cluster was assigned a number, its track.[427]

As the paths of the targets became clear over time, operators observing the map picked tracks heading towards the various fighter groups and forwarded the information to the group headquarters. The group HQs used these reports to recreate a portion of the master map containing just the tracks relevant to them. Commanders at the group headquarters could easily picture the battle and assign fighters to targets. Targets assigned to squadrons within a sector were forwarded in this same fashion to the sector headquarters, which recreated the map at an even smaller scale, using this map to guide their fighters.[427]

By early 1939, the basic system had been built out, and from 11 August 1939, Bomber Command was asked to launch a series of mock attacks using aircraft returning from exercises over France. Reports from No. 11 Group RAF were enthusiastic, stating that "RDF information and plotting throughout the Exercise was consistently first-rate, and enabled interceptions to be effected on the Coast", to which Dowding added "daylight raids were normally tracked and intercepted with ease and regularity".[427]

Description

Filtering

The first improvement Dowding suggested was to add a *filter room* at FCHQ, where all CH reports were sent.[428]

CH stations converted their angle and range measurements into a location on the Ordnance Survey National Grid.[412] A telephone operator, or *teller*, forwarded this location to the filter room, where a *plotter* would place a small coloured marker at that location on a large map covering most of the UK, the colours being the same as those adopted by the Observer Corps to indicate the time of the report. The rapidity of reporting caused plot markers to pile up on the map, which became quite cluttered during larger missions. Since each station had inaccuracies, the plots spread out on the map.[425]

Observers watching the progress of plots, tried to determine which of these represented one group of aircraft. When they were confident that a group of markers was a formation, a wooden block was placed on the map in the middle of the plots and numbers and letters placed on the block, to indicate the aircraft

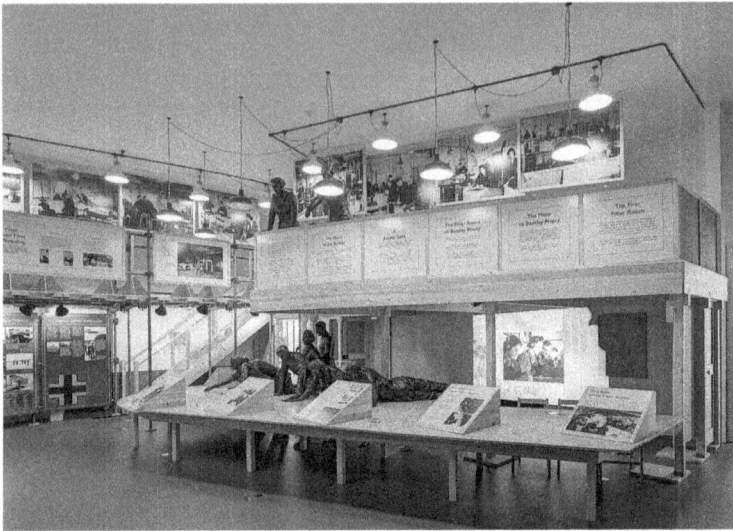

Figure 65: *A museum display of a filter room at Bentley Priory*

type, number and altitude and each block was given a *track number*. The block would be periodically moved or revised as further plot markers were placed on the board and as it moved, plotters left small arrow-shaped pointers to illustrate where it had been. Once created, the entire network used the same track numbers, from the radar operators who could be asked to revise information for a given track, to the pilots intercepting them.[425]

Around and above the map were more tellers who controlled the communications, connecting incoming reports to the plotter on the floor nearest that location on the map or connecting incoming requests for information to another teller who could read the map. Tellers examined the track markers, whose larger print allowed them to see the information, although this sometimes required opera glasses.[429] Sometimes information would have to be plotted that came from an external source, not normally part of the reporting chain; a fighter calling an SOS would report this through his radio on an emergency frequency, which would be picked up by the closest listening post. This information would also flow into the filter room but they were not connected to the plotters on the floor. Operators above the map could mark locations of interest using theatrical spotlights and filters allowed them to change the message being projected.

Figure 66: *11 Group's Operations Room is now known as the Battle of Britain Bunker. On the plotting table are numerous plots. The sector clock on the wall behind the map has coloured 5 minute regions matching the colours on the plots. Above the clock is the main tote board showing the status of the various airfields and their squadrons.*

Reporting hierarchy

The second improvement introduced by Dowding was aimed at reducing the amount of information being sent to the pilots, and speeding its delivery. For this task, Dowding introduced a hierarchy of control and information flow which ensured that only the information the pilots needed was forwarded to them. At the topmost level was FCHQ filter room, located at Bentley Priory. FCHQ maintained an overall view of the entire battlespace. This information was then forwarded one step down a hierarchy, to the Groups.[412]

During the Battle of Britain the defensive fighters were split among four active Groups, 10 through 13. 11 Group, which handled most of the fighting, had its plotting room located in the Battle of Britain Bunker (RAF Hillingdon) at Uxbridge, not far from FCHQ. 12 Group, covering the Midlands, was located at Hucknall (and later Watnall), 13 Group in a quarry in Blakelaw outside Newcastle, and the late-formed 10 Group in the aptly named Box outside Bath.[412]

At the Group HQs another plotting board, covering only the area of interest to that Group, re-created the plots from FCHQ via position reports sent to them

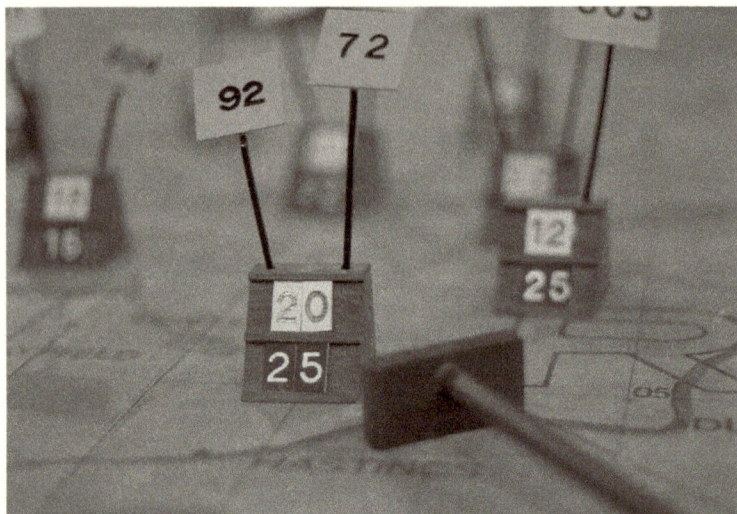

Figure 67: *This close-up of a Group level marker indicates that 25 enemy aircraft at 20,000 ft (6.1 km) are being intercepted by 92 and 72 Squadrons of Biggin Hill.*

over the telephone. This allowed the Groups to re-create the map, but on a scale and location more suitable to their area of operations.[430] Since the information was being pre-filtered, these maps did not have to be changed as often, and a somewhat simpler marker solution was adopted. Small wooden blocks with tags were placed on the map to represent the location of various formations, indicated by the ID number created in the filter room. The tags indicated the ID number, friend or foe status if known ("H" meant "hostile", F for "friendly"), the estimated number of aircraft, and their altitude. The colour of the altitude tags indicated when the report was updated, matching the same sector clock pattern used at FCHQ. This allowed observers to quickly determine whether or not a plot was up to date, and request updates if needed.[431] If a target was assigned squadrons for interception, these were indicated with cocktail stick-like tags with the squadron number on them.[432]

Each Group was split into several Sectors, which handled operations for one or more airfields. This formed the lowest level of the hierarchy, based at the Sector Controls, normally co-located at one of the sector's airfields. For instance, 11 Group was split into sectors A through F running anticlockwise from the south-west to north-east, along with Sector Z to the northwest. A typical sector, Sector C which saw considerable action, was controlled out of Biggin Hill, but also contained another major airbase at West Malling (Maidstone).[412] Telephone links from Sector to Group allowed the Group's version of the map to be re-created at the Sector, again filtering out information that was not of interest in that area.[433]

It was the Sector Controls that were responsible for communication with the pilots, as well as barrage balloon and anti-aircraft batteries, providing early warning of the approach of the enemy or warning them not to fire on friendlies.[412] To combat the problem that the fighter pilots tended to ignore orders from paper pushers, Sector Commanders were normally former pilots themselves, either retired or on medical leave. Dowding, Blackett and Tizard personally drove home the fact that the pilots could not simply hunt for their targets, and had to follow the instructions of the operations centres.[425]

By creating this system, information flow was primarily in one direction, and continued to be split out on the way down. For instance, the filter room might be receiving 15 reports per minute from various CH sites, but these would be about formations that might cover the entire coast of Great Britain. Portions of these reports, say those over Kent, would be sent to 11 Group, while others, the attack on RAF Driffield for instance, would only be relayed to 13 Group. In turn, 11 Group's operations room would relay only those tracks of interest down to the sectors, filtering out tracks that were out of their range, or being handled by other sectors. Finally, the sector operators only had to relay information to the pilots that actually had an effect on their flight – data about other formations was not relayed, freeing the radio time.

Information sources

Chain Home offered an enormous improvement in early detection times compared to older systems of visual or acoustic location. It was not uncommon for CH stations on the southeast coast of Kent to detect enemy raids as they were still forming up over their airfields in France. Additionally, this information was available day or night, in any weather. However, to provide maximum warning time, the CH stations had to be placed as close to the shore as possible. As they could only locate objects in front of them, this meant that CH provided no service over land. This required two additional locating services.[412]

The task of tracking enemy aircraft over land fell to the Royal Observer Corps. Because of the large number of ROC stations and the relatively small areas they covered, information duplication and overload was a concern. For this reason, information from the ROC was sent to a parallel system of Observer Centres, who acted as both filter and communications stations. This pre-filtered information was then sent into the Dowding reporting chain.[412,434]

Likewise, a separate reporting chain was tasked with tracking friendly aircraft through the use of radio direction finding (RDF) on their radio transmissions, using a system known as Huff-Duff (receivers) and pip-squeak (transmitter).[431]

Figure 68: *The tall towers of the Chain Home system allowed them to detect targets as far as 100 miles away, over France.*

Figure 69: *A ROC plotter sights an aircraft with his Post Instrument plotter. ROC reports began to flow in as the enemy approached the shoreline.*

Developing a fix using RDF requires two or more observation locations spread apart by some distance and then using triangulation on their reports. In this case three stations were typically used, located about 30 miles (48 km) apart. This information was reported to a selected Sector Control, who used this to plot their locations and pass on that information to the main operations plot. Controllers could then give directions the squadrons. Locations of the fighters were sent up the chain only as required.[435]

Finally, information on the status of the fighter squadrons was known to the Sectors but needed by the Groups to choose which squadrons to commit. For this task, operations rooms also contained a series of blackboards and electrical lamp systems indicating the force strengths of the fighter squadrons and their current status. Known as the "tote board", this allowed commanders to tell at a glance which units were available to receive commands. The statuses were *Released* (not available); *Available* (able to be airborne in 20 minutes); *Readiness* (airborne in 5 minutes); *Standby* (pilots in cockpit, airborne in 2 minutes); *Airborne and moving into position*; *Enemy sighted*; *Ordered to land*; *Landed and refuelling/rearming*. Next to the tote board was a weather board. It was the responsibility of the Women's Auxiliary Air Force (WAAF) plotters[436] to continually update the tote and weather boards, and relay that information up the chain.[437,438]

Command

The most visible part of the Dowding System were the "operations rooms". The most advanced of these were located at FCHQ and Group HQs. These rooms typically consisted of three layers: a large plotting table on the lowest level, communications operators located at desks around and above the plot, and a second storey above the plot, sometimes behind glass, where commanders could observe and communicate.[431]

Command of the battle was devolved to the group.[428] Observing the map from above, group commanders could track the movements of enemy aircraft through their patch, examine the tote board, select a squadron and called their sector to have them scramble. The orders could be as simple as "Squadron nine-two, intercept hostile two-one".[433] The sector would then phone the office for that squadron (often nothing more than a small shack) and order the aeroplanes to be scrambled.

After forming up, the sector controller asked the squadron to set up their pip-squeak system so they could be tracked. Once their location was measured and transferred to the sector plotting table, the controller would relay instructions to the formation leader. Vectoring was accomplished using the methods developed in the Biggin Hill exercises in 1935, with the sector commander comparing the location of the friendly aircraft with the hostile plots being transferred

Figure 70: *One of the best developed control rooms was for No. 10 Group, located at RAF Box in Wiltshire.*

Figure 71: *The Sector Control room at Duxford controlled the area from London to The Wash. Radio and telephone operators sat on the upper level, with plot operators in chairs around the map.*

Figure 72: *Group 11's operations room was completely under-ground, its entrance is now watched over by a Spitfire gate guard.*

from group and arranging the interception.[419] As the fighters were faster and often reached the interception point first, they orbited the location, giving them time to climb and seek an advantageous position.

Squadrons, bases and enemy formations were assigned code words to ease communication speed and accuracy. Amendments from sector control at Biggin Hill to 72 Squadron would take the general form "Tennis leader this is Tophat control, your customers are now over Maidstone, vector zero-nine-zero, angels two-zero"; the Biggin Hill controller (Tophat) was asking 72 Squadron (Tennis) to fly due east (vector zero-nine-zero) at 20,000 feet (6,100 m) (angels two-zero) to intercept their target. The sector was also responsible for local gun and balloon defences and getting the fighters safely back to an airfield after the sortie.

Physical construction

FCHQ and Group Control centres, in keeping with their importance in the battle, were located in bomb-proof bunkers away from airfields. Most of these were built just before the war. Communications were ensured by hundreds of miles of dedicated phone lines laid by the GPO and buried deep underground to prevent them from being cut by bombs.

Figure 73: *The German Freya early warning radar was a match for British units. Early detection alone was not enough, however; the information needed to be relayed to the pilots.*

Sector Control centres tended to be relatively small, and were mostly housed in brick, single-storey, tile-roofed structures above ground, where they were vulnerable to attack. By 1940, most were semi-protected by an earth bank or "blast wall" surrounding them which reached as high as the eaves. Fortunately, *Luftwaffe* Intelligence was unaware of the importance of these rooms and most were left alone.

The control rooms at Biggin Hill were destroyed by a raid on 31 August, but this was due to a chance bomb hit. As a further precaution, emergency control rooms were set up in different locations away from the airfields, with small loss in efficiency; Kenley, for example, could use an alternative room housed in a butcher's shop in nearby Caterham.[437]

The vulnerability of the earlier rooms was appreciated, and new airfields built during the expansion programme of the 1930s used bombproof Mk. II, L-shaped structures.

Effects on the battle

The effect of this system was profound, and remains a widely used example of the concept of force multiplication.[439]

Before the introduction of radar the task of interception appeared to be increasingly difficult, if not impossible. As bomber speeds and altitudes grew, the time available to arrange an interception was dropping. Although fighter performance was also increasing, certain aspects like getting the pilot into the aircraft and taking off introduced fixed delays that did not improve. With the only detection means being the observers and acoustic location with ranges on the order of 20 mi (32 km) under the very best conditions, the bombers would be over their targets before the spotters could call in the raid and the fighters could climb to their altitude.[411]

Given this lopsided balance of power, fighter operations prior to the introduction of radar were generally in the form of standing patrols or "sweeps", with the fighters being sent up to fly along a pre-arranged path or area in the hopes of encountering the enemy. During World War I interception missions, the vast majority of patrols returned home without ever having seen the enemy. The same was true for all forces during the Battle of France, where 30% interception rates were considered typical, and 50% excellent.[411]

In the case of an attack by a high-speed force, the attackers could pick the time and place of the attack. They would encounter only the aircraft already in the air along that route, so they could outnumber the defenders in any given area. To ensure there were a reasonable number of fighters along any approach route, huge numbers of aircraft would need to be in the air at all times covering all the routes. Since a fighter spends most of its time on the ground being maintained and refuelled, some multiple of the airborne numbers would be needed, along with a similarly huge number of pilots, as each pilot could only be expected to fly so long per day. Such a system was essentially impossible, and was one of the reasons it was widely believed that "the bomber will always get through".

A startling illustration of this scenario was provided by the RAF itself. In the summer of 1934, a series of large-scale exercises with up to 350 aircraft were carried out. About half the number were bombers attempting to approach London, and the other half fighters trying to stop them. The initial results were so dismal that the commanders attempted to improve the results, eventually giving the fighter controllers complete details of the bomber's locations prior to the mission. Even then, 70% of the bombers reached London without having even seen a fighter. The result was, as one RAF commander put it, that "a feeling of defencelessness and dismay, or at all events of uneasiness, has seized the public."

The unified view of the battlespace provided by the Dowding system turned the tables in favour of the defence. By rapidly sending accurate, timely information to the fighters, their ability to find and attack the enemy was dramatically increased, and the time required to do so decreased. The fighters took off, flew directly to their targets, engaged, and returned directly to their bases. In early operations interception rates of 75% were routine, and this number continued to improve as the operators became more familiar with their tasks. By the end of the Battle of Britain, rates of interception over 90% were becoming common, and several raids were met with 100% interception rates.[411] In numerical terms, it was as if Fighter Command had over twice as many fighters, giving them effective parity with the *Luftwaffe*.

While CH was being installed in the UK, the Germans were working on their own radar systems and had deployed an excellent early-warning system known as "Freya". But the complexity of relaying the information from the radars to the fighters had not been addressed and was apparently never seriously considered at the time. During the Battle of the Heligoland Bight in 1939, over 100 German aircraft were scrambled to meet a small force of RAF bombers, but less than half of these found them. This was in spite of a *Luftwaffe* Freya detecting the raid while still one hour out; there was no way for the radar operators to communicate with the fighters. The only radar reports to reach them came from a naval Freya near the target, too late to improve matters.

Likewise, the Opana Radar Site detected the attack on Pearl Harbor about an hour before it reached the island. They telephoned the communications office that was in charge of disseminating such information and made their report. The office had been informed that a flight of B-17 Flying Fortress bombers would be arriving that day, but lacked any sort of information on their location, at that time far to the east. The communications officer, Lt. Kermit Tyler, concluded the radar site had spotted the bombers and failed to pass on the warning. The Japanese attack went unopposed.

It was only through the combination of all of the elements of the Dowding system that an effective defensive network was created. Peter Townsend later noted that:

> *The Germans knew about British radar but never dreamed that what the radar 'saw' was being passed on to the fighter pilot in the air through such a highly elaborate communications system.*[428]

During the early war period, the *Luftwaffe* consistently underestimated the value of the system. A 16 July 1940 *Luftwaffe* intelligence report failed to even mention it, in spite of being aware of it through signals intercepts and having complete details of its World War I predecessor. A later report on 7 August did make mention of the system, but only to suggest that it would tie fighters to their sectors, reducing their flexibility and ability to deal with large raids.[440]

While discussing the events with British historians immediately after the war, Erhard Milch and Adolf Galland both expressed their belief that one or two CH stations might have been destroyed during early raids, but they proved difficult targets. This was true; several stations had been knocked out of service for a time, while others managed to maintain operations in spite of attacks. But the historians interviewing them noted, "neither seemed to realize how important were the RDF stations to Fighter Command technique of interception or how embarrassing sustained attacks upon them would have been."[440]

This realisation must have sunk in over time; after the war Galland noted:

> *From the first the British had an extraordinary advantage, never to be balanced out at any time during the whole war, which was their radar and fighter control network and organization. It was for us a very bitter surprise. We had nothing like it. We could do no other than knock frontally against the outstandingly well-organized and resolute direct defence of the British Isles.*[441]

Problems

Although the Dowding system proved itself in combat, the system and command of the battle had several problems. A huge volume of information flowed through the system, especially into the FCHQ filter room. On 11 January 1940, an operations research report on the Dowding system concluded that the filter room had been intended to correlate radar reports, but had developed into something much more complicated. Too much control took place in the filter room, which was producing results with "appallingly low standards". Given the success of the FCHQ filter room, it is unclear whether the report was inaccurate or if the problems had been solved by the time of the Battle of Britain.[442]

It was known that the filter room could be overwhelmed by a high volume of reports, and it was a constant complaint that it was a single point of failure in reports from OR and in the RAF and Air Ministry. Most critics wanted the filter room to be moved from Bentley Priory to Group commands, lowering the reporting volume at each location and providing duplication. Dowding refused the change, leading to increasing friction with other commanders. Information overload occurred on several occasions and the filter room had to ask certain CH stations to stop reporting. But this had little effect on their capabilities. Later, stations reported information for multiple formations as a single plot.[442]

Radio communications was another problem. The TR.9D HF radio telephone set in fighters at the time of the Battle of Britain had two channels and the operating frequencies of the two could only be selected before take-off. One channel was used for voice communication between the aircraft and the other for with communications with sector control, which was also used by the "pip-squeak" system. With the channels set to squadron-specific frequencies, the TR.9D limited the ability to coordinate with other squadrons. The set was low power, with a range of about 40 miles (64 kilometres) air-to-ground and 5 mi (8.0 km) air-to-air,[443] which presented numerous problems with reception quality. The TR.9 originally operated on a band that was relatively empty, but by the time of the war it was much busier and interference was a constant problem.

Chain Home could only produce information of aircraft in "front" of the antennas, typically off-shore, and the reporting system relied on the OC once the raid was over land. The OC, using sight, could provide little information at night, in bad weather or through overcast. During the Battle of Britain, the weather was unusually good, the so-called "fighter's summer", and the OC was further aided by the fact that German raids took place only when the weather allowed the bombers to see their targets.[444,445] The system failed to work against high-altitude raids that took place late in the battle.

The effectiveness of the system was also influenced by personal and inter-group rivalries within the RAF command, particularly between 11 Group and 12 Groups whose commanders constantly bickered. Trafford Leigh-Mallory, commander of 12 Group, had originally been slated to take over 11 Group command but it went to Keith Park instead. Leigh-Mallory felt further slighted by Dowding because 12 Group had to defend 11 Group airfields while 11 Group attacked the Germans.

Dowding failed to centralise a command structure at FCHQ, which meant that group commanders controlled their own battle and could request, but not demand, support from other groups. During the battle, Leigh-Mallory repeatedly failed to send his fighters to cover 11 Group airfields, preferring instead to build his "Big Wing" formations to attack the *Luftwaffe*. Big Wings took time to assemble and were often incomplete as the Germans flew away, and thus contributed little to the early stages of the battle.

Aftermath

Dowding resisted suggestions to devolve the filter room to the group level to reduce demand on FCHQ. The matter was raised several times, the last time on 27 September, when the Air Council's request was once again dismissed by Dowding. He was then summoned to the Air Staff on 1 October and was forced to implement this change, although he delayed this until all fighters were equipped with new IFF systems.[442]

On 24 November 1940, Dowding was removed from command. This was due partly to his lack of action on ending the feud between Lee-Malory and Park, partly due to his refusal to devolve command, and partly due to the lack of success against the increasing tempo of night bombing, which by this time had become The Blitz.

Figure 74: *GCI radars allowed a station to provide detection, identification (IFF) and fighter direction, eliminating the need for the complex reporting chains of the Dowding system.*

The groups soon had their own filter rooms. The introduction of ground-controlled interception radars (GCI) in the winter of 1940–41 allowed further devolution of command because sector controllers could directly detect and control the aircraft in their area.[442] Working with IFF, now widely used, the GCI display eliminated the need for separate detection and plotting, as well as the communications links and manpower needed to operate the reporting system. The Dowding system remained in use for the rest of the war for daytime missions, both for (rare) defensive situations, as well providing support for aircraft supporting offensive daytime raids during 1943 and later.

After the war, the fighter control system was largely demobilized. The explosion of the Soviet atomic bomb in 1949 and the presence of Tupolev Tu-4 "Bull" aircraft that could deliver it to the UK led to the rapid construction of the ROTOR system. ROTOR re-used many existing GCI and CH systems with more sophisticated control rooms in fortified underground bunkers. ROTOR was itself replaced by AMES Type 80 Master Control rooms and then the Linesman/Mediator system in the 1960s.

References

Bibliography

<templatestyles src="Template:Refbegin/styles.css" />

- Bowen, Edward George (1998). *Radar Days*. CRC Press. ISBN 978-0-7503-0586-0.

- Bungay, Stephen (2010). *Most Dangerous Enemy: An Illustrated History of the Battle of Britain*[446]. Zenith Press. ISBN 978-0-7603-3936-7.

- Burns, Russell (2006). "The Evolution of Modern British Electronics, 1930–1945"[447]. *Transactions of the Newcomen Society*.
- Coakley, Thomas (1992). *Command and Control for War and Peace*[448]. DIANE Publishing. ISBN 978-0-7881-0825-9.

- Corrigan, R. (September 2008). *Airborne minefields and Fighter Command's information system*[449] (PDF). GikII 2008. University of Edinburgh School of Law.

- Gough, Jack (1993). *Watching the Skies: The History of Ground Radar in the Air Defense of the United Kingdom*. Her Majesty's Stationery Office. ISBN 0117727237.

- *The Battle of Britain; August – October 1940*[450]. Ministry of Information on behalf of the Air Ministry. 1941. OCLC 5245114[451].

- Ramsay, Winston, ed. (1989). *The Battle of Britain Then and Now* (Mk V ed.). London: Battle of Britain Prints International. ISBN 978-0-900913-46-4.

- Watson, Jr., Raymond C. (2009), *Radar Origins Worldwide*[452], Trafford Publishing
- Westley, Max (Autumn–Winter 2010). "Pip-Squeak – the Missing Link"[453]. *Duxford Radio Society Journal*.

- Zimmerman, David (2001). *Britain's Shield: Radar and the Defeat of the Luftwaffe*. Sutton. ISBN 978-0-7509-1799-5.

- Zimmerman, David (2013). "Information and the Air Defence Revolution, 1917–40". In Goldman, Emily. *Information & Revolutions in Military Affairs*[454]. Routledge. ISBN 978-1-136-82779-2. First published in: Zimmerman, David (2004). "Information and the Air Defence Revolution, 1917–40". *Journal of Strategic Studies*. **27** (2): 370–394. doi:10.1080/0140239042000255968[455].

Further reading

<templatestyles src="Template:Refbegin/styles.css" />

- "Understanding The Dowding System"[456]. The Association of RAF Fighter Control Officers.

- "The Battle of Britain; August – October 1940"[457]. *Battle of Britain 70th Anniversary*. Royal Air Force.

External links

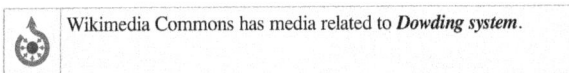

> Wikimedia Commons has media related to *Dowding system*.

- The Filter Room - WW2 - Radar Command[458], World War II film on the role of the Filter Room.

Air-sea rescue

Royal Air Force Marine Branch

RAF Marine Branch	
 Royal Air Force Ensign	
Active	1918 - 8 January 1986
Disbanded	Yes
Country	🇬🇧 United Kingdom
Branch	⊙ Royal Air Force
Motto(s)	The Sea Shall Not Have Them

The **Marine Branch** (1918-1986) was a branch of the Royal Air Force (RAF) which operated watercraft in support of RAF operations. Just days after the creation of the RAF itself, the **Marine Craft Section** (MCS) was created with the transfer of Royal Navy Air Service (RNAS) vessels and personnel to the new service. Originally tasked with the support of RNAS, and later RAF, seaplanes, Marine Craft Section was to achieve its greatest size during the Second World War, and achieved fame for its role in air-sea rescue operations. After the war MCS was granted full branch status on 11 December 1947, however post war the role of the new branch became greatly reduced with the end of the British Empire, the withdrawal of flying boats from service, and the increasing use of helicopters in air-sea rescue. The branch was disestablished on 8 January 1986.

Figure 75: *RAF seaplane tender 1502, in. 2011.*

History

Formation

In 1918 the RAF was established through the merging of the aviation arms of the Royal Navy, the Royal Navy Air Service (RNAS), and that of the Army, the Royal Flying Corps. During the First World War the RNAS had structured its force to protect Britain from both surface sea and air attack. Against surface attack the RNAS had built up a force of seaplanes and in support of these had accumulated between 300 and 500 vessels of various kind including pinnaces, lighters, launches, motorboats, depot ships and other vessels. These were used as primarily as seaplane tenders. The term seaplane tender in British usage being used for small watercraft of launch to pinnace size used as tenders, what in United States usage would be called a seaplane tender the British would call a seaplane depot ship.

These craft were used to ferry crews, stores and supplies between shore and the aircraft, to maintain the buoys used to mark out "taxiways" and "runways" and to keep these clear of debris to prevent foreign object damage, and in the case of emergency to act as rescue craft and airport crash tenders. All those functions that on land would require wheeled ground support equipment had a need for a watercraft equivalent. Other vessels were equipped as high speed target tugs, pickets and for range safety. On the creation of the RAF, along with the seaplanes they served, these RNAS vessels and their crews would become the RAF's Marine Craft Section (MCS), However, the Navy was from the start opposed to and did its best to prevent the creation of the new service, of the vessels that were now theoretically part of the RAF some could not be found; others were carried aboard Royal Navy vessels that were not part of the RNAS transfer, and to which the RAF had no option but to acede to their transfer back to the Navy. The MCS officers tasked with carrying out an inventory of the new service's assets concluded that achieving the transfer of 323 vessels was possible. However, of those boats handed over, because of their war service, some 50% were unserviceable, with some in such a poor state of repair so as to be totally unseaworthy.

Interwar

In the interwar period the MCS contracted to a force of 150 vessels, which in addition to supporting the operation of seaplanes were equipped for rescue operations, with a launch being at the ready whenever an aircraft was flying over water. However, the training and seamanship of the crews, especially with regards to navigation, and the fact that these boats were hard pressed to make 10 kn (19 km/h), meant that the MCS at this time was only capable of inshore rescue operations. The MCS were subdivided into Marine Craft Units (MCU) with individual units assigned to an individual RAF Coastal Command seaplane base. In 1921 the RAF was officially granted its own ensign, to the dissatisfaction of the Navy, and henceforth MCS vessels would fly the Royal Air Force Ensign.

As the vessels it had inherited from the Navy began wear out the MCS began to have built for it launches capable of higher speeds and - in light of the larger crews of some aircraft - greater capacity. The arrival of high speed craft into the MCS was driven in part by T.E. Lawrence, better known as "Lawrence of Arabia", whilst an airman at RAF Mount Batten; Lawrence had previously witnessed the drowning of the crew of a seaplane when the seaplane tender sent to their rescue was too slow in arriving. Working with Hubert Scott-Paine, the designer of the record breaking Miss Britain III and Miss England boats and founder of the British Power Boat Company (BPBC), the 37.5 ft (11.4 m) long ST 200 Seaplane Tender Mk1 was introduced into service. These boats had a range of 140 mi (230 km) when cruising at 24 kn (44 km/h), and could achieve a top speed of 29 kn (54 km/h). As even faster boats became available many of the ST 200s were converted into fireboats.

The work of the BPBC would lead in the late 1930s to the RAF 100 class High Speed Launch (HSL), based on the enlongated hull of a 64ft Motor Torpedo Boat the RAF 100 was designed to have a maximum speed of 35 knots, and achieved over 39 knots during trials, making it one of the fastest boats of the time.

Figure 76: *Whaleback high speed air-sea res-*
cue launch HSL 164 off Ceylon in 1943

However, the internal arrangements of the RAF 100 was to prove vulnerable to combat damage, its high deck made the recovery of aircrew in the water difficult, and for wartime use it was underarmed. These shortcomings were rectified in the Type Two 63 ft HSL, nicknamed the "Whaleback" from its deck shape.

Second World War

As Britain entered the Second World War the MCS found itself ill-prepared for war. During the Battle of Britain the MCS could only keep 10 of 13, HSL launches available for air-sea rescue operations at any one time, the high performance of the craft was brought at the expense of engines which had a service life of only 360 hours. The HSLs were also individually assigned to individual Coastal Command bases, primarily to support the operation of those squadrons based there; and although theoretically available for rescue operations in general this was done on an uncoordinated ad hoc basis. So that even with the help of civilian vessels and the Royal Navy, aircrew who baled out or ditched in the North Sea and English Channel had only a 20% chance of being returned to their squadrons. Between mid July 1940 and October Britain lost 215, hard to replace, pilots and aircrew to the seas.

In light of this, in 1941, an emergency meeting was convened by Air Marshal Sir Arthur "Bomber" Harris. The Royal Navy offered to take over in its entirety the at sea rescue role, the RAF declined and subsequently created the Directorate of Air Sea Rescue on 6 February 1941, which adopted the motto "The sea shall not have them". Operationally it was to become known as Air Sea Rescue Services (ASRS), which later became the RAF Search and Rescue Force. The headquarters of the ASRS was co-located with that of Coastal Command with which it was to operate closely.

As more High Speed Launches became available these were formed into new dedicated Air Sea Rescue Units (ASRU). Together with the expansion of the ASRS component of the MCS, the ASRS worked to improve the survival of aircrews through the development and issue of better individual survival equipment-including one man inflatable dinghies for fighter pilots copied from the Germans; the training of aircrew in ditching drills to maximise their chances of surviving to be retrieved; the development and fielding of air droppable survival equipment; and better coordination and collaboration amongst the different services, branches and units in the locating and retrieval of downed airmen.

The air-sea rescue squadrons of the ASRS flew a variety of aircraft, usually hand me downs rejected or withdrawn from front line service by the RAF's other branches or as in the case of the Walrus begged from the Navy. They used Supermarine Spitfires and Boulton Paul Defiants to patrol for downed aircrew and Avro Ansons to drop supplies and dinghies. Supermarine Walrus and Supermarine Sea Otter amphibious craft were used to pick up aircrew from the water. Larger aircraft were used to drop airborne lifeboats. Although the Walrus and Sea Otters could pick up survivors in calm seas, further out to sea and in rougher waters, it was still not possible for aircraft to routinely pick up survivors, the large flying boats that could do so, such as the Catalinas and Short Sunderlands of Coastal Command, had many other jobs to do and were not always available. The role of aircraft in the ASRS therefore, was to locate downed airmen and to keep them alive, by dropping them survival equipment and stores, until an ASRS launch, or one from the Royal Navy's Naval Sea Rescue Services, arrived to pick them up. Generally MCS launches had responsibility for the Channel and North Sea, and Navy ones for the Western Approaches.

In addition to more and better "whalebacks", the ASRUs would acquire United States built powerboats under Lend-Lease, known as "Miamis" in RAF service, from the name of their builder. These boats were not used in home waters. In addition to High Speed Launches, the MCS would also acquire larger craft, such as the Fairmile D derived "115 Foot Long Range Rescue Craft" (LRRC), these traded outright top speed for much better seakeeping and range. The MCS craft also became much better armed, sporting multiple machine guns in powered turrets derived from those found in the RAF's multi-engined bombers. By convention craft with weapons in front of the deckhouse are not considered rescue craft, and the MCS craft disposed its armament in the amidships, wing, and aft deck positions. This was achieved despite the ship yards and boat builders of Britain coming under the control of the Admiralty, and which ensured that the needs of the Navy were met first, for example the MCS's LRRCs, only being delivered once the naval need for torpedo boats was satisfied.

By the end of the Second World War, more than 8,000 aircrew and 5,000 civilians had been rescued, and the MCS had some 300 HSLs and over a thousand other vessels, located not just in the waters around the United Kingdom, but everywhere around the world. The largest fleet of such rescue craft in the world. This fleet and the RAF sailors that crewed it would contract as Britain entered peacetime, however it continued be found everywhere that the RAF flew over water. On 11 December 1947 the MCS was granted full branch status and on 25 June 1948 the largest of its vessels, of 68 feet or more were, granted the ship prefix His Majesty's Air Force Vessel (HMAFV).

Postwar and demise

As the British withdrew from Empire, and aircraft reliability improved, the need for rescue craft to provide cover for the routes that the troop planes and supply transports flew waned, and with the withdrawal from service of flying boats a large part of the Branch's reason to exist disappeared.

In the early 1950s, helicopters had begun to replace fixed–wing aircraft and supplement the marine craft in the search and rescue role, with the introduction of the Westland Wessex and later the Westland Sea King, it was now possible to consider the replacement of marine craft in all sea and weather conditions. However, even into the 1970s helicopters had not completely replaced RAF marine craft, however by this time the Marine Branch craft were becoming increasingly elderly and service in the Branch increasingly unattractive. Physically isolated from the majority of RAF bases and personnel, with the withdrawal of the flying boats and the absorption of Coastal Command into Strike Command, the majority of RAF bases were now inland; the Marine Branch became largely forgotten and neglected by the rest of the Royal Air Force. The only interaction between the Marine Branch and the rest of the RAF was when the Branch had to draw supplies from another base, or when aircrew arrived at Mount Batten for safety and survival training. Associating the RAF with the conducting of flight operations, other members of the RAF, like the public at large, were often unaware that the RAF had its own marine

Figure 77: *Rescue & Target Towing Launch (RTTL) 2757, built in 1957, in the Grounds of the Royal Air Force Museum London, Hendon.*

Figure 78: *Rescue & Target Towing Launch Mk.3 4003 - Halifax*

craft or why they were needed, and when they did become aware of the fact, found it strange and surprising.

The last roles for the MCS craft were as guard ships and target tugs for the training of the maritime anti-shipping squadrons of the RAF, and its vessels were designated Rescue & Target Towing Launches (RTTL) to reflect this. In 1986 the Marine Branch was disbanded, the last of the RAF's vessels were retired and handed over to civilian contractors for the target towing role, in the rescue role they were replaced by helicopters, and by the RNLI where necessary.

Actions and engagements

In addition to being available for rescue operations on at ready basis, the MCS was tasked with providing a rescue capability for specific operations, including clandestine ones.

* Operation Dynamo
* Battle of Britain
* Dieppe Raid
* Operation Overlord
* Operation Market Garden

Boats and ships

Name	Role	Length	Dis-place-ment	Cruis-ing speed	Top speed	Range	Built	Builder	Notes
MV Dumana	Sea-plane Depot Ship	464 feet	8,428 GRT		13.5 knots		1923	Barclay Curle	Chartered in 1939 for use as a base and maintenance ship in the Mediterranean, sunk in 1943
HMAFV *Adastral*	Sea-plane depot ship								ex HMS Fife Ness a Victory ship, on con-version served as HMAVFS Adastral 1947-1953
HMAFV *Bridport*	Long Range Rescue Craft	162 feet	605 tons		16 knots		1940	William Denny and Brothers	J50 ex Royal Navy Bangor-class minesweeper handed over 1946

HMAFV *Bridlng-ton*	Long Range Rescue Craft	162 feet	605 tons		16 knots		1940	William Denny and Brothers	J65 ex Royal Navy Bangor-class minesweeper handed over 1946
RAFV *Seal*	Long Range Re-covery and Sup-port Craft	120 feet	158 tons full load	17 knots	25 knots	950 miles @ 20 Knots, 2,200 Miles @ 12 Knots.	1967	Brooke Marine	Was to have been the lead ship of a class of ten, curtailed after three were built.
RAFV *Seagull*	Long Range Re-covery and Sup-port Craft	120 feet	158 tons full load	17 knots	25 knots	950 Miles @ 20 Knots, 2,200 Miles @ 12 Knots.	1969	Fairmile	
RAFV *Sea Otter*	Long Range Re-covery and Sup-port Craft	120 feet	158 tons full load	17 knots	25 knots	950 miles @ 20 Knots 2,200 Miles @ 12 Knots.	1970	Fairmile	Transferred to Royal Navy as HMS Redpole (P259)

I+RAF Marine Craft Section ships

Class/Name	Designation	Number	Length	Displacement	Cruising speed	Top speed	Range	Year(s) built	Builder	Notes
ST-200 Mk1	Seaplane Tender	104	37.5feet	4.5 tons	24 knots	29 knots	140 miles@24 knots	1931	British Power Boat Company	Some converted into fire floats(fireboats)
HSL100 Type 1	High Speed Launch	22	64 feet	19 tons		35 knots	500 miles	1936	British Power Boat Company	First of the RAF HSLs, in light of combat experience, contract for further craft cancelled in favour of the Type 2
HSL100 Type 2	High Speed Launch	69	63 feet	21.5 tons		39 Knots		1941	British Power Boat Company	Popularly known as the Whaleback
Canadian Power Boat Company 70 ft HSL	High Speed Launch	11	70 feet			42 knots		1941	Canadian Power Boat Company	Canadian subsidiary of the BPBC, building related designs
British Power Boat 41.5 ft ST	Seaplane Tender	67	41 feet 6 inches			23 knots		1941-4	British Power Boat Company	Used as a general purpose utility craft
Groves and Gutteridge	General Service Pinnace	200	60 feet			13-17 knots		1941-4	Groves & Gutteridge	Designed to replace 56 foot Admiralty type, top speed depended on which engines were fitted, either 3x102hp or 3x130hp engines
Thorneycroft Whaleback	Whaleback High Speed Launch	105	67 feet			25-26 knots		1942-45	John I. Thornycroft & Company	

Hants & Dorset Type 3	High Speed Launch	91	68 feet		28 knots		1942-5	British Power Boat Company	So called because of the large superstructure which was likened to a bus from the local bus company. Became the cornerstone of the postwar ASRUs when other HSLs were demobilised.
Miami	High Speed Launch	39	63 feet		33 knots			Miami Shipbuilding Company	Supplied under Lend-Lease mostly deployed in the Mediterranean, around Africa and the Red Sea
Vosper 73 ft HSL	High Speed Launch	15	73 feet		27 knots		1942	Vosper & Company	Based on the hull of the Fairmile D, acquired for operation in the Western approaches and farther out to sea, better seakeeping than other HSLs but considered slow by crews used to the whalebacks.
Fairmile 115 ft LRRC	Long Range Rescue Craft	40	115 feet		33 knots		1943-4	Fairmile Marine	based on the hull of the Fairmile D, acquired for operation in Far East
43 foot RSL	Range Safety Launch	27	43 feet	12 tons	20 knots	200 miles	1953-56	various	
RTTL Mk II[459]	Rescue & Target Towing Launch		68 feet	34 tons			1956	Vosper	

l+RAF Marine Craft Section boats

External links

| | Wikimedia Commons has media related to *Royal Air Force Search and Rescue Force*. |

- RAF Search and Rescue Force[460] – official site of successor
- ASR and MCS Club[461] - old comrades association

The Kanalkampf

Kanalkampf

Kanalkampf	
Part of the Battle of Britain	
A British convoy under air attack, 14 July 1940	
Date	4 July – 11 August 1940
Location	Southern England and the English Channel 50°N 02°W[462] Coordinates: 50°N 02°W[462]
Result	German victory[463]
Belligerents	
🇬🇧 United Kingdom • Foreign volunteers **Naval support:** Netherlands Norway Canada Poland Belgium	🇩🇪 Nazi Germany
Commanders and leaders	
🇬🇧 Hugh Dowding 🇬🇧 Keith Park 🇬🇧 T. Leigh-Mallory	🇩🇪 Hermann Göring 🇩🇪 Albert Kesselring 🇩🇪 Hugo Sperrle 🇩🇪 W. von Richthofen 🇩🇪 Alfred Saalwächter

Units involved	
11 Group	*Luftflotten* 2 and 3
Casualties and losses	
RAF:	**Luftwaffe**:
115 fighters destroyed	80 fighters destroyed
42 fighters damaged	36 fighter aircraft damaged
71 pilots killed in action	22 Dive bombers destroyed
19 pilots wounded in action	22 dive bombers damaged
4 pilots missing in action	100 medium bombers destroyed
Royal Navy:	33 medium bombers damaged
35 merchant ships sunk	13 naval aircraft destroyed
(including neutral ships)	1 naval aircraft damaged
7 fishing vessels	201 airmen killed
several naval vessels	75 airmen wounded
4 destroyers	277 missing
at least 176 sailors killed	16 airmen captured
∼300 casualties	**Kriegsmarine**:
	∼4

The ***Kanalkampf*** (Channel Battle) was the German name for air operations by the German *Luftwaffe* against the British Royal Air Force (RAF) over the English Channel, which marked the beginning of the Battle of Britain in July 1940, during the Second World War. By 25 June, the Allies had been defeated in Western Europe and Scandinavia. Britain rejected peace overtures and on 16 July, Adolf Hitler issued Directive 16 to the *Wehrmacht* (German armed forces), ordering preparations for the invasion of Britain, under the codename *Unternehmen Seelöwe* (Operation Sea Lion).[464]

The Germans needed air superiority over southern England before the invasion, and the *Luftwaffe* was to destroy the RAF, assume command of the skies and protect the cross-channel invasion from the Royal Navy. To engage RAF Fighter Command, the *Luftwaffe* attacked convoys in the English Channel, which began the Battle of Britain. There is some dispute among historians about the dates for the beginning and end of the battle, and British histories usually treat 10 July as the beginning. British and German writers and historians acknowledge that air battles were fought over the Channel between the Battle of France and Britain; deliberate German attacks against British coastal targets and convoys began on 4 July. During the *Kanalkampf*, the *Luftwaffe* received modest support from the E-Boats of the *Kriegsmarine* (German navy).

Fighter Command could not adequately protect convoys, and the Germans sank several British and neutral ships, at considerable cost to Fighter Command. The Royal Navy was forced to order a cessation of large convoys in Channel waters and close it to ocean-going vessels until more protection could be arranged after several weeks. On 1 August, Hitler issued Directive 17, extending *Luftwaffe* operations to the British mainland and RAF-related targets and on *Adlertag* (Eagle Day, 13 August) the main air offensive against the

RAF began. The *Kanalkampf* had drawn out Fighter Command as intended, and convoy attacks continued for several more days. Both sides had suffered losses, but the *Luftwaffe* failed to inflict a decisive defeat on Fighter Command and the RAF; the *Luftwaffe* had yet to gain air superiority for Operation Sealion.

Background

On 2 July 1940, in the aftermath of the French surrender, Adolf Hitler decided that an invasion of Britain could only begin after achieving air superiority. On 12 July he outlined his reasoning: aerial domination over the invasion area and its sea approaches was necessary to compensate for the weakness of the *Kriegsmarine*. Hitler issued a directive to this end on 16 July, which ordered the *Luftwaffe* to prevent all air attacks on the invasion force, destroy British coast defences at the landing points and break the resistance of the British army.[465]

The campaign did not start against the RAF until August. Throughout the intervening period, the *Luftwaffe* undertook its third major operational move within the space of two months. The first had seen it push forward its Air Fleets into the Low Countries and the second into southern France. Now it was expanded into northern France and Belgium, along the English Channel coast. It took time to establish the signal system in France owing to a shortage of trained staff officers while the units replenished after losses through the *Ergänzungsverbände* (supplemental formations).[466]

The logistics challenge was also evident in the lethargic build up. Matters were not helped by the fact that the *Luftwaffe* and army had to repair the French and Belgian infrastructure which had been badly damaged during the Battle of France. The army was forced to rebuild bridges to supply forward bases. Air bases also required rebuilding after war damage in May and June. This often meant short-range dive bombers and fighters were sent to forward airfields which were urgently in need of electricity and running water for personnel.[467]

Upon the French surrender the *Luftwaffe* supply system was breaking down. For example, on 8 July only 20 of the 84 railway tanks with aviation fuel had reached the main depot at Le Mans. The *transportgruppen* (transport groups) could not cope and barely kept their own units running. Preparations continued at a glacial pace, since the men responsible for the organisation of German air power and its efficient transfer to the Channel, were enjoying the fruits of their new assignments in Paris. Senior staff members were distracted by victory parades and promotions, including Göring who was promoted to *Reichsmarschall*. During the *Kanalkampf* the Germans assembled powerful

Figure 79: *Kesselring, commander of Luftflotte 2.*

air forces to attack convoys in the Channel but it took about forty days after the French capitulation, for the *Luftwaffe* to begin its assault on the Britain.[468]

While many *Luftwaffe* units returned to Germany to replace losses, *Luftflotte* 2 and *Luftflotte* 3 (Air Fleets 2 and 3) sent small numbers of bombers against British sea communications, attacking ships and laying mines. In July, the *Luftwaffe* transferred air units to the European coast from Hamburg to Brest in Brittany on the French Atlantic coast. By 17 July, the two air fleets had reached their intended strength for operations against southern England and the Midlands, with 1,200 medium bombers, 280 dive-bombers, 760 single-engine fighters, 220 twin-engine fighters, 50 long-range reconnaissance aircraft (90 of the medium bombers could fly bomber-reconnaissance sorties against shipping and ports) and 90 short-range reconnaissance aircraft. *Luftflotte* 5 in Norway, with 130 medium bombers, 30 twin-engine fighters and 30 long-range reconnaissance aircraft, exerted an indirect effect on the *Kanalkampf*, by making the RAF keep fighters in the north.[469]

Evolving German strategy

The *Luftwaffe* did not operate over Britain in any force until France was on the brink of collapse. Diversion of effort during the continental campaign ran contrary to the German methods in concentration of force *Schwerpunkt-prinzip* (concentration principle).[470] When German bomber crews flew over the country they did so at night; sorties were recorded in May and June 1940. When it became clear that Britain would not accede to Hitler's demands, the *Luftwaffe* undertook preparations to neutralise the country and end the fighting in Western Europe. This involved the transfer of two *Luftflotten* (Air Fleets)—*Luftflotte 2* and *Luftflotte 3*—into France and Belgium. Over the course of June and July sporadic attacks were carried out at night, both inland and along Britain's east and southern coastlines to keep the civil population awake and to damage British morale. The attacks were ill-directed and German intentions were not clear to the British.[471]

Night operations gave the *Luftwaffe* valuable experience in using night navigation equipment, such at the *Knickebein* (crooked leg). By taking bearings and cross-bearings on German medium-wave transmitters, aircraft could find their position sufficiently accurately to make the discovery of landmarks easy. On the night of 6/7 June, the first *Luftwaffe* bomb to fall on Greater London was dropped on at Addington, and small raids continued through the month. Thirteen airfields, 16 factories and 14 ports were bombed to little effect.[472] By flying at low altitudes, it was possible for British defences to detect German bombers with searchlights.[473] Two were shot down in June by anti-aircraft guns.[474] After this period, the bombers flew too high for anti-aircraft fire to be effective.[475] Fighter Command claimed 21 German bombers at night over Britain in June.[476] Seven German aircraft crashed and were credited to fighters. Fighter Command defences at night were weak. The British lacked a specialised night fighter or widespread use of reliable Airborne interception radar. Coastal radar looked out to sea, once a raider had penetrated into the interior, they became difficult to track. Until the following year, night fighter defences remained ineffective at finding enemy aircraft and shooting them down. At the beginning of The Blitz in October, the *Luftwaffe* flew 5,900 sorties and lost 23—a 0.4 percent loss rate. The failures would cost Air Officer Commanding (AOC) Hugh Dowding, his command in November 1940.[477,478,479,480]

Operations against British sea communications did not appeal to *Reichs-marschall* Hermann Göring. In Göring's view, the *Luftwaffe* was not prepared for naval warfare and this strategy was tantamount to Blockade. Blockade, which was put in effect against Britain from 18 July, required the cooperation of the *Luftwaffe* with the *Kriegsmarine* (German navy). Göring ensured air assistance was not forthcoming.[481] Göring loathed the navy and its Commander-in-Chief *Großadmiral* Erich Raeder. In Göring's eyes, both Raeder and the navy represented the bourgeois clique of German society the National Socialist revolution had pledged to eliminate.[482] Cooperation would not be easy and the *Reichsmarschall* consistently refused to accept the navy's calls for assistance in the war against the Royal Navy and British commerce throughout

the conflict.[483] All of the directives issued to the *Luftwaffe* at this time, by
the *Oberkommando der Luftwaffe* (*OKL*—High Command of the Air Force)
or *Oberkommando der Wehrmacht* (*OKW*—Supreme High Command of the
Armed Forces), expressly stated that sea attacks on warships and shipping must
take second place to "military objectives."[481] The *OKW* did not alter this view
until February 1941.[481]

Göring and the *OKL* intended to strike at the RAF and establish air superiority
or air supremacy. This aspect of future operations was clear in Göring's 30
June directive.[484] The directive stated, "As long as the enemy air force is
not destroyed, it is the basic principle of the conduct of air war to attack the
enemy air units at every possible favourable opportunity—by day and night,
in the air, and on the ground-without regard for other missions."[485] Göring
hoped that a victory in the air battle would preclude an invasion of Britain
by persuading the Churchill Government to either submit to, or reach a peace
settlement with, Germany.[486,487] This was most evident during a conference in
Berlin on 31 July when Hitler outlined Operation Sea Lion and its objectives.
No *Luftwaffe* representative was present and Göring ignored summonses by
Hitler to conferences aimed and inter-service cooperation. While the army
and navy made tentative steps toward planning an amphibious assault, the *OKL*
was engaged in an internal debate about which target sets should be attacked
to attain control of the air as quickly as possible. Though Göring's directive
mentioned cutting off British supplies he did not mention shipping specifically.
On 11 July Chief of the General Staff Hans Jeschonnek ordered that coastal
shipping should be attacked as a prelude to the main battle against the RAF and
its infrastructure. The two *Luftflotten* commanders, Hugo Sperrle and Albert
Kesselring, had already begun such operations as the indecision of the OKL
had left them with little else to do.[488]

The *OKL* decided to pursue coastal targets for several reasons. The first was
that these targets and locations were easier to find than targets inland. The second, was the Royal Air Force (RAF) would suffer a higher degree of attrition
in comparison to fighting over land in defending them, since they would be
fighting over an area which could and would be strongly contested by the bulk
of its enemy. Moreover, RAF pilots that abandoned their aircraft over water
would face the same peril as their German counterparts. Unlike the *Luftwaffe*,
the RAF lacked an air-sea rescue service at that time and consequently the Germans stood to gain more of an advantage under those circumstances. A third
was the obvious advantage in eliminating the English Channel as a conduit
through which British imports could supply Greater London via the Thames
Estuary. Shipping could still travel north of Scotland, but it would slow down
the supply of materials for the British war effort. Air Officer Commanding
Fighter Command, Hugh Dowding preferred the navy to re-route its convoys
that way to ease the burden on his forces.[489,490,491]

Figure 80: *RAF and Luftwaffe bases, group and Luftflotte boundaries, British radar coverage and range of Luftwaffe Bf 109 fighters*

Air Ministry and Admiralty

Relations between the Air Ministry, War Office and the Admiralty had been strained since the independence of the RAF on 1 April 1918. In the early 1920s, the three services competed for resources, influence and the right of the RAF to exist as a separate service. The War Office and the Navy tried to abolish the RAF and regain control of army and naval aviation. By 1940, service rivalry had diminished but the Air Ministry remained suspicious of the intentions of the other services.[492]

Fighter Command cooperated with the navy during the Battle of Dunkirk when the RAF provided fighter cover for the embarkation of the British Expeditionary Force (BEF), which was costly for both services.[493] By 1 June, the RAF reduced its effort to conserve its fighters and a Minesweeper, one transport and three Destroyers were sunk and two destroyers were damaged in their absence.[494] The absence of air cover was not uncommon and the RAF believed itself to be more successful in battle, over-claiming German losses by 4:1. Of the 156 German aircraft lost in the west, about 35 were downed by fire from naval vessels leaving 102, aside from other causes, likely to have been shot down by the RAF against 106 British losses.[495]

Cooperation was hindered by Fighter Command retaining rigid control of its units. The Admiralty complained that RAF methods did not permit direct contact by RAF operational staff liaising with the naval command. Time was lost and the fluidity of aerial warfare, meant that RAF aircraft came into action at the wrong time or place, often in numbers too small to defend the evacuation ships.[496] Vice Admiral Max Horton the Commander-in-Chief Dover, responsible for organising the evacuation (Operation Dynamo), asked to meet Dowding in late June, to prevent the operational difficulties occurring again. Horton was told to put his complaints on paper and send them to Dowding, with a copy to the Air Ministry and they never met. It was felt by the Admiralty that the RAF was fighting a separate war, with little consideration given to joint operations.[497]

The protection of shipping was a source of controversy in the RAF, since it required a substantial commitment of fighters. On average the 12 convoys passing through the Channel waters needed cover every day and roughly one-third were attacked. It became an immediate burden to No. 11 Group RAF under the command of Keith Park which was responsible for defending southwest England. The employment of convoys from the Suffolk coast to Lyme Bay negated the value of using the sea as a protective shield because the location gave tactical advantages to the attacker. Coastal radar could give little advance warning of incoming raids since the proximity of *Luftwaffe* airbases, meant that German aircraft could attack and quickly withdraw, making interception difficult.[498] Standing patrols over convoys could compensate but this exhausted pilots and handed the tactical initiative to the Germans.[499]

Coast and convoy defence had a place in Air Staff fighter defence policy but Dowding had to decide how best to employ Fighter Command to meet the German threat which he did so, apparently without consulting the navy. Before the war, Fighter Command had expected attacks by unescorted German bombers upon the eastern part of the country. The German occupation of France put the west of England in range of German aircraft. Dowding considered that airfields and factories would be attacked as well as convoys and ports, to draw RAF fighter forces into battle and inflict losses.[500] On 3 July, Dowding asked for convoys to be sent around Scotland, to reduce the burden of convoy escort along the south coast, to preserve Fighter Command for the main battle. Four weeks later the Air Ministry (ostensibly after complaints from the Admiralty) instructed him to meet the *Luftwaffe* with large formations over shipping on the south coast route. On 9 August Winston Churchill was still asking the navy to use the convoys as bait to lure German bombers; the tactic succeeded but fighting over the sea caused Fighter Command greater losses.[501]

Signals intelligence

The amount of *Luftwaffe* Enigma messages declined after the Battle of France, when the higher commands returned to the use of land lines but at the end of June, decrypts revealed that the *Luftwaffe* was preparing for operations against Britain from Belgium and Holland and that most bomber *Geschwader* would be ready by 8 July; photographic reconnaissance (PR) showed runways being extended. Since PR had found no invasion shipping in Channel ports, it was considered likely that preliminary operations were contemplated and after about a month of small night raids, the *Luftwaffe* began bigger daylight attacks on ports, coastal convoys and aircraft factories on 10 July. Decrypts in late June enabled the Air Ministry Air Intelligence branch (AI) to predict the beginning of the German offensive and decrypts for several months previous had been uncovering the *Luftwaffe* organisation, order of battle and equipment. The accumulation of information allowed AI and the codebreakers at Bletchley Park to glean strategic intelligence from tactical signals being sent in lower-grade codes by *Luftwaffe* flying units. The British estimate of the number of German bombers was reduced from 2,500–1,250 by 6 July (the true number was 1,500–1,700).[502]

Changes in *Luftwaffe* methods and objectives were communicated via landline but at times could be inferred from Enigma decrypts that changes were afoot. The code-name *Adlertag* and references to the period from 9–13 August, were uncovered but not its purpose. As the *Kanalkampf* continued, Enigma gave more notice of targets, timing and the size raids but this was sometimes too late to be useful and *Luftwaffe* changes at short-notice could negate the information. Tactical information from Enigma was not well co-ordinated with RAF Y-stations (RAF Y), which reported separate to Enigma but RAF Y was able to give warnings of German sightings of coastal convoys and imminent attacks, by eavesdropping on and decrypting *Luftwaffe* wireless transmissions between aircraft and the ground. RAF Y identified airborne bomber units and their bases, occasionally also uncovering the target area, although it was mid-August before this added much to RDF reports.[503]

German voice transmissions by radio telephone (R/T) were collected by stations around Britain based on RAF Kingsdown in Kent by German speaking WAAF and WRNS and sent to local RAF headquarters and Fighter Command HQ, the centre of the Dowding system where they were collated with reports from RDF and the Observer Corps. Voice transmissions could occasionally alert Fighter Command to formations assembling beyond RDF range, give the height of formations, discriminate between fighters and bombers and hear orders being passed to fighter escorts showing main and secondary attacks, *Luftwaffe* judgements about RAF intentions, meeting points and courses for return journeys.[504]

Coastal and Bomber command operations

Coastal Command Spitfires and Lockheed Hudsons of the Photographic Reconnaissance Unit flew from Norway to the Spanish border to photograph
German-occupied ports, looking for signs of invasion preparations. Nothing was revealed until the second week of August, when accumulations of
barges were found and interpreted as an invasion preparation. In the mean-
time, Bomber Command sent its bombers nightly against the German ports,
aircraft industry and airfields when unable to bomb the primary target. The
Blenheims of 2 Group made daylight attacks on airfields occupied by the *Luftwaffe*. In July ports and shipping were made the priority target but until the
ports filled with invasion craft in August, Bomber Command continued to attack industry and *Luftwaffe* ground facilities. The Germans had 400 airfields
available and dispersed aircraft around them, making bombing ineffectual.
These targets were defended by large concentrations of anti-aircraft artillery,
making ground strafing too risky.[505]</ref> The Blenheims were vulnerable
to fighter attack and the crews had orders to abandon raids unless there was
7/10ths cloud and by the end of June, 90 percent of sorties were cancelled. The
Blenheims—with some Fairey Battles returned from France—began to fly on
moonlit nights.[506,507] In July 1940, Bomber Command lost 72 aircraft carrying
out these operations.[508]

Prelude

1–3 July

Luftwaffe attacks on shipping were made much easier by the capture of bases
in France and the Low Countries, while in the North Sea, the Grimsby fishing
fleet was attacked twice in June. Air attacks increased and in July, ship losses
off the east coast exceeded those by naval mines. Attacks on minesweepers,
escort vessels and anti-invasion patrols rapidly increased and was made worse
by a lack of light anti-aircraft guns and the concentration of the air defence
effort in the south-east of England, against a possible invasion. The Admiralty
reserved the right for ships to fire on aircraft on an apparently attacking course,
because it had been found that a high volume of prompt, accurate fire could
reduce the accuracy of bombing and sometimes shoot down the attacker. Hur-
ried training and lack of experience in aircraft recognition among navy crews
led to many RAF aircraft being taken for hostile and fired on, even escorts
for the ships. While demanding close escort, the Admiralty required ships to
engage unidentified aircraft within 1,500 yd (1,400 m), a practice the RAF
considered irresponsible. More training in aircraft recognition and pilots not
flying towards to ships on tracks similar to bomb runs were obvious remedies
and with experience, navy gunners made fewer mistakes.[509]

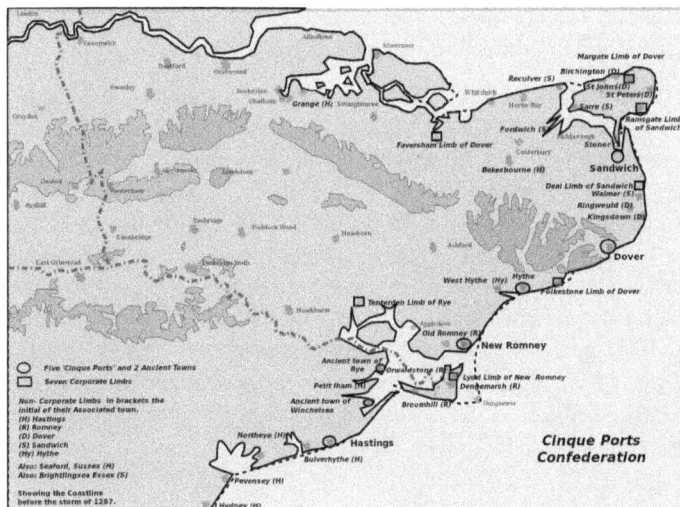

Figure 81: *Map of the Kent coast*

In July, convoys of 20–30 coasters began to sail along the south coast between the Thames and the Bristol Channel. The convoys were slow and in easy range of enemy aircraft flying from France but the south coast ports needed 40,000 long tons (41,000 t) of coal a week and land transport capacity was insufficient. On 25 July, Convoy CW 8 of 21 ships had a standing fighter patrol overhead but so many *Luftwaffe* fighters were airborne that British ground controllers were unable to tell which raids contained strike aircraft, as opposed to fighter aircraft, and the standing patrol was never numerous enough to prevent four dive-bomber attacks, which sank five ships and damaged two destroyer escorts and four coasters. On 26 July, E-boats sank three ships and only eleven passed Dungeness. The German attacks on the convoy showed that far more fighters would be needed to protect convoys in the Straits of Dover.[510]

The German occupation of the Channel Islands began on 30 June 1940 and on Monday 1 July, early morning mist curtailed operations by *Luftflotte 2* and *Luftflotte 3* but reconnaissance sorties by the *Aufklärungsgruppen* took place and two Dornier Do 215s were shot down by British ground defences. A Junkers Ju 88 from 3.(F)/*Aufklärungsgruppe* 121 was also lost to mechanical failure. Several Bristol Blenheims, escorted by Hawker Hurricanes of 145 Squadron reconnoitred Abbeville for no loss.[511] Supermarine Spitfires of 72 Squadron shot down a Heinkel He 59 seaplane and the crew was rescued by a British cruiser, complaining that they were a Red Cross service and should not have been fired upon. The British issued a warning that aircraft operating in the vicinity of convoys did so at their own risk. A scramble was ordered soon afterwards to protect Convoy Juno as it approached Portsmouth; the convoy was attacked by Ju 87s which left before the fighters arrived.[512]

Blenheim If fighters from 235 Squadron claimed a Dornier Do 17 damaged and Spitfires from 64 Squadron engaged and shot down a Do 17 from *Kampfgeschwader* 77 (*KG*: Bomber Wing) that was approaching RAF Kenley. On 2 July, German attacks caught convoy OA177G en route for Gibraltar and *Sturzkampfgeschwader* 2 (*StG*: Dive Bomber Wing) sank the British steamer *Aeneas* (10,058 GRT) south-east of Start Point, Devon; 18 crewmen died and the rest were rescued by the destroyer HMS *Witherington* and later StG2 damaged the British steamer *Baron Ruthven* (3,178 GRT).[513] A German E-Boat, *S-23*, looking for the convoys, was damaged by a mine and sank as it was being towed. *Bijou* (98 GRT) was sunk by air attack at Mistley Quay, near Harwich on 3 July.[514] To be closer to the coast, Dowding transferred 79 Squadron from Biggin Hill to RAF Hawkinge.

Portland and Convoy OA 178

4 July

In the morning of 4 July, the *Luftwaffe* attacked Portland harbour, with Messerschmitt Bf 110s from V.(Z)./*Lehrgeschwader* 1 (*LG*: Experimental Wing) and two *Staffeln* (squadrons) of Messerschmitt Bf 109s from I./*Jagdgeschwader* 1 (*JG*: Fighter Wing) (renamed III./*Jagdgeschwader* 27 -*JG* 27- the next day) were ordered to escort Junkers Ju 87 *Stukas* of II./*Sturzkampfgeschwader* 51 (*StG* 51, renamed II./*Sturzkampfgeschwader* 1 StG 1, the next day).[515] At 08:15 the *Stukas* arrived and with no RAF fighters in sight, attacked HMS *Foylebank* (ex-MV *Andrew Weir*) armed with four twin four-inch high-angle guns, multiple two-pounder Pom-Pom guns and 0.5-inch machine guns. The ship had been sent to Portland on 9 June to protect the harbour but only succeeded in attracting the bulk of the 26 *Stukas*.[515]

Foylebank could not take evasive action, the gunners did not have the time to man their weapons properly and 104 bombs were dropped, many hitting the vessel.[515] *Foylebank's* tender was hit and sank immediately, 176 sailors being killed.[516] Only one four-inch gun got into action, firing 55 rounds against the *Stukas* as they dived steeply at up to 90°. At around 1,500 feet (460 m), the dive-angle was decreased to 45° and the pilot lined up the gun-sight on the ship's stern. The pilot fired the MG 17 machine guns and as the altitude decreased, the gunfire raked the ship. When the rounds struck the water ahead of the bow, the bombs were released and as the *Stuka* pulled out, the rear-gunner opened fire.[517] The *Stukas* sank *Silverdial* and the merchantman *East Wales* (4,358 GRT), *William Wilberforce* (5,004 GRT) and *City of Melbourne* (6,630 GRT) were damaged.[517,518]</ref> Only one RAF aircraft, a

Fairey Battle of No. 10 Bombing and Gunnery School, on a training flight from RAF Warmwell was present and the pilot A. W. Kearsey fled the scene at full speed, apparently unnoticed by the German fighters.[517] The raiders lost a Ju 87 shot down by *Foylebank* gunners, *Leutnant* Schwarze and his gunner being posted missing and another *Stuka* was lightly damaged, both from *StG* 51 and a Bf 109 was damaged.[519]

Convoy OA 178 (*convoy outbound atlantic*) of 14 heavily laden merchantmen left the Thames Estuary, bound for the west coast and passed Dover safely on 3 July. German radar picked up the convoy and the *Luftwaffe* was ordered to intercept the ships after the Portland operation.[520] As smoke was rising over Portland, a Junkers Ju 88 reconnaissance aircraft from 1.(F)/123 flew over the Channel and reported that the convoy was south-west of Portland. I./*StG* 2 took off, led by *Geschwaderkommodore* (Wing Commander) Oskar Dinort, from Falaise with 24 Ju 87s, escorted by a *Staffel* of fighters from I./*JG* 1. The attack was followed by 23 Ju 87s of III./*StG* 51 after they had been hastily re-fuelled and bombed up. The ships were close to the French coast and *Dallas City* was damaged, engulfed in flames and collided with *Flimson* which was also hit and the ships took 15 minutes to disengage; *Dallas City* later sank. *Antonio* limped into Portland Harbour with *Flimson*, where the *Foylebank* was still on fire and sinking. *Deucalion* (1,796 GRT), *Kolga* (3,526 GRT) and *Britsum* (5,225 GRT) were sunk and SS *Canadian Constructor*, was damaged for no *Luftwaffe* loss.

In the late evening, Hurricanes of 79 Squadron scrambled to defend shipping off Dover being attacked by Dornier Do 17s of *Kampfgeschwader* 2 (*KG* 2). Several ships were badly damaged and one freighter was beached to avoid sinking and Bf 109s from II./*Jagdgeschwader* 51 (*JG* 51) shot down a Hurricane. Sergeant Henry Cartwright, a flying ace with five victories, was killed, for one Do 17 damaged.[521] The day had been a victory for the *Luftwaffe*, the attack on Portland inflicting the worst ever loss of life on British military personnel based in Britain.[522,523] Churchill was perturbed and submitted a memo to the Admiralty entitled "Action This Day",

> *Could you let me know on one sheet of paper what arrangements you are making about the Channel Convoys now that the Germans are all along the Channel coast? The attacks yesterday both from the air and by E-boats, were very serious, and I should like to be assured this morning that the situation is in hand and the Air is contributing effectively.*[524]

Horton regarded the episode as a disgrace and the Admiralty complained to the Prime Minister, who demanded that Fighter Command do more to protect Channel shipping.[525]

Figure 82: *Keith Park, AOC No. 11 Group*

5–8 July

The weather over the Channel was poor over the Channel on 5 July. No. 65 Squadron RAF intercepted an 8. *Staffel* Heinkel He 111 of *Kampfgeschwader* 1 (*KG* 1) over the sea and shot it down with the loss of all five crew. Late in the evening, 64 Squadron flew a reconnaissance patrol over Calais. Bf 109s from *JG* 51 intercepted and shot down a Spitfire, its pilot being killed and another was damaged for no loss to the German fighters.[526] Evidence grew that the main *Luftwaffe* attack would fall in the south and as Fighter Command squadrons were rebuilt with pilots from Operational Training Units (OTU), the Air Marshal agreed with Air Officer Commanding (AOC), No. 11 Group, Keith Park and AOC 12 Group, Trafford Leigh-Mallory, to a transfer of some squadrons to bases closer to the coast on 6 July. The Air Staff expected German attacks from the Cherbourg peninsula and 609 Squadron was moved from RAF Northolt to RAF Middle Wallop on Salisbury Plain; 87 Squadron moved to Exeter to cover Bristol, Plymouth and the Western Approaches.[526]

Convoy patrols were resumed on 7 July in defence of CW and CE (west- and east-bound) convoys. 145 Squadron shot down a Do 17P reconnaissance aircraft over the Channel, 43 Squadron shot down another shadowing an east-bound convoy and another Do 17 fell to 601 Squadron later on. *Luftwaffe Jagdgeschwader* (Fighter Wings) were encouraged to embark upon *freie jagd*

Figure 83: *Bristol Channel*

(free hunts) to engage RAF fighters wherever possible. The tactic offered exceptional opportunities for the German fighters, which did not have to worry about protecting bombers. As 54 Squadron prepared to attack a lone He 111, it was "bounced" by Bf 109s and two pilots force-landed and another fighter was damaged, the pilots surviving.[526]

At 19:30 Greenwich Mean Time as the convoy passed Dover, 45 Do 17s from I. and II./*KG* 2 took off from Arras and attacked at 20:15, sinking one ship and damaging three more. The radar stations at Pevensey, Rye and Dover gave good warning of the attack and seven Spitfires from 64 Squadron were ordered up from RAF Kenley, with six more from 65 Squadron at RAF Hornchurch. The fighters took off too late, could not prevent the attack and 65 Squadron was bounced by 70 Bf 109s from *JG* 27. Three Spitfires were shot down, all three pilots being killed and two Bf 109s were claimed destroyed (although neither can be identified through *Luftwaffe* loss records). The fighters of 64 Squadron damaged a Do 17 which crash-landed at Boulogne and another suffered light damage. Before dark, He 111s bombed Portland Harbour near missing the steamer *British Inventor*, killing one man and hitting HMS *Mercury*, whose crew lost four dead and three wounded.[526] Dowding was now in no doubt that the *Luftwaffe* was concentrating on ships and harbours and that the seven coastal convoys and deep-sea convoys at sea would be attacked. Dowding regarded convoy escort as wasteful and feared that Fighter Command would be depleted before main battle. The Germans had lost seven reconnaissance aircraft in a week and the *Jagdgeschwader* were ordered to provide escorts.[526]

On 8 July, the weather was favourable for the *Luftwaffe*, with thick cloud extending from 1,500–20,000 feet (460–6,100 m) shielding the bombers from RAF fighters. A convoy sailing up the Bristol Channel was shadowed by a Do 17, which was intercepted by 92 Squadron and claimed destroyed, though

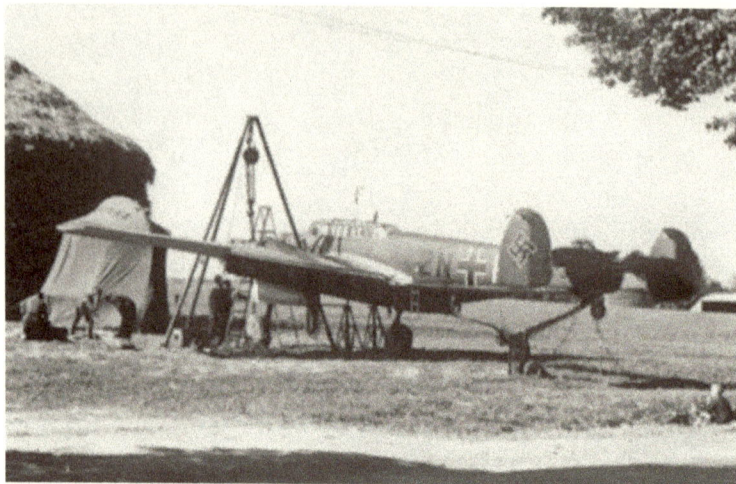

Figure 84: *A Bf 110 of Zerstörergeschwader 76 (ZG 76). The 9 July was the Bf 110's baptism of fire.*

this is not shown in German records. In the early hours a large CW convoy put to sea from the Thames Estuary to pass Dover at 12:00. At 11:30, a He 111 found near the convoy off the North Foreland was claimed shot down by Spitfires of 74 Squadron and appears to have escaped, though seen on fire, undercarriage down, diving into cloud. An hour later, radar picked up considerable aerial activity over the Pas de Calais.[526,527] 610 Squadron intercepted an unescorted *Staffel* of Do 17s off Dover, which dropped their bombs wide of the ships.[526]

The Spitfires damaged a bomber but lost a pilot killed to return fire; six more Spitfires sighted Do 17s escorted by a *Staffel* of Bf 109s and a Bf 109 was claimed without loss. (A II./*JG* 51 Bf 109 force-landed, the pilot wounded.) Hurricanes of 79 Squadron took off from Hawkinge and north of Dover, were attacked and lost two pilots killed to Bf 109s. *Kampfgeschwader* 54 (*KG* 54) Ju 88s made ineffectual attacks and Geoffrey Allard of 85 Squadron shot down a *KG* 1 He 111 (the pilot was killed and the four crew members were posted missing) and 74 Squadron shot down a Bf 109 from 4./*JG* 51 (*Leutnant* Johann Böhm being taken prisoner) and Squadron Leader D. Cooke of 65 Squadron was killed in the afternoon.[526,528,529,530]

9 July

On 9 July Kesselring committed the *Zerstörergeschwader* (Destroyer Wings) to battle en masse, for the first time against the RAF. The first engagement took place when 257 Squadron damaged a *Kampfgeschwader 3* (*KG* 3) Do 17, which crash-landed near Antwerp, Belgium with one crew member dead. A cold front generated thick cloud and caused the *Luftwaffe* to curtail operations. Park ordered section strength (3–4 aircraft) standing patrols over six small coastal convoys and moved 609 Squadron to RAF Warmwell, to cover Portland.[531] A number of single-aircraft raids penetrated the defences and Do 17s bombed docks at Cardiff, damaging the steamers *San Felipe* (5,919 GRT) and *Foxglove*. A local airfield was bombed and two pilots were killed on the ground.[532]

At 12:45, Dover radar detected the build-up of a large formation behind the Pas de Calais and to prevent the *Luftwaffe* from using the cloud cover to approach unseen and attack the convoys from the trailing edge of the cloud base, Park ordered six squadrons from 11 Group into action. At 13:00 he six Hurricanes were ordered up from RAF North Weald, where the station commander, Wing Commander Victor Beamish, became so impatient that he ordered his aircraft to be readied and took off in support, leading 151 Squadron. The Hurricanes were confronted with a formation of 100 bombers and fighters in a stepped up formation, ranging from 12,000–20,000 feet (3,700–6,100 m). The six Hurricanes formed two sections of three, one against the bombers and the others after the 60 Bf 109s and Bf 110s fighters. The German bomber crews exaggerated the number of Hurricanes and split into six formations, one finding itself over the convoy but its bombing was scattered and no ships were hit; a Hurricane was shot down and another damaged; Squadron Leader C. G. Lott was wounded and withdrawn from active service, the Hurricanes probably being shot down by II./*JG* 51. In return III./*Zerstörergeschwader* 26 (*ZG* 26 or Destroyer Wing 26) lost three Bf 110s destroyed and one damaged. Seven crew were posted missing, with one pilot safe, after being intercepted by 43 Squadron. No Bf 109 appears to have been lost and they prevented the RAF fighters from reaching the bombers.[531,533]

Another *Luftwaffe* raid was mounted and Park who had moved three squadrons to RAF Manston, was positioned to intercept. The German raid reached the North Foreland around 15:50, 65 Squadron engaged the formation and shot down one Bf 109 from II./*JG* 51, the pilot posted missing. 17 Squadron Hurricanes reached the area and shot down a *Kampfgeschwader* 53 (*KG* 53) He 111, with the crew killed. Kesselring ordered *Seenotflugkommando* 1 with Heinkel He 59 float planes to rescue survivors, covered by a *Staffel* of Bf 109s. A He 59 found itself above a convoy and was attacked by 54 Squadron Spitfires, led by Al Deere. The He 59 was forced down on the Goodwin Sands and its crew was captured. Two Spitfire pilots were killed by the escorts from II./*JG* 51 for another Bf 109 and its pilot missing.[531,534] The bombers hit the steamer *Kenneth Hawksfield* (1,546 GRT) and *Pol Grange* (804 GRT) with no casualties

Figure 85: *Bf 109s off Dover, 1940. British radar stations can be seen in the background.*

and *Kenneth Hawksfield* was beached, patched up two days later and returned to London docks.[531,535]

The last sorties of the day were flown by 27 I./*Sturzkampfgeschwader* 77 (*StG* 77) Ju 87s, led by *Hauptmann* Friedrich-Karl Lichtenfels, escorted by Bf 110s, which attacked the Portland naval base. Intercepted by 609 Squadron, Lichtenfels was killed with his gunner and a Spitfire pilot was killed by the Bf 110 escort; Lichtenfels was a Knight's Cross of the Iron Cross holder and experienced pilot.[531,536] A Bf 110 escort from 13./*LG* 1 was also lost.[537] The 7,085 GRT freighter *Empire Daffodil* was damaged.[538] Further east, up the North Sea coast, a raid over Norwich by *Kampfgeschwader* 26 (*KG* 26) He 111s killed 26 civilians and 17 Squadron destroyed one of the bombers; all of the crew were killed.[539]

Kanalkampf

Convoy Bread

10 July

Göring's 30 June order had delegated responsibility of attacking shipping to Bruno Loerzer's *Fliegerkorps II* (Air Corps II) and Wolfram Freiherr von

Richthofen's *Fliegerkorps* VIII (Air Corps VIII) since they contained most of the Ju 87 *Stuka* units and Loerzer appointed *Geschwaderkommodore* Johannes Fink, the commander of *KG2* as *Kanalkampfführer* (Channel Battle Leader).[526,540] *JG* 51 (Theo Osterkamp) was based at Wissant, close to *KG* 2 and until other *Jagdgeschwader* could be brought to action *JG* 51 was the *Jagdwaffe* spearhead over England and had been carrying out fighter sweeps over Kent but bomber escort deprived the fighters of freedom of action. Fink devised a compromise in which the Messerschmitt Bf 110 *Zerstörergeschwader* (Destroyer Wings) flew close escort and the Bf 109s roamed, to engage British fighters at a tactical advantage.[540,541] A Do 17 of 4.(F)/121 was sent out to reconnoitre the Channel in thick cloud and rain, accompanied by a *Staffel* of Bf 109s from I./*JG* 51 and 74 Squadron scrambled six Spitfires to intercept, which damaged the Do 17 for two Spitfires damaged by the Bf 109s.[540]

Eight convoys were at sea and the German formation had time to report the composition and heading of a large convoy (Convoy Bread) before being intercepted. The convoy was sailing in ballast from the Thames Estuary and rounded the North Foreland at 10:00. Fink alerted *KG* 2, with III./*ZG* 26 as close escort and *JG* 51 as high cover. While the operation was being prepared, a *Staffel* of Bf 109s on a sweep over Dover shot down a 610 Squadron Spitfire without loss.[540,541,542] Park sent up a patrol over Convoy Bread from 32 Squadron at 13:15 GMT and at 13:30, when it was clear the Germans were mounting a stronger raid, dispatched 56 Squadron, 111 Squadron and 74 Squadron. Twenty minutes later the formations met over the convoy, about 26 Do 17s from I./*KG* 2, all three *Staffeln* of I./*ZG* 26 Bf 110s and two *Staffeln* of I./*Jagdgeschwader* 3 (*JG* 3, which had just arrived in France). Mistaking the Bf 110s for Do 17s, the leader of 32 Squadron reported 60 bombers and called for reinforcements; Park had already ordered three more squadrons into action.[540,541]

A dog-fight between around 100 aircraft broke out; it was difficult for the RAF fighters to co-ordinate attacks, since the radio was full of chatter between pilots and the Bf 109s frustrated British attacks on the bombers. No 111 Squadron made head-on attacks into the Do 17s and a Hurricane collided with a bomber, the body of Pilot Officer Higgs later being washed ashore in the Netherlands. The Do 17, flown *Staffelkapitän* (Squadron Leader) *Hauptmann* Krieger, also crashed with the loss of two crew. (Higgs may have been hit by Walter Oesau of III./*JG* 51 and lost control before the collision.)[540,541] The interception managed to disrupt the bombing and only a 700 GRT sloop was sunk by the 150 bombs dropped. Six 64 Squadron Spitfires arrived and harassed the Germans all the way back to the French coast. A Bf 110 was shot down by 64 Squadron and another by 56 Squadron, a Do 17 was shot down by 111 and 66

Figure 86: *A Heinkel He 59, August 1940. He 59 units
conducted air–sea rescue operations in the Channel.*

squadron aircraft and two more were shot down by 32 Squadron. A Bf 109
of 2./*JG* 3 and one from II./*JG* 51 were shot down and two were damaged,
one pilot being rescued by a He 59 and a Hurricane from 111 Squadron was
damaged.[540,541]

In other attacks, *Luftwaffe* bombers sank the British tanker *Tascalusa* (6,499
GRT) in Falmouth Harbour. The Greek steamer *Mari Chandris* (5,840 GRT)
from convoy HG 33, which had been towed to Falmouth in June after a collision, was set on fire by *Tascalusa*, the crew of the Greek steamer being rescued. (Tascalusa was refloated on 29 August and beached at Mylor Flats for
scrapping.) The British steamer *Waterloo* (1,905 GRT) was sunk by Ju 88s
and the crew rescued. The Dutch steamer *Bill S* (466 GRT), from convoy CW
3 was badly damaged and sank 6.7 miles (10.8 kilometres) off Dungeness, all
the crew surviving. The British tanker *Chancellor* (7,085 GRT), from convoy
OA 170, was damaged by an aircraft off Falmouth and the Dutch salvage tug
Zwarte Zee was sunk by bomb splinters from near-misses.[543,544]

Convoys Booty and Agent

11 July

Von Richthofen ordered *Fliegerkorps VIII* to prepared for operations at first
light and taking off at 07:00 from the Cherbourg Peninsula, Ju 87s from *StG*
2 (*Geschwaderkommodore* Dinort) attacked shipping along the coast. The

Stukas intercepted the British steam yacht HMS *Warrior* (1,124 GRT) and the 36-year-old ship was sunk with one casualty. No. 501 Squadron had scrambled but was engaged by the Bf 109 escort and lost one pilot shot down and drowned; 609 Squadron arrived as the Ju 87s began their dives. The six Spitfires split, one section of three engaging the *Stukas* and the other taking on the escort. Overwhelmed by odds of 6:1, the squadron was routed, with the loss of two pilots killed for no loss to the Germans; none of the merchant vessels were hit.[545]

A relay of German reconnaissance aircraft observed British waters during the morning, *Luftwaffe* aircraft flying as far north as Scotland. Over Yarmouth, a Hurricane was damaged by return fire from a Do 17 and then the Dornier was shot down by Douglas Bader of 242 Squadron based at Coltishall. Squadron Leader Peter Townsend, 85 Squadron, baled out near Harwich after being hit by a Do 17 belonging to II./*KG* 2, which returned with three wounded crew. Encouraged by the relative immunity of the *Stukas* in the morning attack, Hugo Sperrle ordered *Luftflotte* 3 to follow up the attack; Bf 110s from *ZG* 76 would provide escort in place of the Bf 109s.[545] At 11:00 GMT, Hurricanes from 601 Squadron were scrambled to intercept a reconnaissance Do 17, missed it and stumbled into a formation of Ju 87s from III./*StG* 2 escorted by about 40 Bf 110s, that radar had failed to locate. The escorts were too high above the Ju 87s to stop the first attack. Most squadrons in the Middle Wallop sector were re-fuelling but six 238 Squadron Hurricanes were scrambled, with three more from 501 and 87 Squadrons and nine from 213 Squadron near Exeter. None arrived in time to stop the attack on Portland at 11:53 GMT but little damage was done and only one vessel was damaged.[545]

A dog-fight occurred near the Dorset coast, when 87 Squadron attacked the escort out of the sun and the squadron leader, John Dewar, hit the Bf 110 of *Staffelkäpitain Oberleutnant* Gerhard Kadow; the aircraft crash-landed and Kadow tried to destroy his aircraft but was shot by approaching soldiers. *Oberleutnant* Hans-Joachim Göring, nephew of Hermann Göring and his gunner *Unteroffizier* Albert Zimmermann crashed into a cliff top at the Verne Citadel on the Isle of Portland, both being killed. *Leutnant* Friedrich-Wolfgang Graf von und zu Castell tried to help Göring but was killed, four Bf 110s from 9. *Staffel* being lost with their crews. A Ju 87 was destroyed and another force-landed, the light *Stuka* losses were a result of the Bf 110s bearing the brunt of the attacks. One Hurricane was slightly damaged and its pilot unhurt. Hans-Joachim Göring was the first German fighter pilot to die on British soil.[545] The British steamer *Kylemount* (704 GRT) was damaged off Dartmouth and the steamers *Peru* (6,961 GRT) and *City of Melbourne* (6,630 GRT) were damaged in Portland harbour. *Eleanor Brooke* (1,037 GRT) was damaged off Portland and the Dutch steamer *Mies* (309 GRT) was damaged south of Portland Bill.[546,547]

In the evening a He 59 off the Cornish coast was forced down by engine failure and another landed to rescue the crew. Coastguards sighted the Germans
and two destroyers were sent from Plymouth to capture the aircraft. Bristol
Blenheims from 236 Squadron shot down a Ju 88 and damaged a He 111 from
Kampfgeschwader 55 (*KG* 55) that attempted to interfere. A He 59 was lost
and the other evacuated the crew. During the night, raids on Rochester and
Chatham killed 36 people.[545] *KG* 54 was also involved in the convoy operation.[548]

12 July

On 12 July, dawn was showery with grey, overcast skies when Booty, a large
convoy set out from the Thames Estuary steaming south-west off the Essex
coast and Agent another convoy was off the North Foreland. The *Luftwaffe*
and *Regia Aeronautica* (Italian Air Force) attacked Booty and 17 Squadron
took off from RAF Debden to patrol the convoy. While en route, the pilots
were warned of a raid and 85 Squadron from Martlesham, 242 Squadron, led
by Bader, from Coltishall, six Boulton Paul Defiants from 264 Squadron based
at RAF Duxford and eleven Hurricanes of 151 Squadron from North Weald,
were rushed to the area as reinforcements. Two Do 17 *Staffeln* of II./*KG* 2
and III./*Kampfgeschwader* 53 (*KG* 53), were intercepted by 17 Squadron and
attacked at 08:48, as the Germans began to bomb. One He 111 and a Do 17
were shot down, a *Staffelkapitän Hauptmann* Machetzki being killed with his
crew. The bombers flew in a tight formation and their cross-fire damaged several Hurricanes and shot down two, killing a pilot from 85 Squadron. Two
He 111s and two Do 17s were shot down. Trawlers from Booty rescued German aircrew despite the falling bombs.[545,549] A further He 111 from Stab/*KG*
55 was shot down by Spitfires on armed reconnaissance, a crew man being
killed.[550]

The steamer *Hornchurch* (2,162 GRT), from convoy FS 19 was sunk and
the crew rescued by patrol sloop *Widgeon*.[551] The steamer *Josewyn* (1,926
GRT) was damaged 8 nautical miles (15 km; 9.2 mi) west-north-west of St.
Catherine's Point.[552,553] Having missed the chance to attack Agent, *Luftflotte
3* sent out more reconnaissance He 111s and Do 17s to track shipping. A
He 111 from *KG* 55 was lost during the afternoon against 43 Squadron Hurricanes and the *Luftwaffe* failed to find and attack any more convoys. Later
that night *Geschwaderkommodore* Alois Stoeckl led *KG* 55 on a night attack
against Cardiff without loss.[545]

Figure 87: *HMS Vanessa—the first destroyer casualty of the Kanalkampf.*

13–18 July

On 13 July other, smaller convoys ran the gauntlet through the Channel. A II./*Kampfgeschwader* 51 (*KG* 51) Ju 88 was shot down by 43 Squadron Spitfire while shadowing a convoy. The convoy was heading west and was in the area of Lyme Bay when 238 and 609 squadrons, with 12 Hurricanes and three Spitfires were ordered to mount an aerial guard. Convoy CW 5 was late and instead they found no ships but fifty *Luftwaffe* aircraft searching for the convoy. Two Do 17s were shot down for one pilot killed in a force-landing. V./*LG* 1 Bf 110 fighter-bombers attempted to engage but became embroiled in a dogfight with RAF fighters who claimed three damaged for no loss. One damaged claim was filed by John Dundas.[554]

As Bread sailed out of range, the smaller convoy was attacked by *StG* 1 escorted by three *Staffeln* of *JG* 51. 11 Hurricanes of 56 Squadron engaged the Ju 87s before the Bf 109s could react, two Ju 87s were damaged but the escorts shot down two Hurricanes. 54 Squadron Spitfires attacked the Bf 109s and New Zealander Colin Falkland Gray shot down *Leutnant* Hans-Joachim Lange, who was killed. *Luftwaffe* losses amounted to six aircraft destroyed and eight damaged, four Hurricanes were shot down and a Spitfire was shot down in error by the Dover defences. HMS *Vanessa* was disabled by near-misses and was taken under tow by tug *Lady Duncannonand* and repaired in November 1940.[554,555]

Bad weather over the next few days reduced operations and on 14 July, Kesselring sent the IV.(St)/*LG* 1 Ju 87s against convoys, when the escorts from
III./*JG* 3 and II./*JG* 51 shot down a Hurricane from 615 Squadron but only
one Ju 87 and one Bf 109 were destroyed and another force-landed. The air
battle took place over a convoy which was recorded by Charles Gardiner, a
BBC reporter.[556,557] No damage was done to the convoy but an armed merchant cruiser *Esperance Bay*, carrying £10,000,000 in Gold bullion was badly
damaged off Land's End, Lieutenant commander H. Close and six ratings being killed. The Turkish Navy minelaying sloop *Yuzbasi Hakki* was damaged
off Weymouth.[558] Convoys CW 5 and CW 6 were also attacked and the British
Mons (614 GRT) and the 1,129 GRT Norwegian steamer *Balder* were damaged and *Island Queen* (779 GRT) was sunk.[559] The Belgian trawler *Prov-
identia* (139 GRT) blew up with the loss of all hands, probably bombed by
IV.(StG)/*LG* 1.[560]

On 15 July, a Hurricane was shot down and the *Luftwaffe* lost a He 111, a
Ju 88 and a Dornier Do 18 seaplane to RAF fighters.[561] The steamer *Heworth*
(2855 GRT) in convoy FN 223 was damaged and taken in tow for Harwich
but ran aground. Four crew were killed and the survivors were rescued by
the destroyer HMS *Valorous*. Steamer *City of Limerick* (1359 GRT) was sunk
and the destroyers HMS *Mackay* and HMS *Broke* went to rescue the crew.
Two men were killed and the survivors were rescued by Belgian trawler *Roger
Jeannine*. The Polish steamer *Zbaraz* (2,088 GRT) in convoy FN 223, was
badly damaged by German bombs 10 nautical miles (19 km; 12 mi) south of
the Aldeburgh Light Vessel, taken in tow by the tug *ST Olaves* but sank, with
no casualties and the survivors rescued by trawler *Vidonia* and tug *Muria*. The
Portuguese steamer *Alpha* (853 GRT) was sunk and the crew picked up by
destroyers HMS *Bedouin*, HMS *Tartar* and HMS *Mashona*.[562]

On 16 July the RAF had no losses and shot down a *KG* 54 Ju 88, a Do 17
intruder from 5.(Nacht)/*Jagdgeschwader* 1 (*JG* 1) was shot down by RAF
bombers. Next day, a He 111 and Ju 88 from III./*KG* 26 and I./*KG* 51 were
shot down and one 64 Squadron Spitfire was lost with the pilot wounded.[563]
The *Kanalkampf* was having a serious effect on Fighter Command. The number of losses on paper was not high but the attrition of continuous patrols, 80
percent over the sea and poor weather, tired pilots and slowed the training of
replacements. The dispersal by the *Luftwaffe* of its raids kept British pilots in
action rather than resting and Fighter Command lost a disproportionate number of experienced squadron leaders and flight commanders from the 1/3 of
the Fighter Command squadrons engaged.[564] The growing number of Hurricanes in RAF Maintenance Command, meant that each squadron was allotted
18 fighters, allowing two flights of six to operate and keep six in reserve for
training and maintenance.[565]

Figure 88: *Boulton Paul Defiants of No. 264 Squadron RAF, August 1940*

On 18 July, two 609 Spitfires were shot down by Ju 88s from I. and II./*KG* 54 which lost one Ju 88 destroyed and one damaged in return. A 603 Spitfire was damaged by a He 111 while *KG* 27 lost *Geschwaderkommodore Oberst* Bernhard Georgi and his crew killed in action by 145 Squadron Hurricanes for one Hurricane damaged. A 152 Squadron Spitfire was damaged and one 610 Squadron Spitfire was shot down by Bf 109s. One *LG* 1 Ju 88 fell to anti-aircraft fire while a *StG* 77 Do 17 reconnaissance aircraft was destroyed by 152 Squadron over a convoy.[566]

19 July

On 19 July nine convoys were at sea as German aircraft scouted the shipping lanes in the early morning. A Do 17 from 4.(F)/121 was shot down by 145 Squadron at 07:04. No 264 Squadron flying Boulton Paul Defiants, had operated with success over Dunkirk eight weeks earlier and its sister unit, 141 Squadron with twelve aircraft, was moved from West Malling to Hawkinge. The unit was inexperienced and while the aircraft were being fitted with Constant speed propellers in the early summer, the crews had little time to practice in the air; the gunners were uneasy about escaping their turrets in an emergency. Dowding and Park were dubious about the Defiant but ordered 141 Squadron to escort a convoy that morning.[567]

Osterkamp used a break in the weather to lead III./*JG* 51 on a patrol over the Dover area and spotted a formation of RAF aircraft at 12:45. Identifying them as Defiants, they attacked from the rear and below, to avoid return fire from the turret. Four Defiants were shot down on the first pass and another as it sought cloud cover.[568] The Bf 109s were interrupted by 111 Squadron which shot down a Bf 109 into the sea and the four surviving Defiants escaped, one crash-landed, one was written off and the other two were damaged. Osterkamp noted that the pilots' delight with their success was tempered with knowledge of their own mortality after this mission.[569]

Post-battle analysis suggested that the RAF controller failed to get the squadron airborne before the German aircraft arrived, because a scramble had only been ordered when German fighters had been seen by observers at RAF Hawkinge. The Bf 109s loitering with the advantage of height led to disaster for 141 Squadron.[570] The German pilots quickly learned to distinguish the Defiant from other fighters and did not consider it formidable. Dowding reported on the battle to Churchill, telling him that many men had died; Churchill acknowledged Dowding's misgivings with the Defiant and turned away. The surviving Defiants saw very little action for the remainder of the battle; 19 July was the worst defeat of Fighter Command during the battle, the RAF losing ten aircraft against four from the *Luftwaffe*. Encouraged by the *Luftwaffe* successes, Hitler made his last "appeal to reason" that day and millions of copies of the speech were circulated in Britain.[571]

Off Portland harbour, 87 Squadron intercepted Ju 87s without result and 64 Squadron shot down a Heinkel He 115 float plane mining the Thames Estuary. III./*KG* 55 lost a bomber to 145 Squadron and against Bf 109s, 1 and 32 squadrons lost a Hurricane each, 43 Squadron lost two and one damaged, two pilots were seriously wounded and one was killed; 141 Squadron lost ten crew killed and one wounded. Although the losses on this day were small numerically, the British fighters had been defeated in each engagement. The Germans were more experienced, operating in greater numbers and the Bf 109 units were fighting with greater flexibility. Operating at generally higher altitudes, the Finger-four formation tactic used by German fighter pilots proved far more effective than close British formations of British pilots. All the German pilots could scan the air but the British had to rely on the formation leader, while concentrating on tight formation-flying.[572]

At 12:15, *StG* 1 attacked the destroyer HMS *Beagle* off Dover and *Beagle* replied with its anti-aircraft guns and high-speed manoeuvres, to escape the deluge of bombs from 40–50 Ju 87s. Several near misses damaged *Beagle's* gyro and engines but there were no casualties and *Beagle* made it back to Dover. At 16:00, German formations appeared over Dover and nine Do 17's from *KG* 2 and Ju 87s from *StG* 1 bombed the harbour, attacking in shallow dives. Twenty-two bombs were dropped and the oiler *War Sepoy* blew up,

Figure 89: *HMS Brazen, sinking after the 20 July air attack.*

the tug *Simla*, the drifter *Golden Drift* and the destroyer HMS *Griffin* were damaged.[573]

Bosom and other convoys

20 July

Around midnight, a Focke Wulf Fw 200 *Condor* ventured too far inland and was shot down by ground defences near Hartlepool and another was lost over Northern Ireland. German records show the losses on different dates but British sources are clear that both losses occurred this night, while minelaying. Both machines came from *Kampfgeschwader* 40 (*KG* 40). At dawn (05:21), 12 Hurricanes from 54 Squadron were scrambled to engage a 40 German aircraft approaching the Thames Estuary. The *Luftwaffe* group had been ordered to the estuary after a convoy had been sighted but the report was mistaken. The German formation split into smaller groups, searching for the ships and British radar tracked the raiders but Hurricanes from 54 Squadron failed to intercept. Aircraft of 56 Squadron took off at 05:45, intercepted a formation of Ju 88s from *Kampfgeschwader* 4 (*KG* 4), and forced one down near St Osyth.[574]

Several of Lightvessels had been sunk along the coast, the vessels were tethered and the Trinity House crews could not manoeuvre. Radar usually picked up enemy raiders before they reached the target area but in poor light, the ships were very vulnerable. Both Keith Park and Leigh-Mallory were concerned the

Luftwaffe would attack lightships off the East Coast and they decided to put up aerial patrols over the coast near their anchorages.[575] Convoy Bosom sailed from Lyme Bay and Hurricanes from 238 Squadron chased off three Bf 109s; the Hurricanes spotted a *Seenotflugkommando 4* He 59 ambulance at 14:30 and shot it down, killing the four crew. As Bosom steamed eastwards, another He 59 from *Seenotflugkommando 1* arrived and shadowed the convoy and was attacked by 43 Squadron. A Hurricane was shot down and the pilot bailed out but drowned and the He 59 escaped into cloud. Aircraft from 601 Squadron took over and the Heinkel was shot down; the crew bailed out too low and their parachutes failed to open. As Bosom reached the RAF Kenley and RAF Biggin Hill sectors, there had been plenty of time for the He 59s to report it and Park ordered standing patrols of 24 fighters over Bosom, split evenly between Spitfire and Hurricane units.[575]

At 18:00 the *Luftwaffe* sent II./*StG* 1 to attack Convoy Bosom, the first mission for a week. I./*JG* 27 sent around 50 Bf 109s fighter escorts and a few Bf 110s, with Bf 109s from I. and II./*JG* 51 in support. Radar alerted British fighter units in good time and Hurricanes from 32 and 615 squadrons with high cover from 5 and 610 Squadron Spitfires had time to assemble and dive out of the sun. The escorts were unable to prevent the attack which damaged four Ju 87s and accounted for two destroyed, *Leutnant* Roden and his gunner being killed. The *Geschwader* (Wing) also lost its Do 17 reconnaissance machine shot down near the convoy. The Bf 110s stayed out of the action owing to the strength of the opposition but the Bf 109s reacted quickly and a 30-minute battle began over Bosom. Three Bf 109s were shot down by Spitfires from 615 Squadron. One Bf 109 from I. and II./*JG* 51 were lost to 32 and 65 squadrons and 32 Squadron lost a Hurricane and its pilot against *JG* 51 and 501 Squadron lost a fighter and its pilot. A Spitfire from 610 Squadron was written off and its pilot severely wounded.[575] The most notable German loss this day was *Hauptmann* Riegel, commanding officer of I./*JG* 27; James "Ginger" Lacey shot down two Bf 109s.[576] While the RAF fighters were dog-fighting, the Ju 87s attacked the convoy and the coaster *Pulborough* was blown to pieces. The Ju 87s then attacked the destroyer HMS *Brazen*, which was hit several times. *Brazen* snapped in half.[575,577]

21–26 July

On 21 July, Park established standing patrols of twelve fighters over a west-bound convoy that passed through the Strait of Dover that day. A Bf 110 over Goodwood and a Do 17 were shot down by 238 Squadron. The convoy reached the Isle of Wight at daybreak and Do 17s escorted by around 50 Bf 109s and Bf 110s from III./*JG* 27 and V./*LG* 1 attacked the convoy south of the Needles, where 43 Squadron engaged the formation, shooting down a Bf 109 and a Bf 110 for one pilot killed; 238 Squadron claimed the Bf 110 and

Figure 90: *Codrington was sunk on 27 July 1940 by He 111s.*

the Dorniers failed to damage the ships. The only other daylight action was the destruction of a Do 17 from 4.(F)/121 by Hurricanes of 145 Squadron and 23 July was quiet, a Ju 88 from 4.(F)/121 being shot down by 242 Squadron near Yarmouth. A small convoy passed the strait on 24 July and was attacked by Do 17s from *KG* 2. Spitfires from 54 Squadron intercepted the attack, no ships were hit and no aircraft were shot down.[578] In the afternoon, *StG* 1 sank the *Terlings* and the Norwegian steamer *Kollskegg*.[579]

A convoy had set out from Medway at 11:00 and was attacked by 18 Do 17s escorted by 40 Bf 109s from Adolf Galland's III./*Jagdgeschwader* 26 (*JG* 26). No ? Squadron attacked *JG* 26 while six 65 Squadron Spitfires joined in and 610 Squadron scrambled to cut off the return route but 65 Squadron could not destroy any of the Do 17s, because their defensive cross-fire was accurate and the formation kept tight, stopping the British fighters from breaking up the formation. *JG* 26 lost three two Bf 109s; one falling to Colin Falkland Gray, two pilots being killed and one wounded. Running low on fuel, the Bf 109s used the advantage of their fuel-injected engines to dive away. The RAF pilots thought that they had been shot down and claiming six, with eight probables. Bf 109s from III./*Jagdgeschwader* 52 (*JG* 52) covered the withdrawal of *JG* 26, ran into Spitfires from 610 Squadron, lost three and a Spitfire pilot was killed and one wounded during a force-landing. A Ju 88 from I./*LG* 1 and a He 111 from an unidentified unit were lost with their crews.[580]

Luftflotte 2 carefully timed fighter and bomber sweeps throughout 25 July to exhaust the RAF standing patrols. Once British fighter opposition had spent itself against the Bf 109s, large bomber formations could attack the convoys before reinforcements arrived. At noon, 65 Squadron was in action with *JG* 52, the Germans losing one fighter and its pilot for no loss to the British. Nine 32 Squadron Hurricanes and 11 from 615 Squadron engaged more than 40 Bf 109s in a dogfight near Dover and one Hurricane was badly damaged. As the battle receded, Ju 87s from 11.(Stuka)/*LG* 1 and III./*StG* 1 attacked the convoy. Distress calls from the ships were answered by 54 Squadron which sent nine Spitfires but Bf 109 fighters (unit unknown) shot down two Spitfires for no loss.[581]

Park noted the German attempts to saturate the defences and sent only small numbers of fighters over convoys until a bigger attack developed. In the afternoon, eight Spitfires of 64 Squadron engaged 30 Ju 88s from III./*KG* 4 escorted by over 50 Bf 109s. Three more Spitfires from 64 Squadron scrambled followed by 12 Hurricanes from 111 Squadron at Hawkinge, 111 Squadron using head-on attacks to break up the formation, which abandoned the attack with the Bf 109s covered their retreat. Soon afterwards a large raid appeared in the vicinity of Dover and a convoy was attacked by Ju 87s from Ju 87s from 11.(Stuka)/*LG* 1 and III./*StG* 1, off Folkestone, five ships being sunk and four damaged, including the destroyers HMS *Boreas* and HMS *Brilliant* before 56 Squadron arrived. The *Kriegsmarine* sent nine E-Boats against the convoy and hit three with gunfire. Three Spitfires from 64 Squadron and ten from 54 Squadron arrived and the Bf 109s kept the RAF fighters from the Ju 87s and shot down one Spitfire, killing its pilot; some of the Ju 87s were damaged by naval gunfire. Two Bf 109s from *JG* 52 were shot down by 610 Squadron.[581] Squadron Leader Thompson, the commander of 111 Squadron reported that he was twice attacked in error by Spitfires.[582]

On 26 July, *Fliegerkorps* VIII sent 30 Ju 87s to attack Convoy Bacon off Portland, which were intercepted by 238 Squadron Hurricanes, which shot down one before the Bf 109s escorts intervened. A second wave of Ju 87s and Ju 88s were protected by Bf 109s which countered 238 Squadron Hurricanes and 609 Squadron Spitfires, downing one of the later.[583] By dusk, the Admiralty had decided losses to merchant shipping had become prohibitive and cancelled all traffic through the Dover Strait.[499]

A 32 Squadron Hurricane was damaged and a pilot wounded, 54 Squadron lost three Spitfires and two pilots killed, 64 Squadron lost two Spitfires and one damaged with two pilots killed and 152 Squadron, lost a pilot killed by Bf 109s. II./*KG* 51 lost one Ju 88, *StG* 1 one Do 17 and a Ju 87. III./*JG* 27 lost one Bf 109 and *JG* 52 reported the loss of four Bf 109s. A *KG* 4 Ju 88 was lost over the Bristol Channel and a He 111 was shot down off Wick. The following day saw two losses for the *Luftwaffe* and one for the RAF as heavy rains engulfed the Channel.

27–28 July

Early on 27 July news reached *Luftflotte 3* in Paris that a large convoy was departing Portland and 30 Ju 87s from I./*StG* 77 took off from Caen at 08:00, picking up their Bf 109 escort from *JG* 27 en route. No. 10 Group RAF dispatched three Hurricanes from RAF Middle Wallop, arriving just as the Ju 87s began to attack and a Ju 87 was shot down before the Bf 109s intervened. Meanwhile, Bosom reached Swanage at 09:45 and a second wave of Ju 87s arrived to attack the ships. Nine RAF fighters tried to intercept but failed and lost a 610 Squadron pilot killed. Later on, Hurricanes from 615 Squadron shot down another He 59 off Deal. He 111s attacked shipping off Dover and sank the destroyers, HMS *Codrington* at Dover and HMS *Wren* off Aldeburgh with heavy bombs, *KG* 53 taking credit for the latter vessel, for the loss of a *KG* 53 He 111, probably to 504 Squadron.[584] The loss of two destroyers led the Admiralty to abandon Dover as an advanced base for destroyers.[585]

Sunday 28 July was sunny and clear when Spitfires of 234 Squadron were ordered to a plot south of Plymouth, found a II./*LG* 1 Ju 88 and shot it down with only two survivors. Big attacks were anticipated and the Biggin Hill, North Weald and Hornchurch sector controllers moved eight squadrons to Hawkinge, Manston and Martlesham.[586] At 13:50 a large raid was detected forming up and heading to Dover and 74 Squadron took off to intercept. Several other units were sent with instructions for the Hurricanes to attack bombers and Spitfires to engage the fighters. The bombers flew off to the south without bombing and Malan engaged I. and II./*JG* 51, led by *Geschwaderkommodore* Werner Mölders, on his first sortie over England. The Bf 109s were also engaged by 41 Squadron and Malan destroyed one Bf 109, then damaged a second.[587]

Three *JG* 51 Bf 109s were shot down with two pilots killed and one missing, three fighters force-landed, one with 20 percent damage and the other 50 percent; Mölders' machine was 80 percent damaged and he was wounded. 74 Squadron lost three Spitfires, with two pilots wounded and one killed. One Bf 109 from II./*JG* 27 and another from III./*JG* 53 force-landed, the pilots wounded, probably by 41 Squadron. Two Ju 88s from 9./*KG* 4 were damaged by anti-aircraft fire over the Thames Estuary, with one crew member killed and seven wounded. *Seenotflugkommando* 1 and 3 lost two He 59s, rescuing airmen in the Channel. *KG* 4 were engaged in mine laying operations in July.[588]

29 July

The dawn mist cleared and fine weather and cloudless skies promised much German activity. The Kent Sector Operations Room received news of a German build-up over Calais. Two convoys were in the Channel in the 11 Group area but the controllers waited. At 07:20 it became clear as the convoys passed the Dover Strait that Dover was the target and 11 Spitfires from 41 Squadron were ordered to attack the right flank and 12 Hurricanes of 501 Squadron from Hawkinge, the German left. The formation consisted of 48 Ju 87s from six *Staffeln* of IV.(*Stuka*)/*LG* 1, II./*StG* 1 and II./*StG* 3. The escort consisted of 80 Bf 109s from *JG* 51 and III./*JG* 26, the former led by Galland as Mölders was recovering from the wound received the day before.[589]

The leading escort formation was on the extreme right, looking down-sun at the *Stukas* but when 41 Squadron dived to attack the Ju 87s they were not seen by III./*JG* 26. *JG* 51 engaged the RAF fighters and the Spitfires split against the escorts. 41 Squadron lost one Spitfire shot down and its pilot killed, four damaged and forced to crash-land. While 41 Squadron fought the fighters, 501 Squadron attacked the Ju 87s as they began to dive and the harbour suffered little damage. *StG* 1 and *LG* 1 lost two *Stukas* each and II./*StG* 3 reported one damaged, 501 Squadron suffering no losses. The steamer *SS Gronland* was sunk in the outer harbour, having already been damaged in the attacks of 25 July and 19 crew were killed and the patrol yacht *Gulzar* was sunk but the crew were saved; *Sandhurst* was destroyed.[590] (The men of *Sandhurst* received six mentions in dispatches and the Dover port personnel were awarded four George Medals—the last to Tug Harbour Master Captain F. J. Hopgood.)

III./*KG* 76 sent Ju 88s under the British radar, to bomb the convoys from low altitude but the bombers scored no direct or near misses. The *Gruppenkommandeur*, Adolf Genth, was killed when he flew into a balloon cable off Dungeness and another was lost with its crew, when it was shot down by the escort ships. Observers called for fighter assistance and 610 Squadron Spitfires were sent but the Ju 88s were long gone. The other convoy was attacked by *KG* 2 after a Dornier from the Stab. *Staffel* reported its position and was then chased to the French coast by Spitfires from 85 Squadron, damaged and made a forced-landing at Saint-Inglevert Airfield. Eight Bf 110s from 1. *Staffel* and three machines from 2. *Staffel* were met near Dunkirk by 30 Bf 110 escorts from *ZG* 26 and were attacked by 151 Squadron Hurricanes. Two Hurricanes force-landed, the pilots unharmed, an Erpro 210 Bf 110 was damaged and *ZG* 26 suffered no losses, the attackers claiming hits on a 1,000 GRT and an 8,000 GRT ship.

At 19:25 III./*StG* 2 Ju 87s led by *Gruppenkommandeur* Walter Enneccerus sank the destroyer HMS *Delight* 13 nautical miles (24 km; 15 mi) off Portland. The ship was crippled and burning as the *Stukas* left the scene unchallenged

Figure 91: *A Spitfire overflies a ditching Bf 109*

and *Delight* made for the coast off Portland. The destroyers HMS *Vansittart* and *Broke* rescued 147 men and 59 wounded but 19 of the crew were killed. The burning vessel remained afloat until 21:30, when there was a large explosion and it sank. The Admiralty withdrew all destroyer flotillas from the Channel and ordered no convoy to sail the Channel in daylight. This order had been given on 26 July before *Delight* sailed and some sources note that standing orders had been broken.[591,592,593,594,595] The Admiralty had issued instructions to abandon the Dover area as a merchant route on 26 July and on 29 July, RAF reconnaissance discovered that the Germans were assembling long-range guns at Calais, the Admiralty ordered the abandonment of Dover as a base in favour of Harwich and Sheerness.[499] There was no desire on the part of the Admiralty to maintain a Destroyer division at Dover. Only one seaworthy destroyer, HMS *Vivacious*, remained. She was used to escort the crippled HMS *Walpole* and the damaged *Brilliant*, towed by the *Lady Brassey* to Sheerness. HMS *Skate*, the oldest destroyer in the navy, was lent to Dover Command by Portsmouth and the force was reinforced by HMS *Bulldog* until the return of the damaged vessels.[596]

The Germans viewed the British naval withdrawal and suspension of merchant traffic as a success but the lack of targets for the Germans, eliminated the need for Fighter Command to engage the *Luftwaffe* over the Channel. The Germans now had to fly into southern England, which put the Bf 109, the best German fighter, at the limit of its endurance. Hitler's Directive No. 17 expanded the scope of the air offensive from the English Channel to British airfields. When Göring held a meeting with the OKL staff at The Hague on 1 August, he emphasised the need for German fighters to conserve fuel, which remained a severe handicap for the Germans.[597]

The Admiralty suspended convoys until they could be better defended but in the last week of the month, the busiest of the *Kanalkampf*, 103 ships had been escorted in convoy through the straits. Losses to air attack amounted to 24,000 long tons (24,000 t) from 10 July – 7 August, substantially less than sinking caused by mines. Convoy escort was made a combined operation and Fighter Command sent bigger formations over the convoys, since smaller formations had been shown to be too vulnerable against the tactical advantages of greater numbers, height and surprise enjoyed by the *Luftwaffe*. The larger formations could not prevent attacks on convoys but the standing patrols were less likely to be overwhelmed by German fighters. A Mobile Balloon Barrage Flotilla (MBBF) of small ships was established to inhibit air attacks and first sailed with Convoy CW 9 on 4 August and later on kites were used instead of balloons, which were too vulnerable to gunfire. A Channel Guard of sailors was trained at the gunnery school at Portsmouth to use light machine-guns and two to three teams joined each westbound ship on the Thames. After the journey the guard joined eastbound ships or took the train back to Southend.[598]

The size of convoys was reduced by half and modern Hunt-class destroyers, better equipped for anti-aircraft operations, replaced the older escorts. More escorts were provided and convoys had minesweeper trawlers ahead, two destroyers in close escort, 3–4 anti-submarine trawlers, six Motor Anti-submarine Boats (MA/SBs) or Motor Launches, 6–8 MBBF balloon ships and larger formations of fighters overhead. More escorts could not prevent ships being sunk but the greater number of Fighter Command aircraft made dive-bombing much more difficult and losses never again became serious. On 5 August, CE 8 sailed east from Falmouth at night, sheltered in ports during the day and reached the Thames estuary with no losses. On 7 August, Convoy CW 9 sailed from the Thames Estuary with 25 ships and was attacked by E boats during the night, which sank three ships. By morning, when the *Luftwaffe* attacked, the remaining ships were scattered over 10 sq mi (26 km²) but the raid was intercepted by 145 Squadron and no ships were sunk.[599]

30 July – 6 August

On 30 July, Britain was covered in low cloud and continuous rain, Dowding expecting the Germans to use the weather to hide their attacks and patrols were sent over convoys and minesweeper units but the *Luftwaffe* did not operate in strength. He 111s from *KG* 26 harassed the Scottish coast from bases in Norway, near Suffolk two Bf 110s of *Erprobungsgruppe* 210 (ErpGr: development unit) stalking a convoy, were caught by Geoffrey Allard and his wingman and after a long chase one German aircraft was shot down. The following day the weather improved but haze covered southern England. The *Luftwaffe* attempted some raids but could not find their targets, the RAF made two interceptions and Hurricanes from 111 Squadron damaged a Ju 88 from III./*KG* 76.[600]

At 16:00, six squadrons with 30 Spitfires and 24 Hurricanes were scrambled to Dover where Bf 109s were strafing barrage balloons. The 12 Spitfires from 74 Squadron led by Malan, engaged two *Staffeln* of *JG* 2 under the command of Harry von Bülow-Bothkamp. A flight from 74 Squadron engaged the Bf 109s at equal height but the second flight was attacked while climbing and lost two Spitfires and one pilot killed. The day ended with one 7./*JG* 2 Bf 109 destroyed and one pilot wounded, in exchange for two Spitfires lost and one damaged; two RAF pilots were killed.

On 1 August, Dowding returned the establishment of fighter squadrons to the pre-Battle of France figure of 20 aircraft plus two in reserve. The number of Fighter Command pilots also increased and 1,414 pilots were in service in July, compared to the establishment of 1,454. The success of pilot training led Dowding to increase the figure to a minimum of 1,588 pilots, creating a paper deficiency, that led to the belief that Fighter Command was understaffed. The number of operational pilots never fell below the number available at the end of July. Dowding was more concerned by the dilution of pilot quality, losing more than 80 regular pilots and flight commanders, whose place was taken by less experienced men.[601]

A Henschel Hs 126 was shot down by 145 Squadron Hurricanes but the rear gunner killed one of the British pilots; both German airmen were posted missing. I./*KG* 4 crossed the coast near Norfolk, while Wing Commander Walter Beisiegel, the Coltishall Sector Controller, was busy organising convoy protection. The Boulton-Paul factories near Norwich and the Thorpe railway goods yards were damaged and the Germans escaped, despite the 66 and 242 Squadron airfields being 10 minutes flying time away. On 2 August, *KG* 26 He 111s attacked a convoy off Scotland and anti-aircraft fire brought one down on the deck of the steamer *Highlander*, which steamed to Leith, where the aircraft was displayed and another He 111 was shot down. *ErpGr* 210 sank the

590 GRT trawler *Cape Finisterre*. For the next five days both sides suffered virtually no combat casualties.[602]

Convoy Peewit

7 August

At 07:00 on 7 August 1940, Peewit, a coal convoy sailed from Southend and a Do 17 crew of *KG* 2 on patrol over the Channel spotted two minesweepers, which were searching for mines dropped by He 115s of *Küstenflieger-Gruppe* 106. The crew flew north into the North Sea, missing the large convoy approaching from the west and landed soon afterwards.[603] Peewit continued through the Channel and reached Dover at 14:30, with three Hurricanes from 85 Squadron covering the convoy. Winds were light but overhead fog down to 2,000 ft (610 m) gave the convoy cover, with visibility from 2–5 nautical miles (3.7–9.3 kilometres; 2.3–5.8 miles). As Peewit rounded Dover, it was escorted by Hurricanes from 32, 615 and 501 squadrons and just under four hours later, reached Dungeness unseen;As visibility improved, a German radar station at Wissant detected the convoy.

At 18:30 the sighting was relayed to the headquarters of Alfred Saalwächter, Commander-in-Chief of *Kriegsmarine* Group Command West. The information was then passed to Carl-Heinz Birnbacher, commander of 1. *Schnellboot-flottille* (1st Fast Attack Boat Flotilla) in Cherbourg. S-20, S-21, S-25 and S-27 (commanded by Siegfried Wuppermann, Götz Freiherr von Mirbach, Bernd Klug and Hermann Büchting) were ordered to readiness. The British ordered four Motor Torpedo Boats (MTBs) from Dover Command eastwards, to reconnoitre German movements among the French Channel ports. The MTBs sighted the German boats but did not engage, considering their mission was one of reconnaissance. Birnbacher suspected a trap took a position off Beachy Head and Newhaven and at 02:00 on 8 August, the attack began.[604]

Büchting sank SS *Holme Force* with torpedoes within a minute, the cargo of coke spilling into the sea and six of the 13 crew being killed. The British were surprised and thought that the noise of the S-Boats was an air attack; the Norwegian SS *Tres* stopped engines and avoided attracting attention and *Fife Coast* increased speed to 12 nautical miles (22 km; 14 mi) and zig-zagged. With surprise gone, the Germans fired flares to illuminate the ships and *Fife Coast* was seen and sunk. The destroyer *Bulldog* arrived but could do little in the darkness, its gunners struggled to see the fast E-Boats. *Polly M* steamed through the wreckage of *Fife Coast* and threw the Germans off. Her Captain, P. Guy, stated the vessel blew up. SS *Rye* survived an attack by S-27 (It was sunk on 7 March 1941 by the same vessel.) and Wupperman attacked SS *Polly M* and SS *John M*. The captains skilfully evaded torpedoes but Wuppermann

Figure 92: *RAF pilots examine a Ju 87, shot down while attacking a convoy.*

raked SS *Polly* with machine-gun and cannon fire, causing damage and the crew abandoned SS *Polly*. The crew re-boarded the next morning and the ship limped into Newhaven. SS *John* was fired on for nearly two hours but remained afloat. The E-Boat crews claimed to have sunk 17,000 GRT of shipping but only 2,588 GRT was sunk. At 04:20, Bristol Blenheims from 59 Squadron took off from Thorney Island to intercept the E-Boats but returned without success after three hours.

8 August

Next day dawned fine and Peewit was scattered over 10 square miles (26 km[2]), the leading ships with only the barrage balloon vessel HMS *Borealis* to guard against air attack. A Do 17P from 4.(F)/14 had been sent to report on the convoy and found 17 vessels south of Selsey Bill, the Dornier was spotted and the captain said "look, the angel of death". The Dornier reported the ships and *Fliegerkorps* VIII dispatched II. and II./*StG* 1 to attack the convoy.[605]

From 09:00–10:45, the Stukas (commanded by Major Paul-Werner Hozzel and *Hauptmann* Helmut Mahlke) dive-bombed the convoy, covered by Bf 109s from *JG* 27. The Dutch vessel SS *Ajax* (172) carrying a cargo of Wheat was sunk in five minutes, with four men killed and four wounded and SS *Coquetdale* was sunk with two men wounded.[606] 601 Squadron soon arrived for convoy escort but Spitfires from 609 and 234 Squadron arrived too late to engage, despite flying at full speed and three aircraft had to make emergency landings due to fuel shortage. Three Hurricanes from 145 Squadron made contact. Three more from the Squadron assisted. In a confused engagement, III./*StG* 1 lost two Ju 87s, II./*StG* 1 suffered one damaged and three Bf 109s were shot down by 145 Squadron for a loss of two Hurricanes and pilots at 09:00.[607,608]

In the late morning *StG* 2, 3 and 77 from Angers, Caen and St. Malo were escorted by Bf 110s from V./*LG* 1, to attack the convoy south of the Isle of Wight, with about 30 Bf 109s from II. and III./*JG* 27 for high cover. From 12:20, Spitfires of 609 Squadron and Hurricanes from 257 and 145 squadrons attacked the German formations, joined later by 238 Squadron. The Ju 87s severely damaged SS *Surte*, MV *Scheldt* and SS *Omlandia* and sank SS *Balmaha* soon after. SS *Tres* was sunk by *StG* 77. SS *Empire Crusader* in the lead, was hit by *StG* 2 and sank several hours later; four ships were sunk and four were damaged in the attacks. From 20–30 RAF fighters attacked the German aircraft and I. and II./*StG* 2 suffered one damaged Ju 87 each, *StG* 3 lost three Stukas from I. *Gruppe* and two damaged. *LG* 1 lost one Bf 110 and three damaged, *JG* 27 lost three Bf 109s and two damaged, the three lost pilots coming from II. *Gruppe*. Three Hurricanes from 238 Squadron were shot down and two pilots were killed by Bf 109s. Squadron Leader H. A Fenton, was wounded while shooting down a He 59 floatplane and rescued by the trawler HMS *Basset*. 64 Squadron lost a Spitfire and 65 Squadron lost two over Dover from 10:45–12:07, along with the three pilots in unrelated engagements; *JG* 27 lost nine Bf 109s.[609]

I./*StG* 1 tried to locate the convoy and while reporting 9/10 cloud cover, far from ideal for dive-bombing attack and the cloud-base ended from 3,500–4,000 feet (1,100–1,200 m) above the sea and Hozzel abandoned the mission. *Hauptmann* Waldemar Plewig the commander of II./*StG* 77 used his discretion to fly over the convoy from Le Havre in the unit Do 17P reconnaissance aircraft and found the conditions good enough for an attack and 82 Ju 87s from III./*StG* 1, I./*StG* 3 and Stab, II./*StG* 77 were alerted. Major Walter Sigel led *StG* 3 to rendezvous with escorts from Bf 110s from II./*Zerstörergeschwader* 2 (*ZG* 2, Destroyer Wing 2), *LG* 1 and Bf 109s from II./*JG* 27.[610]

III./*JG* 26, II. and III./*JG* 51 flew a fighter sweep to clear the skies before the attack and engaged Nos. 41, 64 and 65 Squadrons, claiming eight Spitfires around 12:55 CET. Among the claimants were Joachim Müncheberg (11th claim) and Gerhard Schöpfel (5th and 6th claims). Schöpfel claimed a Blenheim from 600 Squadron which was lost with its crew, after taking off from Manston in the midst of the battle.[611] A 64 Squadron Spitfire was shot

down with the pilot seriously wounded at 12:07 GMT, the same time and lo-
cation; 41 Squadron suffered no losses and probably damaged a Bf 109 of
II./*JG* 53 and one from III./*JG* 54 that arrived. Two Spitfires were lost by 65
Squadron at 10:45 GMT (earlier than the German claims at 12:55 CET.)[612]

The ships of CW 9 had sailed on and the anti-submarine yachts HMS *Wilna*,
HMS *Rion*, trawlers HMS *Cape Palliser*, *Kingston Chrysoberyl*, *Kingston
Olivine* and *Stella Capella* were attacked, having been sent to rescue survivors.
Cape Palliser and *Rion* were badly damaged; Fighter Command sent 145 and
43 squadrons to defend the convoy. Just after 16:00, three 145 Squadron Hurricanes were lost with their pilots against Bf 110s and three more were lost
from 43 Squadron, five of the pilots being killed. Three *StG* 77 Stukas were
shot down by 145 Squadron and four were damaged by 43 Squadron (two were
70 percent and 80 damaged). *LG* 1 suffered two damaged Bf 110s and three
Bf 109s from II./*JG* 27 were lost, two shot down by 43 Squadron and one was
damaged; no ships were hit and none were sunk. 152 and 238 squadrons tried
to intercept but failed to make contact with the attackers but 152 Squadron
met Bf 109s from *JG* 53 12 miles (19 km) south of Swanage and two Spitfires were damaged and force-landed, the pilots unhurt.[613] II./*JG* 53 claimed
two Spitfires and a Hurricane for no loss. II./*JG* 53 commanded by Günther
Freiherr von Maltzahn flew from Guernsey.[614]

Convoys Booty, Agent and Arena

11 August

The *Luftwaffe* flew few sorties from 9–10 August and *Adlerangriff* (Operation Eagle Attack) had not occurred. The events of 11 August 1940 increased
the ferocity and tempo of German air operations now that a large period of
clear and fine weather was predicted. The day's operation amounted to a co-
ordinated attack on No. 10, 11 and 12 Groups coupled with naval interdiction
activity in the Channel. Kesselring hoped to draw out and disperse Park's defences by sending out large numbers of single *Staffeln*. With the exception of
the early morning, Park did not take the bait. While a high proportion of No.
11 Group aircraft were forced into the air it did not achieve Kesselring's aim
of attracting enforcements from other RAF Groups.[615]

In the morning *Hauptmann* Walter Rubensdörffer led *Erprobungsgruppe* 210
and 17 Bf 110s on a strafing attack on Dover. Covered by a flight of Bf 109s
the escort dispatched three barrage balloons from No. 961 Balloon Squadron.
The Bf 110s released light bombs but did little damage. Park reacted by committing 74 Squadron (Adolph "Sailor" Malan). The unit ran into three *Staffeln*
of Bf 109s from *JG* 51. The closing speed was so fast a fleeting firing pass
was made by opposing the fighters which resulted in one British pilot ditching

Figure 93: *No. 85 Hurricane, by Squadron Leader
Peter Townsend at RAF Castle Camps, July 1940.*

in the sea, later to be rescued and Hurricanes of 32 Squadron tried to engage
the Bf 109s. I./*JG* 2 and 64 Squadron met and two Bf 109s were shot down,
one pilot was wounded and the other killed.

Park soon identified the naval base at Portland as the Germans' main objective
for the day. Radar detected a large build-up over the Cherbourg peninsula. He
ordered No. 609 and No. 1 Squadron up from Warmwell and Tangmere. Six
other units from Middle Wallop and Exeter, Tangmere and Warmwell were
ordered to readiness. Some 53 fighters were now involved. The enemy approached in strength in the late morning. Around 54 Ju 88s from I., and II./*KG*
54 were supported by 20 He 111s from *KG* 27. I., and II./*ZG* 2 provided 61
Bf 110s as escort which were reinforced by 30 Bf 109s from III./*JG* 2 under
the command of Erich Mix. *JG* 27 provided withdrawal cover. It was the
largest raid yet sent against a British target. Within a minute from 10:04, 145,
152, 87, 213 and 238 Squadrons were scrambled to support the two airborne
Squadrons.

The Bf 109s and Bf 110s arrived ahead of the bombers. 609 Squadron attacked, the flight containing future ace John Dundas. The battle commenced
at 23,000 feet (7,000 m). Squadron leader Horace Darley led the Spitfires onto
the flank of the enemy Bf 110s and fired full-deflection shots which enabled his

pilots to avoid the powerful frontal guns of the German heavy fighters. The attack shot down five of the Bf 110s. Among the dead was *Gruppenkommodore Major* Ott, shot down by Noel Agazarian. Most of the British units fell for the trap, and became engaged with the escort with only four 152 Spitfires spotting the bombers as they headed for Portland and Weymouth. The He 111s bombed from 15,000 feet (4,600 m) while the Ju 88s dropped to 10,000 feet (3,000 m) and hit the oil storage tanks. The destroyer HMS *Esk* was damaged at Harwich while HMS *Scimitar* and *Skate* were damaged in Portland. HMS *Windsor* was damaged off Botany Buoy. The armed trawler HMT *Edwardian* was run aground at North Foreland to prevent it sinking. The trawler *Peter Carey* was severely damaged and the steamer *Kirnwood* and tanker *Oil Trader* were hit.[616,617]

JG 27 were involved in combat as they covered the raid's withdrawal. *JG* 27 lost three of its number to 238 and 145 squadrons but the German fighters destroyed four 238 Hurricanes and killed four pilots while damaging another. 145 suffered two damaged and two destroyed and two pilots killed.[618] The massive dogfight resulted in the loss of 16 Hurricanes with 13 pilots killed and two wounded. A 152 Squadron Spitfire was lost and its pilot drowned. German losses amounted to six Bf 110s, five Ju 88s, one He 111 and six Bf 109s. The number of aircraft lost over the Channel prompted both sides to send forces out to locate survivors. Two Blenheims from 604 covered by 152 Squadron Spitfires scouted the Dover–Calais straits. They came across a solitary He 59 protected by Bf 109s. The Spitfires held off the German fighters while the Blenheims destroyed the He 59. 610 also caught and destroyed a He 59 but were attacked in-turn by Bf 109s and lost two pilots killed.

The day's events came to a close with a final German attack on convoys Booty, Agent and Arena. Walter Rubensdörffer led *ErpGr* 210 off the Harwich–Clacton coast at noon GMT. The Germans spotted the ships and began their bombing run against Booty. Rubensdörffer and his *Zerstörer* were accompanied by eight Dornier Do 17s from the specialist 9./*KG* 2, whose crews were trained for low-level attacks. Twenty Bf 110s from *ZG* 26 provided high cover for the bombers. The fighters were intercepted by Spitfires from 74 and 85 squadrons while six Hurricanes from 17 Squadron attacked. 85 Squadron led by Peter Townsend shot down three Bf 110s and the Hurricanes one more; two Bf 110s and three Do 17s were damaged. Rubensdörffer's group attacked and withdrew. It was followed by another raid, designed to catch those fighters already in combat when they were low on fuel and unable to assist. *ZG* 26 destroyed one Hurricane and damaged another from 17 Squadron killing one pilot. Two pilots from 74 Squadron were shot down and killed.[619,620]

The second wave of 45 Do 17s and a *Staffel* of Ju 87s from II./*StG* 1 and IV./*LG* 1 arrived over the Thames Estuary to hit Agent and Arena, which were hugging the coast. The formation was protected by Bf 109s belonging to *JG* 26 and led by Adolf Galland. 111 and 74 Squadrons were scrambled, with Malan leading, who claimed a Bf 109 which crash-landed in France. One *StG* 1 Ju 87 also fell to his unit before the Bf 109s arrived. German records say a 9./*KG* 4 Do 17 was lost to Hurricanes but no corresponding claim can be found in British records. 111 Squadron lost four Hurricanes and one crash-landed; four pilots were killed with two believed drowned. The weather forced the Germans to curtail operations in the early afternoon and the lull lasted until the following morning with *Adlertag*. The raid sank two naval trawlers—*Tamarisk* and *Pyrope* killing 12 seamen.[621]

On 12 August, on the same day *Adlertag* was launched, the Germans began to bombard convoys with heavy guns emplaced at Cap Gris Nez to protect an invasion force. Coaster crews sailing past at 5–6 kn (5.8–6.9 mph; 9.3–11.1 km/h) found the bombardments highly stressful but none of the ships were hit. After the operations against CW 9, the *Luftwaffe* campaign against inland targets and though the coastal convoys remained vulnerable the traffic continued. Losses to the *Luftwaffe* were only a small proportion of the 4,000,000 long tons (4,100,000 t) of shipping which sailed along the south coast during the *Kanalkampf* but at its peak, the *Luftwaffe* anti-shipping campaign damaged or sank $1/3$ of the ships off the south coast. Had losses continued at such a rate, it would have become impossible to find new crews for the ships. S. W. Roskill, the Royal Navy official historian, wrote in 1957, that the operations were costly for both sides; had the RAF failed to increase the convoy protection effort, the route would probably have been abandoned.[622]

Aftermath

Analysis

The *Kanalkampf* was the beginning of the Battle of Britain and occurred because the Germans needed time to establish airfields along the French and Belgian coasts for the air assault on south-east England and replace the losses of May and June. The German High Command and Hitler were also uncertain about how to proceed, and attacking shipping was the only way for the *Luftwaffe* to engage Fighter Command.

Hitler issued directive 16 on 16 July, for the preparation of an invasion fleet but Göring did not see an invasion as the solution to the British problem and failed to attend any of the conferences to improve inter-service co-operation for a landing in Britain before 1 August. Göring may still have believed that the British would negotiate and was content for the Channel battles to continue. On 19 July, Göring decided to escalate the air campaign and approved a directive to destroy British air power. Hitler issued Directive 17 on 1 August, intending the air operation to be a prelude to invasion, which expanded the scope of Göring's 19 July directive. The campaign against the RAF was to begin around 5 August, depending on suitable weather for mass air operations.[623,624]

Göring met his staff officers in The Hague, Netherlands on 1 August. Göring believed the inaccurate German intelligence dossiers from *Abteilung* 5 (the *Luftwaffe* Military Intelligence Branch), under the command of Joseph Schmid, that the RAF defences were weak and could be defeated within days. Göring hoped that an aerial victory would encourage the British to sue for terms, which would preclude a risky cross-Channel invasion against Royal Navy; Göring was confident the battle would be over quickly.[625,626,627,628] In the second week of August, *Luftflotten*, 2, 3 and 5, were ready to begin the assault on England proper. While the Channel battles and the campaign against shipping was sidelined, the air war intensified over English air bases.

Casualties

Kanalkampf

RAF and *Luftwaffe* aircraft losses

4 July – 11 August 1940[629]

Loss	RAF	*Luftwaffe*
shot down	115	215
damaged	42	92
total	157	307

In 1953, Richards wrote that from 10 July to 10 August the RAF shot down 227 *Luftwaffe* aircraft for a loss of 96 fighters.[630] In 1969, Mason wrote that the *Luftwaffe* lost 201 airmen killed, 75 wounded, 277 missing and 16 taken prisoner, 80 fighters destroyed and 36 damaged, 22 *Stuka* Dive bombers shot down and 22 damaged, 100 medium bomber losses and 33 damaged, 13 naval aircraft were destroyed and one damaged. Fighters: 53 Bf 109s were destroyed and 21 damaged, 27 Bf 110s shot down and 15 damaged; medium bombers: 24 Ju 88s shot down, 10 damaged, 28 Do 17s lost and 17 damaged, 33 He 111s destroyed and six damaged; air-sea rescue: 10 He 59s destroyed, one damaged and 3 He 115s destroyed.[631] Four E-boats of the *Kriegsmarine* were damaged or sunk.[632]

Mason listed an RAF loss of 71 pilots killed, 19 pilots wounded and 4 pilots missing; 115 fighters were destroyed and 42 damaged, of which: 45 Spitfires were shot down, 20 were severely damaged and four were lightly damaged, 64

Hurricanes were lost, twelve were severely damaged and six lightly damaged; six Defiants were shot down, 10 aircrew killed and two wounded.[633] The Merchant Navy and neutral states lost 35 ships sunk along with seven fishing vessels and the Royal Navy lost four destroyers, with at least 176 sailors killed among c. 300 casualties.[634]

Bibliography

<templatestyles src="Template:Refbegin/styles.css" />

- Bergström, Christer (2015). *The Battle of Britain: An Epic Conflict Revisited*. Oxford: Casemate. ISBN 978-1612-00347-4.
- Bertke, Donald A.; Kindell, Don; Smith, Gordon. (2011). *World War II Sea War: France Falls, Britain Stands Alone: Day-to-Day Naval Actions from April 1940 through September 1940*. Bertke Publications, Dayton Ohio. ISBN 9780578029412.
- Bishop, Ian. (2009). *Battle of Britain: A Day-to-Day Chronicle, 10 July – 31 October 1940*. Quercus Publishing, London. ISBN 978-1-84916-989-9
- Breffort, Dominique and Jouineau, Andre. (2009). *Messerschmitt Me 110: From 1939 to 1945, Messerschmitt's twin-engined fighters Bf 110, Me 210 and 410*. Histoire and Collections, Paris. ISBN 978-2-35250-144-2
- Bond, Brian. (1990) *France and Belgium, 1939–1940*. Davis-Poynter, London. ISBN 978-0-7067-0168-5
- Cull, Brian. (2013) *First of the Few: 5 June – July 1940*. Fonthill Media. ISBN 978-1781551165
- Bungay, Stephen. (2000) *The Most Dangerous Enemy: A History of the Battle of Britain*. London: Aurum Press. ISBN 978-1-85410-721-3
- Collier, B. (2004) [1957]. Butler, J. R. M., ed. *The Defence of the United Kingdom*[635]. History of the Second World War United Kingdom Military Series (Naval & Military Press ed.). London: HMSO. ISBN 978-1-845-74055-9. Retrieved 15 April 2016.
- Cooksey, Peter. (1983) *1940: The Story of No. 11 Group, Fighter Command*. Hale, London. ISBN 978-0709009078
- De Zeng, Henry L., Stankey, Douglas G. and Creek, Eddie. (2009). *Dive Bomber and Ground Attack Units of the Luftwaffe 1933–45, Volume 1*. Classic Publications, London. ISBN 978-1906537081
- Donnelly, Larry. (2004). *The Other Few: Bomber and Coastal Command Operations in the Battle of Britain*. Red Kite. ISBN 978-0954620127
- Evans, Arthur. (2010). *Destroyer Down: An Account of HM Destroyer Losses 1939–1945*. Pen and Sword, London. 978-1848842700

- Goodrum, Alastair (2005). *No Place for Chivalry: RAF Night Fighters Defend the East of England Against the German Air Force in Two World Wars*. Grub Street London. ISBN 978-1-904943-22-8
- Hague, Arnold. (2000). *The Allied Convoy System, 1939–1945: Its Organization, Defence and Operation*. Naval Institute Press. ISBN 978-1557500199
- Hinsley, F. H. (1994) [1993]. *British Intelligence in the Second World War. Its influence on Strategy and Operations*. History of the Second World War. abridged (2nd rev. ed.). London: HMSO. ISBN 0-11-630961-X.
- Hough, Richard and Denis Richards. (2007). *The Battle of Britain*: Pen & Sword. ISBN 978-1-84415-657-3
- Hooton, E.R.. (1994). *Phoenix Triumphant: The Rise and Rise of the Luftwaffe*. Arms & Armour Press. ISBN 978-1-86019-964-6
- Hooton, E.R.. (1997). *Eagle in Flames: The Fall of the Luftwaffe*. Arms & Armour Press. ISBN 978-1-86019-995-0
- James, T.C.G and Cox, Sebastian. (2000). *The Battle of Britain*. Frank Cass, London. ISBN 978-0-7146-8149-8
- Isby, David. (2005). *The Luftwaffe and the War at Sea, 1939–1945*. Chatham Publishing, London. ISBN 1-86176-256-9
- Korda, Michael. (2009). *With Wings Like Eagles: A History of the Battle of Britain*. Harper Books, London. ISBN 978-0-06-112535-5
- Heinz, Magenheimer. (2015). *Hitler's War: Germany's Key Strategic Decisions 1940–45*. Orion. ISBN 978-1-4746-0275-4
- Murray, Willamson. (1983). *Strategy for Defeat. The Luftwaffe 1935–1945*. Princeton, New Jersey: University Press of the Pacific. ISBN 978-0-89875-797-2.
- Mason, Francis. (1969). *Battle Over Britain*. McWhirter Twins, London. ISBN 978-0-901928-00-9
- Neitzel, Sönke. (2003). *Kriegsmarine und Luftwaffe Cooperation in the War against Britain, 1939–1945*. War in History, Volume 10.
- North, Richard. *The Many Not The Few: The Stolen History of the Battle of Britain* Continuum, London. ISBN 978-0754649113
- Overy, Richard J. *The Bombing War : Europe 1939–1945*. Allen Lane, London & New York. ISBN 978-0-7139-9561-9
- Parker, Nigel. (2013). *Luftwaffe Crash Archive: A Documentary History of Every Enemy Aircraft Brought Down over the United Kingdom*. Red, Kite. ISBN 978-1-906592-09-7
- Parker, Mathew. (2001). *Battle of Britain, July – October 1940*. Headline, London. ISBN 978-0-7472-3452-4
- Parker, Nigel. (2013). *Luftwaffe Crash Archive: Volume 1 1: A Documentary History of Every Enemy Aircraft Brought Down Over the*

United Kingdom, September 1939 – 14 August 1940. Red Kite, London. ISBN 978-1906592097

- Ray, John. (2009). *The Battle of Britain: Dowding and the First Victory, 1940*. London:Cassel Military Paperbacks. ISBN 978-1-4072-2131-1
- Richards, Denis (1974) [1953]. *Royal Air Force 1939–1945: The Fight At Odds*. London, HMSO ISBN 0-11-771592-1
- Roskill, S. W. (1957) [1954]. Butler, J. R. M, ed. *War at Sea*[636]. History of the Second World War United Kingdom Military Series. **I** (4th impr. ed.). London: HMSO. OCLC 881709135[637]. Retrieved 16 April 2016.
- Saunders, Andy. (2013). *Stuka Attack! The Dive-Bombing Assault on England During the Battle of Britain*. Grub Street, London. ISBN 978-1908-117359
- Saunders, Andy. (2010). *Convoy Peewit: August 8, 1940: The First Day of the Battle of Britain?*. Grub Street, London. ISBN 9781906502676
- Smith, Peter. (2007). *Naval Warfare in the English Channel: 1939–1945*. Pen and Sword, London. ISBN 978-1-844155-804
- *The Rise and Fall of the German Air Force*. Public Record Office War Histories. Air 41/10 (repr. ed.). Richmond, Surrey: Air Ministry. 2001 [1948]. ISBN 1-903365-30-9.
- Thompson, Adam. (2013). *Kustenflieger: The Operational History of the German Naval Air Service 1935–1944*. Fonthill Media. ISBN 978-1781552254
- Trevor-Roper, Hugh. (2004). *Hitler's War Directives; 1939–1945*. Birlinn. ISBN 1-84341-014-1
- Ward, John. (2004). *Hitler's Stuka Squadrons: The Ju 87 at War, 1936–1945*. London: Eagles of War. ISBN 978-1-86227-246-0.
- Weal, John. (1999). *Messerschmitt Bf 110 Zerstörer Aces of World War 2*. Botley, Oxford UK: Osprey. ISBN 978-1-85532-753-5.
- Weal, John. (1997). *Junkers Ju 87 Stukageschwader 1937–41*. Oxford: Osprey. ISBN 978-1-85532-636-1.
- Weal, John. (2007). *Jagdgeschwader 53 Pik-As*. Oxford: Osprey. ISBN 978-1-84603-204-2.
- Williamson, Gordon. (2011). *E-Boat Vs MTB: The English Channel 1941–45* Osprey, Oxford. ISBN 978-1849084062

External links

- Charles Gardner News Report Air Battle off Dover 14 July 1940[638]
- Film of a convoy attack, July 1940[639]
- CW convoy details (Convoy Web)[640]
- CE convoy details (Convoy Web)[641]

The blitz

The Blitz

The Blitz	
Part of the Western Front of World War II	

The undamaged St Paul's Cathedral surrounded by smoke and bombed-out buildings and houses in December 1940 in the iconic photo *St Paul's Survives*

Date	7 September 1940 – 11 May 1941 (8 months, 5 days)
Location	United Kingdom 51.50°N 0.12°W[642]Coordinates: 51.50°N 0.12°W[642]
Result	German strategic failure

Belligerents	
United Kingdom	Germany

Commanders and leaders	
• **Winston Churchill** • Hugh Dowding • Frederick Pile • Owen Tudor Boyd • Sir Leslie Gossage	• **Adolf Hitler** • Hermann Göring • Hugo Sperrle • Albert Kesselring • Hans Jeschonnek

Casualties and losses	
~40,000–43,000 civilians dead, ~46,000 injured figures for wounded possibly as high as 139,000	Unknown 3,363 aircrew 2,265 aircraft (Summer 1940 – May 1941)

The Blitz was a German bombing offensive against Britain in 1940 and 1941, during the Second World War. The term was first used by the British press and is the German word for 'lightning'.[643]

The Germans conducted mass air attacks against industrial targets, towns and cities, beginning with raids on London towards the end of the Battle of Britain in 1940, a battle for daylight air superiority between the *Luftwaffe* and the Royal Air Force over the United Kingdom. By September 1940, the *Luftwaffe* had failed and the German air fleets (*Luftflotten*) were ordered to attack London, to draw RAF Fighter Command into a battle of annihilation.[644,645] Adolf Hitler and *Reichsmarschall* Hermann Göring, commander-in-chief of the *Luftwaffe*, ordered the new policy on 6 September 1940. From 7 September 1940, London was systematically bombed by the *Luftwaffe* for 56 out of the following 57 days and nights.[646] Most notable was a large daylight attack against London on 15 September.

The *Luftwaffe* gradually decreased daylight operations in favour of night attacks to evade attack by the RAF, and the Blitz became a night bombing campaign after October 1940. The *Luftwaffe* attacked the main Atlantic sea port of Liverpool in the Liverpool Blitz and the North Sea port of Hull, a convenient and easily found target or secondary target for bombers unable to locate their primary targets, suffered the Hull Blitz. Bristol, Cardiff, Portsmouth, Plymouth, Southampton and Swansea were also bombed, as were the industrial cities of Birmingham, Belfast, Coventry, Glasgow, Manchester and Sheffield. More than 40,000 civilians were killed by *Luftwaffe* bombing during the war, almost half of them in the capital, where more than a million houses were destroyed or damaged.[647]

In early July 1940 the German High Command began planning Operation Barbarossa, the invasion of the Soviet Union.[648] Bombing failed to demoralise the British into surrender or do much damage to the war economy; eight months of bombing never seriously hampered British war production which continued to increase.[649,650] The greatest effect was to force the British to disperse the production of aircraft and spare parts.[651] British wartime studies concluded that cities generally took 10 to 15 days to recover when hit severely but exceptions like Birmingham took three months.

The German air offensive failed because the *Luftwaffe* High Command (*Oberkommando der Luftwaffe*, *OKL*) did not develop a methodical strategy for destroying British war industry. Poor intelligence on British industry and economic efficiency led to *OKL* concentrating on tactics rather than strategy. The bombing effort was diluted by attacks against several sets of industries instead of constant pressure on the most vital.[652]

Background

The *Luftwaffe* and strategic bombing

In the 1920s and 1930s, airpower theorists such as Giulio Douhet and Billy Mitchell claimed that air forces could win wars, obviating the need for land and sea fighting.[653] It was thought that bombers would always get through and could not be resisted, particularly at night. Industry, seats of government, factories and communications could be destroyed, depriving an opponent of the means to make war. Bombing civilians would cause a collapse of morale and a loss of production in the remaining factories. Democracies, where public opinion was allowed, were thought particularly vulnerable. The RAF and the United States Army Air Corps (USAAC) adopted much of this apocalyptic thinking. The policy of RAF Bomber Command became an attempt to achieve victory through the destruction of civilian will, communications and industry.[654]

The *Luftwaffe* took a cautious view of strategic bombing and *OKL* did not oppose the strategic bombardment of industries or cities and believed it could greatly affect the balance of power on the battlefield by disrupting production and damaging civilian morale. *OKL* did not believe air power alone could be decisive and the *Luftwaffe* did not have a policy of systematic "terror bombing". (The *Luftwaffe* did not adopt an official policy of the deliberate bombing of civilians until 1942.)[655]

> *The vital industries and transport centres that would be targeted for shut-down were valid military targets. It could be claimed civilians were not to be targeted directly, but the breakdown of production would affect their morale and will to fight. German legal scholars of the 1930s carefully worked out guidelines for what type of bombing was permissible under international law. While direct attacks against civilians were ruled out as "terror bombing", the concept of attacking vital war industries—and probable heavy civilian casualties and breakdown of civilian morale—was ruled as acceptable.[656]*

From the beginning of the National Socialist regime until 1939, there was a debate in German military journals over the role of strategic bombardment, with some contributors arguing along the lines of the British and Americans.[657] General Walter Wever (Chief of the *Luftwaffe* General Staff 1 March 1935 – 3 June 1936) championed strategic bombing and the building of suitable aircraft, although he emphasised the importance of aviation in operational and tactical terms. Wever outlined five points of air strategy:

1. To destroy the enemy air force by bombing its bases and aircraft factories and defeat enemy air forces attacking German targets.

Figure 94: *Walter Wever*

2. To prevent the movement of large enemy ground forces to the decisive
   areas, by destroying railways and roads, particularly bridges and tunnels,
   which are indispensable for the movement and supply of forces
3. To support the operations of the army formations, independent of railways, i.e., armoured forces and motorised forces, by impeding the enemy
   advance and participating directly in ground operations.
4. To support naval operations by attacking naval bases, protecting German
   naval bases and participating directly in naval battles
5. To paralyse the enemy armed forces by stopping production in armaments factories.[658]

Wever argued that *OKL* should not be solely educated in tactical and operational matters but also in grand strategy, war economics, armament production and the mentality of potential opponents (also known as mirror imaging).
Wever's vision was not realised, staff studies in those subjects fell by the way-
side and the Air Academies focused on tactics, technology and operational
planning, rather than on independent strategic air offensives.[659]

In 1936, Wever was killed in an air crash and the failure to implement his
vision for the new *Luftwaffe* was largely attributable to his successors. Ex-
Army personnel and his successors as Chief of the *Luftwaffe* General Staff,
Albert Kesselring (3 June 1936 – 31 May 1937) and Hans-Jürgen Stumpff (1

Figure 95: *Hitler and Göring, March 1938*

June 1937 – 31 January 1939) are usually blamed for abandoning strategic planning for close air support. Two prominent enthusiasts for ground-support operations (direct or indirect) were Hugo Sperrle the commander of *Luftflotte 3* (1 February 1939 – 23 August 1944) and Hans Jeschonnek (Chief of the *Luftwaffe* General Staff from 1 February 1939 – 19 August 1943). The *Luftwaffe* was not pressed into ground support operations because of pressure from the army or because it was led by ex-soldiers, the *Luftwaffe* favoured a model of joint inter-service operations, rather than independent strategic air campaigns.[660]

Hitler, Göring and air power

Hitler paid less attention to the bombing of opponents than air defence, although he promoted the development of a bomber force in the 1930s and understood it was possible to use bombers for strategic purposes. He told *OKL* in 1939, that ruthless employment of the *Luftwaffe* against the heart of the British will to resist would follow when the moment was right. Hitler quickly developed scepticism toward strategic bombing, confirmed by the results of the Blitz. He frequently complained of the *Luftwaffe*'s inability to damage industries sufficiently, saying, "The munitions industry cannot be interfered with effectively by air raids ... usually the prescribed targets are not hit".[661]

While the war was being planned, Hitler never insisted upon the *Luftwaffe* planning a strategic bombing campaign and did not even give ample warning to the air staff, that war with Britain or even Russia was a possibility. The amount of firm operational and tactical preparation for a bombing campaign was minimal, largely because of the failure by Hitler as supreme commander to insist upon such a commitment.

Ultimately, Hitler was trapped within his own vision of bombing as a terror weapon, formed in the 1930s when he threatened smaller nations into accepting German rule rather than submit to air bombardment. This fact had important implications. It showed the extent to which Hitler personally mistook Allied strategy for one of morale breaking instead of one of economic warfare, with the collapse of morale as an additional bonus.[662] Hitler was much more attracted to the political aspects of bombing. As the mere threat of it had produced diplomatic results in the 1930s, he expected that the threat of German retaliation would persuade the Allies to adopt a policy of moderation and not to begin a policy of unrestricted bombing. His hope was – for reasons of political prestige within Germany itself – that the German population would be protected from the Allied bombings. When this proved impossible, he began to fear that popular feeling would turn against his regime, and he redoubled efforts to mount a similar "terror offensive" against Britain in order to produce a stalemate in which both sides would hesitate to use bombing at all.

A major problem in the managing of the *Luftwaffe* was Göring; Hitler believed the *Luftwaffe* was "the most effective strategic weapon", and in reply to repeated requests from the *Kriegsmarine* for control over aircraft insisted, "We should never have been able to hold our own in this war if we had not had an undivided *Luftwaffe*."[663] Such principles made it much harder to integrate the air force into the overall strategy and produced in Göring a jealous and damaging defence of his "empire" while removing Hitler voluntarily from the systematic direction of the *Luftwaffe* at either the strategic or operational level. When Hitler tried to intervene more in the running of the air force later in the war, he was faced with a political conflict of his own making between himself and Göring, which was not fully resolved until the war was almost over. In 1940 and 1941, Göring's refusal to co-operate with the *Kriegsmarine* denied the entire *Wehrmacht* military forces of the *Reich* the chance to strangle British sea communications, which might have had strategic or decisive effect in the war against the British Empire.[664]

The deliberate separation of the *Luftwaffe* from the rest of the military structure encouraged the emergence of a major "communications gap" between Hitler and the *Luftwaffe*, which other factors helped to exacerbate. For one thing, Göring's fear of Hitler led him to falsify or misrepresent what information was available in the direction of an uncritical and over-optimistic interpretation of

Figure 96: *RAF pilots with one of their Hawker Hurricanes, October 1940*

air strength. When Göring decided against continuing Wever's original heavy bomber programme in 1937, the *Reichsmarschall's* own explanation was that Hitler wanted to know only how many bombers there were, not how many engines each had. In July 1939, Göring arranged a display of the *Luftwaffe's* most advanced equipment at Rechlin, to give the impression the air force was more prepared for a strategic air war than was actually the case.[665]

Battle of Britain

Although not specifically prepared to conduct independent strategic air operations against an opponent, the *Luftwaffe* was expected to do so over Britain. From July until September 1940 the *Luftwaffe* attacked Fighter Command to gain air superiority as a prelude to invasion. This involved the bombing of English Channel convoys, ports, and RAF airfields and supporting industries. Destroying RAF Fighter Command would allow the Germans to gain control of the skies over the invasion area. It was supposed Bomber Command, Coastal Command, and the Royal Navy could not operate under conditions of German air superiority.[666]

The *Luftwaffe's* poor intelligence meant that their aircraft were not always able to locate their targets, and thus attacks on factories and airfields failed to achieve the desired results. British fighter aircraft production continued at a rate surpassing Germany's by 2 to 1.[667] The British produced 10,000 aircraft in 1940, in comparison to Germany's 8,000.[668] The replacement of pilots and aircrew was more difficult. Both the RAF and *Luftwaffe* struggled to replace manpower losses, though the Germans had larger reserves of trained aircrew. The circumstances affected the Germans more than the British. Operating over home territory, British aircrew could fly again if they survived being shot down. German crews, even if they survived, faced capture. Moreover, bombers had four to five crewmen on board, representing a greater loss of manpower.[669] On 7 September, the Germans shifted away from the destruction of the RAF's supporting structures. German intelligence suggested Fighter Command was weakening, and an attack on London would force it into a final battle of annihilation while compelling the British Government to surrender.[670]

The decision to change strategy is sometimes claimed as a major mistake by *OKL*. It is argued that persisting with attacks on RAF airfields might have won air superiority for the *Luftwaffe*.[671] Others argue that the *Luftwaffe* made little impression on Fighter Command in the last week of August and first week of September and that the shift in strategy was not decisive.[672] It has also been argued that it was doubtful the *Luftwaffe* could have won air superiority before the "weather window" began to deteriorate in October.[673] It was also possible, if RAF losses became severe, that they could pull out to the north, wait for the German invasion, then redeploy southward again. Other historians argue that the outcome of the air battle was irrelevant; the massive numerical superiority of British naval forces and the inherent weakness of the *Kriegsmarine* would have made the projected German invasion, Unternehmen Seelöwe (Operation Sea Lion), a disaster with or without German air superiority.[674]

Change in strategy

Regardless of the ability of the *Luftwaffe* to win air superiority, Hitler was frustrated it was not happening quickly enough. With no sign of the RAF weakening and the *Luftflotten* suffering many losses, *OKL* was keen for a change in strategy. To reduce losses further, strategy changed to prefer night raids, giving the bombers greater protection under cover of darkness.[675,676]</ref>

It was decided to focus on bombing Britain's industrial cities, in daylight to begin with. The main focus was London. The first major raid took place on 7 September. On 15 September, on a date known as Battle of Britain Day, a large-scale raid was launched in daylight, but suffered significant loss for no lasting gain. Although there were a few large air battles fought in daylight later in the month and into October, the *Luftwaffe* switched its main effort to night attacks. This became official policy on 7 October. The air campaign soon got under way against London and other British cities. However, the *Luftwaffe* faced limitations. Its aircraft – Dornier Do 17, Junkers Ju 88, and Heinkel He 111s – were capable of carrying out strategic missions[677] but were incapable of doing greater damage because of their small bomb-loads.[678] The *Luftwaffe*'s decision in the interwar period to concentrate on medium bombers can be attributed to several reasons: Hitler did not intend or foresee a war with Britain in 1939; *OKL* believed a medium bomber could carry out strategic missions just as well as a heavy bomber force; and Germany did not possess the resources or technical ability to produce four-engined bombers before the war.[679]

Although it had equipment capable of doing serious damage, the *Luftwaffe* had unclear strategy and poor intelligence. *OKL* had not been informed that Britain was to be considered a potential opponent until early 1938. It had no time to gather reliable intelligence on Britain's industries. Moreover, *OKL* could not settle on an appropriate strategy. German planners had to decide whether the *Luftwaffe* should deliver the weight of its attacks against a specific segment of British industry such as aircraft factories, or against a system of interrelated industries such as Britain's import and distribution network, or even in a blow aimed at breaking the morale of the British population.[680] The *Luftwaffe*'s strategy became increasingly aimless over the winter of 1940–1941.[681] Disputes among *OKL* staff revolved more around tactics than strategy.[682] This method condemned the offensive over Britain to failure before it began.[683]

In an operational capacity, limitations in weapons technology and quick British reactions were making it more difficult to achieve strategic effect. Attacking ports, shipping and imports as well as disrupting rail traffic in the surrounding areas, especially the distribution of coal, an important fuel in all industrial economies of the Second World War, would net a positive result. However, the use of delayed-action bombs, while initially very effective, gradually had less impact, partly because they failed to detonate.[684]</ref> The British had anticipated the change in strategy and dispersed its production facilities, making them less vulnerable to a concentrated attack. Regional commissioners were given plenipotentiary powers to restore communications and organise the distribution of supplies to keep the war economy moving.[685]

Civil defence

Pre-war preparations and fears

London had nine million people – a fifth of the British population – living in an area of 750 square miles (1,940 square kilometres), which was difficult to defend because of its size.[686] Based on experience with German strategic bombing during World War I against the United Kingdom, the British government estimated after the First World War that 50 casualties – with about one third killed – would result for every tonne of bombs dropped on London.

Figure 97: *Barrage balloons flying over central London*

The estimate of tonnes of bombs an enemy could drop per day grew as air-craft technology advanced, from 75 in 1922, to 150 in 1934, to 644 in 1937. That year the Committee on Imperial Defence estimated that an attack of 60 days would result in 600,000 dead and 1.2 million wounded. News reports of the Spanish Civil War, such as the bombing of Barcelona, supported the 50-casualties-per-tonne estimate. By 1938, experts generally expected that Germany would attempt to drop as much as 3,500 tonnes in the first 24 hours of war and average 700 tonnes a day for several weeks. In addition to high-explosive and incendiary bombs, the enemy would possibly use poison gas and even bacteriological warfare, all with a high degree of accuracy.[687] In 1939 military theorist Basil Liddell-Hart predicted that 250,000 deaths and injuries in Britain could occur in the first week of war. London hospitals prepared for 300,000 casualties in the first week of war.

British air raid sirens sounded for the first time 22 minutes after Neville Chamberlain declared war on Germany. Although bombing attacks unexpectedly did not begin immediately during the Phoney War, civilians were aware of the deadly power of aerial attacks through newsreels of Barcelona, the Bombing of Guernica and the Bombing of Shanghai. Many popular works of fiction during the 1920s and 1930s portrayed aerial bombing, such as H. G. Wells' novel *The Shape of Things to Come* and its 1936 film adaptation, and others such as *The Air War of 1936* and *The Poison War*. Harold Macmillan wrote in 1956 that he and others around him "thought of air warfare in 1938 rather as people think of nuclear war today".[688]

Based in part on the experience of German bombing in the First World War, politicians feared mass psychological trauma from aerial attack and the collapse of civil society. In 1938, a committee of psychiatrists predicted there would be three times as many mental as physical casualties from aerial bombing, implying three to four million psychiatric patients.[689] Winston Churchill told Parliament in 1934, "We must expect that, under the pressure of continuous attack upon London, at least three or four million people would be driven out into the open country around the metropolis". Panic during the Munich crisis, such as the migration by 150,000 people to Wales, contributed to fear of social chaos.[690]

The government planned the evacuation of four million people – mostly women and children – from urban areas, including 1.4 million from London. It expected about 90 per cent of evacuees to stay in private homes, conducted an extensive survey to determine the amount of space available and made detailed preparations for transporting evacuees. A trial blackout was held on 10 August 1939 and when Germany invaded Poland on 1 September, a blackout began at sunset. Lights were not allowed after dark for almost six years and the blackout became by far the most unpopular aspect of the war for civilians, even more than rationing.[691] The relocation of the government and the civil service was also planned but would only have occurred if necessary so as not to damage civilian morale.[692]

Much civil-defence preparation in the form of shelters was left in the hands of local authorities and many areas such as Birmingham, Coventry, Belfast and the East End of London did not have enough shelters.[693] The unexpected delay to civilian bombing during the Phoney War meant that the shelter programme finished in June 1940, before the Blitz.[694] The programme favoured backyard Anderson shelters and small brick surface shelters; many of the latter were abandoned in 1940 as unsafe. Authorities expected that the raids would be brief and in daylight, rather than attacks by night, which forced Londoners to sleep in shelters.[695]

Communal shelters

Deep shelters provided most protection against a direct hit. The government did not build them for large populations before the war because of cost, time to build and fears that their safety would cause occupants to refuse to leave to return to work or that anti-war sentiment would develop in large congregations of civilians. The government saw the leading role taken by the Communist Party in advocating the building deep shelters as an attempt to damage civilian morale, especially after the Molotov–Ribbentrop Pact of August 1939.[696]

The most important existing communal shelters were the London Underground stations. Although many civilians had used them for shelter during

Figure 98: *Aldwych tube station being used as a bomb shelter in 1940*

the First World War, the government in 1939 refused to allow the stations to be used as shelters so as not to interfere with commuter and troop travel and the fears that occupants might refuse to leave. Underground officials were ordered to lock station entrances during raids but by the second week of heavy bombing, the government relented and ordered the stations to be opened. Each day orderly lines of people queued until 4:00 pm, when they were allowed to enter the stations. In mid-September 1940, about 150,000 people a night slept in the Underground, although by the winter and spring months the numbers had declined to 100,000 or less. Noises of battle were muffled and sleep was easier in the deepest stations but many people were killed from direct hits on stations.[697] In March 1943, 173 men, women and children were crushed to death at Bethnal Green tube station in a panic after a woman fell down the steps as she entered the station.[698]

Communal shelters never housed more than one seventh of Greater London residents.[699] Peak use of the Underground as shelter was 177,000 on 27 September 1940 and a November 1940 census of London, found that about 4 percent of residents used the Tube and other large shelters, 9 percent in public surface shelters and 27 percent in private home shelters, implying that the remaining 60 percent of the city stayed at home.[700,701] The government distributed Anderson shelters until 1941 and that year began distributing the Morrison shelter, which could be used inside homes.[702]

Figure 99: *A young woman plays a gramophone*
in an air raid shelter in north London during 1940

Public demand caused the government in October 1940 to build new deep shelters within the Underground to hold 80,000 people but the period of heaviest
bombing had passed before they were finished.[703] By the end of 1940 im-
provements had been made in the Underground and in many other large shelters. Authorities provided stoves and bathrooms and canteen trains provided
food. Tickets were issued for bunks in large shelters, to reduce the amount
of time spent queuing. Committees quickly formed within shelters as informal
governments and organisations such as the British Red Cross and the Salvation
Army worked to improve conditions. Entertainment included concerts, films,
plays and books from local libraries.[704]

Although only a small number of Londoners used the mass shelters, when
journalists, celebrities and foreigners visited they became part of the Beveridge
Report, part of a national debate on social and class division. Most residents
found that such divisions continued within the shelters and many arguments
and fights occurred over noise, space and other matters. Anti-Jewish sentiment
was reported, particularly around the East End of London, with anti-Semitic
graffiti and anti-Semitic rumours, such as that Jewish people were "hogging"
air raid shelters.[705] Contrary to pre-war fears of anti-Semitic violence in the
East End, one observer found that the "Cockney and the Jew [worked] together,
against the Indian".[706]

Figure 100: *Office workers make their way to work through debris after a heavy air raid*

No collapse of morale

Although the intensity of the bombing was not as great as pre-war expectations so an equal comparison is impossible, no psychiatric crisis occurred because of the Blitz even during the period of greatest bombing of September 1940. An American witness wrote "By every test and measure I am able to apply, these people are staunch to the bone and won't quit ... the British are stronger and in a better position than they were at its beginning". People referred to raids as if they were weather, stating that a day was "very blitzy".[707]

According to Anna Freud and Edward Glover, London civilians surprisingly did not suffer from widespread shell shock, unlike the soldiers in the Dunkirk evacuation.[708] The psychoanalysts were correct, and the special network of psychiatric clinics opened to receive mental casualties of the attacks closed due to lack of need. Although the stress of the war resulted in many anxiety attacks, eating disorders, fatigue, weeping, miscarriages, and other physical and mental ailments, society did not collapse. The number of suicides and drunkenness declined, and London recorded only about two cases of "bomb neuroses" per week in the first three months of bombing. Many civilians found that the best way to retain mental stability was to be with family, and after the first few weeks of bombing avoidance of the evacuation programmes grew.[709,710,711]

The cheerful crowds visiting bomb sites were so large they interfered with rescue work, pub visits increased in number (beer was never rationed), and 13,000
attended cricket at Lord's. People left shelters when told instead of refusing
to leave, although many housewives reportedly enjoyed the break from house-
work. Some people even told government surveyors that they enjoyed air raids
if they occurred occasionally, perhaps once a week. Despite the attacks, defeat in Norway and France, and the threat of invasion, overall morale remained
high; a Gallup poll found only 3 per cent of Britons expected to lose the war in
May 1940, another found an 88 per cent approval rating for Churchill in July,
and a third found 89 percent support for his leadership in October. Support
for peace negotiations declined from 29 per cent in February. Each setback
caused more civilians to volunteer to become unpaid Local Defence Volunteers, workers worked longer shifts and over weekends, contributions rose to
the £5,000 "Spitfire Funds" to build fighters and the number of work days lost
to strikes in 1940 was the lowest in history.[712]

Civilian mobilisation

The civilians of London had an enormous role to play in the protection of their
city. Many civilians who were unwilling or unable to join the military joined
the Home Guard, the Air Raid Precautions service (ARP), the Auxiliary Fire
Service and many other civilian organisations; the AFS had 138,000 personnel by July 1939. Only one year earlier, there had only been 6,600 full-time
and 13,800 part-time firemen in the entire country.[713] Before the war, civilians were issued with 50 million respirators (gas masks) in case bombardment
with gas began before evacuation.[714] During the Blitz, The Scout Association
guided fire engines to where they were most needed and became known as the
"Blitz Scouts". Many unemployed people were drafted into the Royal Army
Pay Corps and with the Pioneer Corps, were charged with the task of salvage
and clean-up.[715] The Women's Voluntary Services for Civil Defence (WVS)
was established in 1938 by the Home Secretary, Samuel Hoare, who considered it the female branch of the ARP.[716] The WVS organised the evacuation
of children, established centres for those displaced by bombing and operated
canteens, salvage and recycling schemes. By the end of 1941, the WVS had
one million members.

Pre-war dire predictions of mass air-raid neurosis were not borne out. Predictions had underestimated the adaptability and resourcefulness; in addition
there were many new civil defence roles that gave a sense of fighting back
rather than despair. Official histories concluded that the mental health of a
nation may have improved, while panic was a rare.[717]

Pre-war RAF night defence

British air doctrine, since Hugh Trenchard had commanded the Royal Flying Corps (1915–1917), stressed offence as the best means of defence.[718] Defensive strategy was based on offensive tactics, what became known as the cult of the offensive. To prevent German formations from hitting targets in Britain, Bomber Command would destroy *Luftwaffe* aircraft on their bases, aircraft in their factories and fuel reserves by attacking oil plants. This philosophy proved impractical as Bomber Command lacked the technology and equipment necessary for mass night operations, resources having been diverted to Fighter Command in the mid-1930s and it took until 1943 to catch up. Dowding agreed air defence would require some offensive action and that fighters could not defend Britain alone.[719] Until September 1939, the RAF lacked specialist night-fighting aircraft and relied on anti-aircraft units, which were poorly equipped and lacking in numbers.[720]

The attitude of the Air Ministry was in contrast to the experiences of the First World War when German bombers caused physical and psychological damage out of all proportion to their numbers. Around 280 short tons (250 t) (9,000 bombs) had been dropped, killing 1,413 people and injuring 3,500 more. Many people aged 35 or over remembered the bombing and greeted the threat of more with great trepidation. From 1916–1918, German raids had diminished against countermeasures which demonstrated defence against night air raids was possible.[721] Although night air defence was causing greater concern before the war, it was not at the forefront of RAF planning after 1935, when funds were directed into the new ground-based radar day fighter interception system. The difficulty RAF bombers had in night navigation and target finding, led the British to believe that it would be the same for German bomber crews. There was also a mentality in all air forces that flying by day would obviate the need for night operations and their inherent disadvantages.[722]

Hugh Dowding, Air Officer Commanding Fighter Command, defeated the *Luftwaffe* in the Battle of Britain, but preparing day fighter defences left little for night air defence. When the *Luftwaffe* struck at British cities for the first time on 7 September 1940, a number of civic and political leaders were worried by Dowding's apparent lack of reaction to the new crisis.[723] Dowding accepted that as AOC, he was responsible for the day and night defence of Britain but seemed reluctant to act quickly and his critics in the Air Staff felt that this was due to his stubborn nature. Dowding was summoned on 17 October, to explain the poor state of the night defences and the supposed (but ultimately successful) "failure" of his daytime strategy. The Minister of Aircraft Production, Lord Beaverbrook and Churchill distanced themselves. The failure to prepare adequate night air defences was undeniable but it was not

Figure 101: *Map of Knickebein transmitters*

the responsibility of the AOC Fighter Command to dictate the disposal of resources. The general neglect of the RAF until the late spurt in 1938, left few resources for night air defence and the Government, through the Air Ministry and other civil and military institutions was responsible for policy. Before the war, the Chamberlain government stated that night defence from air attack should not take up much of the national effort.

Technology

German night navigation devices

Because of the inaccuracy of celestial navigation for night navigation and target finding in a fast moving aircraft, the *Luftwaffe* developed radio navigation devices and relied on three systems: *Knickebein* (Crooked leg), *X-Gerät* (X-Device), and *Y-Gerät* (Y-Device). This led the British to develop countermeasures, which became known as the Battle of the Beams.[724] Bomber crews already had some experience with the Lorenz beam, a commercial blind-landing aid for night or bad weather landings. The Germans adapted the short-range Lorenz system into *Knickebein*, a 30–33 MHz system, which used two Lorenz beams with much stronger signals. Two aerials at ground stations were rotated so that their beams converged over the target. The German bombers would fly along either beam until they picked up the signal from the other beam. When a continuous sound was heard from the second beam the crew knew they were above the target and dropped their bombs.[725,726]

Knickebein was in general use but the *X-Gerät* (X apparatus) was reserved for specially trained pathfinder crews. *X-Gerät* receivers were mounted in He 111s, with a radio mast on the fuselage. The system worked on 66–77 MHz, a higher frequency than *Knickebein*. Ground transmitters sent pulses at a rate of 180 per minute. *X-Gerät* received and analysed the pulses, giving the pilot visual and aural directions. Three cross-beams intersected the beam along which the He 111 was flying. The first cross-beam alerted the bomb-aimer, who activated a bombing clock when the second cross-beam was reached. When the third cross-beam was reached the bomb aimer activated a third trigger, which stopped the first hand of the clock, with the second hand continuing. When the second hand re-aligned with the first, the bombs were released. The clock mechanism was co-ordinated with the distances of the intersecting beams from the target so the target was directly below when the bombs were released.[727]

Y-Gerät was an automatic beam-tracking system and the most complex of the three devices, which was operated through the autopilot. The pilot flew along an approach beam, monitored by a ground controller. Signals from the station were retransmitted by the bomber's equipment, which allowed the distance the bomber had travelled along the beam to be measured precisely. Direction-finding checks also enabled the controller to keep the pilot on course. The crew would be ordered to drop their bombs either by a code word from the ground controller or at the conclusion of the signal transmissions which would stop. The maximum range of *Y-Gerät* was similar to the other systems and it was accurate enough on occasion for specific buildings to be hit.

British counter measures

In June 1940, a German prisoner of war was overheard boasting that the British would never find the *Knickebein*, even though it was under their noses. The details of the conversation were passed to an RAF Air Staff technical advisor, Dr. R. V. Jones, who started a search which discovered that *Luftwaffe* Lorenz receivers were more than blind-landing devices. Jones began a search for German beams; Avro Ansons of the Beam Approach Training Development Unit (BATDU) were flown up and down Britain fitted with a 30 MHz receiver. Soon a beam was traced to Derby (which had been mentioned in *Luftwaffe* transmissions). The first jamming operations were carried out using requisitioned hospital electrocautery machines.[728] The counter-operations were carried out by British Electronic Counter Measures (ECM) units under Wing Commander Edward Addison, No. 80 Wing RAF. The production of false radio navigation signals by re-transmitting the originals became known as Meaconing using masking beacons (meacons).[685] Up to nine special transmitters directed their signals at the beams in a manner that subtly widened their paths, making it harder for bomber crews to locate targets; confidence in the device was diminished by the time the *Luftwaffe* was ready to conduct big raids.

German beacons operated on the medium-frequency band and the signals involved a two-letter Morse identifier followed by a lengthy time-lapse which enabled the *Luftwaffe* crews to determine the signal's bearing. The meacon system involved separate locations for a receiver with a directional aerial and a transmitter. The receipt of the German signal by the receiver was duly passed to the transmitter, the signal to be repeated. The action did not guarantee automatic success. If the German bomber flew closer to its own beam than the meacon then the former signal would come through the stronger on the direction finder. The reverse would apply only if the meacon were closer.[729] In general, German bombers were likely to get through to their targets without too much difficulty. It was to be some months before an effective night-fighter force would be ready, and anti-aircraft defences only became adequate after the Blitz was over, so ruses were created to lure German bombers away from their targets. Throughout 1940, dummy airfields were prepared, good enough to stand up to skilled observation. An unknown number of bombs fell on these diversionary ("Starfish") targets.

For industrial areas, fires and lighting were simulated. It was decided to recreate normal residential street lighting, and in non-essential areas, lighting to recreate heavy industrial targets. In those sites, carbon arc lamps were used to simulate the flash of tram cables. Red lamps were used to simulate blast furnaces and locomotive fireboxes. Reflections made by factory skylights were created by placing lights under angled wooden panels. The use of diversionary techniques such as fires had to be made carefully. The fake fires could only begin when the bombing started over an adjacent target and its effects were brought under control. Too early and the chances of success receded; too late and the real conflagration at the target would exceed the diversionary fires. Another innovation was the boiler fire. These units were fed from two adjacent tanks containing oil and water. The oil-fed fires were then injected with water from time to time; the flashes produced were similar to those of the German C-250 and C-500 *Flammbomben*. The hope was that, if it could deceive German bombardiers, it would draw more bombers away from the real target.

Figure 102: *Smoke rising from fires in the London docks, following bombing on 7 September*

First phase

Loge and *Seeschlange*

The first deliberate air raids on London were mainly aimed at the Port of London, causing severe damage. Late in the afternoon of 7 September 1940, the Germans began Operation London (*Unternehmen Loge*) (the codename for London) and *Seeschlange* (Sea Snake), the air offensives against London and other industrial cities. *Loge* continued for 57 nights.[730] A total of 348 bombers and 617 fighters took part in the attack.[731,732]

Initially the change in strategy caught the RAF off-guard and caused extensive damage and civilian casualties. Some 107,400 gross tons of shipping was damaged in the Thames Estuary and 1,600 civilians were casualties.[733] Of this total around 400 were killed.[734] The fighting in the air was more intense in daylight. *Loge* had cost the *Luftwaffe* 41 aircraft; 14 bombers, 16 Messerschmitt Bf 109s, seven Messerschmitt Bf 110s and four reconnaissance aircraft.[735] Fighter Command lost 23 fighters, with six pilots killed and another seven wounded.[736] Another 247 bombers from *Luftflotte* 3 (Air Fleet 3) attacked that night.[737] On 8 September the *Luftwaffe* returned; 412 people were killed and 747 severely wounded.

Figure 103: *Heinkel He 111 bomber over the Surrey Commercial Docks in South London and Wapping and the Isle of Dogs in the East End of London on 7 September 1940*

On 9 September *OKL* appeared to be backing two strategies. Its round-the-clock bombing of London was an immediate attempt to force the British government to capitulate, but it was also striking at Britain's vital sea communications to achieve a victory through siege. Although the weather was poor, heavy raids took place that afternoon on the London suburbs and the airfield at Farnborough. The day's fighting cost Kesselring and *Luftflotte 2* (Air Fleet 2) 24 aircraft, including 13 Bf 109s. Fighter Command lost 17 fighters and six pilots. Over the next few days weather was poor and the next main effort would not be made until 15 September 1940.

On 15 September the *Luftwaffe* made two large daylight attacks on London along the Thames Estuary, targeting the docks and rail communications in the city. Its hope was to destroy its targets and draw the RAF into defending them, allowing the *Luftwaffe* to destroy their fighters in large numbers, thereby achieving an air superiority. Large air battles broke out, lasting for most of the day. The first attack merely damaged the rail network for three days,[738] and the second attack failed altogether.[739] The air battle was later commemorated by Battle of Britain Day. The *Luftwaffe* lost 18 percent of the bombers sent on the operations that day, and failed to gain air superiority.[740]

Figure 104: *Bomb damage to a street in Birmingham after an air raid*

While Göring was optimistic the *Luftwaffe* could prevail, Hitler was not. On 17 September he postponed Operation Sea Lion (as it turned out, indefinitely) rather than gamble Germany's newly gained military prestige on a risky cross-Channel operation, particularly in the face of a sceptical Joseph Stalin in the Soviet Union. In the last days of the battle, the bombers became lures in an attempt to draw the RAF into combat with German fighters. But their operations were to no avail; the worsening weather and unsustainable attrition in daylight gave *OKL* an excuse to switch to night attacks on 7 October.[741,742]

On 14 October, the heaviest night attack to date saw 380 German bombers from *Luftflotte* 3 hit London. Around 200 people were killed and another 2,000 injured. British anti-aircraft defences (General Frederick Alfred Pile) fired 8,326 rounds and shot down only two bombers. On 15 October, the bombers returned and about 900 fires were started by the mix of 415 short tons (376 t) of high explosive and 11 short tons (10.0 t) of incendiaries dropped. Five main rail lines were cut in London and rolling stock damaged.[743]

Loge continued during October. 9,000 short tons (8,200 t) of bombs were dropped that month, about 10 percent in daylight, over 6,000 short tons (5,400 t) on London during the night. Birmingham and Coventry were subject to 500 short tons (450 t) of bombs between them in the last 10 days of October. Liverpool suffered 200 short tons (180 t) of bombs dropped. Hull and

Figure 105: *Firefighters tackling a blaze amongst
ruined buildings after an air raid on London*

Glasgow were attacked but 800 short tons (730 t) of bombs were spread out all over Britain. The Metropolitan-Vickers works in Manchester was hit by 12 short tons (11 t) of bombs. Little tonnage was dropped on Fighter Command airfields; Bomber Command airfields were hit instead.[744]

Luftwaffe policy at this point was primarily to continue progressive attacks on London, chiefly by night attack; second, to interfere with production in the vast industrial arms factories of the West Midlands, again chiefly by night attack; and third to disrupt plants and factories during the day by means of fighter-bombers.[745]

Kesselring, commanding *Luftflotte* 2, was ordered to send 50 sorties per night against London and attack eastern harbours in daylight. Sperrle, commanding *Luftflotte* 3, was ordered to dispatch 250 sorties per night including 100 against the West Midlands. *Seeschlange* would be carried out by *Fliegerkorps* X (10th Air Corps) which concentrated on mining operations against shipping. It also took part in the bombing over Britain. By 19/20 April 1941, it had dropped 3,984 mines, ⅓ of the total dropped. The mines' ability to destroy entire streets earned them respect in Britain, but several fell unexploded into British hands allowing counter-measures to be developed which damaged the German anti-shipping campaign.

By mid-November 1940, when the Germans adopted a changed plan, more than 13,000 short tons (12,000 t) of high explosive and nearly 1,000,000 incendiaries had fallen on London. Outside the capital, there had been widespread harassing activity by single aircraft, as well as fairly strong diversionary attacks on Birmingham, Coventry and Liverpool, but no major raids. The London docks and railways communications had taken a heavy pounding, and much damage had been done to the railway system outside. In September, there had been no less than 667 hits on railways in Great Britain, and at one period, between 5,000 and 6,000 wagons were standing idle from the effect of delayed action bombs. But the great bulk of the traffic went on; and Londoners—though they glanced apprehensively each morning at the list of closed stretches of line displayed at their local station, or made strange detours round back streets in the buses—still got to work. For all the destruction of life and property, the observers sent out by the Ministry of Home Security failed to discover the slightest sign of a break in morale. More than 13,000 civilians had been killed, and almost 20,000 injured, in September and October alone,[746] but the death toll was much less than expected. In late 1940, Churchill credited the shelters.[747]

Wartime observers perceived the bombing as indiscriminate. American observer Ralph Ingersoll reported the bombing was inaccurate and did not hit targets of military value, but destroyed the surrounding areas. Ingersol wrote that Battersea Power Station, one of the largest landmarks in London, received only a minor hit.[748] In fact, on 8 September 1940 both Battersea and West Ham Power Station were both shut down after the 7 September daylight attack on London.[749] In the case of Battersea power station, an unused extension was hit and destroyed during November but the station was not put out of action during the night attacks.[750] It is not clear whether the power station or any specific structure was targeted during the German offensive as the *Luftwaffe* could not accurately bomb select targets during night operations.[751] In the initial operations against London, it did appear as if rail targets and the bridges over the Thames had been singled out: Victoria Station was hit by four bombs and suffered extensive damage. The bombing disrupted rail traffic through London without destroying any of the crossings.[752] On 7 November, St Pancras, Kensal and Bricklayers' Arms stations were hit and several lines of Southern Rail were cut on 10 November. The British government grew anxious about the delays and disruption of supplies during the month. Reports suggested the attacks blocked the movement of coal to the Greater London regions and urgent repairs were required.[753] Attacks against East End docks were effective and many Thames barges were destroyed. The London Underground rail system was also affected; high explosive bombs damaged the tunnels rendering some unsafe.[754] The London Docklands, in particular the Royal Victoria Dock, received many hits and Port of London trade was disrupted. In some cases, the

Figure 106: *An anti-aircraft searchlight and crew at the Royal Hospital Chelsea, 17 April 1940*

concentration of the bombing and resulting conflagration created firestorms of 1,000 °C.[755] The Ministry of Home Security reported that although the damage caused was "serious" it was not "crippling" and the quays, basins, railways and equipment remained operational.[756]

Improvements in British defences

British night air defences were in a poor state.[757] Few anti-aircraft guns had fire-control systems, and the underpowered searchlights were usually ineffective against aircraft at altitudes above 12,000 ft (3,700 m).[758,759] In July 1940, only 1,200 heavy and 549 light guns were deployed in the whole of Britain. Of the "heavies", some 200 were of the obsolescent 3 in (76 mm) type; the remainder were the effective 4.5 in (110 mm) and 3.7 in (94 mm) guns, with a theoretical "ceiling'" of over 30,000 ft (9,100 m) but a practical limit of 25,000 ft (7,600 m) because the predictor in use could not accept greater heights. The light guns, about half of which were of the excellent Bofors 40 mm, dealt with aircraft only up to 6,000 ft (1,800 m).[760] Although the use of the guns improved civilian morale, with the knowledge the German bomber crews were facing the barrage, it is now believed that the anti-aircraft guns achieved little and in fact the falling shell fragments caused more British casualties on the ground.[761]

Figure 107: *3.7-inch anti-aircraft guns in Hyde Park London*

Few fighter aircraft were able to operate at night. Ground-based radar was limited, airborne radar and RAF night fighters were generally ineffective.[762] RAF day fighters were converting to night operations and the interim Bristol Blenheim night fighter conversion of the light bomber was being replaced by the powerful Beaufighter, but this was only available in very small numbers. By the second month of the Blitz the defences were not performing well.[763] London's defences were rapidly reorganised by General Pile, the Commander-in-Chief of Anti-Aircraft Command. The difference this made to the effectiveness of air defences is questionable. The British were still one-third below the establishment of heavy anti-aircraft artillery AAA (or ack-ack) in May 1941, with only 2,631 weapons available. Dowding had to rely on night fighters. From 1940 to 1941, the most successful night-fighter was the Boulton Paul Defiant; its four squadrons shot down more enemy aircraft than any other type.[764] AA defences improved by better use of radar and searchlights. Over several months, the 20,000 shells spent per raider shot down in September 1940, was reduced to 4,087 in January 1941 and to 2,963 shells in February 1941.[765]

Airborne Interception radar (AI) was unreliable. The heavy fighting in the Battle of Britain had eaten up most of Fighter Command's resources, so there was little investment in night fighting. Bombers were flown with airborne search lights out of desperation but to little avail. Of greater potential was the GL

Figure 108: *Boulton Paul Defiant night fighter N1671*

(Gunlaying) radar and searchlights with fighter direction from RAF fighter control rooms to begin a GCI system (Ground Control-led Interception) under Group-level control (No. 10 Group RAF, No. 11 Group RAF and No. 12 Group RAF).[766] Whitehall's disquiet at the failures of the RAF led to the replacement of Dowding (who was already due for retirement) with Sholto Douglas on 25 November. Douglas set about introducing more squadrons and dispersing the few GL sets to create a carpet effect in the southern counties. Still, in February 1941, there remained only seven squadrons with 87 pilots, under half the required strength. The GL carpet was supported by six GCI sets controlling radar-equipped night-fighters. By the height of the Blitz, they were becoming more successful. The number of contacts and combats rose in 1941, from 44 and two in 48 sorties in January 1941, to 204 and 74 in May (643 sorties). But even in May, 67 per cent of the sorties were visual cat's-eye missions. Curiously, while 43 per cent of the contacts in May 1941 were by visual sightings, they accounted for 61 percent of the combats. Yet when compared with *Luftwaffe* daylight operations, there was a sharp decline in German losses to one per cent. If a vigilant bomber crew could spot the fighter first, they had a decent chance of evading it.

Nevertheless, it was radar that proved to be critical weapon in the night battles over Britain from this point onward. Dowding had introduced the concept of airborne radar and encouraged its usage. Eventually it would become a success. On the night of 22/23 July 1940, Flying Officer Cyril Ashfield (pilot),

Figure 109: *Coventry city centre following 14/15 November 1940 raid*

Pilot Officer Geoffrey Morris (Observer) and Flight Sergeant Reginald Leyland (Air Intercept radar operator) of the Fighter Interception Unit became the first pilot and crew to intercept and destroy an enemy aircraft using on-board radar to guide them to a visual interception, when their AI night fighter brought down a Do 17 off Sussex.[767] On 19 November 1940 the famous RAF night fighter ace John Cunningham shot down a Ju 88 bomber using airborne radar, just as Dowding had predicted.[768] By mid-November, nine squadrons were available, but only one was equipped with Beaufighters (No. 219 Squadron RAF at RAF Kenley). By 16 February 1941, this had grown to 12; with five equipped, or partially equipped with Beaufighters spread over five Groups.[769]

Second phase

Night attacks

From November 1940 – February 1941, the *Luftwaffe* shifted its strategy and attacked other industrial cities.[770] In particular, the West Midlands were targeted. On the night of 13/14 November, 77 He 111s of *Kampfgeschwader* 26 (26th Bomber Wing, or KG 26) bombed London while 63 from KG 55 hit Birmingham. The next night, a large force hit Coventry. "Pathfinders" from 12 *Kampfgruppe* 100 (Bomb Group 100 or KGr 100) led 437 bombers from KG

Figure 110: *View from St. Paul's Cathedral after the Blitz*

1, KG 3, KG 26, KG 27, KG 55 and *Lehrgeschwader* 1 (1st Training Wing, or LG 1) which dropped 394 short tons (357 t) of high explosive, 56 short tons (51 t) of incendiaries, and 127 parachute mines.[771] Other sources say 449 bombers and a total of 530 short tons (480 t) of bombs were dropped.[772] The raid against Coventry was particularly devastating, and led to widespread use of the phrase "to conventrate". Over 10,000 incendiaries were dropped.[773] Around 21 factories were seriously damaged in Coventry, and loss of public utilities stopped work at nine others, disrupting industrial output for several months. Only one bomber was lost, to anti-aircraft fire, despite the RAF flying 125 night sorties. No follow up raids were made, as *OKL* underestimated the British power of recovery (as Bomber Command would do over Germany from 1943–1945). The Germans were surprised by the success of the attack. The concentration had been achieved by accident.[774] The strategic effect of the raid was a brief 20 percent dip in aircraft production.

Five nights later, Birmingham was hit by 369 bombers from KG 54, KG 26, and KG 55. By the end of November, 1,100 bombers were available for night raids. An average of 200 were able to strike per night. This weight of attack went on for two months, with the *Luftwaffe* dropping 13,900 short tons (12,600 t) of bombs. In November 1940, 6,000 sorties and 23 major attacks (more than 100 tons of bombs dropped) were flown. Two heavy (50 short tons

(45 t) of bombs) attacks were also flown. In December, only 11 major and five heavy attacks were made.[775]

Probably the most devastating attack occurred on the evening of 29 December, when German aircraft attacked the City of London itself with incendiary and high explosive bombs, causing a firestorm that has been called the Second Great Fire of London.[776] The first group to use these incendiaries was *Kampfgruppe* 100 which despatched 10 "pathfinder" He 111s. At 18:17, it released the first of 10,000 fire bombs, eventually amounting to 300 dropped per minute.[777] Altogether, 130 German bombers destroyed the historical centre of London.[778] Civilian casualties on London throughout the Blitz amounted to 28,556 killed, and 25,578 wounded. The *Luftwaffe* had dropped 18,291 short tons (16,593 t) of bombs.[779]

Not all of the *Luftwaffe* effort was made against inland cities. Port cities were also attacked to try to disrupt trade and sea communications. In January, Swansea was bombed four times, very heavily. On 17 January around 100 bombers dropped a high concentration of incendiaries, some 32,000 in all. The main damage was inflicted on the commercial and domestic areas. Four days later 230 tons was dropped including 60,000 incendiaries. In Portsmouth Southsea and Gosport waves of 150 bombers destroyed vast swaths of the city with 40,000 incendiaries. Warehouses, rail lines and houses were destroyed and damaged, but the docks were largely untouched.[780] In January and February 1941, *Luftwaffe* serviceability rates declined, until just 551 of 1,214 bombers were combat worthy. Seven major and eight heavy attacks were flown, but the weather made it difficult to keep up the pressure. Still, at Southampton, attacks were so effective morale did give way briefly with civilian authorities leading people *en masse* out of the city.

Strategic or "terror" bombing

Although official German air doctrine did target civilian morale, it did not espouse the attacking of civilians directly. It hoped to destroy morale by destroying the enemy's factories and public utilities as well as its food stocks (by attacking shipping). Nevertheless, its official opposition to attacks on civilians became an increasingly moot point when large-scale raids were conducted in November and December 1940. Although not encouraged by official policy, the use of mines and incendiaries, for tactical expediency, came close to indiscriminate bombing. Locating targets in skies obscured by industrial haze meant the target area needed to be illuminated and hit "without regard for the civilian population".[781] Special units, such as *KGr* 100, became the *Beleuchtergruppe* (Firelighter Group), which used incendiaries and high explosive to mark the target area. The tactic was expanded into *Feuerleitung* (Blaze Control) with the creation of *Brandbombenfelder* (Incendiary Fields)

Figure 111: *Children in the East End of London, made homeless by the Blitz*

to mark targets. These were marked out by parachute flares. Then bombers carrying SC 1000 (1,000 kg (2,205 lb)), SC 1400 (1,400 kg (3,086 lb)), and SC 1800 (1,800 kg (3,968 lb)) "Satan" bombs were used to level streets and residential areas. By December, the SC 2500 (2,500 kg (5,512 lb)) "Max" bomb was used.

These decisions, apparently taken at the *Luftflotte* or *Fliegerkorps* level, meant attacks on individual targets were gradually replaced by what was, for all intents and purposes, an unrestricted area attack or *Terrorangriff* (Terror Attack).[782] Part of the reason for this was inaccuracy of navigation. The effectiveness of British countermeasures against *Knickebein*, which was designed to avoid area attacks, forced the *Luftwaffe* to resort to these methods. The shift from precision bombing to area attack is indicated in the tactical methods and weapons dropped. *KGr* 100 increased its use of incendiaries from 13–28 percent. By December, this had increased to 92 percent. Use of incendiaries, which were inherently inaccurate, indicated much less care was taken to avoid civilian property close to industrial sites. Other units ceased using parachute flares and opted for explosive target markers. Captured German air crews also indicated the homes of industrial workers were deliberately targeted.

Final attacks

Directive 23: Göring and the *Kriegsmarine*

In 1941, the *Luftwaffe* shifted strategy again. Erich Raeder—commander-in-chief of the *Kriegsmarine*—had long argued the *Luftwaffe* should support the German submarine force (*U-Bootwaffe*) in the Battle of the Atlantic by attacking shipping in the Atlantic Ocean and attacking British ports.[783] Eventually, he convinced Hitler of the need to attack British port facilities.[784] At Raeder's prompting, Hitler correctly noted that the greatest damage to the British war economy had been done through the destruction of merchant shipping by submarines and air attacks by small numbers of Focke-Wulf Fw 200 naval aircraft and ordered the German air arm to focus its efforts against British convoys. This meant that British coastal centres and shipping at sea west of Ireland were the prime targets.[785]

Hitler's interest in this strategy forced Göring and Jeschonnek to review the air war against Britain in January 1941. This led to Göring and Jeschonnek agreeing to Hitler's Directive 23, *Directions for operations against the British War Economy*, which was published on 6 February 1941 and gave aerial interdiction of British imports by sea top priority.[786] This strategy had been recognised before the war, but Operation Eagle Attack and the following Battle of Britain had got in the way of striking at Britain's sea communications and diverted German air strength to the campaign against the RAF and its supporting structures.[787] The *OKL* had always regarded the interdiction of sea communications of less importance than bombing land-based aircraft industries.[788]

Directive 23 was the only concession made by Göring to the *Kriegsmarine* over the strategic bombing strategy of the *Luftwaffe* against Britain. Thereafter, he would refuse to make available any air units to destroy British dockyards, ports, port facilities, or shipping in dock or at sea, lest *Kriegsmarine* gain control of more *Luftwaffe* units.[789] Raeder's successor—Karl Dönitz—would—on the intervention of Hitler—gain control of one unit (KG 40), but Göring would soon regain it. Göring's lack of co-operation was detrimental to the one air strategy with potentially decisive strategic effect on Britain. Instead, he wasted aircraft of *Fliegerführer Atlantik* (Flying Command Atlantic) on bombing mainland Britain instead of attacks against convoys.[790] For Göring, his prestige had been damaged by the defeat in the Battle of Britain, and he wanted to regain it by subduing Britain by air power alone. He was always reluctant to co-operate with Raeder.[791]

Even so, the decision by *OKL* to support the strategy in Directive 23 was instigated by two considerations, both of which had little to do with wanting to destroy Britain's sea communications in conjunction with the *Kriegsmarine*. First, the difficulty in estimating the impact of bombing upon war production was becoming apparent, and second, the conclusion British morale was unlikely to break led *OKL* to adopt the naval option. The indifference displayed by *OKL* to Directive 23 was perhaps best demonstrated in operational directives which diluted its effect. They emphasised the core strategic interest was attacking ports but they insisted in maintaining pressure, or diverting strength, onto industries building aircraft, anti-aircraft guns, and explosives. Other targets would be considered if the primary ones could not be attacked because of weather conditions.

A further line in the directive stressed the need to inflict the heaviest losses possible, but also to intensify the air war in order to create the impression an amphibious assault on Britain was planned for 1941. However, meteorological conditions over Britain were not favourable for flying and prevented an escalation in air operations. Airfields became water-logged and the 18 *Kampfgruppen* (bomber groups) of the *Luftwaffe*'s *Kampfgeschwadern* (bomber wings) were relocated to Germany for rest and re-equipment.

British ports

From the German point of view, March 1941 saw an improvement. The *Luftwaffe* flew 4,000 sorties that month, including 12 major and three heavy attacks. The electronic war intensified but the *Luftwaffe* flew major inland missions only on moonlit nights. Ports were easier to find and made better targets. To confuse the British, radio silence was observed until the bombs fell. X- and Y-*Gerät* beams were placed over false targets and switched only at the last minute. Rapid frequency changes were introduced for X-*Gerät*, whose wider band of frequencies and greater tactical flexibility ensured it remained effective at a time when British selective jamming was degrading the effectiveness of Y-*Gerät*.

By now, the imminent threat of invasion had all but passed as the *Luftwaffe* had failed to gain the prerequisite air superiority. The aerial bombing was now principally aimed at the destruction of industrial targets, but also continued with the objective of breaking the morale of the civilian population.[792] The attacks were focused against western ports in March. These attacks produced some breaks in morale, with civil leaders fleeing the cities before the offensive reached its height. But the *Luftwaffe*'s effort eased in the last 10 attacks as seven *Kampfgruppen* moved to Austria in preparation for the Balkans Campaign in Yugoslavia and Greece. The shortage of bombers caused *OKL* to improvise. Some 50 Junkers Ju 87 *Stuka* dive-bombers and *Jabos* (fighter-bombers) were used, officially classed as *Leichte Kampfflugzeuge*

Figure 112: *Liverpool city centre after heavy bombing*

("light bombers") and sometimes called *Leichte Kesselringe* ("Light Kessel-rings"). The defences failed to prevent widespread damage but on some occasions did prevent German bombers concentrating on their targets. On occasion, only one-third of German bombs hit their targets.[793]

The diversion of heavier bombers to the Balkans meant that the crews and units left behind were asked to fly two or three sorties per night. Bombers were noisy, cold, and vibrated badly. Added to the tension of the mission which exhausted and drained crews, tiredness caught up with and killed many. In one incident on 28/29 April, Peter Stahl of KG 30 was flying on his 50th mission. He fell asleep at the controls of his Ju 88 and woke up to discover the entire crew asleep. He roused them, ensured they took oxygen and Dextro-Energen tablets, then completed the mission.[794]

The *Luftwaffe* could still inflict much damage and after the German conquest of Western Europe, the air and submarine offensive against British sea communications became much more dangerous than the German offensive during the First World War. Liverpool and its port became an important destination for convoys heading through the Western Approaches from North America, bringing supplies and materials. The considerable rail network distributed to the rest of the country.[795] Air attacks sank 39,126 long tons (39,754 t) of shipping, with another 111,601 long tons (113,392 t) damaged. Minister of Home Security Herbert Morrison was also worried morale was breaking, noting the defeatism expressed by civilians. Other sources point out that half of the 144 berths in the port were rendered unusable and cargo unloading capability was reduced by 75 percent. Roads and railways were blocked and ships could not leave harbour. On 8 May 1941, 57 ships were destroyed, sunk or damaged, amounting to 80,000 long tons (81,000 t). Around 66,000 houses were destroyed, 77,000 people made homeless; 1,900 people killed and 1,450 seriously hurt on one night.[796] Operations against London up until May 1941 could also have a severe impact on morale. The populace of the port of Hull became 'trekkers', people who made a mass exodus from cities before, during and after attacks. The *Luftwaffe* attacks failed to knock out railways or port facilities for long, even in the Port of London, a target of many attacks. The Port of London in particular was an important target, bringing in one-third of overseas trade.[797]

On 13 March, the upper Clyde port of Clydebank near Glasgow was bombed. All but seven of its 12,000 houses were damaged. Many more ports were attacked. Plymouth was attacked five times before the end of the month while Belfast, Hull, and Cardiff were hit. Cardiff was bombed on three nights, Portsmouth centre was devastated by five raids. The rate of civilian housing lost was averaging 40,000 people per week dehoused in September 1940. In March 1941, two raids on Plymouth and London dehoused 148,000 people.[798] Still, while heavily damaged, British ports continued to support war industry and supplies from North America continued to pass through them while the Royal Navy continued to operate in Plymouth, Southampton, and Portsmouth.[799] Plymouth in particular, because of its vulnerable position on the south coast and close proximity to German air bases, was subjected to the heaviest attacks. On 10/11 March, 240 bombers dropped 193 tons of high explosives and 46,000 incendiaries. Many houses and commercial centres were heavily damaged, the electrical supply was knocked out, and five oil tanks and two magazines exploded. Nine days later, two waves of 125 and 170 bombers dropped heavy bombs, including 160 tons of high explosive and 32,000 incendiaries. Much of the city centre was destroyed. Damage was inflicted on the port installations, but many bombs fell on the city itself. On 17 April 346 tons of explosives and 46,000 incendiaries were dropped from 250 bombers led by *KG* 26. The damage was considerable, and the Germans also used aerial mines. Over 2,000 AAA shells were fired, destroying two Ju 88s.[800] By the end of the air campaign over Britain, only eight percent of the German effort against British ports was made using mines.[801]

In the north, substantial efforts were made against Newcastle-upon-Tyne and Sunderland, which were large ports on the English east coast. On 9 April 1941 *Luftflotte 2* dropped 150 tons of high explosives and 50,000 incendiaries from 120 bombers in a five-hour attack. Sewer, rail, docklands, and electric installations were damaged. In Sunderland on 25 April, *Luftflotte 2* sent 60 bombers which dropped 80 tons of high explosive and 9,000 incendiaries. Much damage was done. A further attack on the Clyde, this time at Greenock, took place on 6 and 7 May. However, as with the attacks in the south, the Germans failed to prevent maritime movements or cripple industry in the regions.[802]

The last major attack on London was on 10/11 May 1941, on which the *Luftwaffe* flew 571 sorties and dropped 800 tonnes of bombs. This caused more than 2,000 fires. 1,436 people were killed and 1,792 seriously injured, which

Figure 113: *Firefighters at work amongst burning buildings, during the large raid of 10/11 May*

affected morale badly. Another raid was carried out on 11/12 May 1941. Westminster Abbey and the Law Courts were damaged, while the Chamber of the House of Commons was destroyed. One-third of London's streets were impassable. All but one railway station line was blocked for several weeks. This raid was significant, as 63 German fighters were sent with the bombers, indicating the growing effectiveness of RAF night fighter defences.

RAF night fighters

German air supremacy at night was also now under threat. British night-fighter operations out over the Channel were proving successful.[803] This was not immediately apparent.[804] The Bristol Blenheim F.1 carried four .303 in (7.7 mm) machine guns which lacked the firepower to easily shoot down a Do 17, Ju 88 or Heinkel He 111.[805] The Blenheim had only a small speed advantage to overhaul a German bomber in a stern-chase. Added to the fact an interception relied on visual sighting, a kill was most unlikely even in the conditions of a moonlit sky. The Boulton Paul Defiant, despite its poor performance during daylight engagements, was a much better night fighter. It was faster, able to catch the bombers and its configuration of four machine guns in a turret could (much like German night fighters in 1943–1945 with *Schräge Musik*) engage the German bomber from beneath. Attacks from below offered a larger target, compared to attacking tail-on, as well as a better chance of not being seen by the crew (so less chance of evasion), as well as greater likelihood of detonating its bomb load. In subsequent months a steady number of German bombers would fall to night fighters.[806]

Improved aircraft designs were in the offing with the Bristol Beaufighter, then under development. It would prove formidable but its development was slow. The Beaufighter had a maximum speed of 320 mph (510 km/h), an operational ceiling of 26,000 ft (7,900 m), a climb rate of 2,500 ft (760 m) per minute and its battery of four 20 mm (0.79 in) Hispano cannon and six .303 in Browning machine guns was much more lethal.[807] On 19 November, John Cunningham of No. 604 Squadron RAF shot down a bomber flying an AI-equipped Beaufighter, the first air victory for the airborne radar. In November and December 1940, the *Luftwaffe* flew 9,000 sorties against British targets and RAF night fighters claimed only six shot down. In January 1941, Fighter Command flew 486 sorties against 1,965 made by the Germans. Just three and twelve were claimed by the RAF and AA defences respectively.[808] In the bad weather of February 1941, Fighter Command flew 568 sorties to counter the *Luftwaffe* which flew 1,644 sorties. Night fighters could claim only four bombers for four losses.[809]

By April and May 1941, the *Luftwaffe* was still getting through to their targets, taking no more than one- to two-percent losses per mission.[810] On 19/20 April 1941, in honour of Hitler's 52nd birthday, 712 bombers hit Plymouth with a record 1,000 tons of bombs. Losses were minimal. In the following month, 22 German bombers were lost with 13 confirmed to have been shot down by night fighters. On 3/4 May, nine were shot down in one night. On 10/11 May, London suffered severe damage, but 10 German bombers were downed. In May 1941, RAF night fighters shot down 38 German bombers.[811] By the end of May, Kesselring's *Luftflotte* 2 had been withdrawn, leaving Hugo Sperrle's *Luftflotte* 3 as a token force to maintain the illusion of strategic bombing. Hitler now had his sights set on attacking the USSR with Operation Barbarossa, and the Blitz came to end.[812]

Aftermath

Luftwaffe losses

Between 20 June 1940, when the first German air operations began over Britain, and 31 March 1941, *OKL* recorded the loss of 2,265 aircraft over the British Isles, a quarter of them fighters and one third bombers. At least 3,363 *Luftwaffe* aircrew were killed, 2,641 missing and 2,117 wounded.[813] Total losses could have been as high as 600 bombers, just 1.5 per cent of the sorties flown. A significant number of the aircraft not shot down after the resort to night bombing were wrecked during landings or crashed in bad weather.[814]

Effectiveness of bombing

British output index

September 1940 – May 1941[815,816] </ref>

Month	Output
1940	
September	217
October	245
November	242
December	239
1941	
January	244
February	266
March	303
April	284
May	319

The military effectiveness of bombing varied, the *Luftwaffe* dropped around 45,000 short tons (41,000 t) of bombs during the Blitz, which disrupted production and transport, reduced food supplies and shook the British morale. The bombing also helped to support the U-boat blockade, by sinking some 58,000 long tons (59,000 t) of shipping and damaging 450,000 long tons (460,000 t) more. Despite the bombing, British production rose steadily throughout this period although there were significant falls during April 1941, probably influenced by the departure of workers for Easter Holidays, according to the British official history. The official history volume *British War Production* (Postan, 1952) noted that the greatest effect on output of warlike stores, was on the supply of components and dispersal of production rather than complete equipments.[817,818]

In aircraft production, the British were denied the opportunity to reach the planned target of 2,500 aircraft in a month, arguably the greatest achievement of the bombing, as it forced the dispersal of the industry, at first because of damage to aircraft factories and then by a policy of precautionary dispersal.[651] In April 1941, when the targets were British ports, rifle production fell by 25 per cent, filled-shell production by 4.6 per cent and in small-arms production 4.5 per cent. The strategic impact on industrial cities was varied; most took from 10–15 days to recover from heavy raids, although Belfast and Liverpool took longer. The attacks against Birmingham took war industries some three months to recover fully. The exhausted population took three weeks to overcome the effects of an attack.

The air offensive against the RAF and British industry failed to have the desired effect. More might have been achieved had *OKL* exploited the vulnerability of British sea communications. The Allies did so later when Bomber Command attacked rail communications and the United States Army Air Forces targeted oil but that would have required an economic-industrial analysis of which the *Luftwaffe* was incapable. *OKL* instead sought clusters of targets that suited the latest policy (which changed frequently) and disputes within the leadership were about tactics rather than strategy.[819] Though militarily ineffective, the Blitz cost around 41,000 lives, may have injured another 139,000 people and did enormous damage to British infrastructure and housing stock.

RAF evaluation

The British began to assess the impact of the Blitz in August 1941 and the RAF Air Staff used the German experience to improve Bomber Command's offensives. They concluded bombers should strike a single target each night and use more incendiaries, because they had a greater impact on production than high explosives. They also noted regional production was severely disrupted when city centres were devastated through the loss of administrative offices, utilities and transport. They believed the *Luftwaffe* had failed in precision attack and concluded the German example of area attack using incendiaries was the way forward for operations over Germany.

Some writers claim the Air Staff ignored a critical lesson, that British morale did not break and that attacking German morale was not sufficient to induce a collapse. Aviation strategists dispute that morale was ever a major consideration for Bomber Command. Throughout 1933–39 none of the 16 Western Air Plans drafted mentioned morale as a target. The first three directives in 1940 did not mention civilian populations or morale in any way. Morale was not mentioned until the ninth wartime directive on 21 September 1940.[820] The 10th directive in October 1940 mentioned morale by name but industrial cities were only to be targeted if weather prevented raids on oil targets.[821]

The AOC Bomber Command, Arthur Harris, who did see German morale as an objective, did not believe that the morale-collapse could occur without the destruction of the German economy. The primary goal of Bomber Command was to destroy the German industrial base (economic warfare) and in doing so reduce morale. In late 1943, just before the Battle of Berlin, Harris declared the power of Bomber Command would enable it to achieve "a state of devastation

Figure 114: *Women salvaging possessions from*
their bombed house, including plants and a clock

in which surrender is inevitable".[822] A summary of Harris' strategic intentions
was clear,

> *From 1943 to the end of the war, he [Harris] and other proponents of the*
> *area offensive represented it [the bomber offensive] less as an attack on*
> *morale than as an assault on the housing, utilities, communications, and*
> *other services that supported the war production effort.*

—*Hall*

in comparison to the Allied bombing campaign against Germany, casualties
due to the Blitz were relatively low; the bombing of Hamburg alone inflicted
about 40,000 civilian casualties.[823]

Popular imagery and propaganda

A converse popular image arose of British people in the Second World War:
a collection of people locked in national solidarity. This image entered the
historiography of the Second World War in the 1980s and 1990s, especially
after the publication of Angus Calder's book *The Myth of the Blitz* (1991).
It was evoked by both the right and left political factions in Britain during
the Falklands War when it was embedded in a nostalgic narrative in which

the Second World War represented aggressive British patriotism successfully defending democracy.[824,825] This imagery of people in the Blitz was and is powerfully portrayed in film, radio, newspapers and magazines.[826] At the time it was a useful propaganda tool for home and foreign consumption.[827] Historians' critical response to this construction focused on what were seen as over-emphasised claims of righteous nationalism and national unity. In the *Myth of the Blitz*, Calder exposed some of the counter-evidence of anti-social and divisive behaviours. What he saw as the myth – serene national unity – became "historical truth". In particular, class division was most evident.

Raids during the Blitz produced the greatest divisions and morale effects in the working-class areas. Lack of sleep, insufficient shelters and inefficiency of warning systems were causes. The loss of sleep was a particular factor, with many not bothering to attend inconvenient shelters. The Communist Party made political capital out of these difficulties.[828] In the wake of the Coventry Blitz, there was widespread agitation from the Communist Party over the need for bomb-proof shelters. Many Londoners, in particular, took to using the Underground railway system, without authority, for shelter and sleeping through the night. So worried were the Government over the sudden campaign of leaflets and posters distributed by the Communist Party in Coventry and London, that the police were sent to seize their production facilities. The Government, up until November 1940, was opposed to the centralised organisation of shelter. Home Secretary Sir John Anderson was replaced by Morrison soon afterwards, in the wake of a Cabinet reshuffle as the dying Neville Chamberlain resigned. Morrison warned that he could not counter the Communist unrest unless provision of shelters were made. He recognised the right of the public to seize tube stations and authorised plans to improve their condition and expand them by tunnelling. Still, many British citizens, who had been members of the Labour Party, itself inert over the issue, turned to the Communist Party. The Communists attempted to blame the damage and casualties of the Coventry raid on the rich factory owners, big business and landowning interests and called for a negotiated peace. Though they failed to make a large gain in influence, the membership of the Party had doubled by June 1941.[829] The "Communist threat" was deemed important enough for Herbert Morrison to order, with the support of the Cabinet, the stoppage of the *Daily Worker* and *The Week*; the Communist newspaper and journal.[830]

The brief success of the Communists also fed into the hands of the British Union of Fascists (BUF). Anti-Semitic attitudes became widespread, particularly in London. Rumours that Jewish support was underpinning the Communist surge were frequent. Rumours that Jews were inflating prices, were responsible for the Black Market, were the first to panic under attack (even the cause of the panic) and secured the best shelters via underhanded methods, were also widespread. There was also racial antagonism between the small Black, Indian and Jewish communities but there were no race riots despite the mixing of different peoples in confined areas.[831]

In other cities, class conflict was more evident. Over a quarter of London's population had left the city by November 1940. Civilians left for more remote areas of the country. Upsurges in population in south Wales and Gloucester intimated where these displaced people went. Other reasons, including industry dispersal may have been a factor. However, resentment of rich self-evacuees or hostile treatment of poor ones were signs of persistence of class resentments although these factors did not appear to threaten social order.[832] The total number of evacuees numbered 1.4 million, including a high proportion from the poorest inner-city families. Reception committees were completely unprepared for the condition of some of the children. Far from displaying the nation's unity in time of war, the scheme backfired, often aggravating class antagonism and bolstering prejudice about the urban poor. Within four months, 88 per cent of evacuated mothers, 86 per cent of small children, and 43 per cent of school children had been returned home. The lack of bombing in the Phoney War contributed significantly to the return of people to the cities, but class conflict was not eased a year later when evacuation operations had to be put into effect again.

Archive audio recordings

In recent years a large number of wartime recordings relating to the Blitz have been made available on audiobooks such as *The Blitz*, *The Home Front* and *British War Broadcasting*. These collections include period interviews with civilians, servicemen, aircrew, politicians and Civil Defence personnel, as well as Blitz actuality recordings, news bulletins and public information broadcasts. Notable interviews include Thomas Alderson, the first recipient of the George Cross, John Cormack, who survived eight days trapped beneath rubble on Clydeside, and Herbert Morrison's famous "Britain shall not burn" appeal for more fireguards in December 1940.[833]

Bombsite rubble

In one 6-month period, 750,000 tons of bombsite rubble from London were transported by railway on 1,700 freight trains to make runways on Bomber Command airfields in East Anglia. Bombsite rubble from Birmingham was used to make runways on US Air Force bases in Kent and Essex in southeast England.[834] Many sites of bombed buildings, when cleared of rubble, were cultivated to grow vegetables to ease wartime food shortages and were known as victory gardens.[835]

Tables

Bombing raid statistics

Below is a table by city of the number of major raids (where at least 100 tons
of bombs were dropped) and tonnage of bombs dropped during these major
raids. Smaller raids are not included in the tonnages.

Big raids and combined bomb tonnage[836]

City	tons	Raids
London	18,291	71
Liverpool/ Merseyside	1,957	8
Birmingham	1,852	8
Glasgow/ Clydeside	1,329	5
Plymouth	1,228	8
Bristol	919	6
Exeter	75	19
Coventry	818	2
Portsmouth	687	3
Southampton	647	4
Hull	593	3
Manchester	578	3
Belfast	440	2
Sheffield	355	2
Newcastle	155	1
Nottingham	137	1
Cardiff	115	1

Sorties flown

The Blitz: estimated *Luftwaffe* bomber sorties.

Month/year	Day sorties (losses)	Night sorties (losses)	*Luftflotte* 2 sorties	*Luftflotte* 3 sorties	Major attacks	Heavy attacks
October 1940	2,300 (79)	5,900 (23)	2,400	3,500	25	4
November 1940	925 (65)	6,125 (48)	1,600	4,525	23	2

December 1940	650 (24)	3,450 (44)	700	2,750	11	5
January 1941	675 (7)	2,050 (22)	450	1,600	7	6
February 1941	500 (9)	1,450 (18)	475	975	–	2
March 1941	800 (8)	4,275 (46)	1,625	2,650	12	3
April 1941	800 (9)	5,250 (58)	1,500	3,750	16	5
May 1941	200 (3)	3,800 (55)	1,300	2,500	11	3

Notes

Notes

Citations

References

<templatestyles src="Template:Refbegin/styles.css" />

- Addison, Paul and Jeremy Crang. *The Burning Blue: A New History of the Battle of Britain*. London: Pimlico, 2000. ISBN 978-0-7126-6475-2
- Bungay, Stephen. *The Most Dangerous Enemy: A History of the Battle of Britain*. London: Aurum Press, 2000. ISBN 978-1-85410-801-2
- Calder, Angus. *The Myth of the Blitz*. Pimlico, London, 2003. ISBN 978-0-7126-9820-7
- Coates, Tim (1999) [1945]. *Tragedy at Bethnal Green: Report on an Inquiry Into the Accident at Bethnal Green Tube Station Shelter*. London: London Stationery Office. ISBN 978-0-11-702404-5.
- Collier, Richard. *Eagle Day: The Battle of Britain, 6 August – 15 September 1940*. J. M. Dent. 1980. ISBN 978-0-460-04370-0
- Cooper, Matthew. *The German Air Force 1933–1945: An Anatomy of Failure*. New York: Jane's. 1981. ISBN 978-0-531-03733-1
- Corum, James. *The Luftwaffe: Creating the Operational Air War, 1918–1940*. Kansas University Press. 1997. ISBN 978-0-7006-0836-2
- de Zeng, Henry L., Doug G. Stankey and Eddie J. Creek. *Bomber Units of the Luftwaffe 1933–1945: A Reference Source, Volume 1*. Hersham, Surrey, UK: Ian Allen, 2007. ISBN 978-1-85780-279-5.
- de Zeng, Henry L., Doug G. Stankey and Eddie J. Creek. *Bomber Units of the Luftwaffe 1933–1945: A Reference Source, Volume 2*. Hersham, Surrey, UK: Ian Allen, 2007. ISBN 978-1-903223-87-1.

- Faber, Harold. *Luftwaffe: An analysis by former Luftwaffe Generals.* Sidwick and Jackson, London, 1977. ISBN 978-0-283-98516-4
- Field, Geoffrey.[837] Nights Underground in Darkest London: The Blitz, 1940–1941, in *International Labour and Working-Class History.* Issue No. 62, *Class and Catastrophe: September 11 and Other Working-Class Disasters.* (Autumn, 2002), pp. 11–49. OCLC 437133095
- Gaskin, M.J. *Blitz: The Story of the 29th December 1940.* Faber and Faber, London. 2006. ISBN 978-0-571-21795-3
- Goss, Chris. *The Luftwaffe Bombers' Battle of Britain.* Crecy. 2000, ISBN 978-0-947554-82-8
- Hall, Cargill. *Case Studies In Strategic Bombardment.* Air Force History and Museums Program, 1998. ISBN 978-0-16-049781-0.
- Hill, Maureen. *The Blitz.* Marks and Spencer, London, 2002. ISBN 978-1-84273-750-7
- Hinsley, F. H. (1979). *British Intelligence in the Second World War.* History of the Second World War. I. London: HMSO. ISBN 978-0-11-630933-4.
- Holland, James. *The Battle of Britain: Five Months that Changed History.* Bantam Press, London, 2007. ISBN 978-0-593-05913-5
- Hooton, E. R. (1997). *Eagle in Flames: The Fall of the Luftwaffe.* Arms & Armour Press. ISBN 978-1-85409-343-1.
- —— (2010). *The Luftwaffe: A Study in Air Power, 1933–1945.* Classic Publications. ISBN 978-1-906537-18-0
- Hough, Richard and Denis Richards. *The Battle of Britain.* Pen & Sword. 2007. ISBN 978-1-84415-657-3
- Ingersoll, Ralph (1940). *Report on England, November 1940*[838]. New York: Simon and Schuster. OCLC 493444830[839].
- Isby, David. *The Luftwaffe and the War at Sea, 1939–1945.* Chatham, London, 2005. ISBN 978-1-86176-256-6
- James, T. C. G. and Cox, Sebastian. *The Battle of Britain.* Frank Cass, London. 2000. ISBN 978-0-7146-8149-8
- Knickerbocker, H. R. (1941). *Is Tomorrow Hitler's? 200 Questions On the Battle of Mankind*[840]. Reynal & Hitchcock. ISBN 978-1-4179-9277-5. OCLC 1246282[841].
- Levine, Joshua. *Forgotten Voices of the Blitz and the Battle for Britain,* Ebury Press, 2006. ISBN 978-0-09-191003-7
- Mackay, Robert (2002). *Half the Battle: Civilian Morale in Britain during the Second World War.* Manchester: Manchester University Press. ISBN 978-1-84779-020-0.
- Mackay, Ron. *Heinkel He 111* (Crowood Aviation Series). Marlborough: Crowood Press, 2003. ISBN 978-1-86126-576-0

- Mitcham, Samuel W. *Retreat to the Reich: The German Defeat in France, 1944*. Stackpole, 2007, ISBN 978-0-8117-3384-7
- Montgomery-Hyde, H. *British Air Policy Between the Wars*. Heinemann, London, 1976. ISBN 978-0-434-47983-2
- Murray, Williamson (1983). *Strategy for Defeat: the Luftwaffe 1933–1945*. Air University Press. ISBN 978-1-4289-9360-0
- Neitzel, Sönke. *Kriegsmarine and Luftwaffe Co-operation in the War against Britain*. War in History Journal. 2003, Volume 10: pp. 448–463. ISSN 0968-3445[842]
- Nicol, Patricia (2010). *Sucking Eggs*. London: Vintage Books. ISBN 978-0-09-952112-9.
- Overy, Richard. "Hitler and Air Strategy". Journal of Contemporary History 15 (3): 405–421. July 1980 ISSN 0022-0094[843]
- Overy, Richard. *The Air War, 1939–1945*. Potomac Books, Washington, 1980. ISBN 978-1-57488-716-7.
- Price, Alfred. *Battle of Britain Day: 15 September 1940*. Greenhill books. London. 1990. ISBN 978-1-85367-375-7
- Price, Alfred. *Blitz on Britain 1939–45*, Sutton, 2000. ISBN 978-0-7509-2356-9
- Price, Alfred. *Instruments of Darkness: The History of Electronic Warfare, 1939–1945*. Greenhill, London, 1977. ISBN 978-1-85367-616-1.
- Postan, M. M. (1952). *British War Production*. History of the Second World War: United Kingdom Civil Series. London: HMSO. OCLC 459583161[844].
- Raeder, Erich. *Erich Raeder, Grand Admiral*. New York: Da Capo Press. United States Naval Institute, 2001. ISBN 978-0-306-80962-0
- Ramsey, Winston (1988). *The Blitz Then and Now, Volume 2, After the Battle*; First Editions edition. ISBN 978-0-90091-354-9.
- Ray, John. *The Battle of Britain: Dowding and the First Victory, 1940*. London: Cassel Military Paperbacks, 2009. ISBN 978-1-4072-2131-1
- Ray, John. *The Night Blitz: 1940–1941*. Cassell Military, London. 1996. ISBN 978-0-304-35676-8
- Richards, Denis (1974) [1953]. *Royal Air Force 1939–1945: The Fight At Odds*[845]. **I** (paperback ed.). London: HMSO. ISBN 978-0-11-771592-9. Retrieved 22 December 2015.
- Roberts, Andrew. *Chapter 3: Last Hope Island* in *The Storm of War: A New History of the Second World War*. ISBN 978-0-06-122859-9
- Sansom, William. *The Blitz: Westminster at war*. Oxford University Press, 1990. ISBN 978-0-57-127271-6
- Shores, Christopher. *Duel for the Sky: Ten Crucial Battles of World War II*. Grub Street, London 1985. ISBN 978-0-7137-1601-6

- Stansky, Peter. *The First Day of the Blitz*. Yale University Press, 2007. ISBN 978-0-300-12556-6
- Summerfield, Penny and Peniston-Bird, Corina. *Contesting Home Defence: Men, Women and the Home Guard in the Second World War*. Manchester University Press, Manchester, 2007. ISBN 978-0-7190-6202-5
- Taylor, John W.R. *Boulton Paul Defiant: Combat Aircraft of the World from 1909 to the present*. New York: Putnam, 1969. p. 326. ISBN 978-0-425-03633-4
- *The Rise and Fall of the German Air Force*. Public Record Office War Histories. Air 41/10 (repr. HMSO ed.). Richmond, Surrey: Air Ministry (A. C. A. S. [I]). 2001 [1948]. ISBN 978-1-903365-30-4.
- Titmuss, R. M. (1950). *Problems of Social Policy*[846]. History of the Second World War, United Kingdom Civil Series. HMSO. OCLC 1223588[847]. Retrieved 22 December 2015.
- White, Ian. *The History of Air Intercept Radar & the British Night fighter 1935–1939*. Pen & Sword, Barnsley, 2007, ISBN 978-1-84415-532-3
- Tooze, Adam (2006). *The Wages of Destruction: The Making and Breaking of the Nazi Economy*. London: Allen Lane. ISBN 978-0-7139-9566-4.
- Way, T. (2015). *The Wartime Garden: Digging for Victory*. Oxford: Shire. ISBN 978-1-78442-008-6.

Further reading

- Allwright, Lucy (2011). *The War on London: Defending the City From the War in the Air: 1932–1942*[848]. *wrap.warwick.ac.uk* (PhD). Coventry: University of Warwick. OCLC 921053410[849]. EThOS uk.bl.ethos.560239[850]. Retrieved 2 June 2017. ð

External links

	Wikimedia Commons has media related to *The Blitz*.

- The Blitz[851] Original reports and pictures from The Times
- "London Blitz 1940: the first day's bomb attacks listed in full"[852]. The Guardian. 6 September 2010.
- Archive recordings from The Blitz, 1940–41 (audiobook)[853]
- The Blitz: Sorting the Myth from the Reality[854], BBC History

- Exploring 20th century London – The Blitz[855] Objects and photographs from the collections of the Museum of London, London Transport Museum, Jewish Museum and Museum of Croydon.
- Liverpool Blitz[856] Experience 24 hours in a city under fire in the Blitz.
- First Hand Accounts of the Blitz[857] StoryVault Oral History Project
- Forgotten Voices of the Blitz and the Battle for Britain[858]
- War and peace and the price of cat fish[859] World War II diary of resident in south-west London.
- Oral history interview with Barry Fulford, recalling his childhood during the Blitz[860] from the Veteran's History Project at Central Connecticut State University
- Interactive bombing map of London[861]
- Interactive bombing map of a North East Town[862]
- Interactive bombing map of Buckinghamshire[863]
- Childhood Wartime memories[864], form "Memoro – The Bank of Memories"[865] (Joy Irvin)

Battle of Britain Day

<indicator name="good-star"> ⊕ </indicator>

Battle of Britain Day
Part of the Battle of Britain
Dornier Do 17 of Kampfgeschwader 76 falling on Victoria Station, Sunday 15 September 1940

Date	15 September 1940
Location	London, England and English Channel
Result	British victory[866],[867]

Belligerents	
🏴 United Kingdom	卐 Germany
Commanders and leaders	
🏴 Hugh Dowding 🏴 Keith Park	卐 Hermann Göring 卐 Albert Kesselring
Units involved	
▦ Fighter Command	▦ *Luftflotte 2*

Strength	
50,000 observers[868] 630 fighter aircraft[869]	1,120 aircraft (620 fighters and 500 bombers)
Casualties and losses	
29 aircraft destroyed[870] ~ 21 damaged[871] 14[872]–16 killed 14 wounded 1 captured	57[873]–61 aircraft destroyed 20 severely damaged[874] 63–[875] 81 killed 63–65 captured 30–31 wounded 21 missing

Battle of Britain Day[876,877,878,879] is the name given to the day of the large-scale aerial battle that took place on 15 September 1940, during the Battle of Britain.

On this day the Luftwaffe embarked on an all-out attack against London. Around 1,500 aircraft took part in the air battles which lasted until dusk. The action was the climax of the Battle of Britain.[880]

In the aftermath of the raid, Hitler postponed Operation Sea Lion. Having been defeated in daylight, the *Luftwaffe* turned its attention to The Blitz night campaign which lasted until May 1941.[881]

Battle of Britain Day is now an annual commemoration of the battle in the United Kingdom. In Canada, the commemoration takes place on the third Sunday of September.

Background

In June 1940, the *Wehrmacht* had conquered most of Western Europe and Scandinavia. At that time, the only major power standing in the way of a German-dominated Europe was the British Empire and the Commonwealth. After having several peace offers rejected by the British, Adolf Hitler ordered the *Luftwaffe* to destroy the RAF in order to gain air superiority or air supremacy as a prelude to launching Operation Sea Lion, an amphibious assault by the *Wehrmacht* (German armed forces) onto the British mainland.

The Battle of Britain began on 10 July 1940, when the first *Luftwaffe* bomber fleets began attacking convoys and Royal Navy forces in English ports and the Channel. The results were positive and the Germans succeeded in forcing the British to abandon the channel convoy route and to redirect shipping to ports in north-eastern Britain. With this achieved the *Luftwaffe* began the second phase of its air offensive, attacking RAF airfields and supporting structures on the British mainland. The codename of the offensive was *Unternehmen Adlerangriff* ("Operation Eagle Attack"). On 12 August, it flew its first missions in this regard. On 13 August, the *Luftwaffe* carried out its largest attack to date on the mainland. Christened *Adlertag* ("Eagle Day"), the attack was a failure.[882] Nevertheless, the raids continued, at great cost to both sides. The impact of the German offensive on RAF airfields and Fighter Command is disputed. Some historians believe that the attacks were not having much effect and that the Germans were losing the attrition battle,[883,884] while others believe the RAF was faltering.[885]

Either way, Hitler was dissatisfied with the progress being made. Prompted by an RAF raid on Berlin in late August 1940, he ordered the *Luftwaffe* to concentrate its attacks upon London. It was thought the move would draw RAF Fighter Command up into a large, decisive battle.[886] Initially, the change in strategy caught the British off-guard. The first daylight attack of this type occurred on 7 September and caused extensive damage and civilian casualties. Some 107,400 long tons (109,100 t) of shipping was damaged in the Thames Estuary and 1,600 civilians were killed or injured.[887] Still, Hitler was critical of the *Luftwaffe* and its failure to destroy Fighter Command quickly. He dismissed over-optimistic reports from the *Oberkommando der Luftwaffe* (OKL or High Command of the Air Force), particularly the Chief of the *Luftwaffe* general staff Hans Jeschonnek, who asserted the RAF was on its last legs. Confident the RAF was nearly defeated, Jeschonnek requested terror bombing to be enacted as a final blow. Hitler refused, and only allowed attacks on industry, communications and public utility targets.[888]

Over the next few days, bad weather prevented more large attacks. On 9 and 11 September, only smaller raids were carried out. The respite gave Hugh Dowding AOC (Air Officer Commanding) Fighter Command, the chance to prepare and reinforce his forces. The British, possibly through the use of Ultra intelligence, recognised the German change in strategy and duly prepared for further attacks on the capital. Ultra's contribution to the preparations for 15 September is also disputed. The intelligence from Ultra at this stage in the war tended to be fragmented. With the Germans launching attacks whenever there was clear weather, it would not have been difficult for RAF Fighter Command to have predicted an attack on 15 September, which was to be a clear day.[889]

German strategy

On the afternoon of 14 September, Hitler and his command held a conference at the Reich Chancellery in Berlin to discuss the future direction of the war. Göring was not present; he was inspecting *Luftwaffe* units in Belgium. Erhard Milch replaced him. Hitler praised the attacks which had caused heavy damage to the RAF and London. He blamed the failure to achieve more decisive results on the weather. Nevertheless, it was clear to Hitler that victory had still not been attained by the *Luftwaffe*. Under those circumstances, Operation Sea

Lion could not take place. *Großadmiral* Erich Raeder, commander-in-chief of the *Kriegsmarine*, agreed. He argued that Sea Lion should only be carried out as a last resort regardless of gaining air superiority.[890,891,892]

Hitler wanted to maintain the threat of invasion by continuing air attacks on military targets in the British capital. Hans Jeschonnek still pushed for attacks on civilian morale. He argued that military and civilian industries were located too far apart to achieve a collapse of morale by attacking the former. Instead, he pressed for attacks against residential areas. Hitler refused. He ordered that only military targets in London were to be attacked.

The *Luftwaffe* intimated that a period of good weather was now due over France, Belgium and southern Britain. They prepared for an attack along the lines set by Hitler. Staff officers of *Luftflotte* 2 based in Brussels began planning for a two-pronged offensive on 15 September.[893]

The targets were purely military. The first target selected was the Battersea railway station (WLER) West London Extension Railway in Battersea district. The tracks were 12 abreast in some places and linked London to the heavy industries of the West Midlands and other industrial cities on the north and south-east of Britain. The conglomeration of lines included rail-over-rail bridges which were vulnerable to air attack. This was what air planners referred to as "choke points", which if cut could erode enemy communication efficiency.

The second target, for the larger second attack during the afternoon would be the dock areas of the Thames Estuary including the warehouse of the East End of London, Surrey Commercial Docks, south of the river, and Royal Docks (Royal Victoria Dock, West India Docks, Royal Albert Dock and King George V Dock).

Intelligence

The strategy could only be valid if intelligence assessments were correct. To German intelligence, it seemed as if the RAF might be on the verge of collapse. The attacks on London, thus far, seemed to confirm the assumption. None of the *Luftwaffe* bomber formations had encountered the well organised, effective and ferocious defence that had characterised the battles in August 1940. If the German intelligence was correct, then by striking against vital choke points in London that the RAF would be forced to defend, the *Luftwaffe* had the opportunity to destroy the remaining RAF fighter forces. Not only would the attacks allow for the attainment of air superiority, they would eliminate a vital rail network, destroy shipping and supplies brought in from North America, and affect civilian morale by demonstrating London's vulnerability to air power.

The policy of attacking London after the successful 7 September raid quickly became counter-productive, and in this matter the *Luftwaffe* suffered from serious misjudgement resulting from their intelligence service. The crews had been told the RAF was down to its last reserves and that one more assault would clinch victory. This was incorrect which meant bomber crews would be in for a shock on 15 September. The RAF had been given much needed rest after intense operations by the shift in German strategy. British radar, having been virtually untouched, was still able to follow the slow German build ups over France long before the first German aircraft reached British airspace. It would give the rested Fighter Command units plenty of warning. Moreover, by choosing to attack London, it exposed the bombers to greater danger by forcing them to fly greater distances in hostile air space. German crews would be forced to fight all the way to London and back. As it happened, all the German bomber units were at least intercepted on 15 September, and were then scattered as they withdrew.[894]

Hitler was satisfied. The reasoning of the *Luftwaffe* seemed sound. Should the bombing achieve its aim, it offered considerable strategic value. The strike against London meant that most of the fighting on 15 September would take place between *Luftflotte* 2 under Albert Kesselring and Keith Park's No. 11 Group RAF.[895]

British strategy

There was a debate which raged within Fighter Command during the Battle of Britain. It centred around what strategy to pursue against the Luftwaffe. AOC Hugh Dowding and AOC 11 Group Keith Park favoured a strategy of non-attrition. From their perspective, the RAF had to remain intact to win the battle, rather than decimate the Luftwaffe. Both felt that trying to fight a battle of attrition would give the numerically superior enemy the chance to destroy large parts of the Command in one go, thus playing into Göring's hands. Therefore, Park and Dowding advocated the tactic of sending small numbers of fighters to intercept every raid; providing opposition to every raid offered the chance of inflicting continued attrition on German formations while avoiding decisive damage to Fighter Command.

Park's equivalent and another of Dowding's commanders, AOC 12 Group Trafford Leigh-Mallory, held the opposite view. For him, large forces would win the battle by destroying large numbers of the enemy. This attrition strategy would use the concept of the Big Wing as its basis.

Figure 115: *Trafford Leigh-Mallory.*

The Big Wing

Air Vice-Marshal Trafford Leigh-Mallory and Squadron Leader Douglas Bader came to play significant roles in the September fighting. Bader commanded 242 Squadron flying Hurricanes in Leigh-Mallory's 12 Group, which defended the vital industrial targets in the West Midlands. A source of frustration to Leigh-Mallory was the way in which his squadrons were used. During Luftwaffe attacks on south-east England 12 Group units were tasked with protecting 11 Group sector stations north of the Thames Estuary, while Leigh-Mallory believed his units should be in action south of the Thames. Mallory also criticised the way Park and Dowding were conducting the battle. The popular image of outnumbered Spitfires and Hurricanes meeting an enemy with huge numerical strength preyed upon his mind. He favoured a reverse of the image.[896]

Bader was bored and frustrated at being left out of the major actions in the south. To Bader, it did not make sense for 12 Group to apparently sit idle while 11 Group suffered heavy losses and fought at a numerical disadvantage. Bader advocated scrambling 12 Group fighters as soon as German aircraft were detected forming up over France or Belgium. He asserted 12 Group was quick enough to reach 20,000 ft (6,100 m) over the Thames Estuary before the enemy reached the area. He planned to use large forces, three to five squadrons to

Figure 116: *Douglas Bader commanded 242 Squadron during the battle. He also led the Duxford Wing.*

engage the enemy. Should this succeed, 11 Group, following up attacks, might have found broken enemy formations whose crews had lost the determination to press on to their targets. Bader implied that this may reduce the losses of fighter pilots in 11 Group.[897] After the war, Bader insisted that both he and Leigh-Mallory wanted the Big Wing tactic enacted in 12 Group only. They both believed, according to Bader, that it was impractical to use 11 Group as the command was located too close to the enemy and would not have enough time to assemble.[898]

Dowding saw 12 Group as the protector of the Midlands and a reserve for 11 Group. Mallory and Bader wanted to ignore both the defence of the Midlands and keeping a reserve in order to commit 12 Group to battle. In essence, they proposed the opposite of Dowding and resolved to commit the reserves before the front-line units. While this method might have spared 11 Group, it had its problems. Although Mallory and Bader wanted to stop the enemy before it hit RAF airfields, the amount of time it took to position large formations for interception meant that the Big Wing often failed to achieve this. Instead, they engaged the enemy as he withdrew. Prompted by a supporting comment from Leigh-Mallory, to the effect that it did not matter when an interception was made, as long as it accounted for a large number of enemy aircraft, Bader announced that he would rather destroy 50 German bombers after hitting their targets than 10 before. The argument was strong; crippling losses would act as a deterrent, so that damage sustained on an occasion when the Germans did get through would have to be offset against later occasions when they did not even care to try.[899]

The counter-arguments were much stronger. The assumption that the Germans would be put off by losses was wrong; it would have taken severe losses for the OKL to change its mind on target selection. The targets were also vital. The airfields themselves supported the squadrons in the field, while the loss of the vital sector-stations could well have crippled the defence system. Thus the possibility of allowing the bulk of the German bombers to reach their target unscathed was unacceptable. The idea that the Big Wing could inflict heavier losses than had been achieved up until then was based on an overestimate of the numbers of aircraft shot down by the Big Wing. Leigh-Mallory, Sholto Douglas and Bader had based their opinions on claims made by RAF units in battle. However, particularly when a large number of aircraft were engaged, it was possible for the same aircraft to be claimed by more than one pilot. As a result, the RAF claimed 100 or more German aircraft shot down in one day on five occasions, while analysis of Luftwaffe losses has shown that there were only four occasions on which the Luftwaffe lost more than 50 aircraft, and never did they lose 100 or more in a day.[900] Nevertheless, while it is not known whether Mallory and Bader were aware that the claims of the RAF and Big Wings were exaggerated, they certainly tried to use them as a potent tool with which to remove Park and Dowding from command and pursue the Big Wing tactic.[901]

Non-attrition

Keith Park, with endorsement from Dowding, opted for the opposite strategy. Park maintained that it was unimportant to inflict large losses on the Germans in comparison to safeguarding his own forces. Park believed the Germans would give up if they could not achieve their aim of air superiority. This, simply put, meant avoiding the destruction and or depletion of Fighter Command was the primary factor in air defence. This would be achieved by sending small numbers of fighters to intercept, minimising losses in the air. By remaining to offer undiminished and constant air opposition, the RAF ensured the Luftwaffe could not win. As long as some sort of cost was imposed before the enemy dropped his bombs and impaired the defence system, the RAF could remain intact to meet the threat again the next day. To this end, Park favoured the 10 bomber kills before the attack, rather than the 50 shot down after it. The strategy suggested an enemy would give up if he felt he was getting nowhere. For even while his losses remained moderate, it would be senseless to suffer those casualties for no return.[902] Park and Dowding's strategy, under the circumstances, was the wiser choice.[903]

Figure 117: *Keith Park.*

Forces involved

Luftwaffe forces

The *Luftwaffe* had suffered heavy attrition since the opening of the Battle of Britain. Just over a month earlier, it possessed 2,226 operational aircraft on 17 August. By 7 September, it had 1,895 aircraft, a drop of 15 percent. Still, most of the losses were being made good by production. During the battle, the Luftwaffe had undergone a major reorganisation. *Luftflotte* 5 in Norway had sent most of its Messerschmitt Bf 110 and medium bomber units (*Kampfgeschwader* or Bomber Wings) to *Luftflotte* 2 and 3. *Luftflotte* 3 then passed most of its Messerschmitt Bf 109 units to *Luftflotte* 2 which was based in the Netherlands, Belgium and France.[904]

According to the *Luftwaffe* order of battle dated 7 September, the nearest date covered by the list, the three Air Fleets contained 1,895 aircraft. *Luftflotte* 2 had 1,311 machines including; 533 Bf 109s, 107 Bf 110s, 51 reconnaissance and 484 medium bomber aircraft. A further 120 Junkers Ju 87 dive bombers were on the order of battle, but were not used.

Luftwaffe readiness was less than ideal. In August, 211 pilots had been killed, including 105 fighter pilots and 91 bomber pilots. Missing pilots amounted to 132 fighter and 94 bomber pilots alone, with a further respective loss of 47 and 28 wounded.[905] The effect on operational ready crews was significant. Messerschmitt Bf 110 units had 60% of crews against authorised strength. For bomber units, it was 65%, while Bf 109 units had 81% of crews ready, a 5% increase from the 76% level in the first week of September.[906] However, by 14 September, Bf 109 units possessed only 67% of crews against authorised aircraft. In Bf 110 units, it fell to just 46%, and in bomber units it dropped to 59%. One week later, the figures were 64, 52 and 52% respectively.[907]

RAF forces

In the six weeks of intensive combat, RAF strength had been maintained to extent far greater than the *Luftwaffe* intelligence had believed possible. On the evening of 14 September, Fighter Command could muster 269 Supermarine Spitfire and 533 Hawker Hurricane fighters. The two vital groups could put up just over 500 fighters. No. 11 Group RAF had 310 fighters, including 92 Spitfires and 218 Hurricanes. No. 12 Group RAF could field 85 Spitfires and 109 Hurricanes. Should No. 10 Group RAF come into the battle, a further 48 Spitfires and 78 Hurricanes could be committed. Compared with 17 August, there were just 22 fewer Spitfires and Hurricanes.[908]

During the battle, the RAF had suffered a serious loss of experienced pilots. In mid-September, Fighter Command could call upon 1,492 operational pilots against an establishment of 1,662 – a deficiency of 10%. Many of the pilots were ineffective unless led into battle by experienced men. Air Chief Marshal Hugh Dowding's policy was to move in fresh squadrons from quieter areas to replace losses in the units in the south-east as they became exhausted. By early September, the system was breaking down as squadrons were becoming depleted before fresh units could be formed and take their place.[909]

Reluctantly, Dowding defined three categories, A, B and C. Category A units were to bear the brunt of the fighting, and were to be kept at full strength in aircraft and pilots. Only if the A units suffered exceptionally high losses would they be replaced. B units were relief units, to be maintained at operational strength and only used if absolutely necessary. C units were generally stripped down to just five or six pilots. These units were devoted to training new pilots. Although not fit for fighter-fighter action, they could defend quieter areas. The system potentially could have had fatal results for Fighter Command, with C units becoming less and less effective. But the system had not been running long enough by 14 September for it to have a serious impact on Fighter Command's strength. The replacement units were sufficient in number and effectiveness to continue to replace exhausted units. By 15 September, the C units could still give a good account of themselves in battle.

Preliminary engagements

The *Luftwaffe* began its eighth consecutive night of bombing London on 15 September. Soon after midnight, 13 unidentified Dornier Do 17 light bombers attacked the capital. At 00:15 two Junkers Ju 88s followed from *Kampfgeschwader 51* (KG 51, or 51st Bomber Wing). A further 11 Heinkel He 111s from an unidentified unit bombed the city again at 00:50. At 02:00, five He 111s from *Kampfgeschwader 4* (KG 4) bombed the city.[910] A full strike by the *Geschwader* had been planned, but bad weather had forced a cancellation after five He 111s had taken off. Most of the damage was done to residential areas in Fulham, Chelsea and Westminster. Around 19 people were killed and 31 injured. The heaviest casualties were caused when a bomb fell on a church in Chelsea killing 14 and injuring 26. Small raiding forces bombed Cardiff, Bootle (in Liverpool), Leicester and Ipswich. At Bootle, only slight damage was done to rail tracks and facilities at West Alexandra Dock.[911] At sea, a Heinkel He 115 floatplane attacked and sank the 5,548 long tons (5,637 t) freighter *Mailsea River* off Montrose with a torpedo. Soon after, the freighter *Halland* was sunk by the same method in the area. At 03:30, He 115s flew up the Thames Estuary and dropped magnetic anti-shipping mines. Further mines were dropped in the Bristol Channel, Liverpool Bay and Milford Haven and off Hartlepool, Berwick-upon-Tweed and Aberdeen. RAF night fighter defences were still in their infancy. Most fighters lacked radar and in any case, radar was short-range and unreliable. Instead, they flew outside the anti-aircraft guns' fields of fire on likely approach routes using the pilots' vision to locate enemy aircraft. In later years, the night fighter defences would be highly sophisticated. But in 1940, they were not effective. Just 28 sorties were flown against the nocturnal raids.

There was also air activity over German-held territory. RAF Bomber Command flew 92 sorties against German invasion targets at Boulogne, Calais, Ostend, Dunkirk, and Antwerp. The remaining sorties were directed at Brussels marshalling yards, Hamm and Krefeld. One Armstrong Whitworth Whitley failed to return. It was lost to ground fire over the Netherlands. A total of 157 sorties were flown overall. By the September 1940, some 10–13% of invasion barges had been sunk.[912]

The first combat in daylight began just after 08:00. A He 111 from *Aufklärungsgruppe* 51 (Long-range Reconnaissance Group 51), based near Paris, was intercepted and shot down over the Channel by Hurricanes from No. 87 Squadron RAF. A Heinkel He 59 air-sea rescue aircraft was dispatched, but found no trace of the Heinkel or its five crew.[913]

Further flights were made by high altitude Ju 88s. One photographed RAF Sealand, RAF Pembrey and RAF Woodward. It also managed to reach

Figure 118: *Dornier Do 17s. These aircraft were flown by KG 76.*

Manchester, Liverpool and Birkenhead without interception. Another managed to photograph the Thames Haven, RAF Netheravon, RAF Benson and the Royal Navy base at Chatham Dockyard. Interception of these high altitude aircraft was difficult, and none were lost on 15 September 1940.[914]

Noon attack: 10:10 to 13:00

The offensive got underway at 10:10 in the morning. Major Alois Lindmayr *Gruppenkommandeur* (Group Commander) of I./KG 76[915] led the entire formation. Lindmayr was an experienced combat veteran having won the Knight's Cross of the Iron Cross for his effective low-level attacks in France. III./*Kampfgeschwader 76* (KG 76) took off with 19 Do 17s from their base at Cormeilles-en-Vexin.[916] At the same time, 20 mi (32 km) to the north, I./KG 76 took off. Usually a *Gruppe* (Group) could field 27 bombers. After weeks of attrition, I./KG 76 could put up only eight Do 17s. The *Geschwader* had to field two *Gruppen* to do the work of one. Most of the Dorniers were in bad shape, worn down by intensive operations. The two groups rendezvoused at Amiens then proceeded to Cap Gris Nez to pick up their Bf 109 fighter escort. The attacks on Britain had caused heavy losses to the Luftwaffe, German crews and *Geschwader* experimented with innovative ways to defend themselves. One pilot, Feldwebel Rolf Heitsch, had his Dornier fitted with an infantry flame thrower in its tail. If it failed to down a fighter that got too close, it might drive the enemy off: if it worked, it could be fitted to other bombers. After take-off the formation broke up in cloud and was delayed for 10 minutes to allow reforming. Two bombers failed to do and returned to base.[917]

British reaction

Initially, the operations room at RAF Uxbridge was disturbed by a visit from Prime Minister Winston Churchill. Most of the plotting tables were bare, save for a few plots indicating German reconnaissance machines. Most of the Women's Auxiliary Air Force (WAAF) were relaxing, in spite of Churchill's presence (he had ordered that they not behave any differently). However, at 10:30 the first German aircraft triggered the alarm at Chain Home radar station at Dover. The filter room at Stanmore recognised the formation as hostile. The WAAF detailed group and sector commands throughout the south that 40-plus enemy aircraft were entering Kentish airspace.[918]

By 11:04, Lindmayr's Dorniers had reached Calais. Wing Commander Lord Willoughby de Broke, Park's senior fighter controller, watched with the Prime Minister and Park as the Germans moved closer. De Broke had a problem of his own. He had no way of knowing which plots represented bombers and fighters. Bombers had to be intercepted, fighters could be ignored. The trick was to strike a balance and time the interception as well as possible. On one hand he must scramble early and allow enough time to get into a favourable attack position; but on the other hand he had to avoid scrambling them too early lest the fighters run short of fuel before they met the enemy. Park joined de Broke. After a brief discussion he decided to commit several squadrons from RAF Biggin Hill. Park realised the raid could be a trap. Though the target seemed to be London, the aircraft, comprising 120–150 in number, may be an advanced guard of Bf 109s sent to clear the skies or disrupt fighter defences. Still, he gambled and sent nine squadrons into action at 11:15.[919]

No. 92 Squadron RAF and No. 72 Squadron RAF scrambled Spitfires from Biggin Hill. Their orders were to cover the air space over Canterbury at 25,000 ft (7,600 m). De Broke sensed by this time that nothing else was coming in. If this was the main attack, he decided it must be met with force. He ordered squadrons from RAF Northolt, RAF Kenley and RAF Debden to stand by. At 11:20, he ordered RAF Hornchurch and RAF North Weald and No. 10 Group's RAF Middle Wallop into the air. Park now had two squadrons over Canterbury, four over Biggin Hill and Maidstone with further back up of two squadrons over Chelmsford at 15,000 ft (4,600 m).[920]

The plan was for Nos. 72 and 92 to engage the high escort. No. 603 Squadron RAF would arrive on the scene just afterward and get at the close escort (JG 3). The pair from North Weald would go to Maidstone, so if the bombers got

Figure 119: *Spitfire IIA. Although a slightly later variant, its outward appearance was identical to the Mk. I, the mainstay Spitfire of 1940.*

through, they would run into them over London. Despite Park's reservations about Leigh-Mallory's Big Wing, he ordered that it was time for it to be tested. If the Germans attempted to use the Thames Estuary as a navigation aid, as so often before, fighters from 12 Group's RAF Duxford could meet them over Hornchurch at 20,000 ft (6,100 m). They would have a 5,000 ft (1,500 m) height advantage to the west of the bombers and attack out of the Sun, if Leigh-Mallory could get them there in time. The order was sent to Stanmore at 11:20 and Duxford scrambled No. 19, 310, 302 and No. 611 Squadron RAF. No. 242 Squadron RAF's leader, Wing Commander Douglas Bader led the assault with the 56 fighters. They were airborne at 11:22.[921]

Close to contact

The Dorniers were supported by German fighter aircraft that had been sent out in advance of the main strike. *Jagdgeschwader 27* (JG 27) and I./*Jagdgeschwader 52* (JG 52)[922] Bf 109s flew in toward London at 16,000 ft (4,900 m), while *Jagdgeschwader 53* (JG 53) flew top cover over the bombers. Some 30 *Jagdgeschwader 3* (JG 3) flew close escort. The bombers were travelling slowly, forcing the fighters to lower their flaps to stay with the bombers, which made them sitting ducks. They crossed the coast at Folkestone at 11:36. Fighters from II.*Lehrgeschwader 2* (Demonstration Wing 2) were also to form

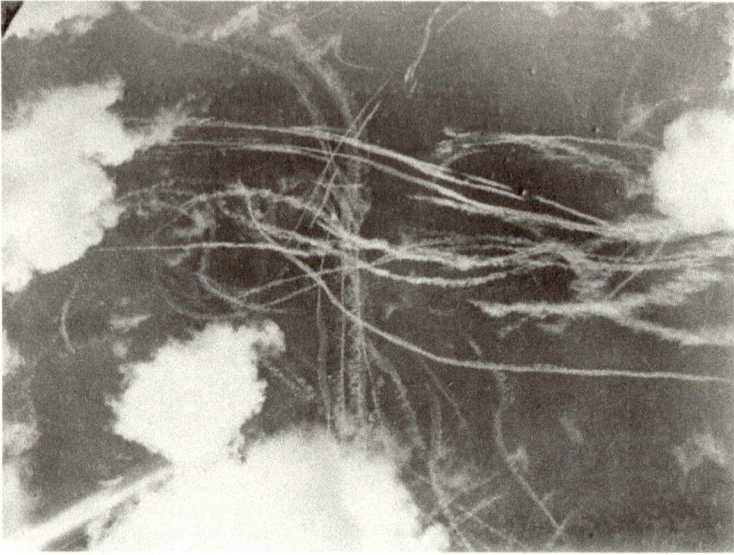

Figure 120: *An air battle, 1940.*

part of the escort. They flew in advance of the main force to drop 550 lb (250 kg) bombs and then resume their role as fighters. The strong head wind slowed the Dorniers, which meant that the Germans took even longer to reach the target while burning up the Bf 109s' limited fuel supplies. It also sped up the RAF fighters coming in from the north.[923,924]

LG 2 took off as the bombers crossed the English coast. Even with bombs, the Bf 109s were expected to overhaul the bombers and attack London a few minutes before the main raids began.[925] Park interpreted the LG 2 raid as a major thrust and was determined to meet the "second wave" as he saw it. He scrambled six more squadrons but kept four reserve squadrons at Hornchurch and RAF Tangmere. As the forces closed, around 120 Bf 109s and 25 Do 17s were facing 245 Spitfires and Hurricanes.

Combat

Park's plan worked. The Biggin Hill squadrons, 72 and 92 Squadrons made contact with the enemy over Canterbury. Arriving at 25,000 ft (7,600 m), they found themselves 3,000 ft (910 m) above the top covering German fighters (JG 53). Beyond Canterbury, they could also see KG 76 and JG 3 over Ashford. At 11:50, they attacked out of the sun. Taken by surprise, four or five of I./JG 53s Bf 109s were hit by the Spitfires.[926] Spitfires of 92 Squadron tried to charge through the fighter screen to get at the Dorniers but were blocked.[927,928] Soon afterwards, No. 603 Squadron joined the fight. Park had broken up the top level escort. Some 23 Hurricanes of Nos. 253 and 501 Squadrons arrived at the same height as the bombers and delivered a head-on attack. Lindmayr's crews were experienced and the formation held its nerve and remained intact. JG 3 in turn attacked the Hurricanes dispatching two from 501 Squadron. Northolt's No. 229 and No. 303 Squadron RAF were also arriving and engaged JG 52. One of 239 Squadrons Hurricanes and a JG 52 Bf 109 collided. The bombers ploughed on and reached Lewisham. However, the formation was now isolated. The escorts were embroiled in dogfights all over Kent and half the RAF fighters were yet to engage. JG 53 were further engaged by several squadrons; Nos. 1, No. 46, No. 249 and No. 605 Squadron RAF. No. 605, led by Archie McKellar broke away and delivered a 12-fighter attack scoring some hits on the bombers.[929] JG 27 meanwhile suffered two casualties, one possibly against No. 19 Squadron. It claimed only one British fighter that day.[930] JG 3 claimed two fighters for one loss.[931]

Up until now, the Bf 109s had successfully blocked attacks on the bombers. However, Park's tactics of attacking the Germans all along the route forced their fighters to use up fuel more quickly in dogfights. When the outskirts of London came into view, they began to depart at 12:07 north of Lewisham.[932]

The North Weald pair, No. 504 and 257 Squadrons engaged the Dorniers with 20 Hurricanes.[933] One German pilot, Feldwebel Robert Zehbe developed engine trouble and lagged half a mile behind the main bomber stream. His Dornier attracted a swarm of fighters. Eventually Ray Holmes of 504 Squadron, out of bullets, rammed the bomber. The tail came off and air pressure snapped off the outer wings short of the engines. The bomber crashed onto the forecourt of London Victoria station. During its spinning dive, the gravitational force on the Dornier caused its bombs to be released, which hit or landed near to Buckingham Palace nearby, damaging the building. Zehbe bailed out and landed near The Oval[934] and was severely wounded by a civilian mob. He was rescued by the British Army but died of his wounds. Holmes' Hurricane was badly damaged, crashing near the grounds of Buckingham Palace. Holmes bailed out injured but survived.[935]

Directly over the target, Bader's Duxford Wing arrived and attacked while the Germans were on the bomb-run. Thirty seconds after the release of the bombs, they hit the target area, the Battersea rail lines next to Battersea Park on the Thames south bank. Each Dornier's payload of twenty 110 lb (50 kg) bombs carved a run 500 yd (460 m) long and 25 yd (23 m) wide. Some fell on the high-density civilian housing. The bombs missed Clapham Junction but fell across the rail network tracks that connected it to Victoria Station north of the Thames and the main line heading north east on the south side of the river.[936] The damage done had cut the tracks in Battersea in several places and a viaduct

Figure 121: *Rudolf Heitsch's Dornier in Castle Farm Shoreham.
The flame throwing device is just visible on the aft fuselage.*[939]

had collapsed over some rails. Rail traffic was halted. Four unexploded bombs delayed repairs.[937] The rail lines were only out of action for three days.[938]

But within minutes, the Do 17 formation had been reduced to 15 aircraft and most of them were damaged. Six had been shot down and four were attempting to make a run for home. The remainder dropped their bombs and were met by a covering force of Bf 109s and landed back in France without further combat. LG 2 meanwhile had been and gone. They saw one rail station and released their bombs and returned home. They saw only one British fighter, No. 46 Squadron's Pilot Officer Gunning who reported the make up of the formation.[940] Park had decided to ignore their raid.

Overall the attackers lost six bombers and 12 Bf 109s, some 12.5% of its strength. However, the British claimed 81 aircraft, 26 by the Duxford Wing. Zehbe's Dornier alone was claimed nine times. Among the German casualties that day was Rolf Heitsch and his flame throwing Dornier;[941] the device had not been tested at high altitude and when used, squirted black oil over Holmes' windshield and attracted the attention of British fighters. Park would not have been pleased that despite being stripped of protection the small force of bombers lost only a quarter of its strength while surrounded by 100 fighters. Still, the operation had been a victory. Fighter Command lost 13 fighters, eight were claimed by JG 52.

Interlude: 13:00 to 13:45

At 13:00, the German formations were plotted making their way back to France. Churchill was delighted with the results. The WAAF had been due to change shift, but the scheduled relief time could not take place during an operation. By 13:05 the fighters were back on the ground. Rearming and refueling

Figure 122: *A formation of He 111Hs, circa 1940*

began immediately to return the machines back to battle ready status as soon as possible, while the pilots wrote their combat reports which included filing claims and details of their battle to the best of their recollections.[942] Bader's Big Wing landed. Owing to battle damage, only 49 of Duxford's 56 fighters were operational by the afternoon.[943]

By this time, the German bombers were touching down in the Pas de Calais. Two were so badly damaged that they were written off in crash landings, bringing the total losses to eight Do 17s. Almost all bore the scars of battle. One machine had sustained 70 hits, another 200.[944]

In the afternoon, RAF Bomber Command abandoned more attacks on invasion ports because of insufficient cloud cover. Six Bristol Blenheims undertook an armed reconnaissance over the North Sea. RAF Coastal Command flew 95 sorties for anti-invasion, anti-submarine, mine laying and reconnaissance missions. Spitfires photographed every port from Antwerp to Cherbourg. They returned with evidence of a gradually increasing buildup of amphibious forces. All the Command's aircraft returned.[945]

Mid-afternoon attack: 13:45 to 15:45

Even before the Do 17s of KG 76 had touched down, the next wave was already just getting airborne. II and III./*Kampfgeschwader 2* (KG 2), (from Boissy-Saint-Léger and Cambrai) II./*Kampfgeschwader 3* (KG 3) (from Antwerp), I and II./*Kampfgeschwader 53* (KG 53) (from Lille) and I and

II./*Kampfgeschwader 26* (from Wevelghem and Gilze en Rijen) took off to target the West India Docks and Royal Victoria Dock north of the Thames as well as the warehouses of the Surrey Commercial Docks in the south. JG 53 and Adolf Galland's *Jagdgeschwader 26* (JG 26) were to escort the bombers. The fighters met them as the bombers formed up over Calais.[946,947]

The phalanx of the German bombers headed for Dungeness. At the head were 43 Do 17s from KG 2; next, a couple of miles behind, came 24 He 111s of KG 53; finally, a couple of miles further behind, came 19 Do 17s from KG 3; followed by 28 He 111s of KG 26. The headwind was present again, and the 114 bombers battled against it. The German fighter pilots kept close escort. They detested the tactic. It handed the initiative to the British regarding how and when to attack. Moreover, if they were bounced by Spitfires, the Bf 109s would take too long to accelerate to full throttle in order to escape.[948]

The German fighter escort consisted of five *Gruppen* from JG 3, JG 53 and *Jagdgeschwader 77* (JG 77). LG 2 Bf 109s flew top cover while Adolf Galland's JG 26 and *Jagdgeschwader 51* (JG 51) conducted fighter sweeps in advance of the main bomber stream. For the sake of appearances (the morale of the bomber crews), *Zerstörergeschwader 26* (Destroyer Wing 26 or ZG 26) flying the Messerschmitt Bf 110 flew close escort to KG 26. It was twice as small as the formation that hit London on 7 September, but instead of having two fighters for every bomber, there were four. Nor could the German pilots complain about being tied to the bombers. Sufficient numbers of fighters were allowed to roam on free-ranging patrols.[949]

At 13:45, Chain Home radar picked up the German raids. No. 11 Group scrambled one Spitfire from RAF Hawkinge on the channel coast. Flown by No. 92 Squadron Pilot Officer Alan Wright, his job was to climb as quickly as possible over the sea and act as a spotter. He was to report on the direction, height, composition and strength of the German formation. The radar operators assessed the strengths of the three largest formations at 30, 50, and 60 plus. Five smaller formations added up to 85 plus. In fact, the British estimate of 225 aircraft proved too small. The German force was 475 aircraft strong. Shortly before 14:00, the German formation left the French coast. Park ordered his forces to repeat the earlier interception tactic. Four pairs of squadrons were ordered to patrol Sheerness, Chelmsford, Hornchurch and RAF Kenley.[950]

RAF scramble

At 14:00, No. 11 Group released 68 fighters. Hornchurch's No. 603 and No. 222 Squadron RAF committed 20 Spitfires to Sheerness at 20,000 ft (6,100 m). The squadrons would fail to find each other and went into action singly. At Debden, No. 17 Squadron RAF, No. 257 Squadron RAF sent 20

Figure 123: *Hawker Hurricane, MK I, from the Battle of Britain.*

Hurricanes to Chelmsford at 15,000 ft (4,600 m). Kenley dispatched No. 501 and 605 Squadrons with 17 Hurricanes to Kenley at just 5,000 ft (1,500 m). North Weald ordered No. 249 and 504 Squadrons to cover Hornchurch at 15,000 ft (4,600 m).[951]

Just five minutes later, the German bombers began splitting into three groups heading for the coast between Dungeness and Dover. Park decided to scramble four more squadrons. When it became apparent that five concentrations of Bf 109s were taking the direct route to London on free-hunting patrols, Park scrambled eight more squadrons. No. 11 Group dispatched Biggin Hill's No. 41 Squadron RAF followed by 92 Squadron. The force could put up 20 Spitfires. They were directed to Hornchurch at 20,000 ft (6,100 m). At 12:10, Northolt No. 1 (Canadian) and 229 Squadrons sent 21 Hurricanes to Northolt. North Weald sent nine Hurricanes of No. 46 Squadrons to the London Docks. Biggin Hill sent another wave, No. 72 and No. 66 Squadron RAF, with 20 Spitfires to Biggin Hill at 20,000 ft (6,100 m). Debden was called into action again and ordered No. 73 Squadron RAF to Maidstone at 15,000 ft (4,600 m). Beginning at 12:15, Kenley dispatched No. 253 Squadron RAF with nine Hurricanes to guard the airfield. RAF Tangmere was in action for the first time, sending Nos. 213 and No. 607 Squadron RAF's 23 Hurricanes to defend Kenley and Biggin Hill. The largest contingent came from No. 12 Group. Duxford, or the "Big Wing", No. 19, 242, 302, 310 and 311

Squadrons with 20 Spitfires and 27 Hurricanes were ordered to Hornchurch at 25,000 ft (7,600 m). Middle Wallop committed No. 238 Squadron and 12 Hurricanes to the Kenley area.[952]

By the time Park decided to launch his third wave, the first engagements were taking place. At 14:20, he ordered No. 11 Group's No. 303 (Polish) Squadron and its nine Hurricanes to Northold at 20,000 ft (6,100 m). Tangmere scrambled No. 602 Squadron RAF and 12 Spitfires to hover over Kenley, Biggin Hill and Gravesend. Meanwhile, No. 10 Group RAF were ordered into action. A request was made for No. 609 Squadron and 13 Spitfires to climb to 15,000 ft (4,600 m) over Kenley. This squadron left Middle Wallop at 14:28.[953]

The RAF now had 276 Spitfires and Hurricanes in the air. The Germans outnumbered the British in this raid by two to one. More seriously, for every two RAF fighters, there were three Bf 109s.

Initial clashes

Over Romney Marsh Nos. 41, 92 and 222 Squadrons engaged JG 26, losing one of their number to the Bf 109s. The second wave of RAF fighters arrived on the scene, comprising 607 and 213 Squadrons with 23 Hurricanes. They initiated a head-on attack against the Do 17s of KG 3. A Hurricane and a Dornier collided, both going down. The Bf 109s did their best to break up attacks and the bombers held a tight formation, putting up withering crossfire. The Bf 109s were not permitted to leave the bombers and chase enemy fighters. Time and again, they were forced to break off and return to the bomber stream, allowing the RAF fighters to return and repeat the process. Soon after, No. 605 and No. 501 Squadron arrived with 14 Hurricanes. One fighter was hit by return fire, but the pilot aimed his aircraft at a Dornier and bailed out. The fighter collided and destroyed the bomber. The German bomber crews had no way of knowing that the crashes were not premeditated. It seemed as if the British were desperate. Nevertheless, they thought the 'tactic' was devastatingly effective. Chastened by losses, the Dorniers closed ranks to snuff out the gaps and continued to their target.[954]

At 14:31, they reached the Thames and British AAA defences opened up. The bombers were forced to evade their fire. One Dornier was damaged. KG 53 lost a He 111 following up KG 3 over the area.

""   **""**

"What other reserves have we?"
"There are none."

— Churchill's question to Park on 15 September 1940[955]

At 14:35, Park and Churchill watched the battle unfold in Uxbridge's operations room. The Prime Minister saw that every squadron was being used and asked what reserves were available. Park said there were none. He was referring only to 11 Group, as there were more aircraft in nearby sectors,[956] but at this point Park was stretched. At Park's request, he had sent all the Squadrons from No. 10 and 12 Group that were adjacent to 11 Group to the capital. If the *Luftwaffe* launched a follow up attack, there were only three Squadrons available, in 12 and 10 Group (based in Norfolk and Dorset) and none in the Kent region. All other day squadrons were based too far away to get involved. Nevertheless, Park knew that a low cloud base over RAF Croydon (2,000 ft (610 m)), Hornchurch (3,000 ft (910 m)), Northolt (3,500 ft (1,100 m)), RAF Hendon (2,100 ft (640 m)) and Biggin Hill (2,000 ft (610 m)) would make a low-level accurate strike the Germans' only option. High-altitude attacks were improbable. Possibly to create a reserve, Park ordered 41, 213 and 605 Squadrons to return early though they had only been airborne for 45 minutes and had plenty of fuel left, even if ammunition was short.[957] The vast bulk of the remaining squadrons were heading to London. A total of 185 fighters in 19 Squadrons were ready to engage. The battle would involve over 600 aircraft.[958]

Main battle

In the vicinity of Gravesend, the right-hand German formation – comprising the Do 17s of KG 3, trailed by the He 111s of KG 26 – would bear the brunt of the next attack from 63 fighters from 17, 46, 249, 257, 504 and 603 Squadrons. The Hurricanes of 249 and 504 squadrons went into action first. Their first pass saw three Do 17s go down, including *Hauptmann* Ernst Püttmann, leading *5. Staffel* of KG 3 (5./KG 3). The Bf 109s escorting KG 26 could only watch, forbidden to leave their Heinkel charges. As the first attack finished, No. 257 Squadron led by Squadron Leader Robert Stanford Tuck attacked the Heinkels with nine Hurricanes. The escorts had their work cut out and were scattered.[959] No. 257 targeted the badly protected bombers.[960]

As 257 engaged KG 26, KG 53 came under attack from No. 1 (Canadian), 66, 72, 229 Squadrons. No. 66 attacked first followed by 72 and 229. Some Spitfires climbed over the bombers to seek cover from the Bf 109s. The British were surprised to see an unidentified formation of Bf 109s continue on without interfering. Two He 111s were forced back to France and another was shot down. Nine Bf 109s were providing close escort for I./JG 3. They claimed

Figure 124: *Heinkel He 111 bomber over the Surrey Commercial Docks in South London and Wapping and the Isle of Dogs in the East End of London on 7 September 1940*

one Canadian Hurricane and one Spitfire from No. 66 Squadron. KG 2 in the left-hand column came under attack from 23 Hurricanes from Nos. 73, 253 and 303 Squadrons. JG 53 were alert to the danger and shot down one 303 Hurricane and damaged five more. No. 73 Squadron made a head-on attack damaging one bomber.[961]

Meanwhile, Park was hoping for Bader's Wing to turn up and deliver its promised results. As soon as the Duxford Wing did arrive it was intercepted. Arriving between Kenley and Maidstone at varying altitude (15,000–16,000 ft (4,600–4,900 m)), it emerged from cloud in the vicinity of KG 2's stream. Galland's JG 26 was directly above it. In a reversal of their roles, the Hurricanes engaged the Bf 109s while the Spitfires went for the bombers. While they failed to deliver their anti-bomber attacks, they drew in the Bf 109 escorts and free-hunting German fighters making it easier for other RAF fighters to reach the bombers. No. 310 Squadron lost two Hurricanes to JG 26, one to Adolf Galland, as the battle became a confusing mess of combats. By 14:40, the bombers reached London. KG 3 had lost three Do 17s destroyed and two damaged while KG 26 had suffered only one damaged bomber. KG 53 in the central column had lost one and three more forced to turn back owing to battle

damage, while only one KG 2 machine had been forced to do the same. Despite the British presence, 100 bombers with 120 tons of bombs prepared to
drop their bombs.[962]

One of the reasons the bombers had sustained so little damage was the cloud
base. Its density had made it difficult for RAF fighter controllers to direct
their squadrons with accuracy. The same cloud that helped shield the bombers
was to obscure the target area. Its base started at 2,000 ft (610 m) and its top
reached 12,000 ft (3,700 m). The bombers reached the Victoria Docks, but it
and the other targets were covered. The skies were clear over West Ham and
the bombers concentrated on the borough, in particular the Bromley-by-Bow
gas works. KG 3, 26 and 53 dropped their bombs at 14:45.[963]

Most of the targeted area was three square miles in extent, bounded on the
north by the over ground railway of the District line, on the west by the River
Lea, on the east by the Plaistow Marshes and on the south by the Royal Victoria Dock. The gas works were targeted by KG 26. Heavy high explosive
bombs severely damaged the plant. Upton Park tube station was also hit and
an electric sub-station was hit causing a black out. Residential areas were badly
damaged. KG 2 was unable to find the Surrey Commercial Docks. It turned
away and dropped its bombs over a wide area.[964] According to West Ham borough records, 17 people were killed, or died of wounds sustained in the attack.
Another 92 were seriously injured, while 40 were slightly injured.[965] As the
Germans retreated back out over the channel, some bomber groups scattered
while others formed uneven formations and were pursued by RAF fighters.
With fuel dwindling, the Bf 109s headed back to France, unable to help the
hard-pressed bombers.[966]

The German bombers that had been forced out of formation attempted to make
it to France using the cloud as cover. However virtually all were destroyed.
Four Do 17s and six He 111s were shot down by fighters that were now swarm-
ing over Kentish air space.[967] The main formations withdrew as more RAF
squadrons closed in. The escort plan held up, and 50 Bf 109s met the withdrawing units. Still, there were gaps in the formation. Nos. 238, 602 and
609 Squadrons exploited them. No. 238 Hurricanes engaged KG 53 while the
others shot down two Do 17s from KG 2. Bader's squadron also took part
shooting down one Dornier. Two RAF fighters were lost to the escorts. Another source indicated the German fighters sent to cover the retreat made little
impact and were hardly noticed by RAF fighters. It appears I./ *Lehrgeschwader
1* (LG 1) formed part of the withdrawal force. It lost three Bf 110s to No. 303
(Polish) Squadron RAF at 15:50. No. 303 Squadron claimed three Dorniers
and two Bf 110s while No. 602 claimed seven bombers and two fighters. Still,
the RAF grossly over-claimed German losses. They claimed 77 bombers and
29 fighters.[968]

German losses on that raid had been heavy. KG 2 had lost eight Do 17s and seven damaged. Personnel losses of the unit amounted to 19 crew killed, nine captured and 10 wounded. KG 3 had fared little better, losing six destroyed and four damaged. Personnel losses in II./KG 3, 15 were killed, 10 were captured and four were wounded. The He 111s were to suffer lightly. One He 111 was lost, its crew was captured. Three more were damaged and two crewmen were wounded. KG 53 lost six Heinkels with another two damaged. It lost 12 aircrew killed, 18 captured and four wounded including Major Max Gruber, II./KG 53's *Gruppenkommandeur* (Group Commander). The German fighter screen suffered as well. In the battle, JG 51 lost two Bf 109s, JG 52 a single Bf 109, JG 53 lost seven Bf 109s and one damaged, JG 77 lost one and one damaged, while LG 2 lost two Bf 109s. Having lost two Bf 109s in the first raid, two more were lost owing to the pilots running out of fuel or being shot down in combat.[969]

In total, the *Luftwaffe* had lost 21 bombers destroyed, and scores damaged. It also lost at least 12 fighters. The RAF had lost 15 fighters destroyed while 21 were damaged. Another source puts German fighter losses at 23.

From 15:00, III./*Kampfgeschwader 55* (KG 55) took off from Villacoublay led by Major Schlemell. It headed towards Southampton before diverting to bomb Royal Navy targets at Portland. British radar reported them as six intruders. There were actually more than 20 He 111s without fighter escort.[970] They were intercepted by six Spitfires from No. 152 Squadron from RAF Warmwell. The bombers dropped their ordnance but only five fell among naval installations causing minor damage. The RAF fighters claimed one destroyed and another damaged. KG 55 *9 Staffel* lost one He 111P-2 (one survivor) and *8 Staffel* suffered one bomber damaged and one of the crew killed.[971]

Evening and night actions

There was one more noteworthy operation before the Germans ceased their attacks for the day. At 17:40, 20 aircraft from *Erprobungsgruppe 210* took off. It was picked up just off the Cherbourg peninsula as it made its way across the central Channel to the Isle of Wight. By 17:50, it had reached St. Catherine's Point. Nos. 213 and 602 Squadrons were patrolling nearby at Tangmere, where they were kept for the duration of the raid. No. 607 Squadron, also from Tangmere, was flying to the airfield over Southampton at 15,000 ft (4,600 m) and No. 609 Squadron was on its way from Middle Wallop to patrol Portsmouth. At 18:00, by which time the German operation was virtually over, the British dispositions were completed when No. 238 Squadron took off from Middle Wallop to patrol the airfield.[972]

Figure 125: *Messerschmitt Bf 110Cs of 1. Staffel/LG 1. The type attacked Southampton in the afternoon.*

The German target was the Spitfire factory at Woolston. They arrived near it at 17:55. The Southampton guns engaged them for the entire time over the target. When the Germans retired, RAF fighters appeared. Fortunately for the British, the Germans missed the factory.[973] They did manage to rupture a number of gas and water mains while damaging nearby residential areas. There was slight damage done to the shipbuilding yard in Southampton Harbour. According to German records, 10–11 t (11–12 short tons) of bombs were dropped. Had they succeeded in hitting the Spitfire factory, they could have seriously impacted British fighter production.[974] As it was, nine civilians were killed, 10 seriously injured, and 23 slightly injured in the attack.[975]

The make up of the formation is unclear. An eye-witness, air enthusiast Alexander McKee, 22, was drinking tea at a cafe in Stoneham when the attack began:

> *....I went outside on hearing enemy planes. I counted them aloud. Ten. They dived straight on Southampton, without any preliminaries, through a barrage of gunfire, one after the other. Alfred saw a bomb released, then handed the glasses (Binoculars) to me. The aircraft had twin-rudders, and might have been Dorniers or Jaguars [a bomber version of the Bf 110 thought to be in use at the time]. The dives were fast but shallow, and they pulled out of them at about 2,000 feet. It was not a dive-bombing attack proper. Soldiers passing made inane remarks about 'nothing could live in*

that barrage', although the Germans were living in it, too. The barrage was quite good, but none of the Huns were brought down....Very quickly and efficiently the Germans re-formed and disappeared into the cloud. I have never seen a better bit of flying than those Nazi pilots [sic – German] put up – they got into formation like a well-drilled team, in the teeth of guns.

Nos. 607 and 609 Squadrons engaged the Germans south-west of The Needles. The British reported 30–40 Bf 110s with 15 Do 17s in support. The tonnage of bombs dropped suggested there were fewer bombers than claimed. The RAF fighters claimed four Do 17s. The fact remains that the Germans penetrated the airspace without interception and came very close to inflicting critical damage to the Spitfire factory. The radar had done its job and alerted No. 11 and 10 Group 20 minutes before the bombs started to fall. The fault lay either with the No. 10 or 11 Group controllers who were late in ordering their Squadrons to scramble.

More interceptions took place in the evening. The interception of two separate He 111s near London at 19:00 signalled the last engagement of daylight. It is likely they were on reconnaissance missions to assess the damage done in the attacks. The interception was made by No. 66 Squadron RAF. One of the He 111s was chased out to sea and was last seen flying on one engine. It was likely to have belonged to I./*Kampfgeschwader 1* (KG 1), which reported one He 111 destroyed upon crash landing back in France after combat.[976]

Small groups of German bombers attempted to attack London in the afternoon, causing little damage. II./*Kampfgeschwader 4* (KG 4) had one He 111 crash land near Eindhoven after combat with the crew unhurt. The bomber was 30 percent damaged. *6 Staffel Kampfgeschwader 30* (KG 30) lost one Junkers Ju 88 to fighters when it crashed in France and another force landed after combat. I. and II./*Kampfgeschwader 51* (KG 51) lost one Ju 88 each and another damaged. In the lost Ju 88s, all crews were reported missing.

Kampfgeschwader 27 (KG 27) bombed Liverpool during the night at 10:48. Widespread damage was caused in the city and neighbouring Birkenhead, but only nine casualties were inflicted. Elsewhere damage was reported at Eastbourne, Worthing, Bournemouth, Cardiff, Avonmouth, Manchester, Warrington, Bootle and Preston. RAF night fighters flew 64 sorties and intercepted two bombers. Neither the fighters or ground defences claimed any successes.[977]

Aftermath

Overclaiming and propaganda

Overclaiming in aerial warfare is not uncommon. During the Second World War, pilots often claimed more aircraft shot down than was actually the case. The Air Ministry released a press statement on 15 September that 175–185 German aircraft had been shot down. The actual number of aircraft destroyed was ⅔ lower and significantly less than the number of German losses on 15 and 18 August (The Hardest Day), in which the *Luftwaffe* lost 75 and 69 respectively.[978]

At 20:00, Churchill, who had returned to 10 Downing Street, was awoken. He received bad news from the navy. In the Atlantic sinking of shipping had been bad, but his Secretary informed him that all had been redeemed in the day's air battle. He was told the RAF had downed 183 enemy aircraft for under 40 losses.[979,980]

On 16 September, a British flying boat arrived in New York City delivering news of a "record bag" of 185 enemy aircraft. The German Embassy tried in vain to correct the total. The Germans were ignored and *The New York Times* ran several excited stories calling for a military alliance with Britain and her Commonwealth. The Germans were slower in putting their story together. On 17 September, the Nazi Party newspaper *Völkischer Beobachter* announced that attacks had caused considerable damage to London. It claimed the *Luftwaffe* destroyed 79 RAF aircraft for 43 losses. This was also a severe over claim. RAF losses amounted to 29 fighters.

AOC 11 Group Keith Park was livid with the claim returns. As far as he was concerned, claiming 200 on one day was nonsense. He placed particular blame on Leigh-Mallory's Big Wing which had claimed one third, around 60, of the 185 'victories' (total claims were 81 in the morning and 104 in the afternoon). More damage should have been done to German bombers inbound to the target rather than destroying stragglers that were no military threat as they made their way to the coast. He complained that there were too many inexperienced leaders and interceptions were being missed. Things needed "tightening up", that was Park's lesson for 15 September. Park was aware the ratio of losses was 2:1 in the British favour. It had been a decent performance, but not Fighter Command's best.

Evaluation of the day's events

In the two main engagements, the fighter losses had been about equal. The big difference was the bombers losses. Fighter Command had had greater success against the afternoon attack rather than the morning assault, which it out numbered 2:1. The ratio of German fighters to bombers had been 3:1 in the morning but 5:1 in the afternoon, so there were more targets. The more bombers Kesselring sent, the more were lost.

Kesselring was back where he started. Park's handling of the actions was a masterpiece of aggressive defence, yet he was not under the same pressure as he had been in the battles during August when air battles were so confusing they were hard to control. A big set-piece offensive played into his hands.

Leigh-Mallory claimed the Big Wings had destroyed entire formations of enemy aircraft upon seeing them. He even claimed the RAF outnumbered their opponents in several engagements. In the afternoon battle, he claimed that the Wing could not get into position to break up the bombers in time and was intercepted by German fighters. Still, while that was true he also claimed his units had shot down 105 enemy aircraft and probably destroyed a further 40. He claimed another 18 damaged for the loss of 14 and six pilots.

The claims were a massive exaggeration. But while the Big Wing had proven physically ineffective for the most part, its biggest contribution to the day had been its use as a psychological weapon.[981] German aircrews had been told the RAF was a defeated force and the German bomber units that had seen the Big Wing form up were quite shocked, and those crews in the badly hit units, including KG 2 and KG 3, that had witnessed head-on collisions with German aircraft were badly shaken.[982]

A German victory on the Battle of Britain Day was unlikely. It could only have been possible if Park had made crass errors and had been caught on the ground. Stephen Bungay postulates that had the loss rates been reversed, Dowding could have replaced those with reinforcements from his C units and carried on. Moreover, during both major engagements Fighter Command had used less than ½ of its strength. It would have been able to meet the *Luftwaffe* again on the morrow.

Hermann Göring met his staff at Karinhall the following day for a conference. Their assessments of the air battle verged on pure fantasy. They concluded the RAF had withdrawn all available fighter units from all over the country to concentrate on London. The fact that the Western afternoon raids against ports were uncontested led them to believe the enemy was breaking. Another four or five days, they thought, would be sure to break them.

The OKL believed that the British were down to their last 300 fighters, with only 250 being produced. To stop fighter production, factories in Bristol were to be attacked. London was also to be subjected to round the clock bombing.[983]

Theo Osterkamp pointed to the massed formations used by the British (Big Wing), and put their use down to the ineffectiveness of the 15 September raids. Göring was delighted with the news that the British were committing mass formations to battle. The Big Wing's use would allow the German fighters to engage and destroy RAF fighters in large numbers. However, the Germans had not realised this stratagem was by no means *the* uniform strategy in Fighter Command. Nevertheless, the OKL were still confident of victory. It blamed the bad weather and RAF's last-minute change of strategy for prolonging summer operations. Still, the *Luftwaffe* bomber crews were ordered to prepare winter quarters. The campaign turned to London for the duration of 1940. It would witness some large-scale daylight air battles, but it gradually turned to a campaign by night. It would become known as The Blitz.

Hitler's reaction and Strategic overview

Hitler did not seem overly bothered with the outcome of the air battle. For him, *Sea Lion* had also been a huge risk, even with air superiority, and he had been convinced since the end of August the *Luftwaffe* would not achieve it anyway. The war with Britain would have to go on. He would maintain the threat of invasion until 1941 through the use of strategic bombing. Then, he would turn against the Soviet Union and eliminate Britain's last possible ally in Europe. With the Soviets defeated, he believed the British would negotiate. On 17 September, he sent out a directive to the three armed services informing them of *Sea Lion's* delay. On this date, the date for S-Day had been 21 September. It was now postponed until further notice. It is likely that Hitler did not want to gamble his new-found military prestige by launching a hazardous venture across the Channel unless the *Luftwaffe* had crushed all opposition.[984] At the beginning of December 1940, Hitler told the *Oberkommando der Wehrmacht* (OKW) that they could forget *Sea Lion*, although he did not formally cancel the operation until 3 March 1942.[985]

Göring had never believed in *Sea Lion*, while Hitler had never believed *Adler* could achieve victory without *Sea Lion*. Both went their own ways. Hitler needed someone to keep up the pressure on Britain, and Göring was willing to do it. On 19 September, Hitler ordered that no further barges were to be added to *Sea Lion* ports, but those under assembly were to continue. But the damage being done by RAF Bomber Command now meant sustaining the army in readiness was becoming a strain. The invasion forces were broken up and moved East on the understanding it could be reassembled with only three weeks notice.[986]

There was no clear solution to combating Britain from the air. Göring had not given up hope of winning a victory by airborne assault. He discussed the possibility of invading Ireland (Fall Grün, or Operation Green) with Kurt Student in January 1941, in order to surround Britain by land, sea and air. The operation was shelved. Instead, the *Luftwaffe*, with varying degrees of success, carried out the strategic bombardment of British industrial cities. The lack of RAF night defences in this stage of the war enabled the German bombers to inflict extensive damage without suffering the heavy losses of the daylight campaign. It is estimated that the *Luftwaffe* lost around 500 aircrews during the *Blitz* in comparison to the Battle of Britain in which it lost around 2,800 killed, 340 wounded, 750 captured. Overall losses were cut by one-third of daylight operations.

Still, perennial problems with spares meant serviceability rates remained at about 50%. The *Luftwaffe*'s bomber crews had never been trained for bad weather or night operations. To support them, navigation aids in the form of *Knickebein* (Crooked Leg) were made available. They allowed German crews to navigate effectively to their targets. For the most part, crews were confident in using them, with the exception of poorer quality replacement crews. These systems were responsible for a few very successful attacks, such as the Coventry operation on 14 November.[987] Operations against Liverpool were also successful. Some 75% of the port's capacity was reduced at one point, and it lost 39,126 long tons (39,754 t) of shipping to air attacks, with another 111,601 long tons (113,392 t) damaged. Minister of Home Security Herbert Morrison was also worried that morale was breaking, noting the defeatism expressed by civilians. Operations against London up until May 1941 could also have a severe impact on morale.[988]

The campaign's ultimate limitation was the poor formulation of military strategy. The types of targets selected from one operation to the next differed radically and no sustained pressure was put on any one type of British target. The *Luftwaffe*'s strategy became increasingly aimless.[989] Disputes among the OKL staff revolved more around tactics than strategy.[990] This method condemned the offensive over Britain to failure before it had begun.[991]

The end result of the air campaign against Britain in 1940 and 1941 was a decisive failure to end the war. As Hitler committed Germany to ever increasing military adventures, the *Wehrmacht* became increasingly overstretched and was unable to cope with a multi-front war. By 1944, the Allies were ready to launch Operation Overlord, the invasion of Western Europe. The Battle of Britain ensured that the Western Allies had a base from which to launch the campaign and that there would be a Western Allied presence on the battlefield to meet the Soviet Red Army in central Europe at the end of the war in May 1945.[992,993]

Figure 126: *The Battle of Britain anniversary parade at Buckingham Palace in 1943.*

Commemoration

Battle of Britain Day is now an annual commemoration of the battle in the United Kingdom, specially commemorated on 15 September. In Canada, the commemoration takes place on the third Sunday of September.Wikipedia:Citation needed

Within the Commonwealth, Battle of Britain Day has been observed more usually on the third Sunday in September, and even on the 2nd Thursday in September in some areas in the British Channel Islands.Wikipedia:Citation needed

The day has been observed by many artists over the years, often with works that show the battle itself. Many mixed media artists have also created pieces in honour of the Battle of Britain.

References

Citations

Bibliography

<templatestyles src="Template:Refbegin/styles.css" />

- Addison, Paul and Jeremy Crang. *The Burning Blue: A New History of the Battle of Britain*. London: Pimlico, 2000. ISBN 0-7126-6475-0.
- Bergström, Christer (2007), *Barbarossa – The Air Battle: July–December 1941*, London: Chervron/Ian Allen . ISBN 978-1-85780-270-2.
- Bishop, Ian. *Battle of Britain: A Day-to-day Chronicle, 10 July-31 October 1940*. Quercus Publishing, London. 2009. ISBN 978-1-84916-989-9
- Bungay, Stephen. *The Most Dangerous Enemy: A History of the Battle of Britain*. London: Aurum Press, 2000. ISBN 1-85410-721-6 (hardcover), 2002, ISBN 1-85410-801-8 (paperback)
- Collier, Richard. *Eagle Day: The Battle of Britain, 6 August – 15 September 1940*. J.M Dent and Sons Ltd. 1980. ISBN 0-460-04370-6
- Cooper, Mathew (1981), *The German Air Force 1933–1945: An Anatomy of Failure*. New York: Jane's Publishing Incorporated . ISBN 0-531-03733-9
- Corum, James. *The Luftwaffe: Creating the Operational Air War, 1918–1940*. Kansas University Press. 1997. ISBN 978-0-7006-0836-2
- Dierich, Wolfgang. *Kampfgeschwader "Edelweiss": The history of a German bomber unit, 1935–45*. Allan; London. 1975. ISBN 978-0-7110-0601-0
- de Zeng, Henry L., Doug G. Stankey and Eddie J. Creek. *Bomber Units of the Luftwaffe 1933–1945: A Reference Source, Volume 1*. Hersham, Surrey, UK: Ian Allen Publishing, 2007. ISBN 978-1-85780-279-5.
- de Zeng, Henry L., Doug G. Stankey and Eddie J. Creek. *Bomber Units of the Luftwaffe 1933–1945: A Reference Source, Volume 2*. Hersham, Surrey, UK: Ian Allen Publishing, 2007. ISBN 978-1-903223-87-1.
- Goss, Chris. *The Luftwaffe Bombers' Battle of Britain*. Crecy Publishing. 2000, ISBN 0-947554-82-3
- Hall and Quinlan (2000). *KG55*. Red Kite. ISBN 0-9538061-0-3.
- Hough, Richard and Denis Richards. *The Battle of Britain* :Pen & Sword. 2007. ISBN 1-84415-657-5
- Hooton, E.R.. *Phoenix Triumphant: The Rise and Rise of the Luftwaffe*. Arms & Armour Press. 1994. ISBN 1-86019-964-X
- Hooton, E.R.. *Eagle in Flames: The Fall of the Luftwaffe*. Arms & Armour Press. 1997. ISBN 1-86019-995-X
- Hooton, E.R.. Hooton, E.R. *The Luftwaffe: A Study in Air Power, 1933–1945*. Classic Publications, London. 2010. ISBN 978-1-906537-18-0

- James, T.C.G and Cox, Sebastian. *The Battle of Britain*. Frank Cass, London. 2000. ISBN 0-7146-8149-0
- Korda, Michael. *With Wings Like Eagles: A History of the Battle of Britain*. Harper Books, London. 2009. ISBN 978-0-06-112535-5
- Mason, Francis. *Battle Over Britain*. McWhirter Twins Ltd, London. 1969. ISBN 978-0-901928-00-9
- Murray, Willamson. *Strategy for Defeat. The Luftwaffe 1935–1945*. Princeton, New Jersey: University Press of the Pacific, 1983. ISBN 0-89875-797-5.
- Price, Alfred. *Battle of Britain Day: 15 September 1940*. Greenhill books. London. 1990. ISBN 978-1-85367-375-7
- Overy, Richard. "Hitler and Air Strategy". Journal of Contemporary History 15 (3): 405–421. 1980
- Parker, Mathew. *Battle of Britain, July – October 1940*. Headline, London, 2001. ISBN 978-0-7472-3452-4
- Terraine, John. *The Right of the Line: The Royal Air Force in the European War, 1939–1945*. London: Sceptre Publishing, 1985. ISBN 0-340-41919-9
- Trevor-Roper, Hugh. *Hitler's War Directives; 1939–1945*. Birlinn Ltd. 2004. ISBN 1-84341-014-1
- Ray, John. *The Battle of Britain: Dowding and the First Victory, 1940*. London:Cassel Military Paperbacks, 2009. ISBN 978-1-4072-2131-1
- Reynolds, David: *Churchill in 1940: The Worst and Finest Hour*. In *Churchill*, ed. Blake, Robert and Louis, Wm. Roger. Oxford:Clarendon Press, 1993. ISBN 978-0198203179
- Wood, Derek and Derek Dempster. *The Narrow Margin: The Battle of Britain and the Rise of Air Power*. London: Tri-Service Press, third revised edition, 1990. ISBN 1-85488-027-6.

Attrition statistics

Confirmation and overclaiming of aerial victories during World War II

In aerial warfare, the term **overclaiming** describes a combatant (or group) that claims the destruction of more enemy aircraft than actually achieved. The net effect is that the actual losses and claimed victories are unequal.

Overclaiming by individuals can occur when more than one person attacks the same target and each claims its destruction, when an aircraft appears to be no longer in a flying condition but manages to land safely, or when an individual simply wishes to claim unjustified credit for downing an opponent. In some instances of combat over friendly territory a damaged aircraft may have been claimed as an aerial victory by its opponent while the aircraft was later salvaged and restored to an operational status. In this situation the loss may not appear in the records while the claim remains confirmed.[994]

Overclaiming can also occur for political or propaganda reasons. It was common for both sides to inflate figures for "kills" or deflate figures for losses in broadcasts and news reports. Overclaiming during World War II has been the centre of much scrutiny, partly because of the significant amount of air combat relative to other conflicts.

German methodology for confirming aerial victories

The *Luftwaffe*'s aerial victory confirmation procedure was based on directive 55270/41 named "Confirmation of aerial victories, destructions and sinking of ships" (German: *Anerkennung von Abschüssen, Zerstörungen und Schiffsvernichtung*) and was issued by the *Oberbefehlshaber der Luftwaffe*. This directive was first issued in 1939 and was updated several times during World War

II.[995] In theory, this approval process for the confirmation of aerial victories was very stringent and required a witness.[996] The final destruction or explosion of an enemy aircraft in the air, or bail-out of the pilot, had to be observed either on gun-camera film or by at least one other human witness. The witness could be the German pilot's wingman, another in the squadron, or an observer on the ground.

In the 1990s, the German archives made available microfilm rolls of wartime records, not seen since January 1945, available to the public.[997] These showed that while in theory the Luftwaffe did not accept a kill without a witness, which was considered only a probable, in practice some units habitually submitted unwitnessed claims and these sometimes made it through the verification process, particularly if they were made by pilots with already established records. In theory the Luftwaffe did not accept shared claims, but it happened. In theory each separate claim should have referred to a particular aircraft, but in practice some victories were awarded to other pilots who had claimed the destruction of the same aircraft. In 1943 the daily OKW communiques of this period habitually overstated American bomber losses by a factor up to two. Defenders of German fighter pilots have always maintained that these were reduced during the confirmation process. But the microfilms prove this not to be the case. 80 to 90 percent of the claims submitted were confirmed or found to be "in order" for confirmation up to the time the system broke down altogether in 1945.

Examples of overclaiming

Date	Unit/Air Force	Notes
10 July 1940	Luftwaffe	III./ZG 26 claimed 12 Hawker Hurricanes. The RAF recorded one lost Hurricane in a collision with a Dornier Do 17[998]
13 July 1940	Royal Air Force	No. 56 Squadron RAF claimed seven Ju 87s from *Sturzkampfgeschwader 1* destroyed over Portland. StG 1 recorded the loss of only two Ju 87s shot down.[999]
12 August 1940	Luftwaffe	The Germans claimed 22 British aircraft destroyed, actual British losses were 3. In one engagement Bf 109s from JG 2 claimed six RAF fighters, while bombers from KG 54 claimed 14. Only one fighter was shot down and six damaged.[1000]
18 August 1940	Luftwaffe Royal Air Force	The Germans claimed 147 aircraft destroyed, recorded British losses were 68, the British claimed 144 aircraft destroyed, recorded German losses were 69.[1001]
15 September 1940	Royal Air Force	On the day termed as the "Battle of Britain Day", the RAF claimed 185 German aircraft shot down. German recorded losses were 60.

1940	Luftwaffe Royal Air Force	Overall, the Germans claimed the shot down of about 3,600 aircraft, nearly two and a half time higher than the actual British losses. The RAF Fighter Command reported the shot down of 2,692 German aircraft in the Battle of Britain, actual German combat losses; including to ground fire, was only about half as many as claimed.[1002]
June 1941 - December 1941	Soviet Air Force	The Soviets of the South Western Front claimed 85 Bf 109s. A further 53 were claimed by anti-aircraft units in October and another 54 in November. Only 31 Bf 109s were recorded as lost by the Luftwaffe in this period. VVS claims on the Eastern Front amount to 3,879, anti-aircraft units claimed 752, and a further 3,257 were claimed destroyed on the ground.[1003] The Luftwaffe reported the loss of 3,827 aircraft to all causes on the Eastern Front in 1941. The VVS overclaiming more than 100%.[1004]
June 1941 - December 1941	Royal Air Force	During this period RAF Fighter Command launched a sustained 'fighter offensive' over Northern Europe, designed to tie down Luftwaffe fighter units, and hence indirectly take pressure off the Eastern Front, and to hopefully draw those Luftwaffe units encountered into a war of attrition. Fighting exclusively over enemy territory, and thus usually unable to accurately verify their pilot's combat reports, Fighter Command claimed 711 Luftwaffe fighters shot down, while losing 411 of its own fighters. The loss to JG 2 and JG 26, the principal opponents, were reportedly just 103 fighters.[1005]
6 April 1942	Soviet Air Force	A Red Air Force unit claimed seven Finnish Brewsters shot down in a single action over Tiiksjärvi-Rukajärvi area and four destroyed on the ground. Not a single Finnish aircraft was confirmed by Finnish records. Soviet pilot V. I. Solomatin claimed to have shot down five Brewster fighters and was later honoured with Hero of the Soviet Union.[1006,1007] Finns claimed to have shot down 2 bombers and 12 fighters; actual USSR air losses were 1 bomber and 6 fighters Wikipedia:Citation needed
8 June 1942	Soviet Air Force	6 GIAP/VVS ChF claimed nine German aircraft shot down in a single action. Not a single German aircraft of any type was recorded as lost.[1008]
4 June 1942	Japanese Imperial Navy	In the attack on Midway Island Japanese Zero pilots claimed more than 40 American fighters shot down and several probably destroyed. The U.S. Marine Corps squadron, VMF-221, had sent up 25 Brewster Buffalos and Grumman F4F Wildcats, losing 15.[1009]
20 July 1942 - 10 August 1942	Luftwaffe	During this period, *Fliegerkorps VIII* claimed to have shot down 606 Soviet aircraft while destroying another 107 on the ground. Actual losses of 8 VA were 230 aircraft - 114 fighters, 70 *Shturmoviks*, 29 Pe-2s, four Su-2s and 13 night bombers.[1010]
26 July 1942	434 IAP and 512 IAP	These units claimed 18 and 12 kills against Macchi C.200s of the Italian *21 Gruppo Autonomo C.T.* during *Fall Blau*. The Italian unit lost three Macchis.[1011]
15 September 1942	Luftwaffe Desert Air Force	*Jagdgeschwader 27* claimed 19-20 aerial victories while Royal Australian Air Force and RAF records report the loss of five aircraft (a further Allied fighter was lost to friendly ground fire).[1012] The Allies claimed two destroyed, two probables and three damaged in the same engagement.[1013] The Germans lost Lt. Hoffmann of *I. Gruppe* and Uffz. *Prien* to a midair collision, killing Prien. No further losses had been reported.[1014]
15 December 1942	Imperial Japanese Army Air Force	Burma: 50th Sentai pilots submitted claims for six Hawker Hurricanes shot down over Chittagong. Not one Hurricane was even damaged.[1015]

25 December 1942	United States Army Air Forces	Burma: 16th Fighter Squadron, 23rd Fighter Group pilots submitted claims for ten enemy aircraft shot down, five probable, and one damaged. The 64th Sentai lost one Ki-43 and three Ki-48s from 8th Sentai were damaged.[1016]
2 March 1943	No. 54 Squadron RAF & No. 457 Squadron RAAF; 202nd Kōkūtai, Imperial Japanese Navy Air Service	Each side claimed three enemy aircraft destroyed. Neither side suffered any losses.[1017]
17 April 1943	United States Army Air Forces	During a mission against the Focke Wulf plant near Bremen, the 91st and 306th Bomb Groups claimed 63 German fighters destroyed, plus 15 probable and 17 damaged. Only two were confirmed destroyed, with nine damaged.[1018]
18 April 1943	United States Army Air Forces	During the Operation Vengeance mission to kill Admiral Isoroku Yamamoto, the 339th Fighter Squadron claimed to have shot down three twin-engined Betty bombers and two Zero fighters. In fact, the Japanese lost two bombers, and no fighters.
5 July 1943 - 8 July 1943	Soviet Air Force: 2.VA, and 16.VA	During the Battle of Kursk, the Soviet unit 2.VA claimed 487 aircraft from *Fliegerkorps VIII* shot down. German records show the Luftwaffe lost only 41. According to the *Generalquartiemeister der Luftwaffe* 58 were lost to *all* causes. The 16 VA unit claimed 391 against *Luftflotte 6*. Actual losses were 39. The Soviets claimed a total of 878 German aircraft destroyed. Losses were 97.[1019]
17 August 1943	United States Army Air Forces, Luftwaffe	After the Schweinfurt-Regensburg mission Gunners on the bombers claimed 288 fighters shot down. Spitfire pilots claimed another 7 German fighters shot down and P-47 pilots claimed 14.[1020] Luftwaffe records show 40 aircraft lost. The Luftwaffe claimed 101 bombers and five fighters shot down, however only 60 B-17s and no fighters were reported lost.[1021] {58-95 bombers were damaged}Wikipedia:Please clarify
14 October 1943	United States Army Air Forces, Luftwaffe	After the Second Raid on Schweinfurt Gunners aboard the B-17 bombers claimed to have shot down 138 German fighters.[1022] German records state only 38 were lost + 20 damaged.[1023] German fighters claimed 121 bombers, the actual figure was 60[1024] bombers & 1 fighter lost; 17 bombers scrapped, and 121 bombers damaged.
6 November 1943	Luftwaffe	On this date Soviet army pushed retreating Germans to the west from city of Kiev Luftwaffe tried to hold the line, and Yak fighters of 256 iad were ordered to patrol west from Kiev. Erich Rudorffer of II./JG54 claimed 13 and his wingman Tangermann 5 near in city of Kiev. Soviet data is suggesting total loss of 5 Yak-fighters of which one by AA-fire and one Yak-1 of l-t Khalatjan, slightly damaged on c/m and bellylanded on friendly territory, pilot returned home[1025]
6 January 1944	United States Army Air Forces	On this date bomber crews claimed 210 German fighters and their escorts claiming 31, for a total of 241 claims. German losses amounted to 39 in total.[1026]
3 March 1944	United States Army Air Forces, Luftwaffe	On a bombing mission to Berlin the Eighth Air Force dispatched the 1st and 2nd Air Divisions, comprising 95th, 100th and 390th Bomb Groups. The B-17 gunners claimed 97 German fighters on this mission. American fighters claimed a further 82 destroyed. German losses amounted to 66. German claims amounted to 108 bombers and 20 fighters. USAAF losses were 69 bombers and 11 fighters.[1027]

? April 1944	United States Army Air Forces vs RAF	An unusual incident involving friendly fire occurred during the Burma campaign when the crew of a US B-25 fired at two approaching aircraft and later claimed to have shot down two Japanese fighters. The fighters were RAF Spitfires, one of which was piloted by New Zealand ace Alan Peart who was recorded by a ground radio unit saying, "Keep clear. The bastards are shooting at us." Both Spitfires returned safely to base, without damage.[1028]
14 June 1944	United States Army Air Forces Vs Hungarian Air Forces	During the Oil Campaign of World War II fifteen P-38 Lightning escorts from 49th Squadron, 14 FG was engaged by 32 Bf 109G-6s from the 101. Honi Légvédelmi Vadászrepülő Osztály, Royal Hungarian Air Force over central Hungary. American fighter pilots claimed 13 Bf 109s destroyed, 1 probable destroyed and 5 damaged. In the preliminary report the Hungarian fighter pilots filed claims for twelve probably destroyed P-38s, and ultimately filed claims for seven; five were eventually claimed confirmed. The actual losses of the day: five P-38s were shot down, with pilots missing, two were severely damaged, while several aircraft were lightly damaged; one Bf 109G was destroyed in air combat (pilot kiled), one Bf 109G destroyed in a forced landing as a result of air combat (pilot safe); one Bf 109G damaged during a landing accident.[1029]
18 June 1944	Luftwaffe	The Luftwaffe claimed 39 B-24s and five P-51s shot down over Schleswig-Holstein. Just 13 B-24s and two P-51s were lost.[1030]
10 June to 1 August 1944	Soviet Air Force	Just one Red Air Force unit, 324th fighter division claimed 39 Finnish Curtiss, 18 Brewster, 6 Morane and 1 Bf-109 shot down during Svir-Petrozavodsk Offensive. Finnish records are showing just 4 Morane and 2 Brewster shot down by Soviet air craft. 3 Morane and 3 Curtiss were shot down by anti aircraft artillery. Soviet 324th fighter division with 3 regiments was not only Soviet fighter unit there operating north from Lake Ladoga. Other units were 197th, 435th, 415th, 773th, 152rd, 195th, 19th Guards and 20th Guards fighter regiments.[1031]
4 July 1944	Luftwaffe III./JG5 versus Soviet 7 VA	Pilots of III./JG5 claimed 26 (at 18.59-19.30). Soviet data checked by Rune Rautio and Yuri Rybin found 2 Soviet aircraft lost in that action. Most of 7 VA aircraft had been deployed further south against Finnish forces in Svir-Petrozavodsk Offensive[1032]
25 July 1944	31st Fighter Group vs Luftwaffe	31st FG HQ/307th Fighter Squadron/308th Fighter Squadron/309th Fighter Squadron vs Hans Rudel's SG.2 and Hungarian Stukas of 102/-2. Dive Squadron and I./Stg 77. USAF Claims of 26 to 28 Enemy aircraft.Wikipedia:Citation needed German/Hungarian losses were 8Wikipedia:Citation needed
17 August 1944	Luftwaffe III./JG5 versus Soviet 7 VA	Pilots of III./JG5 claimed 40 Soviet aircraft during that day (35 found in 'supplementary claim from lists') . Soviet data checked by Rune Rautio and Yuri Rybin: 4 shot down by German fighters, 7 shot down by AA and one destroyed for unknown reason. From early June to late August just 2 Soviet fighter regiments were operating in sector of III./JG5[1033]

28 October 1944	Luftwaffe II./JG54 and 2./JG54 vs Soviet Air Force 8 GvShAP/47 ShAP in Libau	Pilots of II./JG54 Broch, Rudorffer, Tangermann and Thyben claimed 14 Il-2 shot down at 11.44-11.56 and Ludwig Böes of 2./JG54 two other Il-2 (half hour later). Soviet losses of that day in Libau area where just three Il-2. Two Il-2 of 47 ShAp were shot down more likely by Rudorffer or Tangermann or both (or one by Thyben). 8 GvShAP lost one Il-2 and most likely shot down by Broch. None of claims of Ludwig Böes can be found on Soviet loss data of that day. Total German claims were 16 Il-2. Soviet confirmed losses of 3 Il-2. 47 ShAp logbook states: *"8 Il-2 came under attack of 8 Fw190 and lost 2 a/c. Both Il-2 were shot up by fighters, and crashed in flames in the sea 8-9 km SW from Libau. Both crew killed."*[1034] On the other hand Soviet sources have confirmed Soviet losses been 28 aircraft failed to return and 10 force landed. Total German claims of that day in Courland: 28 by fighters, 31 by AA-troops. Details of Soviet losses are missing.[1035]
1944–1945	Luftwaffe	Oberleutnant Kurt Welter, claimed perhaps 25 Mosquitoes shot down by night and two further Mosquitoes by day while flying the Me 262, adding to his previous seven Mosquito kills in "hot-rodded" Bf 109G-6/AS or Fw 190 A-8 fighters. As far as can be ascertained, just three of his Me 262 claims over Mosquitoes coincide with RAF records.[1036]
1 January 1945	Luftwaffe	On this date German pilots overclaimed by between 4 and 3:1 .[1037] During Operation Bodenplatte the Luftwaffe claimed 55 destroyed and 11 probably destroyed in air-to-air combat (according to document: *Fernschreiben II.Jakolc Nr.140/44 geh.vom 3.1.1945*). Other German sources (according to document: *Luftwaffenführungsstab Ic, Fremde Luftwaffen West, Nr. 1160/45 g.Kdos.vom 25.2.1945*), quote 65 claims and 12 probables. Just 31 Allied aircraft were hit. 15 were shot down in aerial combat, two were destroyed whilst on take-off and seven were damaged by enemy action.[1038,1039]
24 March 1945	U.S. Army Air Force	The 332nd Fighter Group was awarded a Distinguished Unit Citation (DUC) for a mission flown on 24 March 1945, escorting B-17s to bomb the Daimler-Benz tank factory at Berlin, Germany. The American pilots were credited with destroying three Me-262 jets of the Luftwaffe's all-jet Jagdgeschwader 7, despite the American unit initially claiming 11 Me 262s.[1040] Upon examination of *JG 7* records, just four Me 262s were lost and all of their pilots survived. The bombers also made substantial claims, making it impossible to tell which units were responsible for those individual four kills.[1041]

References

Bibliography

<templatestyles src="Template:Refbegin/styles.css" />

- Bergström, Christer (2007). *Barbarossa - The Air Battle: July–December 1941*. London: Chervron/Ian Allan. ISBN 978-1-85780-270-2.
- Bergstrom, Christer (2007). *Stalingrad - The Air Battle: November 1942 - February 1943*. London: Chervron/Ian Allan. ISBN 978-1-85780-276-4 .
- Bergström, Christer (2007). *Kursk - The Air Battle: July 1943*. London: Chervron/Ian Allan. ISBN 978-1-90322-388-8.
- Bergström, Christer (2015). *The Battle of Britain: An Epic Conflict Revisited". London: Casemate Books. ISBN 978-1-61200-347-4*

- Brown, Russell (2000). *Desert Warriors: Australian P-40 Pilots at War in the Middle East and North Africa, 1941-1943*. Maryborough, Queensland, Australia: Banner Books. ISBN 1-875593-22-5.
- Bungay, Stephen (2000). *The Most Dangerous Enemy: a History of the Battle of Britain*. ISBN 1-85410-801-8
- Caldwell, Donald & Muller, Richard (2007). *The Luftwaffe over Germany: Defense of the Reich*. London: Greenhill Books. ISBN 978-1-85367-712-0
- Hess, William N. (1994). *B-17 Flying Fortress: Combat and Development History*. St. Paul, Minnesota: Motorbook International. ISBN 0-87938-881-1
- Hinchcliffe, Peter. *The Other Battle: Luftwaffe Night Aces vs Bomber Command*. London: Zenith Press, 1996. ISBN 0-7603-0265-0.
- Lorant, Jean Yves; Goyat, Richard (2005). *Jagdgeschwader 300 "Wilde Sau" — Volume One: June 1943 – September 1944*. Hamilton, Montana: Eagle Edition. ISBN 978-0-9761034-0-0.
- Manrho, John, Putz, Ron. *Bodenplatte: The Luftwaffe's Last Hope–The Attack on Allied Airfields, New Year's Day 1945*. Ottringham, United Kingdom: Hikoki Publications, 2004. ISBN 1-902109-40-6
- Peart, Alan. "From North Africa to the Arakan". Grub Street Publishing, 2008. ISBN 190650203X
- Prien, Jochen & Rodeike, Peter & Stemmer, Gerhard (1998). *Messerschmidt Bf 109 im Einsatz bei Stab und I./Jagdgeschwader 27 1939 - 1945*. struve-druck, Eutin. ISBN 3-923457-46-4
- Iván, Pataki - László, Rozsos - Gyula, Sárhidai: Légi háború Magyarország felett. Második kötet. Budapest: Zrínyi Kiadó, 1988. ISBN 963-327-163-0
- Spick, Mike (1996). *Luftwaffe Fighter Aces*. New York: Ivy Books. ISBN 0-8041-1696-2.
- Shores, Christopher (2005) *Air War for Burma*. London: Grub Street ISBN 1-904010-95-4.
- Thomas, Andrew. *Griffon Spitfire Aces*. London: Oxford. ISBN 978-1-84603-298-1
- Tillman, Barrett. *Wildcat: The F4F in WW II*. Annapolis: Naval Institute Press (1990). ISBN 0-87021-789-5
- Ward, John. (2004). *Hitler's Stuka Squadrons: The Ju 87 at war, 1936 - 1945*. Eagles of War. London. ISBN 1-86227-246-8
- Weal, John (2006). *Bf 109 Defence of the Reich Aces*. Oxford: Osprey. ISBN 1-84176-879-0
- Weal, John. *Messerschmitt Bf 110 Zerstörer Aces World War Two*. London: Osprey, 1999. ISBN 1-85532-753-8.

Appendix

References

[1] The British date the battle from 10 July to 31 October 1940, which represented the most intense period of daylight bombing.<ref name = "Foreman 1989 8">

[2] For example: Terraine states that the outcome was "decisive"; quoting *Luftwaffe* General Werner Kreipe, who described it as a "strategic (Luftwaffe) failure" and "turning point in the Second World War". It also states the "German Air Force was bled almost to death, and suffered losses that could never be made good throughout the course of the war". Quoting Dr (Karl) Klee "The invasion and subjugation of Britain was made to depend on that battle, and its outcome therefore materially influenced the further course and fate of the war as a whole".<ref>

[3] Stacey, p.256: "Even as Britain braced itself to meet the attack of the Luftwaffe, the nice legalities of Commonwealth cooperation had to be observed. But the R.C.A.F., like the Canadian Army, was determined that there should be no possibility of these formalities conferring any advantage on the enemy. To avoid misunderstanding, delay and perhaps embarrassment, and doubtless to emphasize the point that No. 1 Squadron was, after all, a Canadian unit, Air Commodore Walsh early brought the necessity of conforming to the Visiting Forces Acts to the attention of the Air Officer Commanding No. 11 Group R.A.F., under whom the squadron would fight..."

[4] The Polish, Czech and most other national contingents were, at this time, incorporated into the RAF itself: the Polish Air Force, for example, was not given sovereignty until June 1944.<ref>

[5] 754 single-seat fighters, 149 two-seat fighters, 560 bombers and 500 coastal aircraft. The RAF fighter strength given is for 0900 1 July 1940, while bomber strength is for 11 July 1940. UNIQ-ref-0-4259e51a55961309-QINU

[6] Figures taken from Quartermaster General 6th Battalion returns on 10 August 1940. According to these, the *Luftwaffe* deployed 3,358 aircraft against Britain, of which 2,550 were serviceable. The force was made up by 934 single-seat fighters, 289 two-seat fighters, 1,482 medium bombers, 327 dive-bombers, 195 reconnaissance and 93 coastal aircraft, including unserviceable aircraft. The number of serviceable aircraft amounted to 805 single-seat fighters, 224 two-seat fighters, 998 medium bombers, 261 dive-bombers, 151 reconnaissance and 80 coastal aircraft.<ref name="Wood and Dempster 2003, p. 318.">Wood and Dempster 2003, p. 318.

[7] The *Luftwaffe* possessed 4,074 aircraft, but not all of these were deployed against Britain. The force was made up of 1,107 single-seat fighters, 357 two-seat fighters, 1,380 medium bombers, 428 dive-bombers, 569 reconnaissance and 233 coastal aircraft, including unserviceable aircraft. The *Luftwaffe* air strength given is from the Quartermaster General 6th Battalion numbers for 29 June 1940.<ref name="Bungay p. 107">

[8] 544 aircrew (RAF Fighter Command), 718 (RAF Bomber Command), 280 (RAF Coastal Command) killed UNIQ-ref-1-4259e51a55961309-QINU <ref>

[9] "Battle of Britain RAF and FAA Roll of Honour." http://www.raf.mod.uk/history/ BattleofBritainRollofHonour.cfm *RAF.*. Retrieved: 14 July 2008.

[10] Wood and Dempster 2003, p. 309.

[11] 1,220 fighters (per type: 753 Hurricane, 467 Spitfire)<ref>

[12] Hans Ring, "Die Luftschlacht über England 1940", Luftfahrt international Ausgabe 12, 1980 p.580

[13] 812 fighters (per type: 569 Bf 109, 243 Bf 110)

822 bombers (per type: 65 Ju 87, 271 Ju 88, 184 Do 17, 223 He 111, 29 He 59, 24 He 159, 34 Others)

343 non combat (per type: 76 Bf 109, 29 Bf 110, 25 Ju 87, 54 Ju 88, 31 Do 17, 66 He 111, 7 He 59, 7 He 159, 48 Others)The British date the battle from 10 July to 31 October 1940, which represented the most intense period of daylight bombing.<ref name = "Foreman 1989 8">

[14] "92 Squadron – Geoffrey Wellum." https://web.archive.org/web/20090302084417/http://www. raf.mod.uk/bbmf/theaircraft/92sqngeoffwellum.cfm *Battle of Britain Memorial Flight* via *raf.mod.uk.*. Retrieved: 17 November 2010, archived 2 March 2009.

[15] Overy 2013, pp. 73–74.

[16] Bungay 2000, pp. 31–33.

[17] The strategic bombing commenced after the Germans bombed London on 14 September 1940, followed by the RAF bombing of Berlin and of German air force bases in France. Adolf Hitler withdrew his directive not to bomb population centres and ordered attacks on British cities.<ref>

[18] Bungay 2000.

[19] Stacey 1955, p.18

[20] Bishop 2010, pp. 14–18.

[21] Bishop 2010, pp. 18, 24–26.

[22] Murray 2002, pp. 6–7 http://www.ibiblio.org/hyperwar/AAF/AAF-Luftwaffe/AAF-Luftwaffe-1.html#cn32.

[23] Murray 2002, pp. 7–9 http://www.ibiblio.org/hyperwar/AAF/AAF-Luftwaffe/AAF-Luftwaffe-1.html#cn36.

[24] Bungay 2000, pp. 36–39.

[25] Overy 2013, pp. 42–43.

[26] Bishop 2010, pp. 18–24.

[27] Deighton 1996, pp. 12–13.

[28] Bishop 2010, p. 26.

[29] Bungay 2000, pp. 39–40.

[30] "Their Finest Hour." http://winstonchurchill.org/learn/speeches/speeches-of-winston-churchill/1940-finest-hour/122-their-finest-hour *The Churchill Centre*. Retrieved: 17 January 2012.

[31] "Battle of Britain – finest hour speech" https://www.youtube.com/watch?v=QArc2c_umzc on Youtube. Retrieved: 1 February 2015.

[32] Bungay 2000, pp. 27–31.

[33] Shirer 1964, pp. 589–593.

[34] Shirer 1964, pp. 712–713.

[35] , Directive No. 6 for the Conduct of the War http://der-fuehrer.org/reden/english/wardirectives/06.html, Berlin, 9 October 1939

[36] , Directive No. 9 – Instructions For Warfare Against The Economy Of The Enemy http://der-fuehrer.org/reden/english/wardirectives/09.html, Berlin, 29 November 1939.

[37] , Directive No. 13 http://der-fuehrer.org/reden/english/wardirectives/13.html, Headquarters, 24 May 1940

[38] Bungay 2000, pp. 31–33, 122.

[39] Bungay 2000, pp. 110–114.

[40] Overy 2013, p. 72.

[41] Directive No. 17 – For the conduct of air and sea warfare against England http://www.alternatewars.com/WW2/WW2_Documents/Fuhrer_Directives/FD_17.htm, Führer Headquarters, 1 August 1940.

[42] Overy 2001, pp. 87–89.

[43] Overy 2013, p. 90.

[44] Bungay 2000, pp. 9–13, 33.

[45] Bishop 2010, pp. 114–115.

[46] Overy 2013, pp. 68–69.

[47] Bungay 2000, p. 13.

[48] Overy 2001, p. 109.

[49] Bungay 2000, p. 32.

[50] Bungay 2000, p. ii.

[51] Bungay 2000, pp. 31, 110, 122.

[52] Operation Sea Lion – The German Invasion Plans section (David Shears) Thornton Cox 1975 – p. 156

[53] Bishop 2010, pp. 106–107.

[54] Bishop 2010, pp. 70–71.

[55] Deighton 1996, p. 51.

[56] Bungay 2000, p. 111.

[57] Bishop 2010, pp. 107–108.

[58] Bungay 2000, pp. 113–114.

[59] Overy 2013, pp. 42–43, 60–65.

[60] Heinz Magenheimer 2015, p. 20 https://books.google.com/books?id=fsFACgAAQBAJ&pg=PT20.

[61] Overy 2013, pp. 66–67, 70, 75, 690.

[62] Bungay 2000, p. 114.

[63] "Report on Comparative Trials of Hurricane versus Messerschmitt 109." http://www.wwiiaircraftperformance.org/hurricane/hurricane-109.pdf *wwiiaircraftperformance.org*. Retrieved: 19 March 2015.

[64] Lloyd, p.139

[65] "Calibration of Hurricane L1717 Merlin II Engine." http://www.wwiiaircraftperformance.org/hurricane/hurricane-11717-cal.jpg *wwiiaircraftperformance.org*. Retrieved: 19 March 2015.

[66] "RAE Chart of Spitfire I, Merlin III." http://www.spitfireperformance.com/spitfire-I-rae-12lbs.jpg *wwiiaircraftperformance.org*. Retrieved: 19 March 2015.

[67] Harvey-Bailey 1985, p. 135.

[68] Bf 109E-3 and E-4s had this armament, while the E-1, which was still used in large numbers, was armed with four 7.92mm machine guns.

[69] RAF yearbook 1978 p61

[70] Wood and Dempster 2003, p. 228.

[71] The inboard position of the upper wing roundels on the Spitfire strongly suggests this was a re-painted captured Spitfire or a photo-reconnaissance model, at least one of which was captured in France.

[72] "Fairey Battle." http://airlandseaweapons.devhub.com/blog/61173-fairey-battle/ *airlandseaweapons.devhub.com*, 16 August 2009. Retrieved: 3 November 2010.

[73] "But night after night. the Battles and the Blenheims, the Wellingtons, the Whitleys and the Hampdens went forth."<ref name="richards1953">

[74] The pilots occupying these administrative positions included such officers as Dowding, Park and Leigh-Mallory and the numbers actually fit to serve in front line fighter squadrons are open to question.

[75]

[76] Polish units in the composition of the RAF taking part in the Battle of Britain In the Battle of Britain, first in composition, and then alongside the RAF fought four Polish squadrons: two bomber (300 and 301), 2 Hunting (302 and 303) and 81 Polish pilots in British squadrons, a total of 144 Polish pilots (killed 29), representing 5% of all the pilots of the RAF taking part in the battle. Poles shot down about 170 German aircraft, damaged 36, representing about 12% of the losses of the Luftwaffe. Squadron 303 was the best unit air, taking part in the Battle of Britain – reported shot down 126 Luftwaffe planes.

[77] "The Airmen of the Battle of Britain" http://bbm.org.uk/the-airmen/ *bbm.org.uk*. Retrieved: 29 January 2017.

[78] Owen, R.E, *New Zealanders with the Royal Air Force*. http://www.nzetc.org/tm/scholarly/tei-WH2-1RAF-c4.html Wellington, New Zealand: Government Printer, 1953, Volume 1, Chapter 4, p. 71.

[79] Olson and Cloud 2003

[80] Zaloga and Hook 1982, p. 15.

[81] Gretzyngier and Matusiak 1998, p. 25.

[82] Overy 2013, pp. 67–68, 71, 80, 92.

[83] Overy 2001, pp. 61–62, 65–66.

[84] Bungay 2000, p. 122.

[85] Bishop 2010, pp. 82–83.

[86] Bungay 2000, pp. 123–125.

[87] Overy 2001, pp. 56–57, 61–62.

[88] Overy 2013, pp. 82–83.

[89] Overy 2013, p. 85.

[90] Overy 2001, pp. 78–89.

[91] This was the turning radius of a Bf 109, meaning that both aircraft, if necessary, could turn together at high speed.

[92] This formation was developed based on principles formulated by the First World War ace Oswald Boelcke in 1916. In 1934 the Finnish Air Force adopted similar formations, called *partio* (patrol; two aircraft) and *parvi* (two patrols; four aircraft),<ref>Nikunen, Heikki. ""The Finnish Fighter Tactics and Training Before and During the WW II." http://www.saunalahti.fi/~fta/fintac-1.htm FI: *Saunalahti*, January 2006. Retrieved: 26 April 2008.

[93] Wood and Dempster 2003, p. 216.

[94] "Lt Col Earle Lund, USAF, p. 13." http://ftp1.us.proftpd.org/hyperwar//ETO/BOB/BoB-German/ *ProFTPd*. Retrieved: 13 June 2008.

[95] *Abteilung V* Intelligence Appreciation of the RAF (see "Appendix 4") http://ftp1.us.proftpd.org/hyperwar//ETO/BOB/BoB-German/BoB-German-A.html . *ProFTPd.*. Retrieved: 13 June 2008.

[96] Allen 1974

[97] Overy 2013, pp. 79–80.

[98] "RAF History: Air/Sea Search and Rescue – 60th Anniversary." http://www.raf.mod.uk/history_old/sar601.html UK: *RAF*. Retrieved: 24 May 2008.

[99] Overy 2013, pp. 241–245.

[100] This account is from *Warner 2005, p. 253* Another source, *Ramsay 1989, p. 555*, lists no aircrew casualties and three 109s in total destroyed or damaged.

[101] "Speech of 20 August 1940." http://www.winstonchurchill.org/i4a/pages/index.cfm?pageid=420 *Winston Churchill*. Retrieved: 16 April 2008.

[102] Overy 2001, pp. 61–62.

[103] Overy 2001, pp. 63–65.

[104] Overy 2001, pp. 47–49, 61.

[105] Bishop 2010, p. 54.

[106] Overy 2013, pp. 71–72.

[107] Overy 2001, p. 66.

[108] Bishop 2010, pp. 80–81.

[109] Overy 2013, p. 80.

[110] Overy 2013, pp. 82–83, 85.

[111] "Satellite" airfields were mostly fully equipped but did not have the sector control room which allowed "Sector" airfields such as Biggin Hill to monitor and control RAF fighter formations. RAF units from Sector airfields often flew into a satellite airfield for operations during the day, returning to their home airfield in the evenings.

[112] "Document 32. http://www.battleofbritain1940.net/document-32.html *Battle of Britain Historical Society*. Retrieved: 19 March 2015.

[113] Overy 2013, pp. 81–82.

[114]

[115] Overy 2013, p. 82.

[116] Putland, Alan L. "19 August – 24 August 1940." http://www.battleofbritain1940.net/0029.html *Battle of Britain Historical Society*. Retrieved: 12 August 2009.

[117] Zaloga and Hook 1982, p. 15.

[118] Holland 2011, pp. 760. 657–658.

[119] the PRO, AIR 19/60.

[120] Dye, Air Vice Marshal Peter. *Aeroplane*, Issue July 2010, p. 33.

[121] Wood and Dempster 2003, pp. 212–213.

[122] Overy 2013, pp. 84–85.

[123] Wood and Dempster 2003, p. 193.

[124] Irving 1974, p. 117 Note: OKW War diary, 6–9 September 1940.

[125] Hough and Richards 2007, p. 245.

[126] Overy 2013, p. 83.

[127] Putland, Alan L. "7 September 1940." http://www.battleofbritain1940.net/0036.html *Battle of Britain Historical Society*. Retrieved: 12 August 2009.

[128] Putland, Alan L. "7 September 1940 – The Aftermath." http://www.battleofbritain1940.net/0037.html *Battle of Britain Historical Society*. Retrieved: 12 August 2009.

[129] Overy 2013, pp. 83, 87.

[130] Putland, Alan L. "8 September – 9 September 1940." http://www.battleofbritain1940.net/0038.html *Battle of Britain Historical Society*. Retrieved: 12 August 2009.

[131] Wagner and Nowarra 1971, p. 229.

[132] Wagner and Nowarra 1971, p. 235.

[133] Murray 1983, p. 52.

[134] *Irving 1974, pp. 118–119*: Irving's sources were General Franz Halder and the OKW War Diary for 14 September 1940. Keitel's notes, ND 803-PS, record the same.

[135] Bungay refers to the 14 September meeting with Milch and Jeschonnek. Hitler wanted to keep up the "moral" pressure on the British Government, in the hope it would crack. Bungay indicates that Hitler had changed his mind from the day before, refusing to call off the invasion for the time being.<ref>

[136] Overy 2001, p. 88.

[137] Overy 2013, p. 91.

[138] Overy 2013, p. 71.

[139] Overy 2001, pp. 78–89, 95–96.

[140] Jeffrey Quill wrote of his combat experience whilst flying with No. 65 Squadron: *Nearly all our engagements with Me 109s took place at around 20,000 – 25,000 ft. The Spitfire had the edge over them in speed and climb, and particularly in turning circle. (...) One engagement with several Me 109s at about 25,000 ft over the Channel sticks in my memory...I was now convinced that the Spitfire Mk I could readily out-turn the 109, certainly in the 20,000 ft region and probably at all heights.*<ref name="spitfireperformance">

[141] Bf 109 leaking valves, supercharger faults/failure.<ref>Kesselring as cited in A. van Ishoven, Messerschmitt Bf 109 at War, (Ian Allan, Shepperton, 1977), p. 107.

[142] Steinhilper, op. cit., p.280,282, 295–297.

[143] Overy 2001, pp. 95–97.

[144] Green, Ron and Mark Harrison. "Forgotten frontline exhibition tells how Luftwaffe fought with soldiers on Kent marshes." https://web.archive.org/web/20141203142439/http://www.kentonline.co.uk/kent/news/forgotten-frontline-exhibition-t-a93111/ *Kent Online*, 30 September 2009. Retrieved: 21 August 2010.

[145] Overy 2013, pp. 90–93.

[146] This proposal has since been confused, or conflated, with a possible flight by HMG in exile.

[147] "George VI and Elizabeth during the war years." http://www.royal.gov.uk/textonly/Page4081.asp UK: *Royal government*. Retrieved: 30 June 2008.

[148] Hough and Richards 2007, p. 229.

[149] Wood and Dempster 2003, p. 314.

[150] Wood and Dempster 2003, p. 306.

[151] Wood and Dempster 2003, p. 313.

[152] Deighton 1996, introduction by A.J.P. Taylor, pp. 12–17.

[153] Evans, Richard J. "Immoral Rearmament". *The New York Review of Books*, No. 20, 20 December 2007.

[154] The exact percentage was 28. The Luftwaffe deployed 5,638 aircraft for the campaign. 1,428 were destroyed and a further 488 were damaged, but were repairable.<ref>Hooton Vol 2. 2007, pp. 48–49.

[155] Wood and Dempster 2003, p. 80.

[156] Speech to the House of Commons on 20 August 1940.

[157] "Battle of Britain Day" http://www.bbc.co.uk/history/events/battle_of_britain_day. *BBC*. Retrieved: 18 March 2015.

[158] "Battle of Britain 70th Anniversary" http://www.britishlegion.org.uk/remembrance/battle-of-britain-70th-anniversary . *The Royal British Legion*. Retrieved: 18 March 2015.

[159] Battle of Britain: Special Edition DVD (1969) http://www.bbc.co.uk/films/2004/05/19/battle_of_britain_SE_1969_dvd_review.shtml BBC. Retrieved: 22 December 2011

[160] "Churchill's Island." http://www.nfb.ca/playlist/its-oscar-time/viewing/Churchills_Island/ *NFB.ca*, National Film Board of Canada. Retrieved: 17 February 2009.

[161] "Dreaming Spires." https://www.economist.com/blogs/easternapproaches/2010/09/battle_britain_1 *The Economist* via *economist.com*, 16 September 2010. Retrieved: 29 September 2010.

[162] //en.wikipedia.org/w/index.php?title=Battle_of_Britain&action=edit

[163] Moreton, Cole. "Hollywood updates history of Battle of Britain: Tom Cruise won it all on his own." http://arts.independent.co.uk/film/news/article55566.ece *The Independent*, 11 April 2004. Retrieved: 28 December 2007.

[164] https://web.archive.org/web/20100926072822/http://www.aflma.hq.af.mil/lgj/index.asp

[165] http://www.aflma.hq.af.mil/lgj/index.asp

[166] http://www.timesonline.co.uk/tol/news/world/europe/article617574.ece

[167] https://www.telegraph.co.uk/news/main.jhtml?xml=/news/2006/08/24/nbattle24.xml

[168] https://archive.org/stream/ReportOnEngland#page/n7/mode/2up

[169] http://www.ibiblio.org/hyperwar/AAF/AAF-Luftwaffe/

[170] http://www.nzetc.org/tm/scholarly/tei-WH2-1RAF.html

[171] http://muse.jhu.edu/login?uri=/journals/journal_of_military_history/v070/70.4peszke.html

[172] http://www.ibiblio.org/hyperwar/UN/Canada/CA/OpSumm/OpSumm-2.html

[173] http://www.cmp-cpm.forces.gc.ca/dhh-dhp/his/oh-ho/detail-eng.asp?BfBookLang=1&BfId=31

[174] http://www.battleofbritain1940.com

[175] http://battleofbritainblog.com

[176] http://battleofbritain1940.net/bobhsoc/index.html

[177] https://www.youtube.com/watch?v=cSZnFo7JORo

[178] http://www.life.com/image/first/in-gallery/24892/wwii-the-battle-of-britain

[179] https://web.archive.org/web/20031201065135/http://www.raf.mod.uk/bob1940/bobhome.html

[180] http://www.battleofbritainmemorial.org

[181] http://news.bbc.co.uk/hi/english/static/in_depth/uk/2000/battle_of_britain/default.stm

[182] http://www.bbc.co.uk/learningzone/clips/churchill-this-was-their-finest-hour-audio/6981.html

[183] http://www.radionz.co.nz/national/programmes/anzacday/20080425

[184] http://spitfiresite.com/2010/04/battle-of-britain-in-the-words-of-air-chief-marshal-hugh-dowding.html

[185] https://web.archive.org/web/20060520190343/http://www.remuseum.org.uk/corpshistory/rem_corps_part16.htm

[186] http://www.shoreham-aircraft-museum.co.uk

[187] http://www.tangmere-museum.org.uk/

[188] https://web.archive.org/web/20080325212017/http://www.kbobm.org/index.htm

[189] https//web.archive.org

[190] http://www.pillboxesuk.co.uk

[191] http://surfcity.kund.dalnet.se/falco_bob.htm

[192] http://www.northwealdairfieldhistory.org/content/battle-britain

[193] https://archive.is/20101113033622/http://www.celebratebritain.com/

[194] http://www.nzhistory.net.nz/war/battle-of-britain

[195] http://nzetc.victoria.ac.nz/tm/scholarly/tei-WH2-2Epi-t1-g1-t3.html

[196] http://www.battleforbritain.net

[197] https://web.archive.org/web/20111125155937/http://members.multimania.co.uk/hampshire7/ukairfields.html

[198] Führer Directive 16 http://ww2db.com/doc.php?q=316 , July 16, 1940.

[199] Deighton 1996, pp. 23–26.

[200] , Directive No. 6 for the Conduct of the War http://der-fuehrer.org/reden/english/wardirectives/06.html , Berlin, 9 October 1939

[201] Ansel, p.43

[202] , Directive No. 9 – Instructions For Warfare Against The Economy Of The Enemy http://der-fuehrer.org/reden/english/wardirectives/09.html , Berlin, 29 November 1939.

[203] Ansel, pp.47–49

[204] Bishop 2010, pp. 106–107.

[205] Bungay 2000, pp. 31–33.

[206] Overy 2013, pp. 68–69.

[207] Murray, Williamson & Millet, Alan *A War To Be Won* (Harvard: Belknap Press, 2000), p.66.

[208] Murray & Millet, p.84.

[209] Bungay 2000, pp. 9–13.

[210] Murray 2002, pp. 44–45 http://www.ibiblio.org/hyperwar/AAF/AAF-Luftwaffe/AAF-Luftwaffe-2.html#cn76.

[211] Bungay 2000, p. 110.

[212] Bungay 2000, pp. 110–111.

[213] Bungay 2000, p. 111.

[214] Bishop 2010, pp. 107–108.

[215] Cox, p.159

[216] Cox, p.160

[217] Cox, p.157

[218] Cox, p.161

[219] Bungay 2000, pp. 112–113.

[220] Bungay 2000, p. 113.

[221] Burdick and Jacobsen 1988, p. 255.

[222] Bungay 2000, pp. 113–114.

[223] Bungay 2000, p. 114.

[224] Collier 1962, pp. 219-220.

[225] Wood and Dempster 2003, pp. 212–213.

[226] Bungay 2000, pp. 368–369.

[227] Hooton 2010, p. 80.

[228] Corum 1997, pp. 283–284.

[229] Larew 1992, pp. 245–247.

[230] Messerschmitt Bf 110 Bombsights Over England: Erprobungsgruppe 210 in the Battle of Britain by John Vasco

[231] Cox, p.158

[232] Macksey, Kenneth, *Beda Fomm: The Classic Victory*, p. 35. Ballantine, New York, 1971.

[233] Von der Porten, p.111

[234] Dönitz 1958 (1997 edition), p. 114.

[235] Raeder 2001, pp. 324–325.

[236] Evans & Mcgeoch 2014, pp. 87–88.

[237] Schenk, pp.22–25

[238] Schenk, p.29

[239] Schenk, p.67

[240] Schenk, pp.65–74

[241] Schenk, p.99

[242] Schenk, pp.105–107

[243] Schenk, pp.94–98

[244] Schenk, p.95

[245] Schenk, p.113

[246] Schenk, p.111

[247] Schenk, pp.110–111

[248] Evans, p.121

[249] Alderney at War. Brian Bonnard. 1993.. pp106-108. Alan Sutton Publishing.

[250] Schenk, p.139

[251] Schenk, pp.132–133

[252] Schenk p.183

[253] p. 183 Schenk

[254] Anthony Tucker-Jones, Hitlers Great Panzer Heist, Pen & Sword Books, 2007, p.59 & p. 155

[255] Schenk p. 183

[256] Peter Fleming says on page 229 that the number of horses was reduced to 4,200 for the first wave (466 per division) and 7,000 for the second wave.

[257] p. 185 Schenk

[258] p. 184 Schenk

[259] "M M Evans, Invasion!: Operation Sea Lion, 1940, p. 181; "German Airborne Troops" by Roger Edwards (1974) p. 32"

[260] Schenk, p.231

[261] Shears, David. *Operation Sealion*, p.162.

[262] Booth, Owen, and Walton, John. *The Illustrated History of World War II* (1998), p.70.

[263] Rob Wheeler, Rob Wheeler, ed. *German Invasion Plans for the British Isles 1940* (Bodleian Library 2007), p.9.

[264] Schenk, p.323

[265] Schenk, p.324

[266] Schenk, pp.325–327

[267] Cox, pp.149–150

[268] Hewitt, Nick p. 109

[269] Hewitt, Geoff p. 41

[270] Bishop 2010, pp. 70–71.

[271] John Colville, *The Fringes of Power* (1986), diary notes on Churchill's 11 July meetings; in

[272] Deighton 1996, p. 51.

[273] Reagan, Geoffrey. Military Anecdotes (1992) p. 210, Guinness Publishing

[274] Overy 2010, pp. 87–88.

[275] Hayward, James. *Myths and Legends of the Second World War*, p. 214

[276] Shirer 1960, p. 927.

[277] Overy 2010, p. 88.

[278] Bungay 2000, p. 339.

[279] Fleming, Peter.,*Invasion 1940* (Readers Union, London, 1958), p. 273.

[280] Bungay, Stephen *The Most Dangerous Enemy: A History of the Battle of Britain* (2000) p. 337

[281] World At War, pt5, "Alone" (Thames Television 1973).

[282] Operation Sea Lion – The German Invasion Plans section (David Shears), p. 160

[283] Operation Sea Lion – The German Invasion Plans section (David Shears) Thornton Cox 1975 – p. 156

[284] Dönitz 1958 (1997 edition), p. 114

[285] Bungay, Stephen (2000). *The Most Dangerous Enemy : A History of the Battle of Britain.* London: Aurum Press. (hardcover), 2002, (paperback) p.110-114

[286] Bird, Keith W. *Erich Raeder: Admiral of the Third Reich* (2006) p. 171

[287] Churchill, Winston, abridged by Denis Kelly. *Memoirs of WWII*(Bonanza, 1978), p.355.

[288] Churchill, *Memoirs of WWII*, p.345.

[289] Deighton, Len (1980) *Battle of Britain* London: Jonathan Cape

[290] *RUSI Journal* https://rusi.org/commentary/battle-britain-naval-perspective (retrieved 27 December 2017)

[291] Macksey 1990, pp. 144–146.

[292] Macksey 1990, pp. 209–210

[293] Fleming, p.237

[294] Handbook on German military forces - Google Books p.VI-17 - VI-18

[295] Kieser, pp. 226

[296] Fleming, pp. 257–258

[297] Fleming, p. 259

[298] Cox, p. 187

[299] German Invasion Plans for the British Isles, Ed Rob Wheeler, Bodleian Library 2007, p. 10

[300] Wheeler, text of plate 7

[301] The Sandhurst wargame was fictionalised in Richard Cox (ed.), *Operation Sea Lion* (London: Thornton Cox, 1974.). An analysis by F-K von Plehwe, "Operation Sea Lion 1940", was published in the Journal of the Royal United Services Institution, March, 1973.

[302] Rich, Norman (1974). Hitler's War Aims vol. II, p. 397

[303] Goodall, H. Lloyd (2006). *A need to know: the clandestine history of a CIA family* https://books.google.com/books?id=XtARAmgYrTsC&pg=PA175. Left Coast Press, Inc., p. 175

[304] Mazower, Mark (2008). *Hitler's Empire: How the Nazis ruled Europe*, p. 109. The Penguin Press, New York.

[305] Kieser, p.249

[306] Fleming (1957), pp. 260–261.

[307] Shirer, p. 792,

[308] Shirer, p.965

[309] Kieser, p.251

[310] Kieser, p.247

[311] Rich (1974), p. 398

[312] Shirer, p. 943

[313] Shirer, p. 782

[314] Shirer, p. 949

[315] Otto Bräutigam: "*So hat es sich zugetragen...*" (Holzner Verlag, Germany 1968, p. 590)

[316] Adolf Hitler: table talk November 5th, 1941 (in: *Hitler's Table Talk*, Weidenfeld & Nicolson, 1953)

[317] https://books.google.com/books?id=fHQABAAAQBAJ&pg=PT87

[318] http://www.pillboxesuk.co.uk

[319] https://web.archive.org/web/20070504034219/http://www.flin.demon.co.uk/althist/seal1.htm

[320] https://web.archive.org/web/20080416031713/http://alternatehistory.com/gateway/essays/Sealion.html

[321] http://www.spartacus-educational.com/2WWsealoin.htm

[322] http://www.militaryhistoryonline.com/wwii/articles/sealionvsoverlord.aspx

[323] http://www.historylearningsite.co.uk/operation_sealion.htm

[324] http://www.bbc.co.uk/history/worldwars/wwtwo/invasion_ww2_02.shtml

[325] http://www.kartengruppe.it

[326] https://www.youtube.com/watch?v=Ux-J8B8fURk

[327] https://warisboring.com/its-startling-how-close-the-nazis-came-to-invading-britain-ff491fee31e6#.cipfc9l03

[328] http://archiv-akh.de/video_files_mp4/M2395_WEB.mp4

[329] RAF Box http://www.subbrit.org.uk/rsg/sites/r/rudloe_manor_1/

[330] RAF Uxbridge http://www.subbrit.org.uk/rsg/sites/u/uxbridge/index.html

[331] RAF Watnall http://www.subbrit.org.uk/rsg/sites/w/watnall/index.html

[332] RAF Newcastle http://www.subbrit.org.uk/rsg/sites/k/kenton_bar/

[333] Fighter Command Aerodromes and Sectors. http://www.raf.mod.uk/Bob1940/stations.html Retrieved: 28 May 2008

[334] Price, Alfred *The Hardest Day*, 1980, pp. 208-211.

[335] Note: Also used by Sector D

[336] Note: Also used by Sector E

[337] Note: The primary source used to list the Squadron names (e.g.; 152 "Hyderabad" Sqn.), unit code letters, radio call signs and aircraft types of the 71 Officially Accredited Battle of Britain Fighter Command Squadrons and other units which served under Fighter Command is *Ramsay 1989, p.255*.

[338] Note: The squadron code letters QJ were the same as those of 92 Squadron. The codes changed to YQ in 1941

[339] http://www.battle-of-britain.com/BoB2/Diary/Order/order_Luftwaffe.htm

[340] Note: de Zeng, Stanket and Creek provide much of the information presented in this article. Some of the information is sourced from Bungay, 2000, pp. 408-418. In turn Bungay cites Balke, Ulf. *Der Luftkrieg in Europa - Die Operativen Einsätze des Kampgeshwaders 2 im Zweiten Weltkrieg*. Germany: Bernard and Graefe, 1989. and the records of Luftflotte 3 (RL7/89 and 90), although much of this has been superseded by the research of de Zeng et al..

[341] de Zeng *et al.* 2007, Vol 1, p. 14.

[342] de Zeng *et al.* 2007, Vol 1, p. 28.

[343] de Zeng *et al.* Vol 1, 2007, p. 188.

[344] de Zeng *et al.* Vol 1, 2007, p. 194.

[345] Note: Vollbracht scored two victories each in World War I and World War II

[346] de Zeng *et al.* Vol 1 2007, p. 122.

[347] Note: Detached from rest of ZG 76 based in France, Luftflotte 2.

[348] Note: On 15 August the Bf 110 of Hptm. Restemeyer and crewmember Hptm. Hartwich was shot down over the North Sea during Luftflotte 5's attempted attack on North East England.

[349] http://www.battle-of-britain.com/BoB2/Diary/Order/order_Luftwaffe.htm

[350] Ramsay, 1989, pp.252–255

[351] 41 Squadron's Battle of Britain pilots comprised 49 men aged from 18 to 32. Forty-two were British, three Irish, two were Canadian and two were New Zealanders. Casualties were sustained by almost half the men: eleven (22.5%) were killed and twelve (24.5%) were wounded, and one of the squadron's ground crew was killed in the Blitz.

[352] Note: The squadron code letters QJ were the same as those of 92 Squadron. The codes changed to YQ in 1941

[353] *Poznański*

[354] *Warszawski im. Tadeusza Kościuszki*

[355] in normal naval use flown with a navigator, these were flown solo

[356] http://www.battle-of-britain.com/BoB2/Diary/Order/order_Luftwaffe.htm

[357] http://www.raf.mod.uk/bob1940/squadrons.html

[358] Citizens of the British Empire possessed the status of being British subjects and so held British Nationality.

[359] "World War Two." http://www.airforce.gov.au/History/ww2.aspx *Royal Australian Air Force*, 2008. Retrieved: 24 September 2010.

[360] Eather 1995, p. 106.

[361] Coulthard-Clark 2001, p. 173.

[362] Eather 1995, p. 41.

[363] De Vos 2001, p. 86.

[364] Veranneman 2014, p. 69.

[365] "Canada at War." http://wwii.ca/index.php?page=Page&action=showpage&id=48 *WWII: The Battle of Britain.* Retrieved 28 May 2011.

[366] "4 Wing." http://www.airforce.gc.ca/4wing/news/releases_e.asp?cat=90&id=681 *Canada's Air Force/* Retrieved 28 May 2011.

[367] Polak et al. 2006, pp. 6, 7.

[368] Czechoslovak pilots in France shot down 78 enemy planes and with another 14 probables (12 percent of all the French victories during Battle of France). They paid for this success with the loss of 27 pilots killed, out of 135 who flew in France.Wikipedia:Citation needed

[369] Polak et al. 2006, pp. 5, 8.

[370] Czech Pilots and the Battle of Britain (History Learning Site, UK, 2010) http://www. historylearningsite.co.uk/czech_pilots_battle_britain.htm

[371] http://yorkshireairmuseum.org/latest-news/french-raf-battle-of-britain-pilots-honoured-in-paris/

[372] http://www.ambafrance-uk.org/Free-French-Air-Forces-remembered-at-WWII-commemorations.

[373] "Brendan Eamon Fitzpatrick 'Paddy' Finucane." http://www.acesofww2.com/UK/aces/Paddy_Finucane.htm *Aces of World War 2*, 2011. Retrieved: 1 November 2011.

[374] "Battle of Britain Memorial - Paddy Finucane." http://www.bbm.org.uk/as-finucane.htm *bbm.org.* Retrieved: 28 May 2011.

[375] Byrne, Maurice. "Spitfire Paddy: A rose named after a Battle of Britain pilot." http://www.bbm. org.uk/FinucaneRose.htm *bbm.org.* Retrieved: 28 May 2011.

[376] The Airmen's Stories: P/O H Capstick http://www.bbm.org.uk/Capstick.htm BATTLE OF BRITAIN LONDON MONUMENT

[377] The Dominion of Newfoundland became part of Canada in 1949 and today is part of the Canadian province of Newfoundland and Labrador.

[378] The Airmen's Stories: P/O R A Howley http://www.bbm.org.uk/Howley.htm BATTLE OF BRITAIN LONDON MONUMENT

[379] "Keith Park — Battle of Britain." http://news.bbc.co.uk/2/hi/uk_news/7837196.stm *BBC.* Retrieved: 19 August 2010.

[380] Air Vice Marshal Keith Park was played by the actor Trevor Howard in the film *Battle of Britain* (1969).

[381] "Brian Carbury." http://www.the-battle-of-britain.co.uk/pilots/Ca-pilots.htm *The Battle of Britain.* Retrieved: 19 August 2010.

[382] Sergeant Toni Glowacki also achieved this feat. After the war he went to live permanently in New Zealand and joined the RNZAF.

[383] Olson & Cloud 2003, p. 95.

[384] Olson & Cloud 2003, pp. 96-101.

[385] Olson & Cloud 2003, pp. 108-12.

[386] Olson & Cloud 2003, pp. 144-7.

[387] Olson, Lynne. "A Question of Honor." http://www.lynneolson.com/questionofhonor/ *lynneolson.com*. Retrieved: 19 August 2010.

[388] Olson & Cloud 2003, p. 145.

[389] Reagan, Geoffrey. Military Anecdotes (1992) p. 76. Guinness Publishing

[390] Olson & Cloud 2003, p. 154.

[391] Shores and Williams 1994, p. 399.

[392] Salt 2001, pp. 107, 187.

[393] Wood & Dempster 1967, p. 518.

[394] Saunders 2003, pp. 46–47.

[395] Salt 2001, p. 187.

[396] "Billy Fiske." http://www.thehistorychannel.co.za/site/tv_guide/full_details/British_history/programme_2903.php *thehistorychannel.co.za*. Retrieved: 19 August 2010.

[397] //www.worldcat.org/oclc/459294

[398] https://web.archive.org/web/20150822121641/http://www.bbm.org.uk/participants.htm

[399] http://www.belfasttelegraph.co.uk/news/local-national/lets-praise-our-battle-of-britain-heroes-28546347.html

[400] http://www.bbm.org.uk/pilots-ir.htm

[401] Hough, Richard, and Richards, Denis, *The Battle of Britain*, page 305

[402] There is still much confusion about the involved units, depending on the sources they were for sure No.46 and 257 Sqn, that made some claims to BR.20s; often cited are also No. 245, 249 and No.17, plus one or more Spitfire from No.41 Sqn; Gustavson quotes No.257, 17, 46, 249, but apparently only No.46, 249 and 257 made contact with italians, plus one or more Spitfire from No.41. (source) http://surfcity.kund.dalnet.se/italy_ruzzin.htm

[403] Ramsey (1988), p. 313

[404] Time Magazine, Daily Damage http://www.time.com/time/magazine/article/0,9171,764937,00.html

[405] Mrazek, Group Captain Karel in *Wings of war* 1983, p. 91.

[406] Haining 2005, p. 86.

[407] Haining 2005, p. 160.

[408] http://surfcity.kund.dalnet.se/falco_bob.htm

[409] http://www.time.com/time/magazine/article/0,9171,764937,00.html

[410] The term *Dowding system* is a modern one, there was no official name for the network at the time and it was variously referred to as "the reporting system", or simply "the system". Gough also mentions "the C and R system", but this appears to refer to the operational manning of the system and its associated radars, not the system itself.<ref name="FOOTNOTEGough19934">Gough 1993, p. 4.

[411] Ministry 1941, The British Fighter Force on Guard.

[412] Bungay 2010, p. 47.

[413] Zimmerman 2013, p. 178.

[414] Zimmerman 2013, p. 182.

[415] Watt added Watson to his name in 1942, becoming Robert Watson-Watt. He remained Watt during the period covered in this article.

[416] Watson 2009, p. 45.

[417] Zimmerman 2013, p. 184.

[418] Burns 2006, p. 225.

[419] Corrigan 2008, p. 5.

[420] In *Fighter*, Len Deighton suggests that Grenfell developed the equal angles method. All sources included here give precedence to Tizard but do not specifically state that he introduced it to Grenfell.

[421] Zimmerman 2013, p. 186.

[422] Zimmerman notes that the reason for this drop in success rate was due to a lack of DF sets. It is not entirely clear why the lack of direction information would be affected by altitude.

[423] Bowen 1998, p. 24.

[424] The Observer Corps added 'Royal' to their name in 1941 and were properly known simply as the Observer Corps during the period covered by this article.

[425] Corrigan 2008, p. 4.

[426] Bowen 1998, p. xiii.

[427] Zimmerman 2013, p. 190.

[428] Coakley 1992, p. 30.

[429] Zimmerman 2013, p. 196.

[430] Zimmerman 2013, pp. 190-191.

[431] Bungay 2010, p. 49.

[432] See images.

[433] Zimmerman 2013, p. 191.

[434] There is considerable disagreement among references on who the Observer Centres reported to. Some illustrations show them reporting to the FCHQ, and this includes the description given by Bungay in the text. Others, including the *image* in Bungay, describe them reporting to the Sector Controls. This includes the RAF's own page on the system, as well as the wartime image found in this article. The later is likely because the ROC data is important during the attack phase, when the information needs to be relayed to the fighters as rapidly as possible. It is also possible they had links to both centres, switching as the battle progressed. The ROC centre in Horsham may have also provided a middle-layer, collating reports and forwarding them to FCHQ.

[435] Westley 2010.

[436] The plotters were jokingly referred to as "the beauty chorus" and there are rumours that commanders hand-picked the best looking women to run their ops rooms. The movie *Angels One Five* makes prominent mention of both.

[437] Ramsay 1989, pp. 14–28.

[438] The tote board is visible in the images; note the use of coloured lights to indicate the status of each "section" within the squadron. Squadrons typically had two or three sections, identified by colour codes.

[439] Coakley 1992, p. 29.

[440] Zimmerman 2001.

[441] Bungay 2010, p. 51.

[442] Zimmerman 2013, p. 252.

[443] The great difference in range for air-to-ground and air-to-air is a side-effect of the size of the antennas; on the ground they were much larger and had better gain.

[444] Ministry 1941, Phase I.

[445] Several all-time sunshine records were set during the summer of 1940.

[446] https://books.google.com/books?id=6Zoxm33nNE0C

[447] https://dx.doi.org/10.1179/037201806X119822

[448] https://books.google.com/books?id=VrQtiwiRKZMC&pg=PA31

[449] http://www2.law.ed.ac.uk/ahrc/gikii/docs3/corrigan.pdf

[450] http://www.stelzriede.com/ms/html/batlbrt1.htm

[451] //www.worldcat.org/oclc/5245114

[452] https://books.google.com/books?id=_AHn6smb4zEC

[453] http://www.duxfordradiosociety.org/equiphist/pip-squeak/pip-squeak.html

[454] https://books.google.com/books?id=ka_dAAAAQBAJ

[455] //doi.org/10.1080/0140239042000255968

[456] http://www.raffca.org.uk/cms/utds.html

[457] http://www.raf.mod.uk/history/fightercontrolsystem.cfm

[458] https://www.youtube.com/watch?v=Gq8y-O6eANU&spfreload=10

[459] http://navigator.rafmuseum.org/results.do?id=74357&db=object&pageSize=1&view=detail

[460] http://www.raf.mod.uk/rafsearchandrescue/

[461] http://www.asrmcs-club.com/welcome.htm

[462] //tools.wmflabs.org/geohack/geohack.php?pagename=Kanalkampf&params=50_N_02_W_type:waterbody_scale:2500000

[463] Smith 2007, pp. 98–99.

[464] Trevor-Roper 2004, pp. 74–79.

[465] Collier, 2004, pp. 159–160

[466] Hooton 2010, p. 74.
[467] Hooton 1997, pp. 13–14.
[468] Hooton 2010, pp. 74–75.
[469] AIR, 2001, p.76
[470] James and Cox 2000, p. 17.
[471] James and Cox 2000, pp. 17–19.
[472] Collier, 2004, pp. 156–158, 163
[473] Ray 2009, pp. 129–130.
[474] Parker 2013, pp. 43–51.
[475] Ray 2009, p. 129.
[476] Foreman 2003, pp. 77-90.
[477] Orange 2011, pp. 206–210.
[478] Goodrum 2005, pp. 4–142.
[479] Ray 2009, pp. 124–144.
[480] Bergström 2015, p. 286.
[481] Isby 2005, pp. 109–110.
[482] Hooton 1997, p. 42.
[483] Neitzel 2003, pp. 448–463.
[484] Hooton 1997, p. 17.
[485] Murray 1983, p. 45.
[486] Shores 1985, p. 34.
[487] Bungay 2000, p. 337.
[488] Bungay 2000, pp. 122–124.
[489] Isby 2005, p. 126.
[490] James and Cox 2000, pp. 20–21.
[491] Bungay 2000, p. 155.
[492] Hyde 1978, pp. 98–150.
[493] Smith 2007, p. 45.
[494] Smith 2007, pp. 55–60.
[495] Smith 2007, p. 67.
[496] Smith 2007, p. 68.
[497] Smith 2007, p. 93.
[498] Ray 2009, pp. 66–67.
[499] Bungay 2000, p. 179.
[500] Ray 2009, pp. 51–52.
[501] Ray 2009, p. 67.
[502] Hinsley, 1994, p. 37
[503] Hinsley, 1994, pp. 38–40
[504] Hinsley, 1994, p. 40
[505] The *Luftwaffe* developed an effective *flak* arm to defend army, air, and industrial targets. When low-level attacks were tried at Sedan in May 1940, heavy casualties were incurred.<ref>Ray 2009, p. 56.
[506] Richards, 1974, pp. 161–162
[507] Donnelly 2004, pp. 11–115.
[508] Bergström 2015, p. 281.
[509] Roskill, 1957, pp. 322–323
[510] Roskill, 1957, pp. 323–324
[511] Mason 1969, p. 133–138.
[512] Mason 1969, pp. 133–138.
[513] Bertke, Kindell and Smith 2011, p. 349.
[514] Bertke, Kindell and Smith 2011, p. 340.
[515] Saunders 2013, p. 18.
[516] Saunders 2013, p. 19.
[517] Saunders 2013, p. 20.
[518] Leading Seaman Jack Foreman Mantle on *Foylecastle* manned one of the guns unjammed it and opened fire but was mortally wounded by machine gun fire. Captain H. P. Wilson praised

Mantle in an after-report to the Commander-in-Chief, Portsmouth and Mantle was awarded the Victoria Cross.<ref name="Smith 2007, p. 94">Smith 2007, p. 94.

[519] Mason 1969, p. 141.
[520] Saunders 2013, pp. 21–22.
[521] Shores 1985, p. 36.
[522] Weal 1997, pp. 66–67.
[523] Ward 2004, p. 105.
[524] Smith 2007, p. 95.
[525] Saunders 2013, p. 22.
[526] Mason 1969, pp. 142–150.
[527] Robinson 1987, p. 136.
[528] Goss 2000, p. 51.
[529] Weal 2006, p. 25.
[530] Robinson 1987, p. 137.
[531] Mason 1969, pp. 150–155.
[532] Cull 2013, p. 181.
[533] Breffort and Jouineau 2009, p. 22.
[534] Cull 2013, p. 184.
[535] Cull 2013, p. 182.
[536] Weal 1997, p. 69.
[537] Cull 2013, p. 186.
[538] de Zeng *et al.* 2009, p. 129.
[539] Cull 2013, p. 183.
[540] Bungay 2000, p. 149.
[541] Mason 1969, pp. 156–158.
[542] de Zeng *et al.* 2007, p. 29.
[543] Bertke, Kindell and Smith 2011, p. 351.
[544] North 2012, p. 23.
[545] Mason 1969, pp. 159–166.
[546] Smith 2007, p. 100.
[547] Bertke, Kindell and Smith 2011, p. 352.
[548] de Zeng *et al.* 2007, p. 179.
[549] de Zeng *et al.* 2007, p. 171.
[550] Parker 2013, p. 72.
[551] North 2012, p. 28.
[552] North 2012, p. 29.
[553] Bertke, Kindell and Smith 2011, p. 342.
[554] Mason 1969, pp. 166–168.
[555] Cooksley 1983, p. 112.
[556] Mason 1969, pp. 168–170.
[557] Bergström 2015, pp. 79–80.
[558] Bertke, Kindell and Smith 2011, p. 335.
[559] Bergström 2015, p. 79.
[560] Saunders 2013, p. 35.
[561] Mason 1969, pp. 170–172.
[562] North 2012, p. 44.
[563] Mason 1969, pp. 172–174.
[564] Mason 1969, p. 167.
[565] Mason 1969, pp. 172–173.
[566] Mason 1969, pp. 174–176.
[567] Mason 1969, p. 178.
[568] Weal 2006, p. 26.
[569] Bungay 2000, p. 157.
[570] James and Cox 2000, p. 35.
[571] Mason 1969, p. 180.
[572] Mason 1969, pp. 179–180.

[573] Smith 2007, p. 101.
[574] Mason 1969, pp. 181–182.
[575] Mason 1969, p. 182.
[576] Bergström 2015, p. 81.
[577] Weal 1997, pp. 70–71.
[578] Mason 1969, pp. 184–191.
[579] Smith 2007, p. 102.
[580] Mason 1969, pp. 190–191.
[581] Mason 1969, pp. 191–193.
[582] Robinson 1987, pp. 224–225.
[583] Bishop 2010, p. 132.
[584] Mason 1969, pp. 195–198.
[585] Smith 2007, p. 108.
[586] Mason 1969, pp. 196–197.
[587] Legend has it that this was Mölders but post-war research suggests that he was hit by a 41 Squadron Spitfire. UNIQ-ref-0-4259e51a55961309-QINU
[588] de Zeng et al. 2007, p. 129.
[589] Saunders 2010, pp. 198–200.
[590] Saunders 2013, p. 43.
[591] Evans 2010, p. 40.
[592] North 2012, p. 83.
[593] Mason 1969, p. 199.
[594] Saunders 2013, pp. 39–43.
[595] Smith 2007, p. 111.
[596] Smith 2007, pp. 108–109.
[597] Bungay 2000, pp. 180–181.
[598] Roskill, 1957, pp. 324–325
[599] Roskill, 1957, p. 325
[600] Mason 1969, p. 200.
[601] Mason 1969, p. 204.
[602] Mason 1969, pp. 207–212.
[603] Saunders 2010, pp. 26–36.
[604] Saunders 2010, pp. 37–61.
[605] Saunders 2010, pp. 62-63.
[606] Saunders 2013, pp. 46–47.
[607] Mason 1969, pp. 217–218.
[608] Saunders 2010, pp. 62-76.
[609] Saunders 2010, pp. 77–99.
[610] Saunders 2010, pp. 100–112.
[611] Caldwell 1998, pp. 50–51.
[612] Mason 1969, pp. 217–219.
[613] Saunders 2013, p. 76.
[614] Weal 2007, p. 27
[615] Mason 1969, pp. 222–226.
[616] North 2012, p. 117.
[617] Mason 1969, p. 179.
[618] Mason 1969, pp. 227–229.
[619] Mackay 2000, p. 50.
[620] Shores 1985, p. 46.
[621] North 2012, p. 119.
[622] Roskill, 1957, p. 325–326
[623] Bungay 2000, pp. 337, 180–181.
[624] Bergström 2015, p. 13.
[625] Murray 1983, pp. 45, 46.
[626] Bungay 2000, pp. 187–188.
[627] Hooton 1994, pp. 19–20.

[628] Ray 2009, pp. 46–47.

[629] Mason 1969, pp. 141–230.

[630] Richards, 1974, p. 159

[631] Mason 1969, pp. 141, 142, 144, 146, 147, 150, 155, 158, 159, 162, 163, 165, 167, 168, 170, 173, 171, 174, 177, 180, 181, 183, 185, 187, 188, 191, 193, 194, 195, 196, 197, 198, 200, 201, 202, 207–213, 218, 219, 220, 227, 228–230.

[632] Williamson 2011, pp. 74–75.

[633] Mason 1969, pp. 141, 142, 144, 146, 150, 155, 158, 162, 165, 167, 171, 174, 177, 180, 183, 185, 187, 188, 191, 193, 194, 195, 197, 200, 201, 207, 208, 209, 217, 218, 227, 228.

[634] Hooton 1997, p. 43.

[635] http://www.ibiblio.org/hyperwar/UN/UK/UK-Defence-UK/index.html

[636] http://www.ibiblio.org/hyperwar/UN/UK/UK-RN-I/index.html

[637] //www.worldcat.org/oclc/881709135

[638] http://www.bbc.co.uk/archive/battleofbritain/11431.shtml

[639] https://www.youtube.com/watch?v=hNpjDuGPmL4

[640] http://www.convoyweb.org.uk/cw/index.html?cw.php?convoy=5!~cwmain

[641] http://www.convoyweb.org.uk/ce/index.html?ce.php?convoy=5!~cemain

[642] //tools.wmflabs.org/geohack/geohack.php?pagename=The_Blitz&params=51.50_N_0.12_W_

[643] BBC History http://www.bbc.co.uk/history/events/the_blitz

[644] Price 1990, p. 12.

[645] Ray 2009, pp. 104–105.

[646] Stansky 2007, p. 28.

[647]

[648] Bungay, Stephen (2000). The Most Dangerous Enemy : A History of the Battle of Britain. London: Aurum Press. (hardcover), 2002, (paperback). p. 112-3

[649] Cooper 1981, p. 174.

[650] Cooper 1981, p. 173.

[651] Hooton 1997, p. 38.

[652] Overy 1980, pp. 34, 36.

[653] Cox and Gray 2002, p. xvii.

[654] Montgomery-Hyde 1976, p. 137.

[655] Corum 1997, p. 7.

[656] Corum 1997, p. 240

[657] Corum 1997, pp. 238–241.

[658] Corum 1997, p. 138.

[659] Corum 1997, p. 252.

[660] Corum 1997, p. 248.

[661] Overy July 1980, p. 410.

[662] Overy July 1980, p. 411.

[663] Overy July 1980, p. 407.

[664] Corum 1997, p. 280.

[665] Overy July 1980, p. 408.

[666] McKee 1989, pp. 40–41.

[667] Faber 1977, p. 203.

[668] McKee 1989, p. 294.

[669] Faber 1977, pp. 202–203.

[670] Price 1990, p. 12; McKee 1989, p. 225.

[671] Wood and Dempster 2003, pp. 212–213.

[672] Bungay 2000, pp. 368–369.

[673] Corum 1997, p. 283.

[674] Corum 1997, pp. 283–284; Murray 1983, pp. 45–46.

[675] Ray 1996, p. 101.

[676] Williamson Murray's *Strategy for Defeat* indicated a serious decline in operational readiness. In mid-September, Bf 109 units possessed only 67 per cent of crews against authorised aircraft, Bf 110 units just 46 per cent and bomber units 59 per cent.<ref name="FOOTNOTEMurray198352">Murray 1983, p. 52.

677 Corum 1997, p. 282.

678 Overy 1980, p. 35.

679 Murray 1983, pp. 10–11.

680 Murray 1983, p. 54; McKee 1989, p. 255.

681 Overy 1980, pp. 34, 37.

682 Hooton 1997, p. 38; Hooton 2010, p. 90.

683 Bungay 2000, p. 379.

684 This was caused by moisture ruining the electrical fuzes. German sources estimated 5–10 per cent of bombs failed to explode; the British put the figure at 20 per cent.<ref name="FOOTNOTEHooton201084">Hooton 2010, p. 84.

685 Hooton 2010, p. 84.

686 Titmuss 1950, p. 11.

687 Titmuss 1950, pp. 4–6,9,12–13.

688 Mackay 2002, pp. 39–41.

689 Titmuss 1950, p. 20.

690 Titmuss 1950, p. 31.

691 Titmuss 1950, p. 34–42, 90, 97.

692 Mackay 2002, pp. 51, 106.

693

694 Mackay 2002, p. 35.

695 Field 2002, p. 14.

696 Mackay 2002, p. 34.

697 Field 2002, p. 15.

698 Coates, 1999 p. 19

699 Titmuss 1950, pp. 342–343.

700 Field 2002, p. 44.

701 Harrison 1990, p. 112.

702 Mackay 2002, p. 190.

703 Mackay 2002, pp. 189–190.

704 Field, 2002, pp. 15–20.

705 Mackay, 2002, p. 83

706 Field 2002, pp. 15–18.

707 Mackay 2002, pp. 75, 261

708 Ingersol, 1940, pp. 114,117–118

709 Field 2002, pp. 15-20.

710 Titmuss 1950, pp. 340, 349.

711 Mackay 2002, pp. 80–81.

712 Mackay2002, pp. 60–63, 67–68, 75, 78–79, 215–216

713 Ray 1996, p. 51.

714 Ray 1996, p. 50.

715 Hill 2002, p. 36.

716 Summerfield and Peniston-Bird 2007, p. 84.

717 Edgar Jones, et al. "Civilian morale during the Second World War: Responses to air raids re-examined." *Social History of Medicine* 17.3 (2004): 463-479.

718 Hyde 1976, pp. 138, 223–228.

719 Ray 2009, p. 127.

720 Ray 1996, pp. 127–128.

721 Ray 2009, p. 125.

722 Ray 2009, p. 126.

723 Ray 2009, p. 124.

724 Ray 1996, p. 194.

725 Air, 2001, p. 93

726 Hinsley, 1979, pp. 315–328

727 Mackay 2003, p. 89.

728 Mackay 2003, pp. 88–89.

729 Mackay 2003, p. 91.

[730] Bungay 2000, p. 313.
[731] Bungay 2000, p. 309.
[732] Shores 1985, p. 52.
[733] Hooton 1997, p. 26.
[734] Stansky 2007, p. 95.
[735] Bungay 2000, p. 310.
[736] Bungay 2000, p. 311.
[737] Collier 1980, p. 178.
[738] Goss 2000, p. 154.
[739] Price 1990, pp. 93–104.
[740]
[741] Shores 1985, p. 55.
[742] McKee 1989, p. 286.
[743] Ray 1996, p. 131.
[744] James and Cox 2000, p. 307.
[745] James and Cox 2000, p. 308.
[746] Richards 1954, p. 206.
[747] *Knickerbocker*, 1941, pp. 372–373
[748] Ingersoll, 1940, pp. 79–80, 174
[749] Ray 2004, p. 125.
[750] Ramsay 1988, p. 280.
[751] Sansom 1990, p. 28.
[752] Sansom 1990, p. 162.
[753] Ray 2004, p. 150.
[754] Sansom 1990, pp. 28, 81.
[755] Ray 2004, p. 177.
[756] Cooper 1981, p. 166.
[757] Shores 1985, p. 56.
[758] Hooton 1997, p. 33.
[759] Richards 1954, p. 201.
[760] Richards 1954, p. 202.
[761] Gaskin 2006, pp. 186–187.
[762] Price 1990, p. 20.
[763] Dobinson 2001, p. 252.
[764] Taylor 1969, p. 326.
[765] Ray 1996, p. 193.
[766] Hooton 1997, p. 32.
[767] White 2007, pp. 50–51.
[768] Holland 2007, pp. 602–603.
[769] Ray 1996, p. 189.
[770] Cooper 1981, p. 170.
[771]
[772] Hooton 1997, p. 35.
[773] Gaskin 2005, p. 156.
[774] Price 1977, pp. 43–45.
[775] Hooton 2010, p. 87.
[776] Hooton 1997, p. 36.
[777] Gaskin 2005, p. 193.
[778] Mackay 2003, p. 94.
[779] Stansky 2007, p. 180.
[780] Ray 1996, p. 185.
[781]
[782] Hooton 2010, p. 85.
[783] Raeder 2001, p. 322.
[784] Over 1980, p. 36.
[785] Isby 2005, p. 110.

[786] Hooton 2010, p. 88.
[787] Ray 1996, p. 195.
[788] Isby 2005, p. 109.
[789] Overy 1980, p. 37.
[790] Murray 1983, p. 136.
[791] Murray 1983, p. 135.
[792] Murray 1983, p. 52.
[793] Hooton 2010, pp. 88–89.
[794] Hooton 1997, p. 37.
[795] Ray 1996, p. 205.
[796] Ray 1996, p. 207.
[797] Ray 1996, p. 16.
[798] Calder 2003, p. 37.
[799] Calder 2003, p. 119.
[800] Ray 1996, pp. 215, 217.
[801] Neitzel 2003, p. 453.
[802] Ray 1996, p. 225.
[803] Faber 1977, p. 205.
[804] Mackay 2003, p. 88.
[805] Mackay 2003, pp. 86–87.
[806] Mackay 2003, p. 87.
[807] Mackay 2003, p. 93.
[808] Ray 1996, p. 190.
[809] Ray 1996, p. 191.
[810] Mackay 2003, p. 98.
[811] Ray 1996, p. 208.
[812] Air, 2001, pp. 95–96
[813] Hooton 2010, p. 89.
[814]
[815] Postan 1952, p. 174.
[816] Ministry of Supply index of output of warlike stores; baseline was the average output September–December 1939 and set at 100.<ref name="FOOTNOTEPostan1952174">Postan 1952, p. 174.
[817] Postan, 1952, pp. 164–166
[818]
[819] Hooton 2010, p. 90.
[820] Hall 1998, p. 118.
[821] Hall 1998, p. 119.
[822] Hall 1998, p. 120, 137.
[823] Tooze, 2006, p. 601
[824] Summerfield and Penistion-Bird 2007, p. 3.
[825] Field 2002, p. 12.
[826] Summerfield and Penistion-Bird 2007, p. 4.
[827] Calder 2003, pp. 17–18.
[828] Calder 2003, pp. 125–126.
[829] Calder 2003, pp. 83–84.
[830] Calder 2003, p. 88.
[831] Field 2002, p. 19.
[832] Calder 2003, pp. 129–130.
[833] Hayward 2007, www.ltmrecordings.com/blitz1notes.html
[834] Nicol, 2010 p. 237
[835] Way, 2015, p. 59
[836] Ray, 1996, p. 264
[837] http://www.cercles.com/n17/special/field.pdf
[838] https://archive.org/stream/ReportOnEngland#page/n97/mode/2up
[839] //www.worldcat.org/oclc/493444830

[840] https://books.google.com/books?id=RwGwpIBHhgcC&pg=PA372
[841] //www.worldcat.org/oclc/1246282
[842] https://www.worldcat.org/search?fq=x0:jrnl&q=n2:0968-3445
[843] https://www.worldcat.org/search?fq=x0:jrnl&q=n2:0022-0094
[844] //www.worldcat.org/oclc/459583161
[845] http://www.ibiblio.org/hyperwar/UN/UK/UK-RAF-I/UK-RAF-I-5.html
[846] http://www.ibiblio.org/hyperwar/UN/UK/UK-Civil-Social/index.html
[847] //www.worldcat.org/oclc/1223588
[848] http://wrap.warwick.ac.uk/49641/
[849] //www.worldcat.org/oclc/921053410
[850] http://ethos.bl.uk/OrderDetails.do?uin=uk.bl.ethos.560239
[851] http://www.timesonline.co.uk/tol/system/topicRoot/The_Blitz/
[852] https://www.theguardian.com/news/datablog/2010/sep/06/london-blitz-bomb-map-september-7-1940
[853] http://www.ltmrecordings.com/blitz1notes.html
[854] http://www.bbc.co.uk/history/british/britain_wwtwo/blitz_01.shtml
[855] http://www.20thcenturylondon.org.uk/server.php?show=conInformationRecord.87
[856] https://web.archive.org/web/20070311005143/http://www.liverpoolmuseums.org.uk/nof/blitz/
[857] http://www.storyvault.com/video/taggedwith?tag=BLITZ
[858] https://web.archive.org/web/20070928044740/http://www.forgottenvoices.co.uk/
[859] http://myunclefred.blogspot.com/
[860] http://content.library.ccsu.edu/u?/VHP,5873
[861] http://www.bombsight.org
[862] http://www.hullblitz.org
[863] https://web.archive.org/web/20120424150324/http://www.buckscc.gov.uk/bcc/archives/ea_Blitz.page
[864] http://www.memoro.org/uk-en/video.php?ID=6158
[865] http://www.memoro.org/uk-en/home.php
[866] Murray 1983, pp. 52–54
[867] Hough and Richards 2007, p. 283.
[868] Collier 1980, p. 196.
[869] Bungay 2000, p. 319.
[870] Terraine 1985, p. 211.
[871] Price 1990, p. 106.
[872] Bungay 2000, p. 333.
[873] Killen 2003, p. 147.
[874] Overy 2001, p. 86.
[875] Price 1990, pp. 154–163.
[876] Bungay 2000, pp. 318, 334.
[877] Mason 1969, p. 386.
[878] Price 1990, p. 128.
[879] Terraine 1985, p. 210.
[880] Murray 1983, p. 52.
[881] Murray 1983, p. 54.
[882] Bungay 2000, p. 211.
[883] Bungay 2000, pp. 368–369.
[884] Price 1990, p. 7.
[885] Wood and Dempster 2003, pp. 212–213.
[886] Hooton 1997, p. 25.
[887] Hooton 1997, p. 26.
[888] Hooton 1997, p. 27.
[889] Price 1990, pp. 136–138.
[890] Price 1990, p. 11.
[891] Raeder 1954, p. 322.
[892] Bungay 2000, p. 317.
[893] Price 1990, p. 12.

894 Ray 2009, pp. 104–105.
895 Price 1990, p. 17.
896 Terraine 1985, p. 196.
897 Terraine 1985, p. 199.
898 Ray 2000, p. 2009, p. 99.
899 Terraine 1985, p. 202.
900 Terraine 1985, p. 203.
901 Ray 2009, p. 108.
902 Bungay 2000, p. 134.
903 Addison and Crang 2000, p. 65.
904 Price 1990, p. 13.
905 Murray 1983, p. 50.
906 Murray 1983, p. 51.
907 Murrary 1983, p. 52.
908 Price 1990, p. 14.
909 Price 1990, pp. 15–17.
910 .Price 1990, p. 152.
911 Price 1990, p. 20.
912 Addison and Crang 2000, p. 62.
913 Price 1990, pp. 23–25.
914 Price 1990, p. 25.
915 de Zeng 2007 (Vol 2), p. 231.
916 de Zeng 2007 (Vol 2), p. 236.
917 Price 1990, pp. 26–28.
918 Price 1990, pp. 28–29.
919 Price 1990, pp. 30–31.
920 Bungay 1990, pp. 320–321.
921 Addison and Crang 2000, p. 134.
922 Weal 2004, p. 33.
923 Price 1990, pp. 29–30.
924 Bungay 2000, p. 321.
925 Price 1990, pp. 35–36.
926 Bungay 2000, p. 324.
927 Price 1990, p. 41.
928 Hough and Richards 2007, p. 278.
929 Price 1990, pp. 44–45.
930 Weal 2003, pp. 35, 37.
931 Prien and Stemmer 2002, pp. 78–79
932 Price 1990, pp. 46–47.
933 Price 1990, p. 47.
934 Hooton 1997, p. 30.
935 Bungay 2000, p. 325.
936 Price 1990, pp. 49–52.
937 Price 1990, p. 65.
938 Goss 2000, p. 154.
939 Goss 2000, p. 152.
940 Price 1990, p. 45.
941 Goss 2005, p. 68.
942 Price 1990, pp. 70–71.
943 Addison and Crang 2000, p. 135.
944 Price 1990, pp. 69–70.
945 Price 1990, p. 71.
946 Goss 2000, p. 153.
947 Price 1990, p. 72.
948 Price 1990, pp. 74–75.
949 Bungay 2000, p. 326.

[950] Price 1990, p. 73.
[951] Price 1990, p. 74.
[952] Price 1990, pp. 76–77.
[953] Price 1990, p. 80.
[954] Price 1990, pp. 81–83.
[955] Price 1990, pp. 83–84.
[956] Reynolds 1993, p. 252
[957] Price 1990, p. 84.
[958] Price 1990, p. 85.
[959] Bungay 2000, p. 329.
[960] Price 1990, pp. 85–87.
[961] Price 1990, p. 87.
[962] Price 1990, pp. 86–92.
[963] Price 1990, p. 93.
[964] Price 1990, pp. 93–94.
[965] Price 1990, p. 104.
[966] Mason 1969, p. 390.
[967] Price 1990, pp. 94–98, 99.
[968] James and Cox 2000, p. 265.
[969]
[970] James and Cox 2000, p. 226.
[971] Hall and Quinlan 2000, pp. 90–91.
[972] James and Cox 2000, p. 266.
[973] Hough and Richards 2007, p. 280.
[974] James and Cox 2000, p. 267.
[975] Price 1990, p. 110.
[976] Price 1990, p. 111.
[977] Price 1990, p. 112.
[978] Bungay 2000, p. 332.
[979] Bungay 2000, p. 331.
[980] Hough and Richards 2007, p. 282.
[981] Bungay 2000, p. 335.
[982] Bungay 2000, p. 334.
[983] Bungay 2000, p. 336.
[984] Hooton 1997, p. 28.
[985] Hooton 1997, p. 29.
[986] Bungay 2000, p. 337.
[987] Hooton 1997, p. 31.
[988] Hooton 1997, p. 37.
[989] Overy 1980, pp. 34, 37.
[990] Hooton 1997, p. 38.
[991] Bungay 2000, p. 379.
[992] Addison and Crang 2000, p. 270.
[993] Bungay 2000, pp. 393–394.
[994] Spick 1996, p. 217.
[995] Lorant & Goyat 2005, p. vi.
[996] Brown 2000, pp. 281–282.
[997] Caldwell & Muller 2007, p. 96."
[998] Weal 1999. p. 45.
[999] Ward 2004, p. 97.
[1000] Bungay 2000, p. 208.
[1001] Military History Journal - Vol 5 No 1 Myths of the Battle of Britain by Major D. P. Tidy https://web.archive.org/web/20070420131221/http://rapidttp.com/milhist/vol051dt.html
[1002] Bergström p. 280
[1003] Bergstrom 2007, p. 117.
[1004] Bergstrom 2007, p. 118.(*Barbarossa title*)

[1005] Caldwell, Don. *The JG 26 War Diary, Volume 1* (Grub Street, 1996) p. 199.

[1006] Hannu Valtonen: Luftwaffen pohjoinen sivusta : Saksan ilmavoimat Suomessa ja Pohjois-Norjassa 1941-1944. Hannu Valtonen: The north flank of Luftwaffe

[1007] Geust C-F.: Geust C-F, 4/1997 page 16, airbattle in Tiiksjärvi 6th of April 1942

[1008] Bergstrom 2007, p. 47.(*Stalingrad title*)

[1009] Tillman 1990, p. 53

[1010] Bergstrom 2007, p. 62.(*Stalingrad title*)

[1011] Bergstrom 2007, p. 58.(*Stalingrad title*)

[1012] Christopher Shores and Hans Ring (*Fighters over the Desert*, 1969), cited by Brown 2000, p. 258.

[1013] Brown, pp. 166–167.

[1014] Prien, Rodeike and Stemmer 1998, p. 175.

[1015] Shores, 2005 p.40

[1016] Shores 2005, p. 45.

[1017] Thomas 2008, p. 71.

[1018] Weal 2006, p. 22-23.

[1019] Bergstrom 2007, p. 120. (*Kursk title*)

[1020] Hess 1994, p. 60.

[1021] Caldwell and Muller 2007, p. 114.

[1022] url =http://www.historynet.com/world-war-ii-eighth-air-force-raid-on-schweinfurt.htm

[1023] Caldwell and Muller 2007, p. 136.

[1024] Caldwell 2007, p. 137.

[1025] https://forum.il2sturmovik.com/topic/17292-russian-air-force-ww2-would-they-was-so-bad/

[1026] Hess 1994, p. 71.

[1027] Hess 1994, p. 84.

[1028] Peart, 2008. Highlight Loc 1925-29.

[1029] Pataky-Rozsos-Sárhidai, 1988. pp. 41-53.

[1030] Caldwell & Muller 2007, p. 211.

[1031] Hannu Valtonen: Luftwaffen pohjoinen sivusta : Saksan ilmavoimat Suomessa ja Pohjois-Norjassa 1941-1944. Hannu Valtonen: The north flank of Luftwaffe

[1032] Hannu Valtonen: Luftwaffen pohjoinen sivusta : Saksan ilmavoimat Suomessa ja Pohjois-Norjassa 1941-1944. Hannu Valtonen: The north flank of Luftwaffe

[1033] Hannu Valtonen: Luftwaffen pohjoinen sivusta : Saksan ilmavoimat Suomessa ja Pohjois-Norjassa 1941-1944. Hannu Valtonen: The north flank of Luftwaffe

[1034] https://forum.il2sturmovik.com/topic/17292-russian-air-force-ww2-would-they-was-so-bad/

[1035] http://forum.12oclockhigh.net/showthread.php?t=3824&page=3

[1036] Hinchcliffe 1996

[1037] Manrho and Pütz 2004, p. 272-73.

[1038] Manrho and Pütz 2004, p. 287.

[1039] Manrho and Pütz 2004, p. 290.

[1040] Caldwell and Muller 2007, p. 276.

[1041] "Air Force Historical Study 82." http://afhra.maxwell.af.mil/numbered_studies/916794.pdf *AFHRA Maxwell AFB*, 1969. Retrieved: February 16, 2007.

Article Sources and Contributors

The sources listed for each article provide more detailed licensing information including the copyright status, the copyright owner, and the license conditions.

Battle of Britain *Source:* https://en.wikipedia.org/w/index.php?oldid=853712475 *License:* Creative Commons Attribution-Share Alike 3.0 *Contributors:* 72, A D Monroe III, ANode, Acroterion, Actismar, Alaney2k, Alex Shih, Anotherclown, Audaciter, AustralianRupert, BD2412, Bellerophon5685, Binksternet, BokicaK, Borhammer, Brigade Piron, Bslay22222222, CLCStudent, Catrìona, Charles lindberg, Clarityfiend, ClueBot NG, Coltsfan, Crystallizedcarbon, CubeSat4U, Damwiki1, Dave souza, David J Johnson, DavidCane, Denniscabrams, Denniss, DrZygote214, Drabkikker, Eagleash, Edknol, EdmundT, EdwardUK, Ehrenkater, Eleuther, Ernilandia, Flamingo1, Frenzie23, Fustos, Fuziion, GeneralizationsAreBad, Gigas Devil, Gilliam, GreenMeansGo, Gulumeemee, GünniX, Haakonsson, Hebrides, Hobart's Voice, Hohum, Howcheng, Icd, IdreamofJeanie, Irondome, J31ox, Jan olieslagers, Jandalhandler, Jdaloner, Jennica, JimmyBlackwing, Jiten D, John, John of Reading, Junior5a, JustinSmith, K.e.coffman, KTo288, Keith D, Kind Tennis Fan, LakesideMiners, Laytar1, Leaky caldron, Lesliewoot, MONGO, MPS1992, Mabzilla, Mahdi Mousavi, ManasV, MarshallEdin, MilborneOne, Milktaco, Mrflip, Mukogodo, Mullone, NOTkayla101, Natg 19, Nigholith, Notreallydavid, Oshwah, Ost316, PBS-AWB, PeacePeace, Peepeeelover, Person who formerly started with "216", Rklawton, Rodericksilly, Roger 8 Roger, Scorpius1975, Serols, Shellwood, Shenme, Silesianus, SilverTW, Sodacan, The PIPE, The Rambling Man, TiltuM, Tobby72, Tom.Reding, TwinkleMore, Uffizi98, VivaSlava, WOSlinker, WikiPoetser, Woodensuperman, YankeeBrit79, Ylee, Yoza823, Zawed, Zocke1r, 168 anonymous edits ... 1

Operation Sea Lion *Source:* https://en.wikipedia.org/w/index.php?oldid=852490028 *License:* Creative Commons Attribution-Share Alike 3.0 *Contributors:* 93, A D Monroe III, Abelmoschus Esculentus, Alansplodge, Alfie Gandon, All Hallow's Wraith, America789, Antandrus, Anthony Appleyard, Bender235, Bergenga, Beyond My Ken, Bgwhite, Bigturtle, Binksternet, Bis9vgrp2, Blurryman, BobAnrews, Brigade Piron, CV9933, Caealn, CambridgeBayWeather, Chaheel Riens, CharltonChiltern, Chris troutman, ChrisGualtieri, Clarityfiend, ClueBot NG, Cplakidas, Cyberbot II, Czyrko, DanielPeggoty, Dave souza, Davidelit, Dedrick Edsel, DenygDengue, Dick Kimball, Dissident93, DuncanHill, Earl Marischal, Ehrenkater, EnigmaMcmxc, ErichMilhoffer, FRibeiro66, FanuArtist, Favonian, FenixFeather, Finlay McWalter, Finnusertop, Fnorp, Foofbun, Fuortu, Garfield Garfield, GeneralizationsAreBad, GeorgeJefferys, Gob Lofa, Graeme Bartlett, HMSLavender, Hamiltondaniel, Hannu-san, Harfarhs, Hogyn Lleol, Hugo999, Ich, Irondome, J 1982, Jjdany, Joel Mc, John of Reading, Joshualouie711, Jss199, JustinSmith, Katieh5584, Keith-264, Kimozy, Kiteinthewind, KylieTastic, LilHelpa, Lucasjohansson, LynxTufts, MWAK, Machho, MartinSteinmetz, Materialscientist, Mauls, Medalofdead, Meeepmep, MisterBee1966, MisterShiney, Morris1834, NKogel, Nocality, North Shoreman, Osomite, Panzlms, Patsw, Petercascio, Pretender, Qbli2mHd, Quizman1967, RaiderAspect, Red Jay, Robert Treat, Sau226, Serols, Sevius, SheriffIsInTown, Silesianus, Simhedges, Sitalkes, Skysmith, Slatersteven, TalispinMarcahnt, Textorus, The PIPE, Tim!, Trappist the monk, Trekphiler, Trumpet marietta 45750, Urgayppl, WereSpielChequers, Werieth, Wtmitchell, Xepath, Ylee, Zarcadia, Zawed, ÄDA - DÄP, 130 anonymous edits ... 77

RAF Fighter Command Order of Battle 1940 *Source:* https://en.wikipedia.org/w/index.php?oldid=822114957 *License:* Creative Commons Attribution-Share Alike 3.0 *Contributors:* Andrew Gray, CS46, Chris the speller, Dl2000, Dlsnider, Dormskirk, Excirial, Greenshed, HoraceCoker, Hugo999, John, John of Reading, Kbthompson, KizzyB, Klemen Kocjancic, LittleWink, Londonclanger, LtNOWIS, Materialscientist, Maury Markowitz, Milavia, MilborneOne, Minorhistorian, Motmit, Nthep, R'n'B, Ravacki, Robert Brukner, SPB41Sqn, Tom harrison, 25 anonymous edits ... 111

Luftwaffe Order of Battle August 1940 *Source:* https://en.wikipedia.org/w/index.php?oldid=787171737 *License:* Creative Commons Attribution-Share Alike 3.0 *Contributors:* Abel29a, Adiespeleta, AxelHarvey, Charvex, Colonies Chris, Dapi89, Davidcannon, Dl2000, DocYako, Fdewaele, Harryurz, Hmains, Hugo999, JHunterJ, Jeff3000, Klemen Kocjancic, Kolindigo, M-le-mot-dit, Max-78, Minorhistorian, MisterBee1966, Niceguyedc, Nihiltres, Redrose64, Rich Farmbrough, Rjwilmsi, Yngvadottir, Zumalabe, Zyxw, 1 anonymous edits ... 118

List of Battle of Britain squadrons *Source:* https://en.wikipedia.org/w/index.php?oldid=844194275 *License:* Creative Commons Attribution-Share Alike 3.0 *Contributors:* AustralianRupert, Buckshot06, Catrìona, Colonies Chris, Dl2000, Excirial, Fustos, Gavbadger, GraemeLeggett, HoraceCoker, Hugo999, KizzyB, LtNOWIS, Minorhistorian, Mrg3105, SPB41Sqn, Tim!, 12 anonymous edits ... 131

Non-British personnel in the RAF during the Battle of Britain *Source:* https://en.wikipedia.org/w/index.php?oldid=848112442 *License:* Creative Commons Attribution-Share Alike 3.0 *Contributors:* 15sqnadj, Abductive, Alansplodge, Altenmann, Amyntas123, AnonMoos, Anotherclown, Askave, AustralianRupert, Bartledan, Brendiano, Brigade Piron, Brookesward, BrownHairedGirl, Brutaldeluxe, Bzuk, CaribDigita, Catrìona, Cliftonian, ClueBot NG, Colonies Chris, Cossde, Dave1185, Davidcannon, Davshul, De728631, Dl2000, DocYako, Dominik92, Drutt, Ecthelion2, Ehistory, EnigmaMcmxc, Everyking, EyeSerene, Fahrenheit666, Gbawden, GraemeLeggett, Grant65, Greenshed, Hardtanker, Harryurz, Hugo999, Iridescent, JackyR, Jacurek, JanSuchy, Jevansen, John of Reading, Jørdan, K.e.coffman, Kaiwhakahaere, KizzyB, Kolonoskopia, LMB, Leandrod, Legobot II, Lesliewoot, LilHelpa, Londonclanger, LukaszKatlewa, LukeSurl, M.V.E.i., MFIreland, Maberyroad, Mark Arsten, McMuff, MilborneOne, Minorhistorian, Mogism, Niceguyedc, Nick Cooper, Nick-D, Nyttend, Pettefar, Pyroclastic, Qertis, RASAM, RobotEater, Rodw, Sf, Shimbo, Slatersteven, Sodacan, StalwartUK, The Banner, Thorek329, Trident13, Tulkolahten, Wallie, Woohookitty, XLerate, Юкке, 77 anonymous edits ... 137

Corpo Aereo Italiano *Source:* https://en.wikipedia.org/w/index.php?oldid=839196020 *License:* Creative Commons Attribution-Share Alike 3.0 *Contributors:* 100menonmars, 1m9a9c1, Academic Challenger, Anotherclown, Bchristo, Brigade Piron, Brutaldeluxe, Capt Jim, Catsmeat, Christopher Bryan, Clarityfiend, Cunibertus, DagosNavy, Dawkeye, Dl2000, Elagatis, Esprit15d, Gaia Octavia Agrippa, Gian piero milanetti, GraemeLeggett, Grant65, IAC-62, Ja 62, Jaraalbe, Kbaughan1, Klemen Kocjancic, Kurt Leyman, Lightmouse, Lotje, Lucifero4, MarioMartelli, Mirokado, Mkpumphrey, Mukkakukaku, R'n'B, Richard Keatinge, Sam Sailor, Tabletop, Tdslk, Threecharlie, 11 anonymous edits ... 153

Dowding system *Source:* https://en.wikipedia.org/w/index.php?oldid=845825191 *License:* Creative Commons Attribution-Share Alike 3.0 *Contributors:* Arjayay, Chris the speller, Cornellrockey, Dawnseeker2000, Dl2000, Felix116, GraemeLeggett, Hmains, JEH, Jheald, John of Reading, JoshDonaldson20, Keith-264, Ken Heaton, Kencf0618, Lord Belbury, Lord Mauleverer, Maury Markowitz, Mikenlesley, Mirokado, MrDemeanour, Ninjalectual, Ora Stendar, Philip Trueman, Rcbutcher, Rjwilmsi, Wavelength, Xanzzibar, 24 anonymous edits ... 159

Royal Air Force Marine Branch *Source:* https://en.wikipedia.org/w/index.php?oldid=838355792 *License:* Creative Commons Attribution-Share Alike 3.0 *Contributors:* 23W, Davidships, Dewritech, Dl2000, Gavbadger, GraemeLeggett, John of Reading, JustBerry, KTo288, Lakun.patra, Lightlowemon, Morrispeter, Niceguyedc, Ranger Steve, Robevans123, Tim!, Tom.Reding, 3 anonymous edits ... 183

Kanalkampf *Source:* https://en.wikipedia.org/w/index.php?oldid=847858478 *License:* Creative Commons Attribution-Share Alike 3.0 *Contributors:* AustralianRupert, Bgwhite, Brigade Piron, Chris the speller, Colonies Chris, Cyclopaedic, Dapi89, Dave souza, Davidcannon, Djmaschek, Dl2000, Dpmuk, GünniX, Hohum, Indy beetle, JJMC89, Jbergner, Johnuniq, Keith-264, LilHelpa, LittleWink, Manxruler, MisterBee1966, MrDemeanour, Nick-D, PKT, Rayshade, The Quixotic Potato, Uli Elch, WOSlinker, Wavelength, WereSpielChequers, Ânes-pur-sàng, ÄDA - DÄP, 14 anonymous edits ... 195

The Blitz *Source:* https://en.wikipedia.org/w/index.php?oldid=853385441 *License:* Creative Commons Attribution-Share Alike 3.0 *Contributors:* A D Monroe III, A.Thaliana, Acroterion, Alonso de Mendoza, AprilShowersBringMayFlowers, Benjimenji03, Berean Hunter, Beyond My Ken, Binksternet, Blue520, Byteflush, Bæsj 2, CambridgeBayWeather, Charlesdrakew, Chymicus, ClueBot NG, Cnering, Cnwilliams, Dapi89, Dawnseeker2000, Dlohcierekim, Dmol, Docben, Dohertra, Dstone66, Duncan.Hull, El C, Elmeter, Eric Corbett, Excirial, Favonian, Flyer22 Reborn, FriendorFoe, Gapfall, Gilliam, Glpinagelpinagel, Gog the Mild, Graham.Fountain, GrindtXX, Gulumeemee, Heegey, Hohum, Hux, Irondome, JJBers Public, Jackfork, JimTylerwood, Jiten D, Joey Babalabony, John, Jonesey95, Jprg1966, Keith D, Keith-264, Keswick.from.kidderminster, Kieronoldham, KylieTastic, L293D, Laszlo Panaflex, Laytar1, Londonclanger, MRD2014, Mandruss, MarcBell, Materialscientist, Maury Markowitz, Mecklin, MeinKampf69, MelbourneStar, Mild Bill Hiccup, MisterBee1966, NFLisAwesome, NSPanamera, Naviguessor, NeilN, Neptune's Trident, Neveselbert, Newzild, Nick-D, North Shoreman, Optakeover, Oshwah, PBS, Patrick Neylan, Philip Trueman, Pincrete, Quinton Feldberg, Qzd, RDavidson, Rjensen, Shellwood, Shenme, Simplexity22, The Anomebot2, The PIPE, The Rambling Man, Thewolfchild, Topbanana, Trekphiler, Widr, Wvs, Ylee, 136 anonymous edits ... 241

Battle of Britain Day *Source:* https://en.wikipedia.org/w/index.php?oldid=851048283 *License:* Creative Commons Attribution-Share Alike 3.0 *Contributors:* Acroterion, Alaney2k, Ammarpad, Anotherclown, ArnoldReinhold, BD2412, Beetstra, Biografer, Brigade Piron, Chowbok, Chris the speller, Cplakidas, Cyfal, DZ, Dapi89, Davidcannon, Dawnsky24, Diannaa, Dl2000, Dpmuk, E-Kartoffel, EoGuy, Epicgenius, Geoffrey Matthews, Grant65, GreenReaper, Greenshed, Grover cleveland, HMSSolent, Harrison49, Howcheng, JHunterJ, Jamesx12345, Jennica, Jllatimer, John of Reading, Jpjohnsn, Kinigi, MWAK, MX, MZMcBride, Magus732, Marc Kupper, Maury Markowitz, Mike Rosoft, Minorhistorian, MisterBee1966, Mx. Granger, Neun-x, Nick-D, Piledhigheranddeeper, ProjectHorizons, Ruby Murray, Scarecrow47, StAnselm, Tesscass, The Anome, The PIPE, The Rambling Man, TheGeneralUser, Trahelliven, Travelpleb, TwinkleMore, UConnHusky7, Very Odd Bod, Wavelength, Womboy, Woohookitty, Xyl 54, Ylee, Zet7699348, ÄDA - DÄP, Шуфель, 71 anonymous edits ... 288

Confirmation and overclaiming of aerial victories during World War II *Source:* https://en.wikipedia.org/w/index.php?oldid=853182438 *License:* Creative Commons Attribution-Share Alike 3.0 *Contributors:* BD2412, BerelZ, Binksternet, Boris0192, Btillman, Dapi89, Dircovic, Gavbadger, Georgejdorner, GraemeLeggett, Grant65, Harryurz, K.e.coffman, Kevin Murray, Kintaro, Kurfürst, Kuru, LilHelpa, Markus Becker02, MatiasGerlich, MisterBee1966, Neunhist, Newzild, Nick-D, Pablozeta, Redrose64, ShelfSkewed, Soundofmusicals, Sturmvogel 66, Tabletop, Tarkkis, Tesscass, Tramonte, Trekphiler, Winston365, Xyl 54, YUL89YYZ, 46 anonymous edits ... 323

Image Sources, Licenses and Contributors

The sources listed for each image provide more detailed licensing information including the copyright status, the copyright owner, and the license conditions.

Figure 37 *Source:* https://en.wikipedia.org/w/index.php?title=File:Air_Raid_Shelter_Under_the_Railway_Arches,_South_East_London,_England,_1940_D1587.jpg *License:* Public Domain *Contributors:* Fæ, Labattblueboy, Oxyman, Rcbutcher 54
Figure 38 *Source:* https://en.wikipedia.org/w/index.php?title=File:Battle_of_britain_firefighting.jpg *License:* Public Domain *Contributors:* BotMultichill, Consequentially, Delusion23, Hohum, MartinD, Oneblackline, 1 anonymous edits 55
Figure 39 *Source:* https://en.wikipedia.org/w/index.php?title=File:Dorniervictoriastation.jpg *License:* Public Domain *Contributors:* Dapi89, Hohum, Travelpleb 56
Figure 40 *Source:* https://en.wikipedia.org/w/index.php?title=File:Spitfires_camera_gun_film_shows_tracer_ammunition.jpg *License:* Public Domain *Contributors:* No. 609 Squadron RAF 57
Figure 41 *Source:* https://en.wikipedia.org/w/index.php?title=File:Never_was_so_much_owed_by_so_many_to_so_few.jpg *License:* Public Domain *Contributors:* H.M. Stationery Office 64
Figure 42 *Source:* https://en.wikipedia.org/w/index.php?title=File:Battle_of_Britain_Anniversary,_1943_-_RAF_Parade_at_Buckingham_Palace_Art.IWMARTLD3911.jpg *License:* Public Domain *Contributors:* 14GTR, Fæ, Labattblueboy, BoенTex 64
Figure 43 *Source:* https://en.wikipedia.org/w/index.php?title=File:Monument_of_Polish_Pilots_in_Northolt.JPG *License:* Creative Commons Zero *Contributors:* Darekm135, KoczoPL 66
Image *Source:* https://en.wikipedia.org/w/index.php?title=File:OperationSealion.svg *License:* Public Domain *Contributors:* User:Wereon 77
Figure 44 *Source:* https://en.wikipedia.org/w/index.php?title=File:D.Adm.66_Der_Kanal_Ost_Blatt_by_www.kartengruppe.it.jpg *License:* Creative Commons Attribution-Sharealike 3.0 *Contributors:* User:Pino Esposito 86
Figure 45 *Source:* https://en.wikipedia.org/w/index.php?title=File:Bundesarchiv_Bild_101II-MN-1369-10A,_Wilhelmshaven,_Prahme_für_"Unternehmen_Seelöwe".jpg *License:* Creative Commons Attribution-Sharealike 3.0 Germany *Contributors:* Martin H., Pibwl, WerWil 88
Figure 46 *Source:* https://en.wikipedia.org/w/index.php?title=File:Bundesarchiv_Bild_101II-MN-2781-19,_Russland,_Landungsboot_mit_Zugkraftwagen.jpg *License:* Creative Commons Attribution-Sharealike 3.0 Germany *Contributors:* BotMultichill, Cirt, Fallschirmjäger, Martin H., Motacilla, Pibwl, SuperTank17, Wieralee, 1 anonymous edits 88
Figure 47 *Source:* https://en.wikipedia.org/w/index.php?title=File:Bundesarchiv_Bild_101II-MW-5674-45,_Übungen_mit_Panzer_III_für_Unternehmen_Seelöwe.jpg *License:* Creative Commons Attribution-Sharealike 3.0 Germany *Contributors:* BotMultichill, Brakeet, Bukvoed, Gandvik, Paul.Matthies 92
Figure 48 *Source:* https://en.wikipedia.org/w/index.php?title=File:210_mm_Railway_Gun.jpg *License:* Public Domain *Contributors:* 1989, Peter-Jewell, Rcbutcher, Roo72 97
Figure 49 *Source:* https://en.wikipedia.org/w/index.php?title=File:Six-franz-nuremberg.jpg *License:* Public Domain *Contributors:* BotMultichill, Doctorbigtime∼commonswiki, Frank-m, Jcb, Lotje, Mtsmallwood, Mutter Erde, P199 105
Image *Source:* https://en.wikipedia.org/w/index.php?title=File:Commons-logo.svg *License:* logo *Contributors:* Anomie, Callanecc, CambridgeBayWeather, Jo-Jo Eumerus, RHaworth 108
Figure 50 *Source:* https://en.wikipedia.org/w/index.php?title=File:Spitfire_and_He_111_during_Battle_of_Britain_1940.jpg *License:* Public Domain *Contributors:* Australian armed forces 132
Image *Source:* https://en.wikipedia.org/w/index.php?title=File:Flag_of_Poland.svg *License:* Public Domain *Contributors:* Anomie, Jo-Jo Eumerus, Mifter 137
Image *Source:* https://en.wikipedia.org/w/index.php?title=File:Flag_of_New_Zealand.svg *License:* Public Domain *Contributors:* Achim1999, Adabow, Adambro, Arria Belli, Avenue, Bawolff, Bjankuloski06en, ButterStick, Cycn, Denelson83, Denniss, Donk∼commonswiki, Duduziq, EugeneZelenko, Fred J, FreshCorp619, Fry1989, George Ho, GoldenRainbow, Hugh Jass, Ibagli, Jusjih, Klemen Kocjancic, MAXXX-309, Mamndassan, Mattes, Mindmatrix, Nightstallion, O, Ozgurnarin, Peeperman, Pembe karadeniz, Poco a poco, Poromiami, Reisio, Rfc1394, Salvabl, Salvaeditor, Sarang, Shizhao, SiBr4, Steinsplitter, Tabasco∼commonswiki, TintoMeches, Transparent Blue, Voyager, Väsk, Xufanc, Yann, Zscout370, 43 anonymous edits 137
Image *Source:* https://en.wikipedia.org/w/index.php?title=File:Flag_of_the_Czech_Republic.svg *License:* Public Domain *Contributors:* -xfi-, Alkari, Andres gb.ldc, AwOc, Benzoyl, Bjankuloski06en, C41n, Cycn, Denelson83, Denniss, Dzordzm, EZBELLA, Er Komandante, Fedor204, Fibonacci, FreshCorp619, Fry1989, Future Perfect at Sunrise, Gumruch, Homo lupus, JuTa, Klemen Kocjancic, Leyo, Li-sung, MAXXX-309, Madden, Miraceti, NeverDoING, Nightstallion, Pfctdayelise, Phlegmatic, Pseudomoi, Pumbaa80, Ratatosk, Ricordisamoa, Saibo, Sangjinhwa, Sarang, Shybird, SiBr4, Stephanie∼commonswiki, V-ball, Wiki-vr, علی المزارقه, 43 anonymous edits 137
Image *Source:* https://en.wikipedia.org/w/index.php?title=File:Flag_of_Belgium_(civil).svg *License:* Public Domain *Contributors:* Allforrous, Andres gb.ldc, Bean49, Cathy Richards, David Descamps, Dbenbenn, Denelson83, Evanc0912, FreshCorp619, Fry1989, Gabriel trzy, Howcome, IvanOS, Jdx, Mimich, Ms2ger, Nightstallion, Oreo Priest, Pitke, Ricordisamoa, Rocket000, Rodejong, Sarang, SiBr4, Sir Iain, ThomasPusch, Warddr, Zscout370, ייהליזוישמר, 15 anonymous edits 137
Image *Source:* https://en.wikipedia.org/w/index.php?title=File:Flag_of_Australia.svg *License:* Public Domain *Contributors:* Anomie, Jo-Jo Eumerus, Mifter 137
Image *Source:* https://en.wikipedia.org/w/index.php?title=File:Flag_of_South_Africa_(1928–1982).svg *License:* Public Domain *Contributors:* Parliament of South Africa (Vector graphics image by Denelson83) 137
Image *Source:* https://en.wikipedia.org/w/index.php?title=File:Flag_of_Free_France_(1940-1944).svg *License:* Public Domain *Contributors:* Alkari, Cycn, DIREKTOR, Denelson83, Illegitimate Barrister, Man vyi, Olivier, Quistnix, Sarang, Sir Iain, TCY, Turbothy, Zscout370, 3 anonymous edits 137
Image *Source:* https://en.wikipedia.org/w/index.php?title=File:Flag_of_Ireland.svg *License:* Public Domain *Contributors:* User:SKopp 137
Image *Source:* https://en.wikipedia.org/w/index.php?title=File:Flag_of_the_United_States_(1912-1959).svg *License:* Public Domain *Contributors:* Created by jacobolus using Adobe Illustrator. 137
Image *Source:* https://en.wikipedia.org/w/index.php?title=File:Flag_of_Southern_Rhodesia_(1923-1964).svg *License:* GNU Free Documentation License *Contributors:* Greentubing 137
Image *Source:* https://en.wikipedia.org/w/index.php?title=File:Flag_of_Jamaica_(1906-1957).svg *License:* Public Domain *Contributors:* Thommy 137
Image *Source:* https://en.wikipedia.org/w/index.php?title=File:Flag_of_Barbados_(1870–1966).svg *Contributors:* User:Sodacan 137
Image *Source:* https://en.wikipedia.org/w/index.php?title=File:Dominion_of_Newfoundland_Red_Ensign.svg *License:* Creative Commons Attribution-Sharealike 3.0 *Contributors:* User:Lrenhrda 137
Image *Source:* https://en.wikipedia.org/w/index.php?title=File:Flag_of_Northern_Rhodesia_(1939-1953).svg *Contributors:* - 137
Figure 51 *Source:* https://en.wikipedia.org/w/index.php?title=File:Royal_Air_Force_Fighter_Command,_1939-1945._CH10109.jpg *License:* Public Domain *Contributors:* Brigade Piron, Fæ, Labattblueboy 140
Figure 52 *Source:* https//en.wikipedia.org *License:* Public Domain *Contributors:* Brian Crawford, De728631, Ducksoup, Fæ, Labattblueboy, PeterWD, Rcbutcher 141
Figure 53 *Source:* https://en.wikipedia.org/w/index.php?title=File:Royal_Air_Force_Fighter_Command,_1939-1945._D10206.jpg *License:* Public Domain *Contributors:* Fæ, JanSuchy, Labattblueboy, Rcbutcher 143
Figure 54 *Source:* https://en.wikipedia.org/w/index.php?title=File:Finucane.jpg *License:* Public Domain *Contributors:* Bzuk 144
Figure 55 *Source:* https://en.wikipedia.org/w/index.php?title=File:Sir_Keith_Park.jpg *License:* Public Domain *Contributors:* Royal Air Force official photographer 145
Figure 56 *Source:* https://en.wikipedia.org/w/index.php?title=File:Piloci_303.jpg *License:* Public Domain *Contributors:* Ardfern, Cobatfor, Eric Shalov, File Upload Bot (Magnus Manske), Henryk Borawski, JanSuchy, Jarekt, KTo288, PeterWD, Rcbutcher, Sylwia Zagórska, 6 anonymous edits 147
Figure 57 *Source:* https://en.wikipedia.org/w/index.php?title=File:Sir_Christopher_Quintin_Brand.jpg *License:* Public Domain *Contributors:* Bzuk, FSII, Greenshed, 2 anonymous edits 149
Figure 58 *Source:* https://en.wikipedia.org/w/index.php?title=File:Billy_Fiske.JPG *License:* Attribution *Contributors:* Original photograph taken by an employee of the British government. 150
Figure 59 *Source:* https://en.wikipedia.org/w/index.php?title=File:Fiat_CR.42_-Belgium.jpg *License:* Public Domain *Contributors:* Brigade Piron, PeterWD, Tambo, Thib Phil 154
Figure 60 *Source:* https://en.wikipedia.org/w/index.php?title=File:BR.20M_242_Squadriglia_Colori.jpg *License:* Public Domain *Contributors:* Regia Aeronautica 155
Figure 61 *Source:* https://en.wikipedia.org/w/index.php?title=File:Crashed_Fiat_CR42_near_Lowestoft_1940.jpg *License:* Public Domain *Contributors:* Australian armed forces 157
Figure 62 *Source:* https://en.wikipedia.org/w/index.php?title=File:Operations_Control_from_1941_pamphlet.jpg *License:* Public Domain *Contributors:* UK Air Ministry (Life time: 70 years from publication (see http://www.caret.cam.ac.uk/copyright/Page171.html)) 160
Figure 63 *Source:* https://en.wikipedia.org/w/index.php?title=File:Chain_home_coverage.jpg *License:* Public Domain *Contributors:* British Official Histories (History of the Second World War) 162
Figure 64 *Source:* https://en.wikipedia.org/w/index.php?title=File:Hugh_Dowding.jpg *License:* Public Domain *Contributors:* Ministry of Information official photographer 163
Figure 65 *Source:* https://en.wikipedia.org/w/index.php?title=File:Filter_Room_at_Bentley_Priory_(geograph_4484366).jpg *License:* Creative Commons Attribution-Share Alike 2.0 Generic *Contributors:* David P Howard 166
Figure 66 *Source:* https://en.wikipedia.org/w/index.php?title=File:Plotting_Table.jpg *License:* Creative Commons Zero *Contributors:* Kelly, Maury Markowitz, OgreBot 2, Rcbutcher 167

License

Index

Free Belgian Forces, 137
Free French Forces, 49, 137
Freight train, 282
French Air Force, 146
Freya radar, 38, 176
Friedrich-Karl Freiherr von Dalwigk zu Licht-
enfels, 126, 212
Friedrich Kless, 125
Friendly fire, 142, 224, 327
Führer, 77
Führer Directive, 81
Führer Directives, 196
Fulham, 298
Fuze, 347
F. W. Winterbotham, 34, 70

Galeazzo Ciano, 85
Gallipoli, 95
Gallup poll, 255
Gasoline direct injection, 13
Gate guard, 173
Gauleiter, 104
Generale di Squadra Aerea, 153
Generalfeldmarschall, 99, 100
Generalmajor, 121, 130
Generaloberst, 22
General Post Office, 161
Geneva Convention, 29
Geoffrey Allard, 210
Geographic coordinate system, 195, 241
George Cross, 58
George Denholm, 114
George Goodman (RAF officer), 151
George Medal, 226
George VI, 58
Gerald Stapleton, 149
Gerd von Rundstedt, 99, 100
Gerhard Kollewe, 128
Gerhard Schöpfel, 232
German aims and directives, 20
German Army (Wehrmacht), 10, 79, 94
German battleship Bismarck, 82
German battleship Tirpitz, 82
German language, 2, 77, 323
German occupation of Norway, 4
German occupation of the Channel Islands, 205
German-occupied Europe, 137, 289
German strategic bombing during World War I,
249
German systems, 318
Geschwader, 298
Geschwaderkommodore, 26, 46, 207
Ghent, 119, 120
GHQ Line, 103
GikII, 180
Gilze en Rijen, 306

Giulio Douhet, 3, 243
Glasgow, 104, 263
Glasgow Blitz, 242, 283
Gliding, 3
Gloster Gauntlet, 163
Gloster Gladiator, 113, 133, 135
Gloucester, 97, 282
Gold bullion, 218
Goodwin Sands, 211
Goodwood, West Sussex, 222
Gosport, 270
Gotthard Handrick, 121
Götz Freiherr von Mirbach, 230
Grand Admiral, 199
Gravesend Airport, 49
Gravesend, Kent, 309
Great Britain, 84
Greater London, 199, 200, 264
Great Yarmouth, 223
Great Yarmouth (borough), 215
Greece, 273
Greeks, 214
Greenock Blitz, 275
Greenwich Mean Time, 209
Grimbergen, 118
Großadmiral, 78
Ground-controlled interception, 159, 179
Ground support equipment, 184
Grumman F4F, 135
Grumman F4F Wildcat, 325
Gruppenkommandeur, 299, 312
Guernsey, 233
Guildford, 43
Guînes, 122
Gun camera, 57
Günther Freiherr von Maltzahn, 127, 233
Günther Lützow, 24
Guyancourt, 127
Gyrocompass, 93

Haamstede, 39
Haifa, 151
Hamilton Road Cemetery, Deal, 155
Hamm, 298
Handley-Page Hampden, 16
Hannes Trautloft, 122
Hans Geisler, 128
Hans Jeschonnek, 20, 56, 81, 200, 241, 245,
290
Hansjürgen Reinicke, 78
Hans-Jürgen Stumpff, 1, 22, 127, 244
Hans-Jürgen von Cramon-Taubadel, 127
Hans Korte (general), 125
Hans Rudel, 327
Hans von Hahn, 121
Haren Airport, 39